My Heavenly Hockey Club

5

Ai Morinaga

Translated and adapted by Athena Nibley and Alethea Nibley

Lettered by North Market Street Graphics

BALLANTINE BOOKS · NEW YORK

My Heavenly Hockey Club volume 5 is a work of fiction. Names, characters, places, and incidents are the products of the author's imagination or are used fictitiously. Any resemblance to actual events, locales, or persons, living or dead, is entirely coincidental.

A Del Rey Manga/Kodansha Trade Paperback Original

Published in the United States by Del Rey Books, an imprint of The Random House Publishing Group, a division of Random House, Inc., New York.

Publication rights arranged through Kodansha Ltd.

First published in Japan in 2006 by Kodansha Ltd., Tokyo as *Gokuraku Seishun Hockeybu*

ISBN 978-0-345-50198-1

Printed in the United States of America

www.delreymanga.com

9 8 7 6 5 4 3 2 1

Translator/Adapter—Athena Nibley and Alethea Nibley
Lettering—North Market Street Graphics

Contents

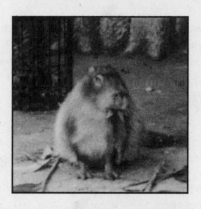

A capybara from the Shanghai Zoo, Mogo'o-kun (named by me).
I just love how under his nose is so long. *Huff, huff.* But when
I think that he's a rat, I don't like it so much. This photo is from
almost ten years ago, so he may no longer be in this world. Rest in
peace, Mogo'o. If you're still alive, I'm sorry. Er, he might be a girl.
—Ai Morinaga

Honorifics Explained

Throughout the Del Rey Manga books, you will find Japanese honorifics left intact in the translations. For those not familiar with how the Japanese use honorifics and, more important, how they differ from American honorifics, we present this brief overview.

Politeness has always been a critical facet of Japanese culture. Ever since the feudal era, when Japan was a highly stratified society, use of honorifics—which can be defined as polite speech that indicates relationship or status—has played an essential role in the Japanese language. When addressing someone in Japanese, an honorific usually takes the form of a suffix attached to one's name (example: "Asuna-san"), is used as a title at the end of one's name, or appears in place of the name itself (example: "Negi-sensei," or simply "Sensei!").

Honorifics can be expressions of respect or endearment. In the context of manga and anime, honorifics give insight into the nature of the relationship between characters. Many English translations leave out these important honorifics and therefore distort the feel of the original Japanese. Because Japanese honorifics contain nuances that English honorifics lack, it is our policy at Del Rey not to translate them. Here, instead, is a guide to some of the honorifics you may encounter in Del Rey Manga.

-san: This is the most common honorific and is equivalent to Mr., Miss, Ms., or Mrs. It is the all-purpose honorific and can be used in any situation where politeness is required.

-sama: This is one level higher than "-san" and is used to confer great respect.

-dono: This comes from the word "tono," which means "lord." It is an even higher level than "-sama" and confers utmost respect.

-kun: This suffix is used at the end of boys' names to express familiarity or endearment. It is also sometimes used by men among friends, or when addressing someone younger or of a lower station.

-chan: This is used to express endearment, mostly toward girls. It is also used for little boys, pets, and even among lovers. It gives a sense of childish cuteness.

Bozu: This is an informal way to refer to a boy, similar to the English terms "kid" and "squirt."

Sempai/Senpai: This title suggests that the addressee is one's senior in a group or organization. It is most often used in a school setting, where underclassmen refer to their upperclassmen as "sempai." It can also be used in the workplace, such as when a newer employee addresses an employee who has seniority in the company.

Kohai: This is the opposite of "sempai" and is used toward underclassmen in school or newcomers in the workplace. It connotes that the addressee is of a lower station.

Sensei: Literally meaning "one who has come before," this title is used for teachers, doctors, or masters of any profession or art.

-[blank]: This is usually forgotten in these lists, but it is perhaps the most significant difference between Japanese and English. The lack of honorific means that the speaker has permission to address the person in a very intimate way. Usually, only family, spouses, or very close friends have this kind of permission. Known as *yobisute*, it can be gratifying when someone who has earned the intimacy starts to call one by one's name without an honorific. But when that intimacy hasn't been earned, it can be very insulting.

My Heavenly Hockey Club

5

Ai Morinaga

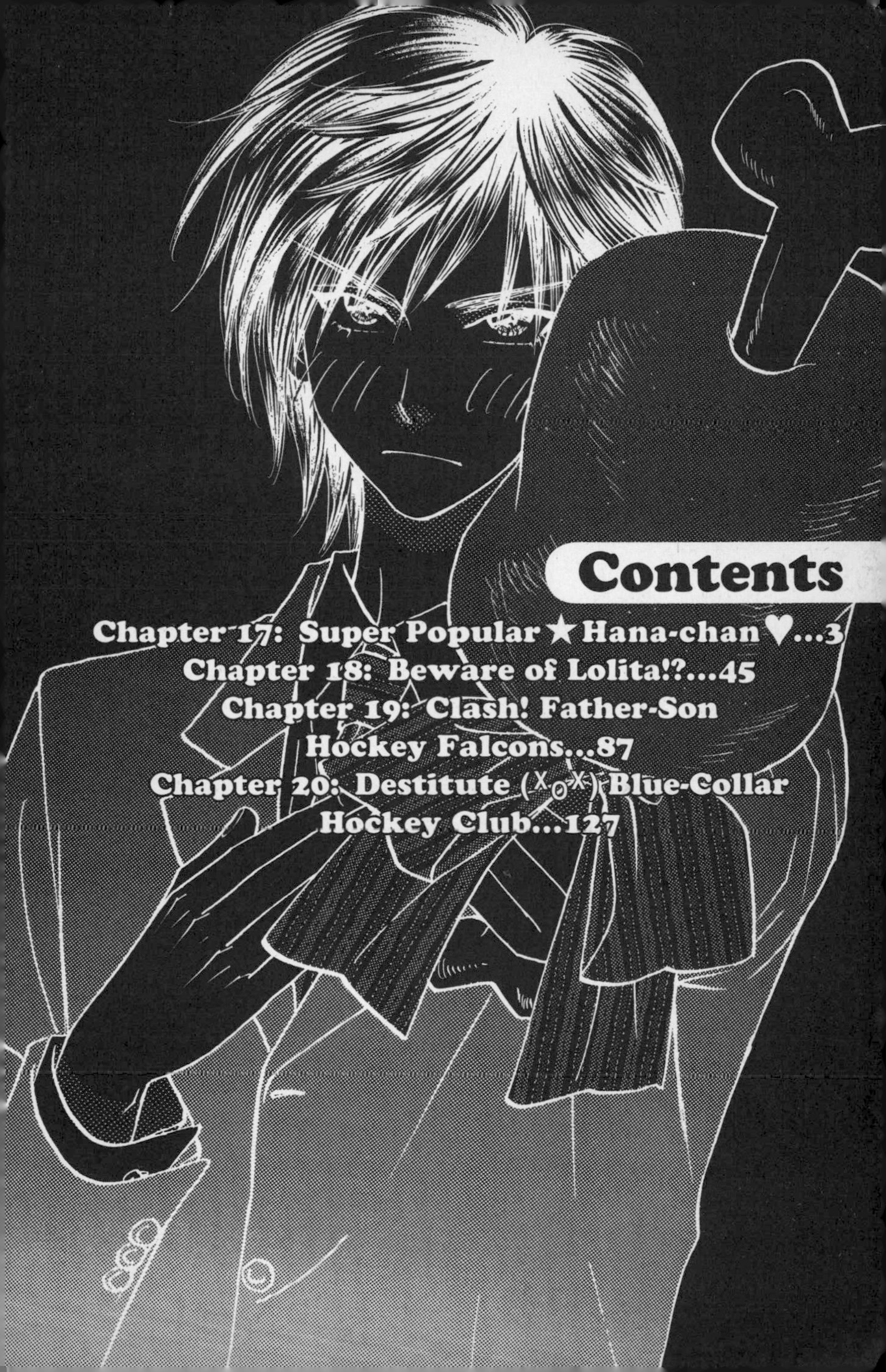

Contents

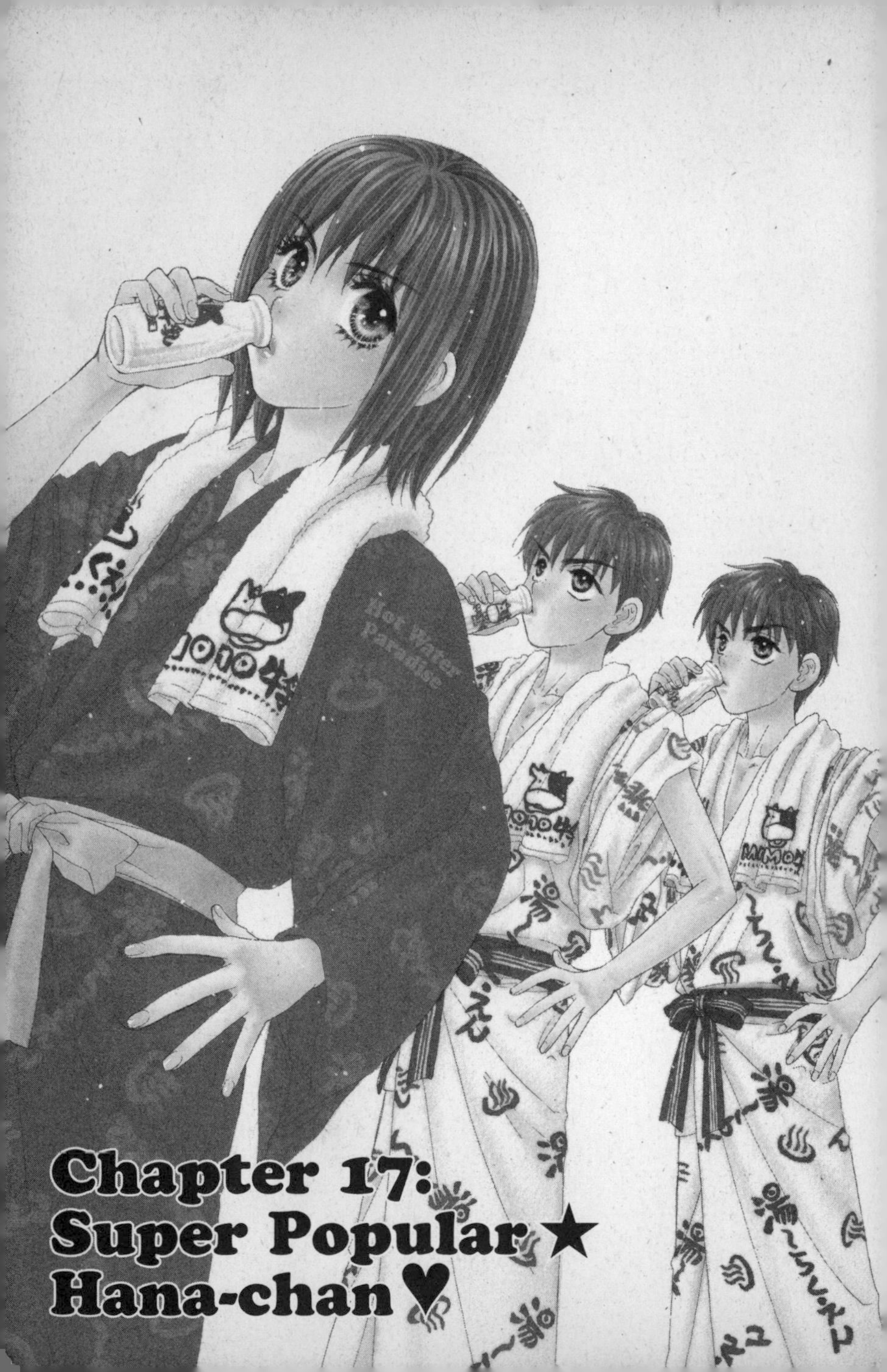
Hot Water
Paradise

Chapter 17: Super Popular ★ Hana-chan ♥

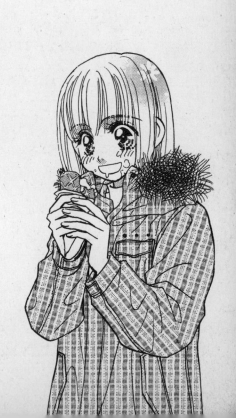

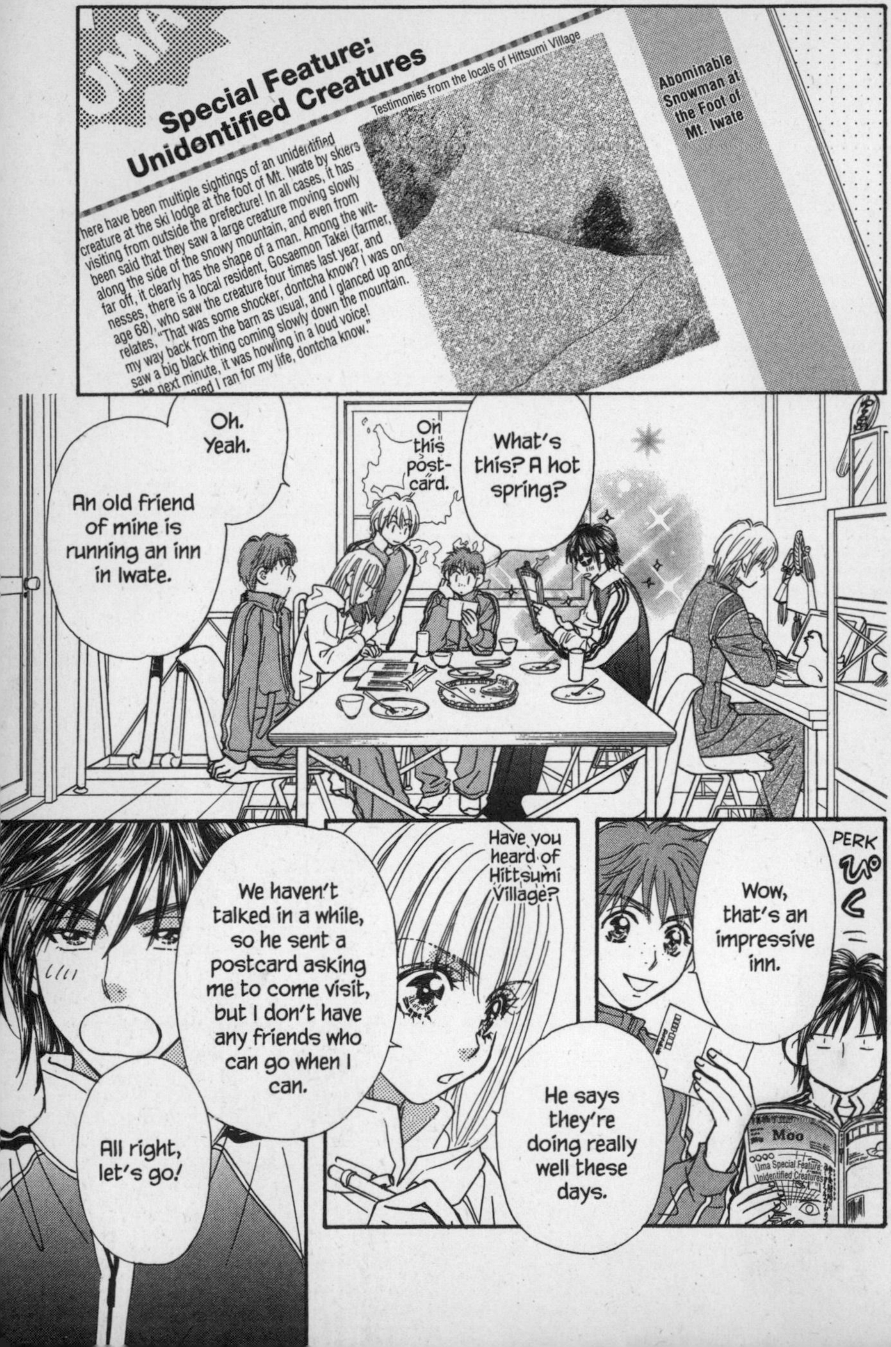
UMA
Special Feature: Unidentified Creatures
Testimonies from the locals of Hittsumi Village
Abominable Snowman at the Foot of Mt. Iwate
here have been multiple sightings of an unidentified creature at the ski lodge at the foot of Mt. Iwate by skiers visiting from outside the prefecture! In all cases, it has been said that they saw a large creature moving slowly along the side of the snowy mountain, and even from far off, it clearly has the shape of a man. Among the witnesses, there is a local resident, Gosaemon Takei (farmer, age 68), who saw the creature four times last year, and relates, "That was some shocker, dontcha know? I was on my way back from the barn as usual, and I glanced up and saw a big black thing coming slowly down the mountain. The next minute, it was howling in a loud voice! ...ared I ran for my life, dontcha know."
What's this? A hot spring?
On this postcard.
Oh. Yeah.
An old friend of mine is running an inn in Iwate.
PERK
Wow, that's an impressive inn.
Moo
Uma Special Feature: Unidentified Creatures
He says they're doing really well these days.
Have you heard of Hittsumi Village?
We haven't talked in a while, so he sent a postcard asking me to come visit, but I don't have any friends who can go when I can.
All right, let's go!

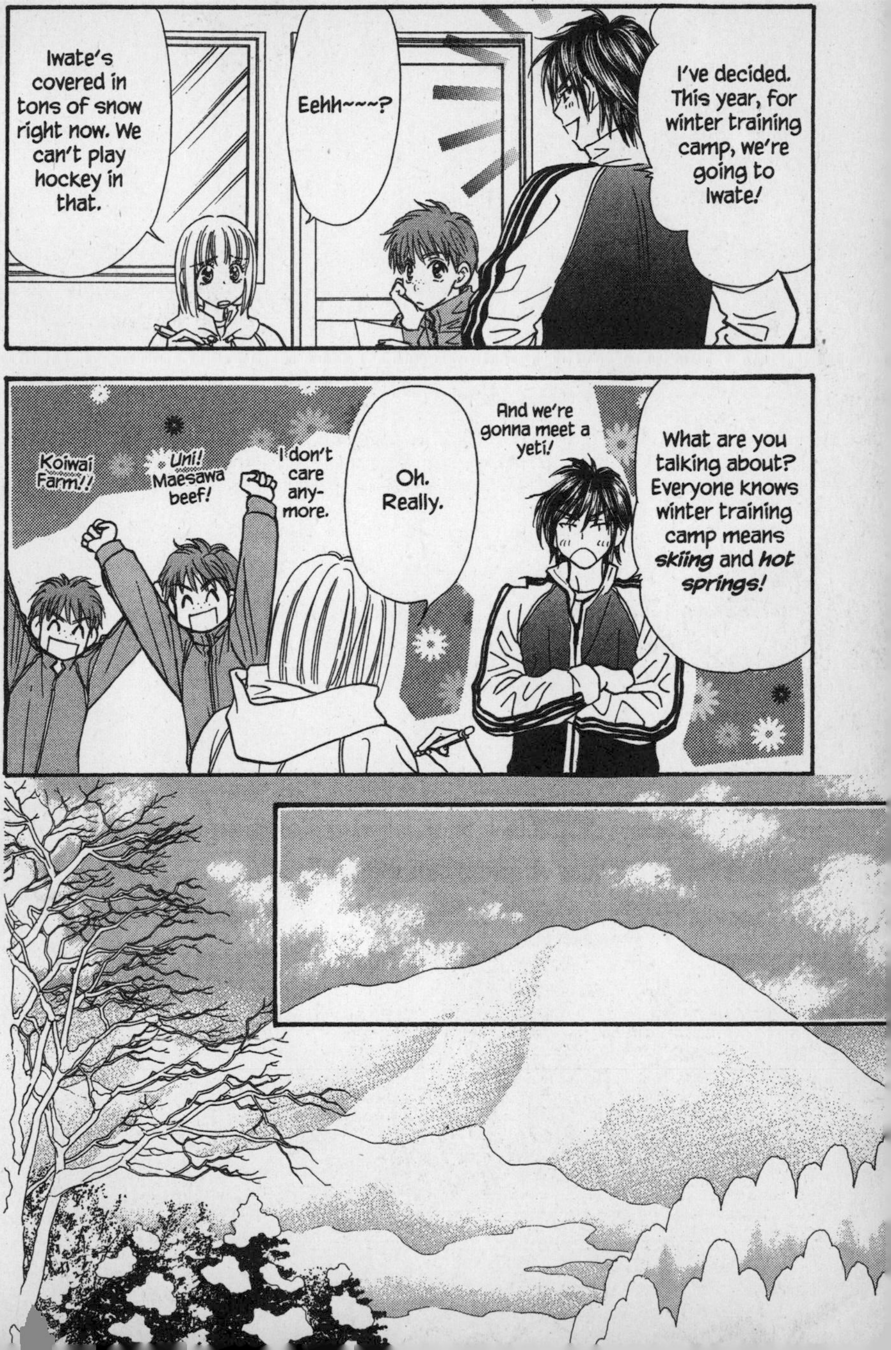
I've decided. This year, for winter training camp, we're going to Iwate!
Eehh~~~?
Iwate's covered in tons of snow right now. We can't play hockey in that.
What are you talking about? Everyone knows winter training camp means *skiing* and *hot springs!*
And we're gonna meet a yeti!
Oh. Really.
I don't care any-more.
Uni! Maesawa beef!
Koiwai Farm!!

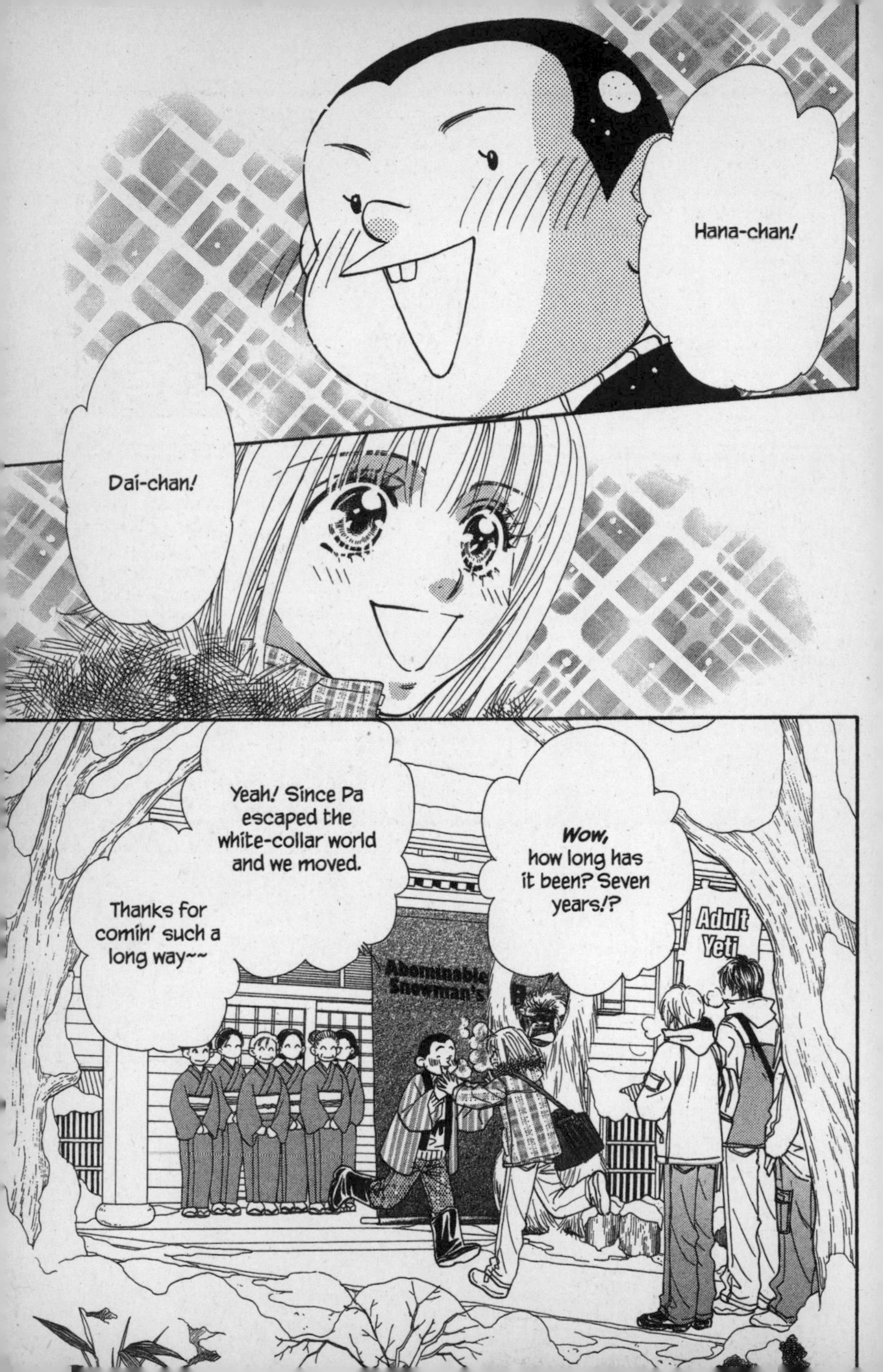
Hana-chan!
Dai-chan!
Wow, how long has it been? Seven years!?
Yeah! Since Pa escaped the white-collar world and we moved.
Adult Yeti
Thanks for comin' such a long way~~
Abominable Snowman's

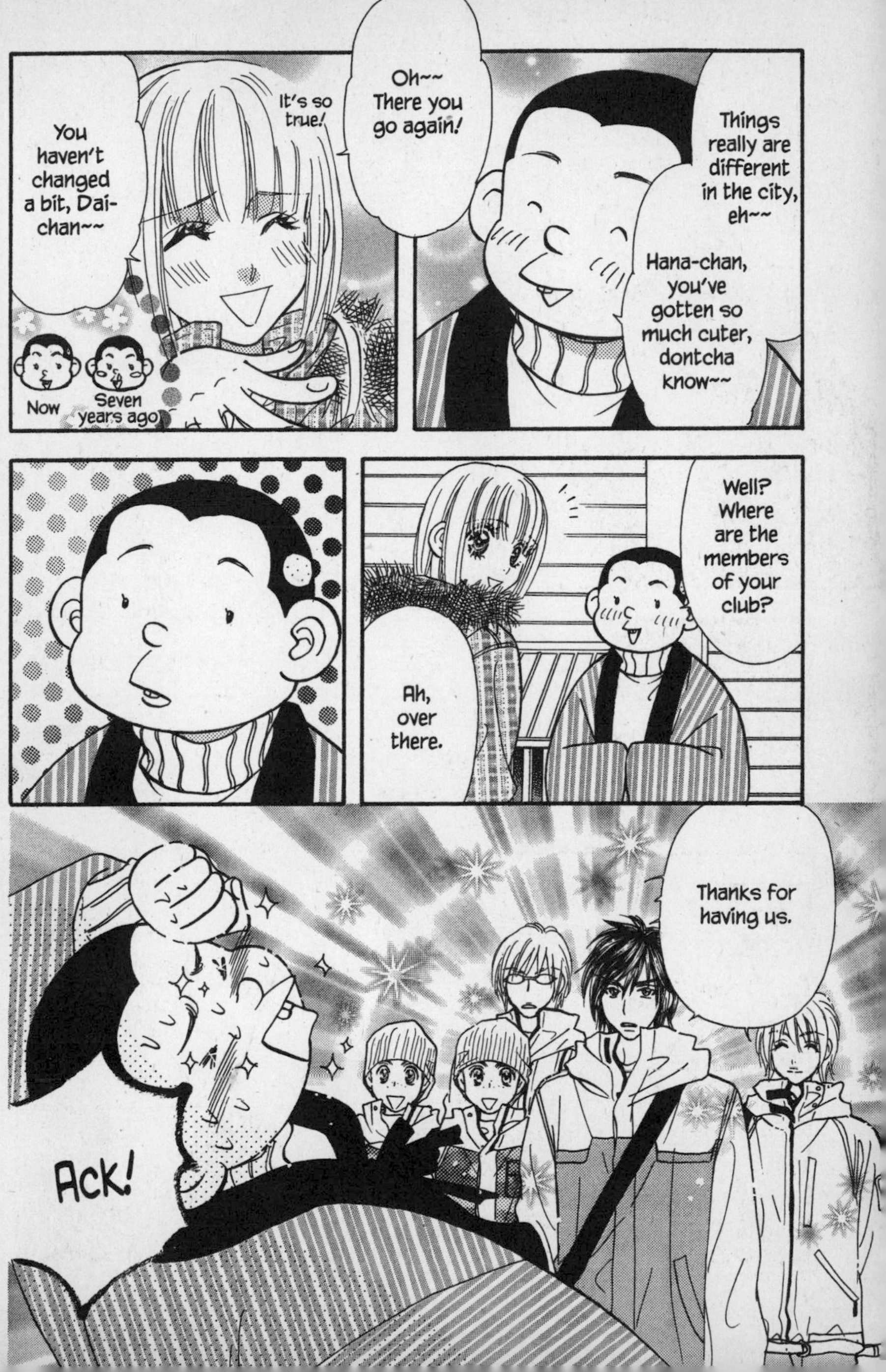
Things really are different in the city, eh~~
Hana-chan, you've gotten so much cuter, dontcha know~~
Oh~~ There you go again!
It's so true!
You haven't changed a bit, Dai-chan~~
Now
Seven years ago
Well? Where are the members of your club?
Ah, over there.
Thanks for having us.
ACK!

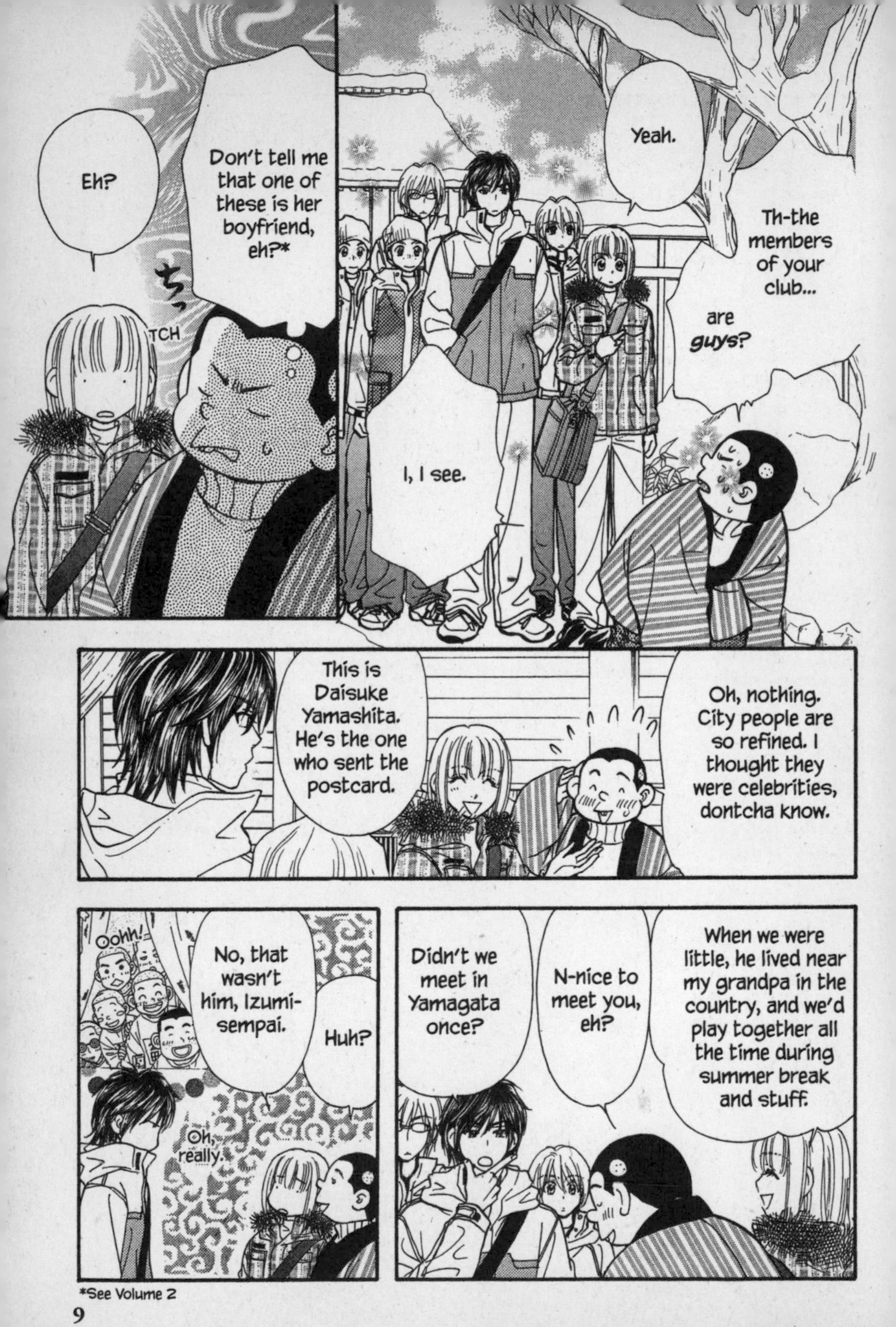
Th-the members of your club...
are guys?
Yeah.
I, I see.
Don't tell me that one of these is her boyfriend, eh?*
TCH
Eh?
Oh, nothing. City people are so refined. I thought they were celebrities, dontcha know.
This is Daisuke Yamashita. He's the one who sent the postcard.
When we were little, he lived near my grandpa in the country, and we'd play together all the time during summer break and stuff.
N-nice to meet you, eh?
Didn't we meet in Yamagata once?
Huh?
No, that wasn't him, Izumi-sempai.
Oohh!
Oh, really.

*See Volume 2

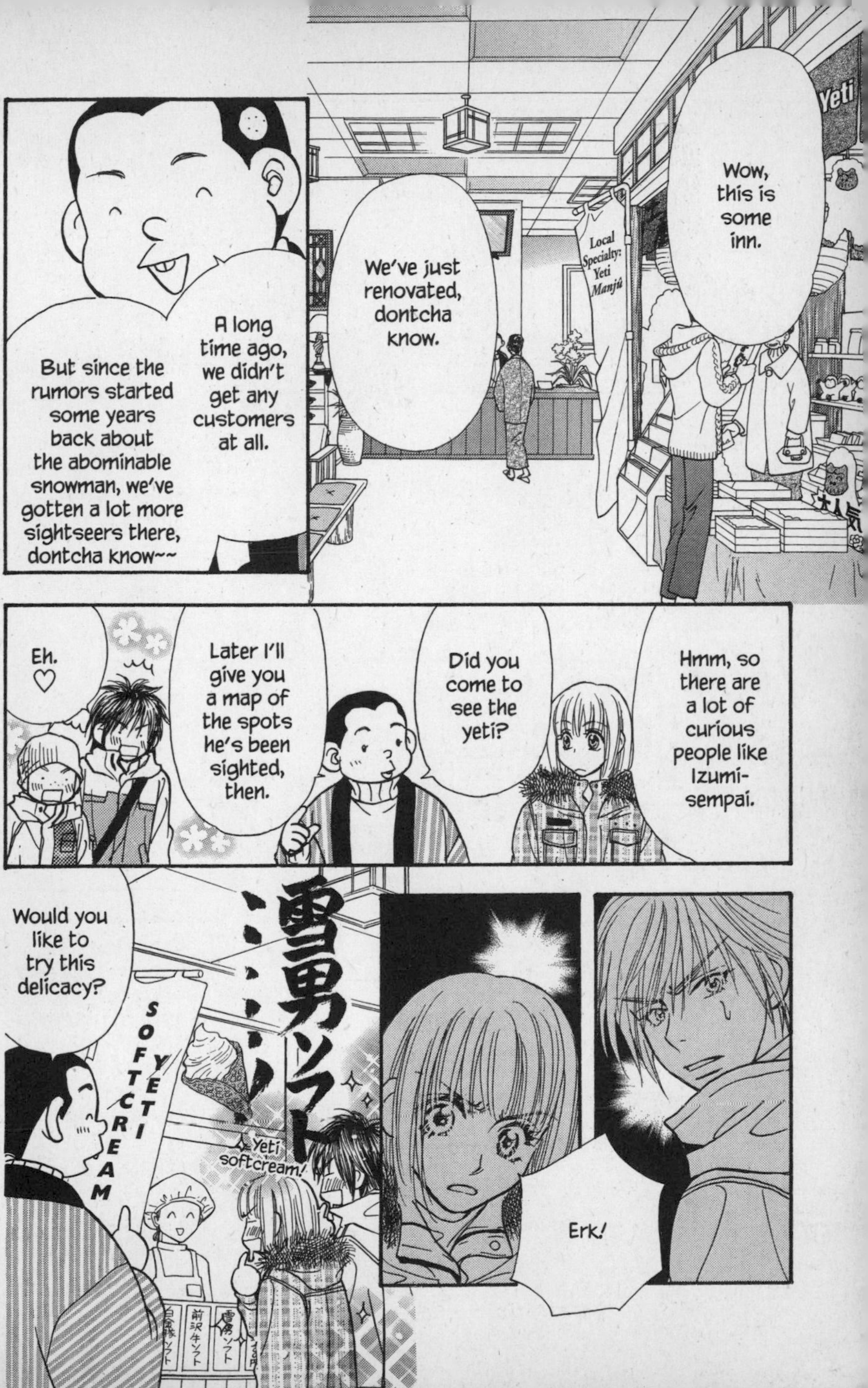
Yeti
Wow, this is some inn.
Local Specialty: Yeti Manjū
We've just renovated, dontcha know.
A long time ago, we didn't get any customers at all.
But since the rumors started some years back about the abominable snowman, we've gotten a lot more sightseers there, dontcha know~~
Hmm, so there are a lot of curious people like Izumi-sempai.
Did you come to see the yeti?
Later I'll give you a map of the spots he's been sighted, then.
Eh. ♡
Erk!
Would you like to try this delicacy?
雪男ソフト
SOFTCREAM
YETI
Yeti softcream!

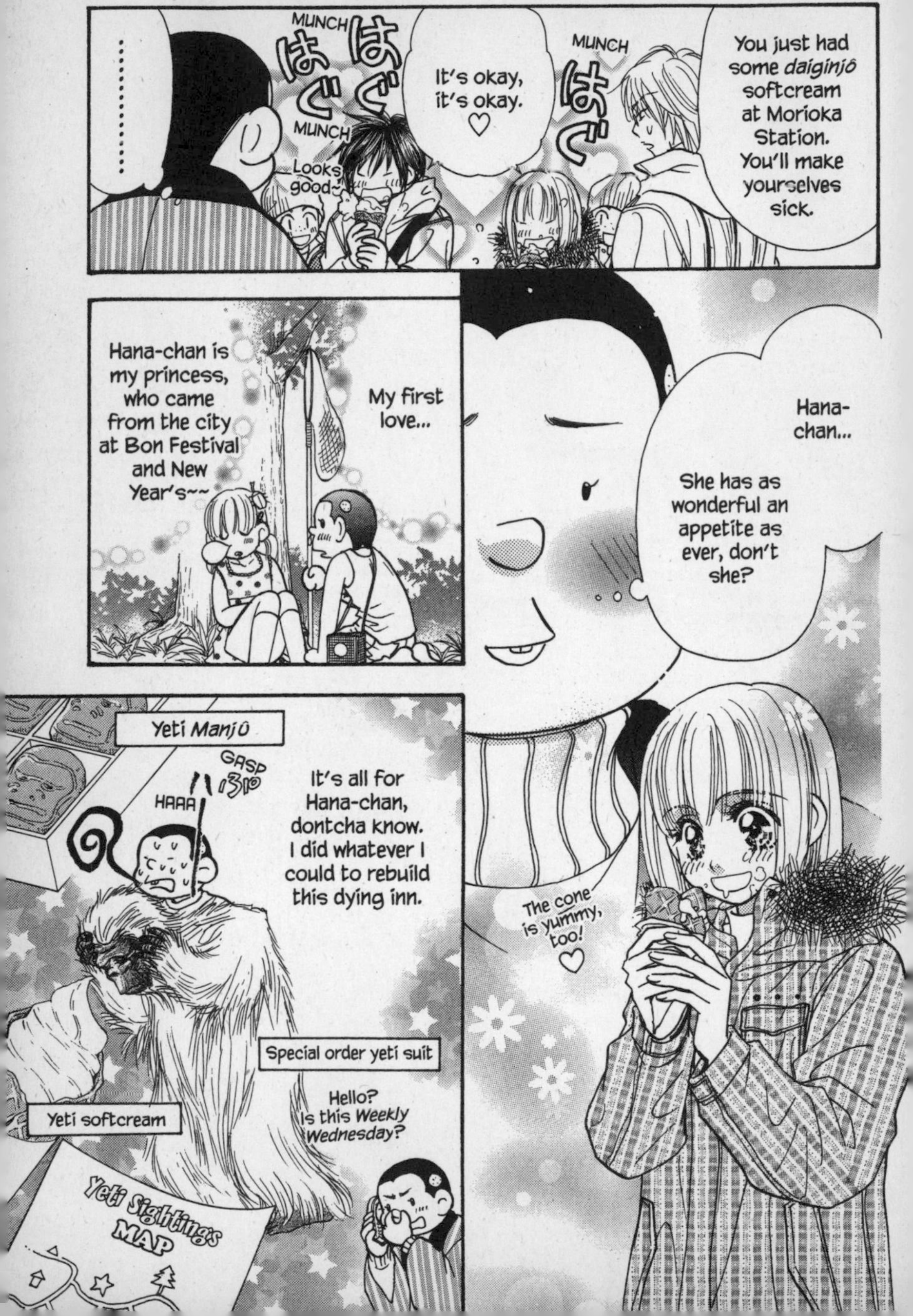
You just had some *daiginjô* softcream at Morioka Station. You'll make yourselves sick.
MUNCH
はぐ
It's okay, it's okay. ♡
MUNCH
はぐ
MUNCH
はぐ
Looks good~
......
Hana-chan... She has as wonderful an appetite as ever, don't she?
The cone is yummy, too! ♡
My first love...
Hana-chan is my princess, who came from the city at Bon Festival and New Year's~~
It's all for Hana-chan, dontcha know. I did whatever I could to rebuild this dying inn.
GASP
HAAA
Yeti *Manjû*
Special order yeti suit
Hello? Is this *Weekly Wednesday*?
Yeti softcream
Yeti Sightings MAP

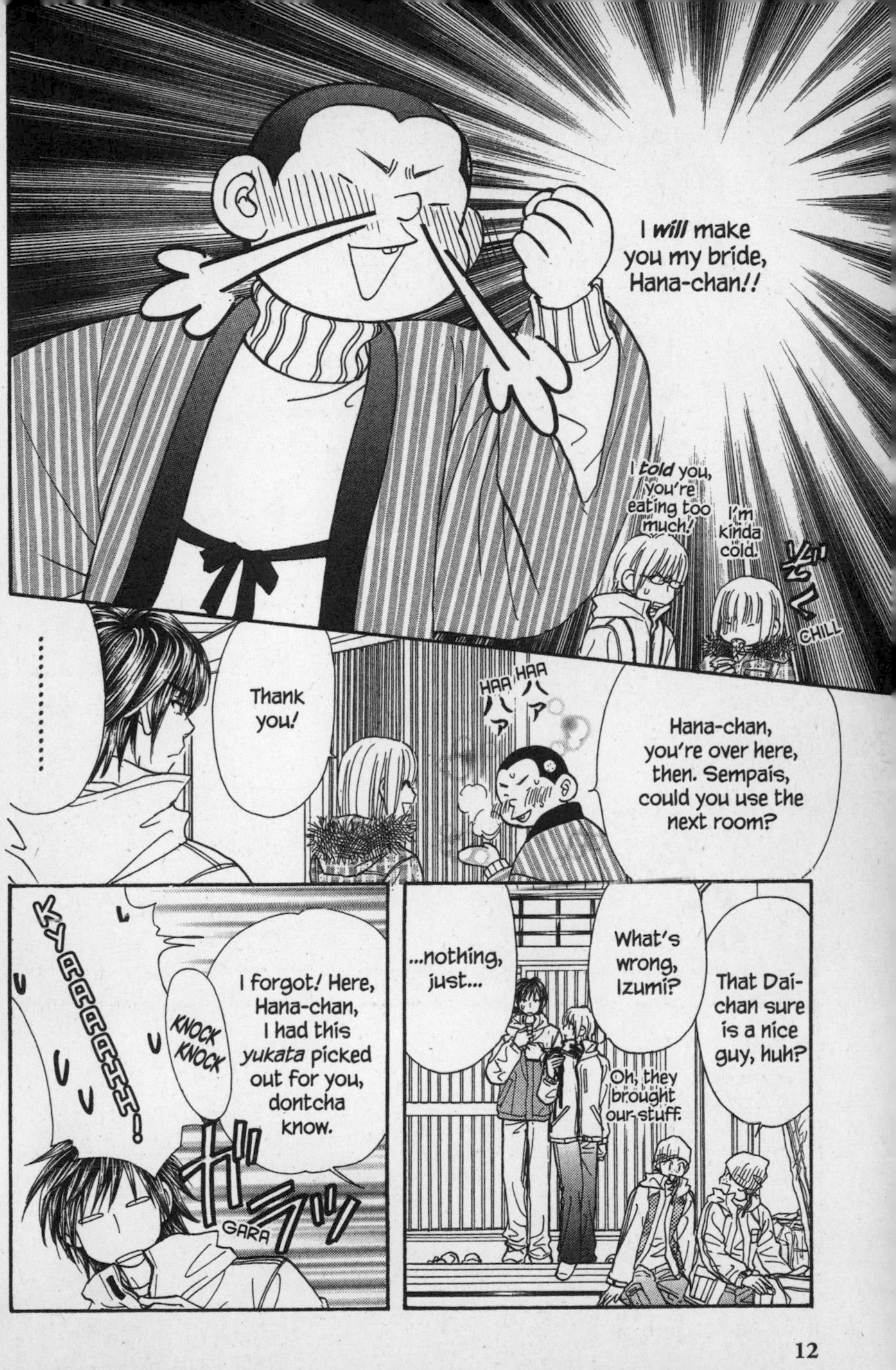

I will make you my bride, Hana-chan!!
I told you, you're eating too much!
I'm kinda cold.
CHILL
Hana-chan, you're over here, then. Sempais, could you use the next room?
HAA HAA
Thank you!
......
That Dai-chan sure is a nice guy, huh?
What's wrong, Izumi?
...nothing, just...
Oh, they brought our stuff.
I forgot! Here, Hana-chan, I had this yukata picked out for you, dontcha know.
KNOCK KNOCK
GARA
KYAAAAAHH!

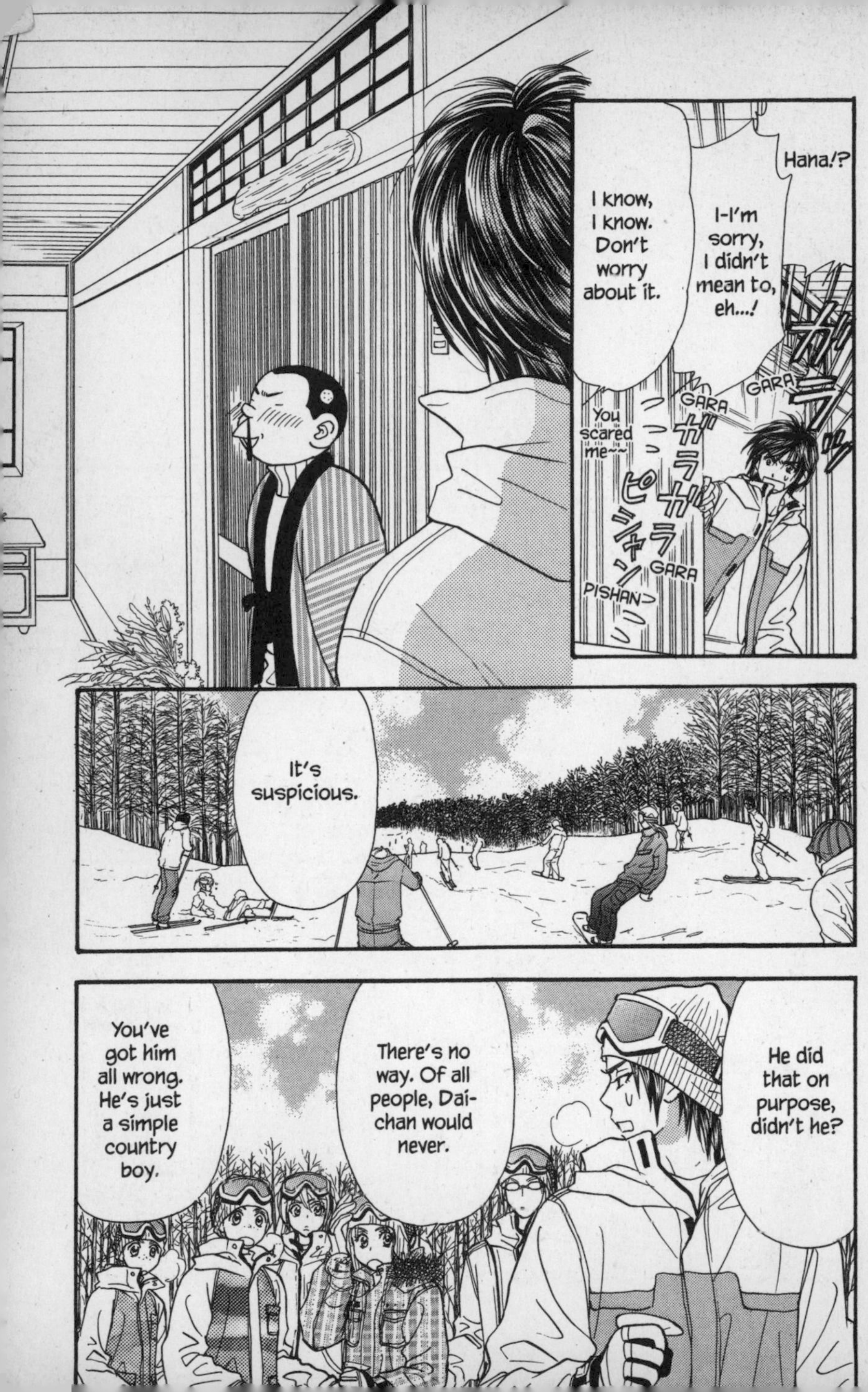
Hana!?
I-I'm sorry, I didn't mean to, eh...!
GARA
GARA
I know, I know. Don't worry about it.
You scared me~~
GARA
PISHAN
It's suspicious.
He did that on purpose, didn't he?
There's no way. Of all people, Dai-chan would never.
You've got him all wrong. He's just a simple country boy.

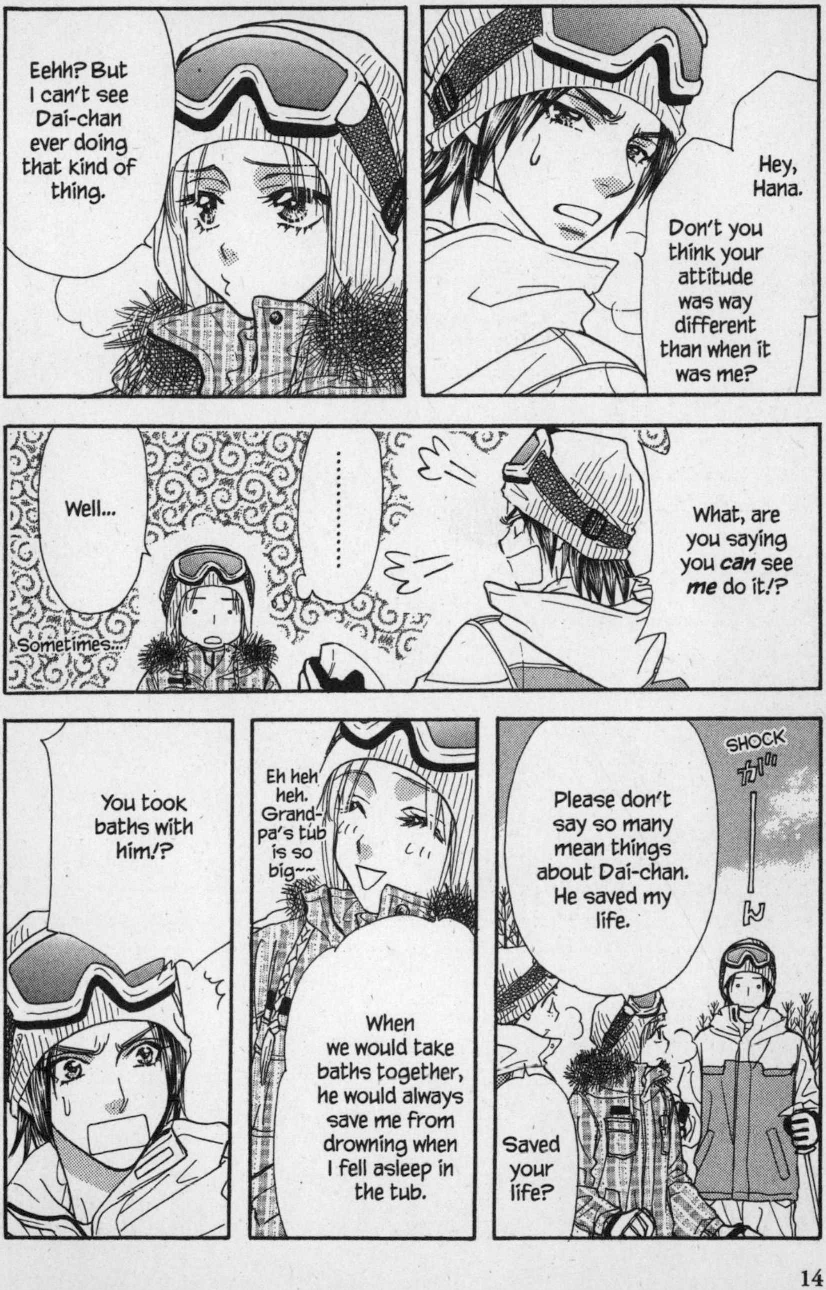
Hey, Hana.
Don't you think your attitude was way different than when it was me?
Eehh? But I can't see Dai-chan ever doing that kind of thing.
What, are you saying you *can* see *me* do it!?
......
Well...
Sometimes...
SHOCK
Please don't say so many mean things about Dai-chan. He saved my life.
Saved your life?
Eh heh heh. Grand-pa's tub is so big~~
When we would take baths together, he would always save me from drowning when I fell asleep in the tub.
You took baths with him!?

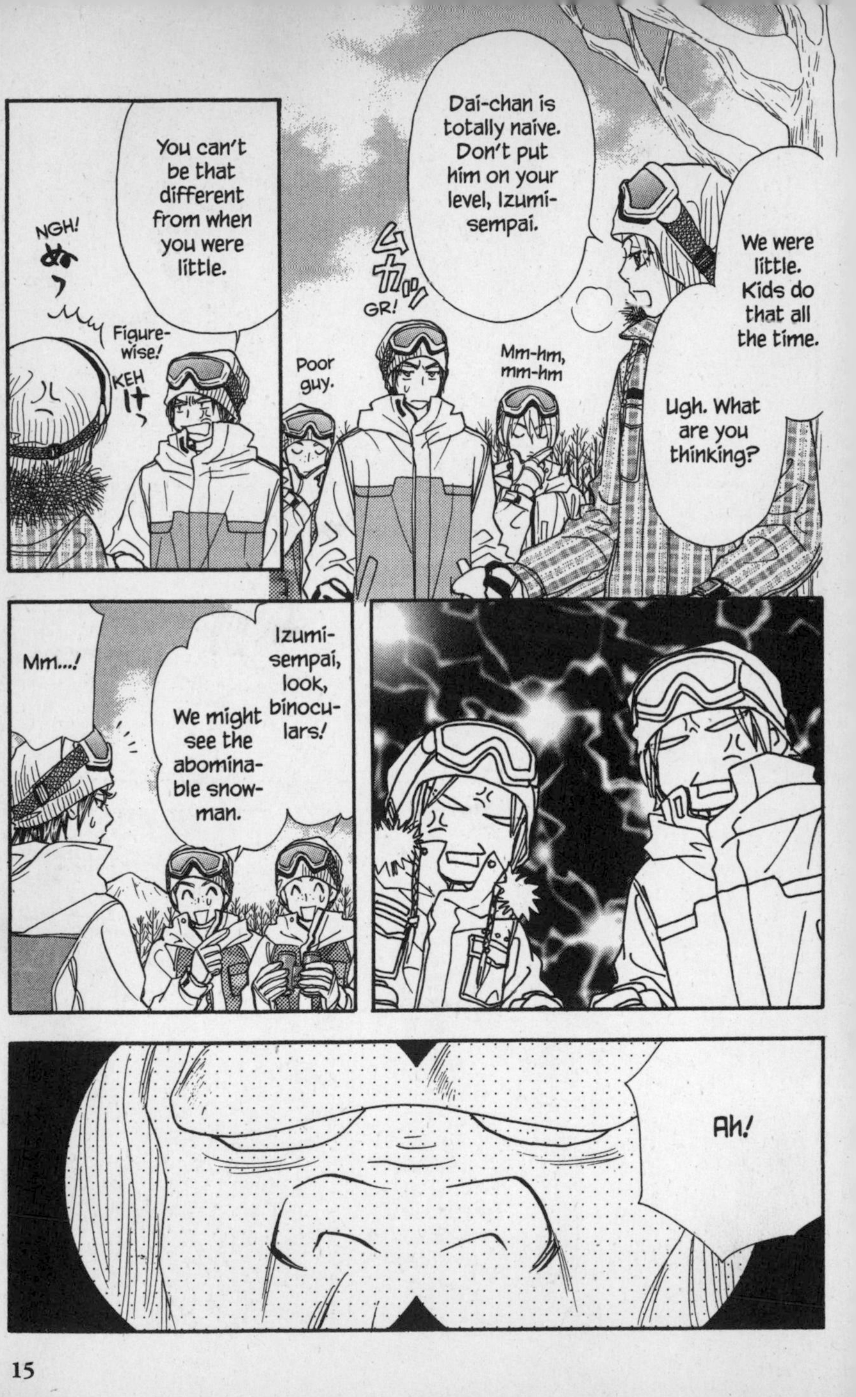
We were little. Kids do that all the time.
Dai-chan is totally naive. Don't put him on your level, Izumi-sempai.
ムカッ
GR!
Ugh. What are you thinking?
Mm-hm, mm-hm
Poor guy.
You can't be that different from when you were little.
NGH!
ぬっ
Figure-wise!
KEH
け
Izumi-sempai, look, binoculars!
We might see the abominable snowman.
Mm...!
Ah!

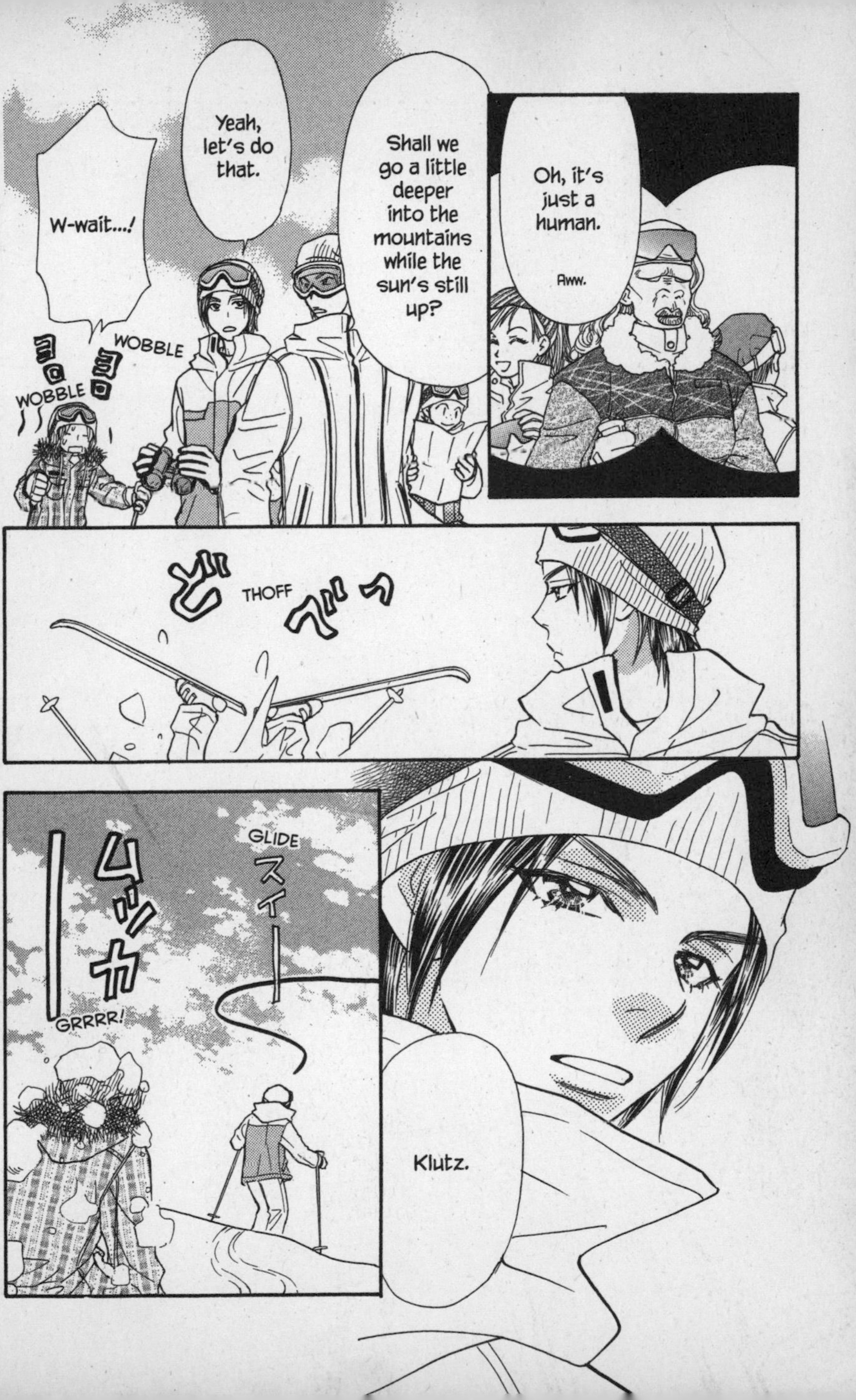
Oh, it's just a human.
Aww.
Shall we go a little deeper into the mountains while the sun's still up?
Yeah, let's do that.
W-wait...!
WOBBLE
WOBBLE
どべっ
THOFF
Klutz.
スイー
GLIDE
ムッカー
GRRRR!

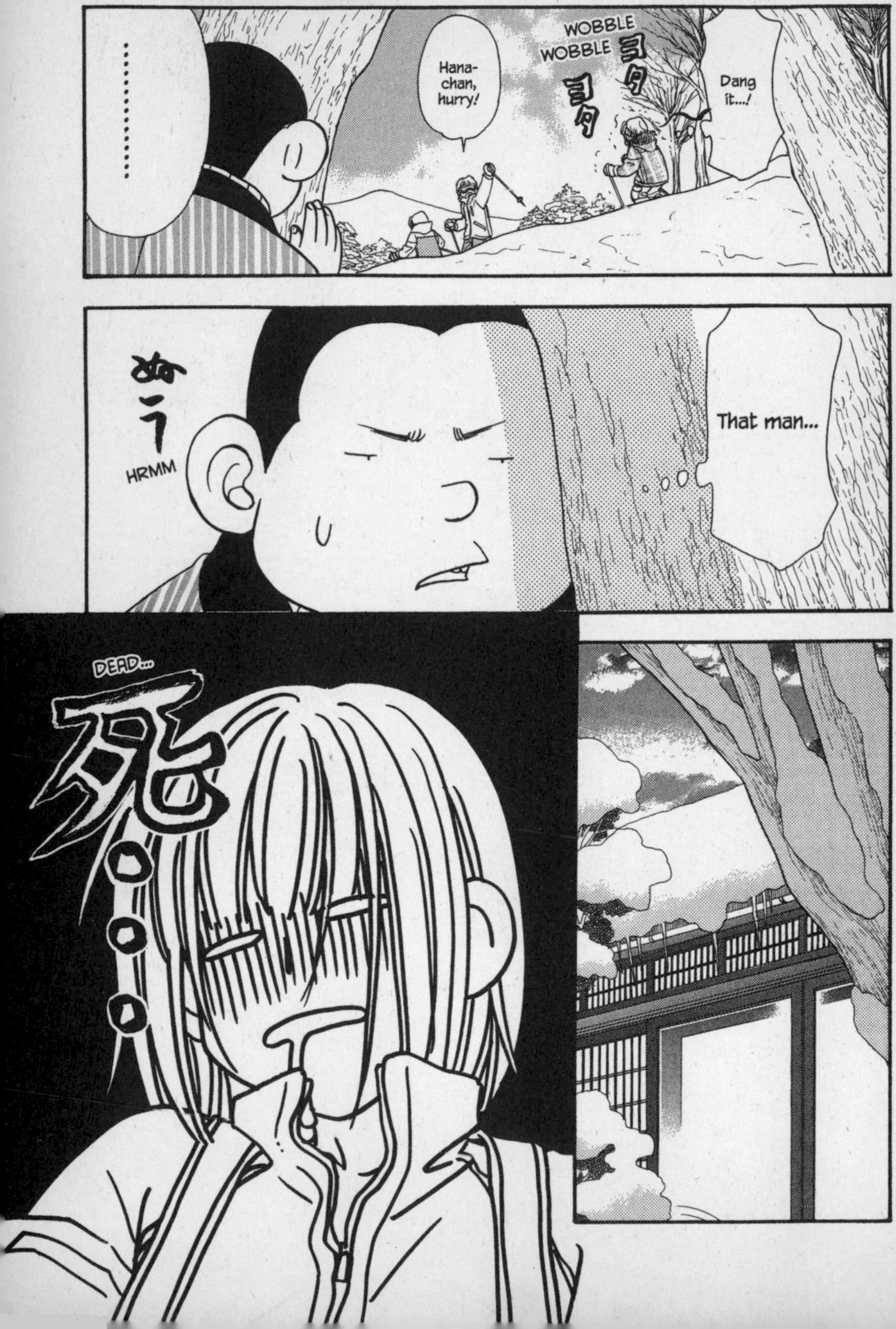

Dang it...!
WOBBLE WOBBLE ヨタヨタ
Hana-chan, hurry!
......
That man...
ぬう
HRMM
DEAD...
死

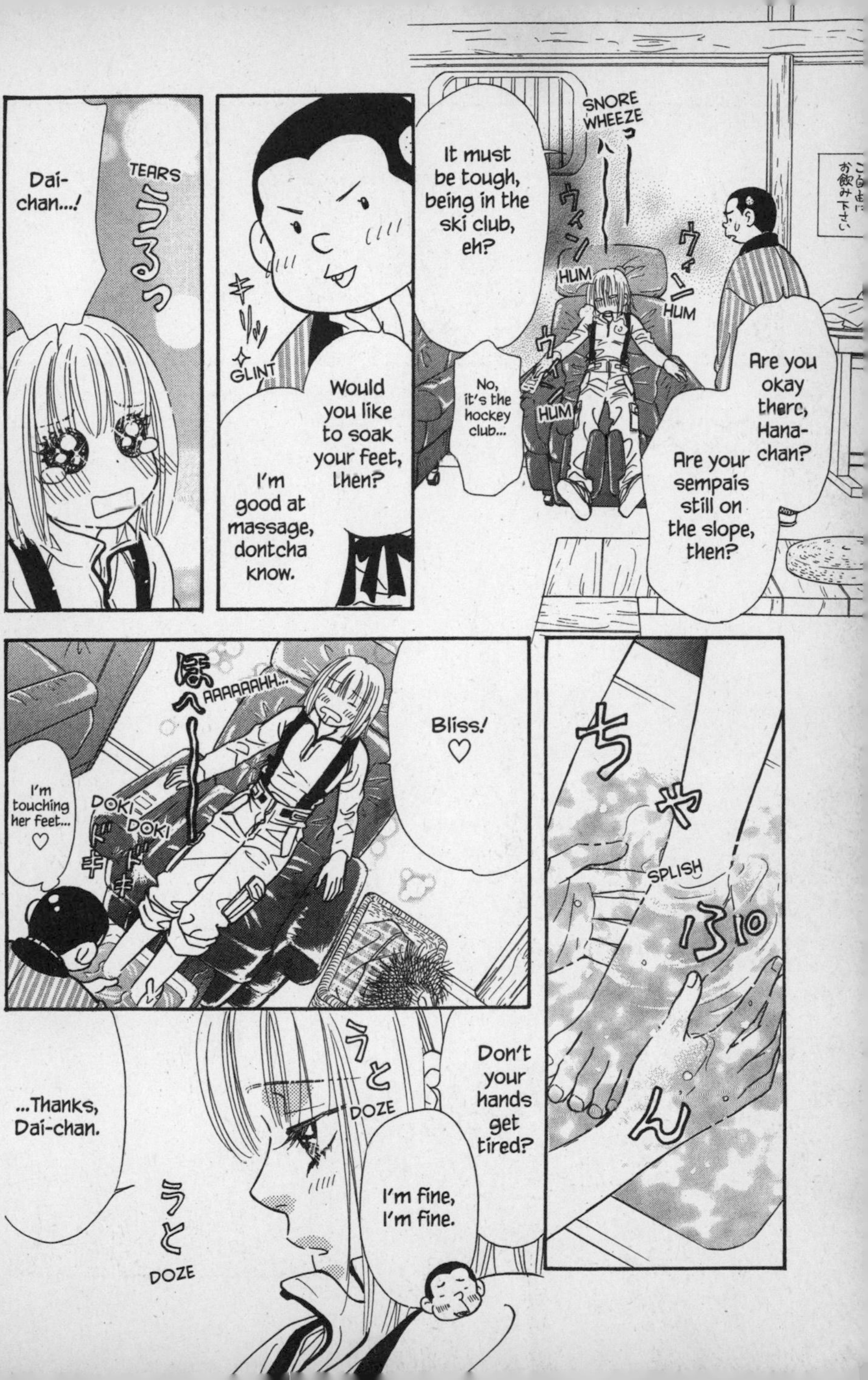

ご自由に お飲み下さい
SNORE WHEEZE
HUM
HUM
HUM
Are you okay there, Hana-chan?
Are your sempais still on the slope, then?
No, it's the hockey club...
It must be tough, being in the ski club, eh?
GLINT
Would you like to soak your feet, then?
I'm good at massage, dontcha know.
TEARS
Dai-chan...!
SPLISH
Bliss! ♡
AAAAAAAHH...
DOKI DOKI
I'm touching her feet... ♡
Don't your hands get tired?
I'm fine, I'm fine.
DOZE
DOZE
...Thanks, Dai-chan.

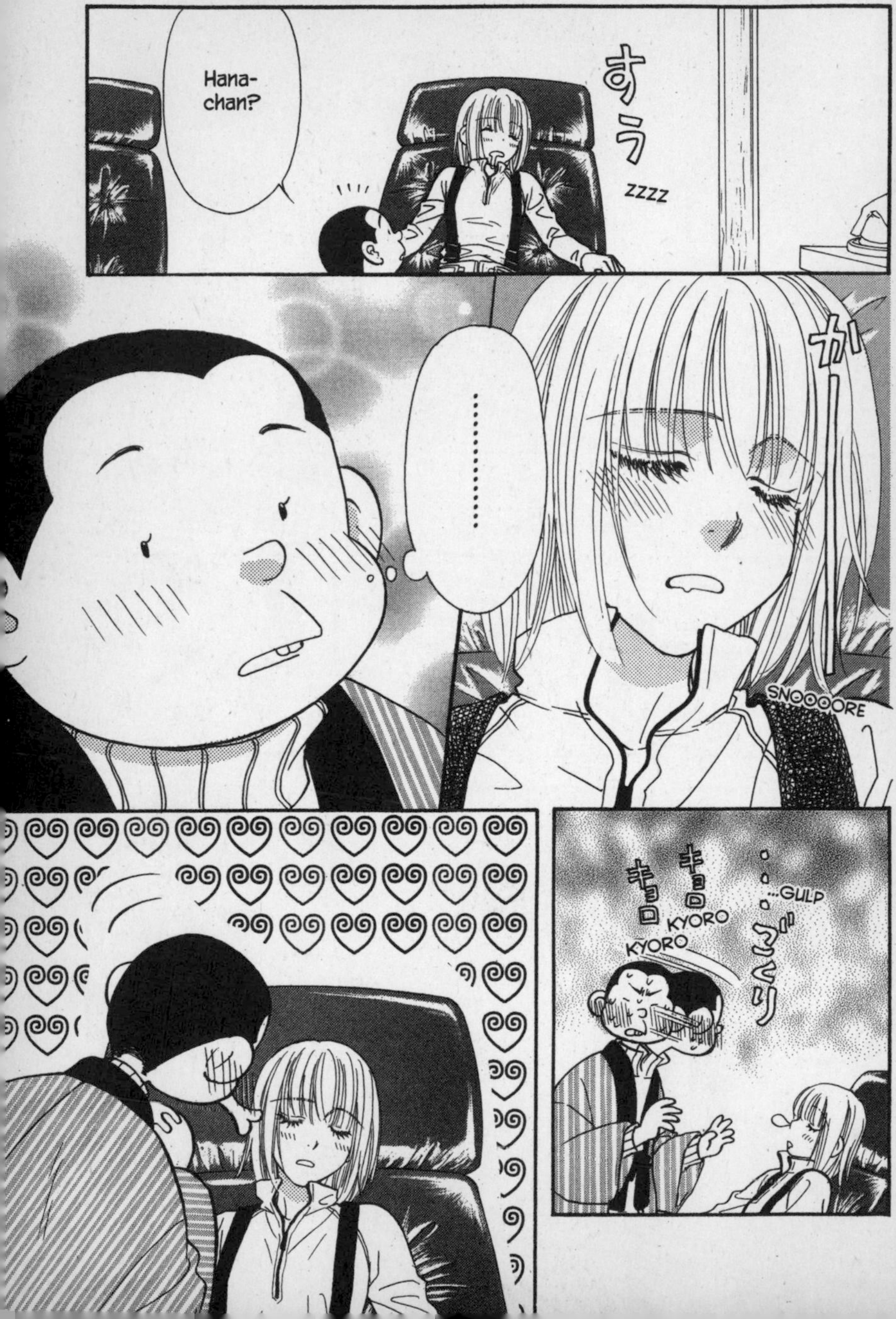
すう
ZZZZ
Hana-chan?
かー
SNOOOORE
……
ごくり
...GULP
キョロ
KYORO
キョロ
KYORO

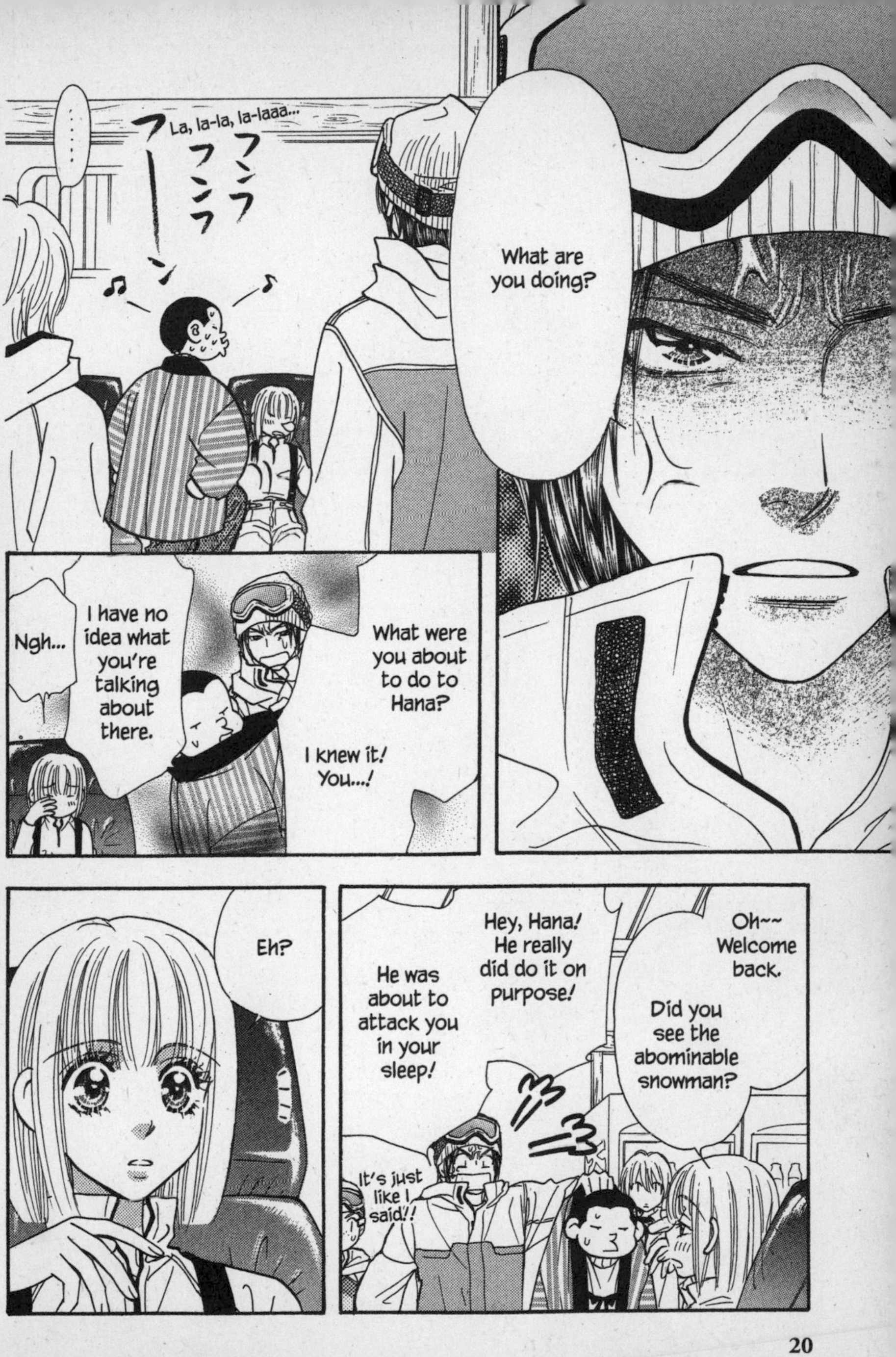
What are you doing?
La, la-la, la-laaa...
フンフ フンフ フーン
......
What were you about to do to Hana?
I knew it! You...!
I have no idea what you're talking about there.
Ngh...
Oh~~ Welcome back.
Did you see the abominable snowman?
Hey, Hana! He really did do it on purpose!
He was about to attack you in your sleep!
It's just like I said!!
Eh?

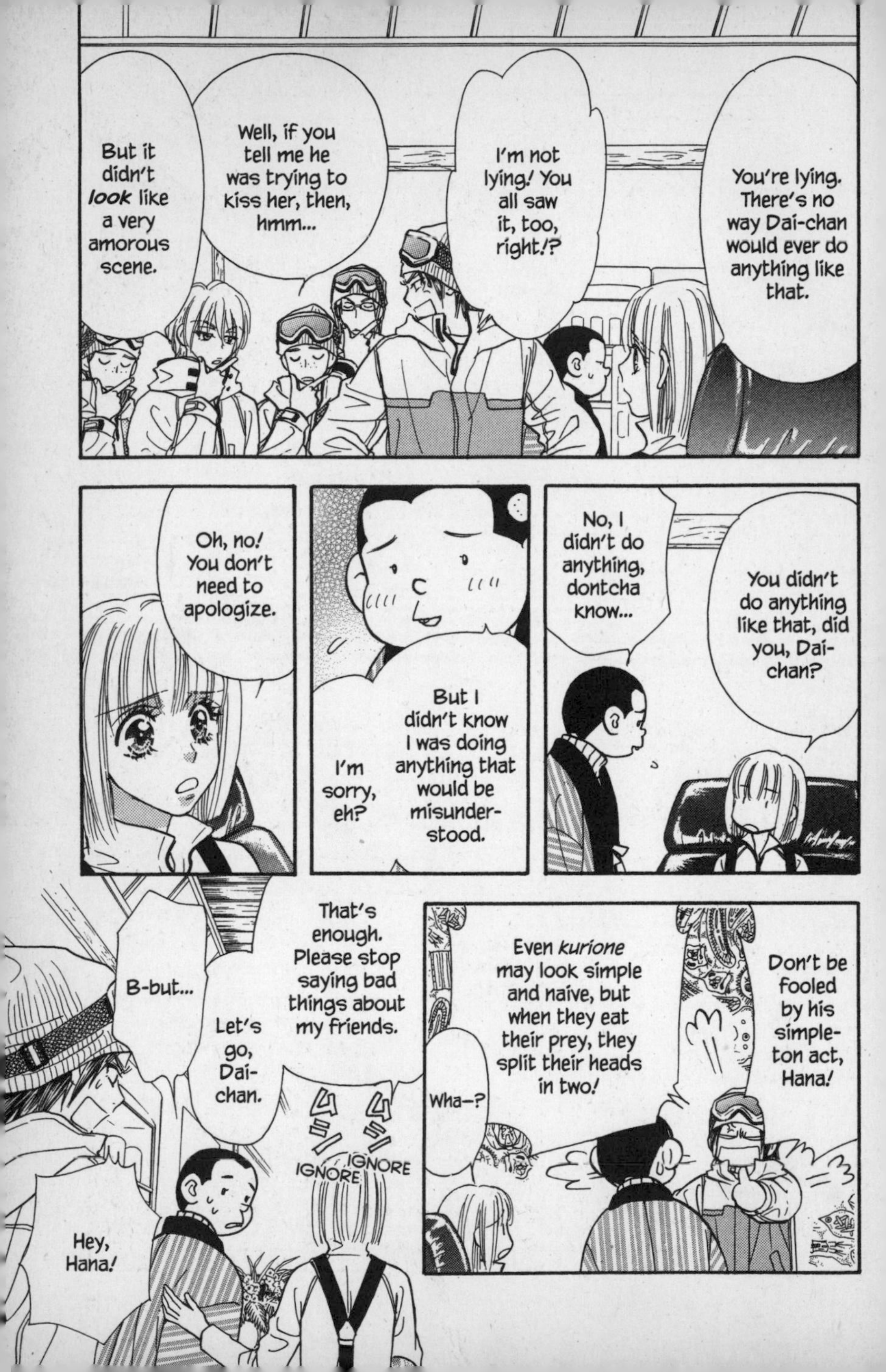
You're lying. There's no way Dai-chan would ever do anything like that.
I'm not lying! You all saw it, too, right!?
Well, if you tell me he was trying to kiss her, then, hmm...
But it didn't *look* like a very amorous scene.
You didn't do anything like that, did you, Dai-chan?
No, I didn't do anything, dontcha know...
But I didn't know I was doing anything that would be misunderstood.
I'm sorry, eh?
Oh, no! You don't need to apologize.
Don't be fooled by his simpleton act, Hana!
Even *kurione* may look simple and naive, but when they eat their prey, they split their heads in two!
Wha–?
That's enough. Please stop saying bad things about my friends.
IGNORE
IGNORE
Let's go, Dai-chan.
B-but...
Hey, Hana!

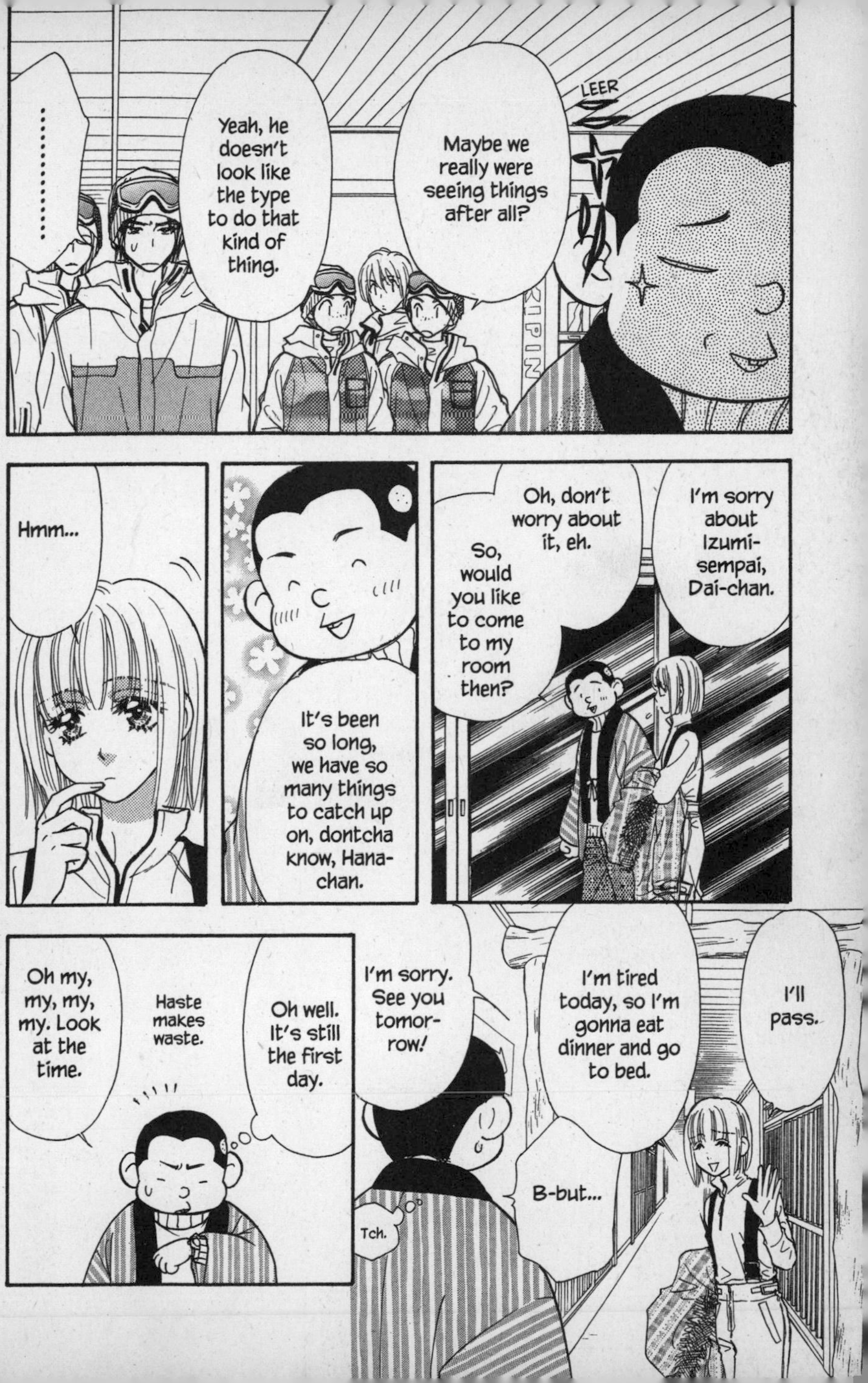
LEER
Maybe we really were seeing things after all?
Yeah, he doesn't look like the type to do that kind of thing.
……
I'm sorry about Izumi-sempai, Dai-chan.
Oh, don't worry about it, eh.
So, would you like to come to my room then?
It's been so long, we have so many things to catch up on, dontcha know, Hana-chan.
Hmm...
I'll pass.
I'm tired today, so I'm gonna eat dinner and go to bed.
I'm sorry. See you tomor-row!
B-but...
Tch.
Oh well. It's still the first day.
Haste makes waste.
Oh my, my, my, my. Look at the time.

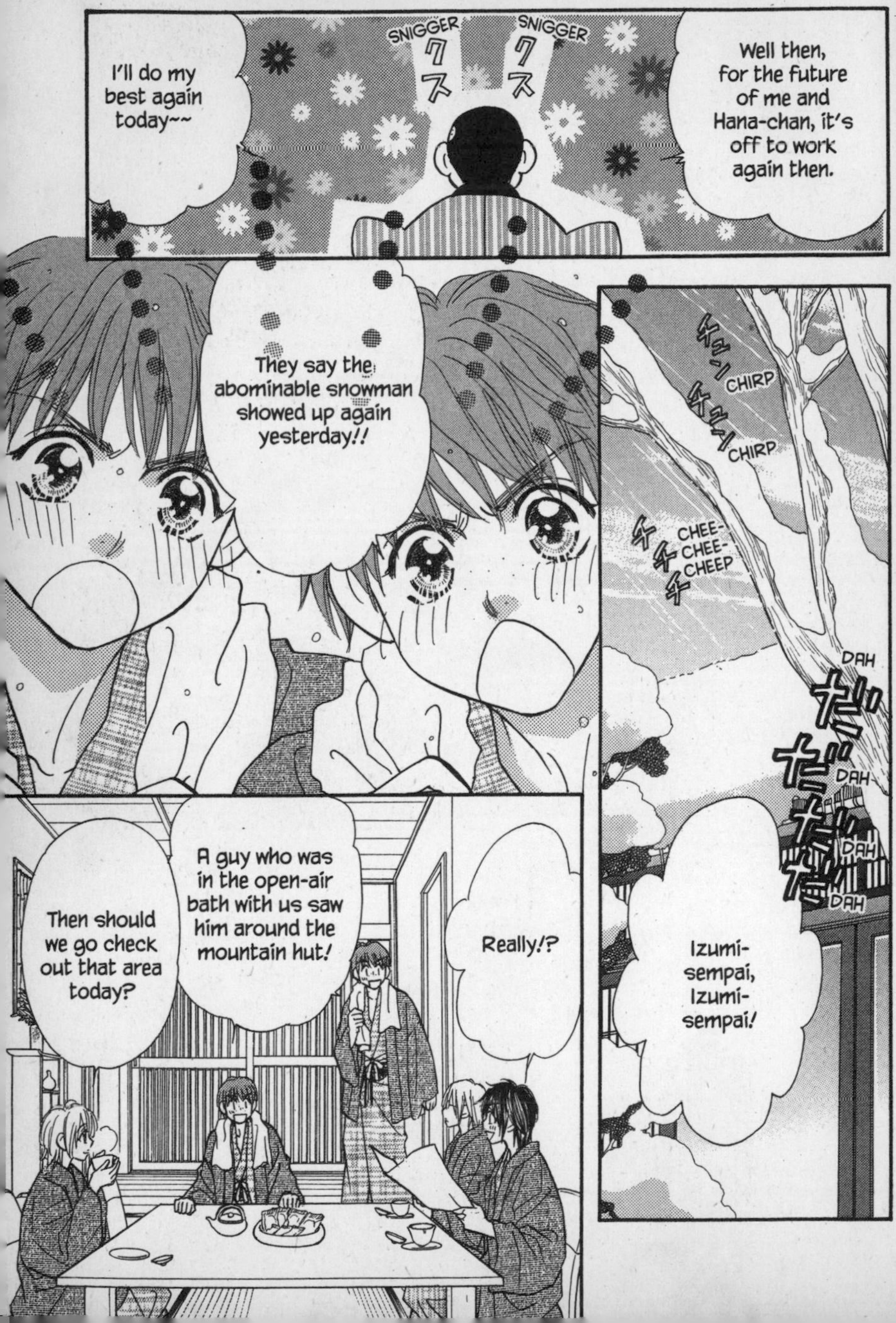
Well then, for the future of me and Hana-chan, it's off to work again then.
SNIGGER
ク
ス
SNIGGER
ク
ス
I'll do my best again today~~
CHIRP
CHIRP
チ
チ
チ
CHEE-CHEE-CHEEP
DAH
DAH
DAH
DAH
Izumi-sempai, Izumi-sempai!
They say the abominable snowman showed up again yesterday!!
Really!?
A guy who was in the open-air bath with us saw him around the mountain hut!
Then should we go check out that area today?

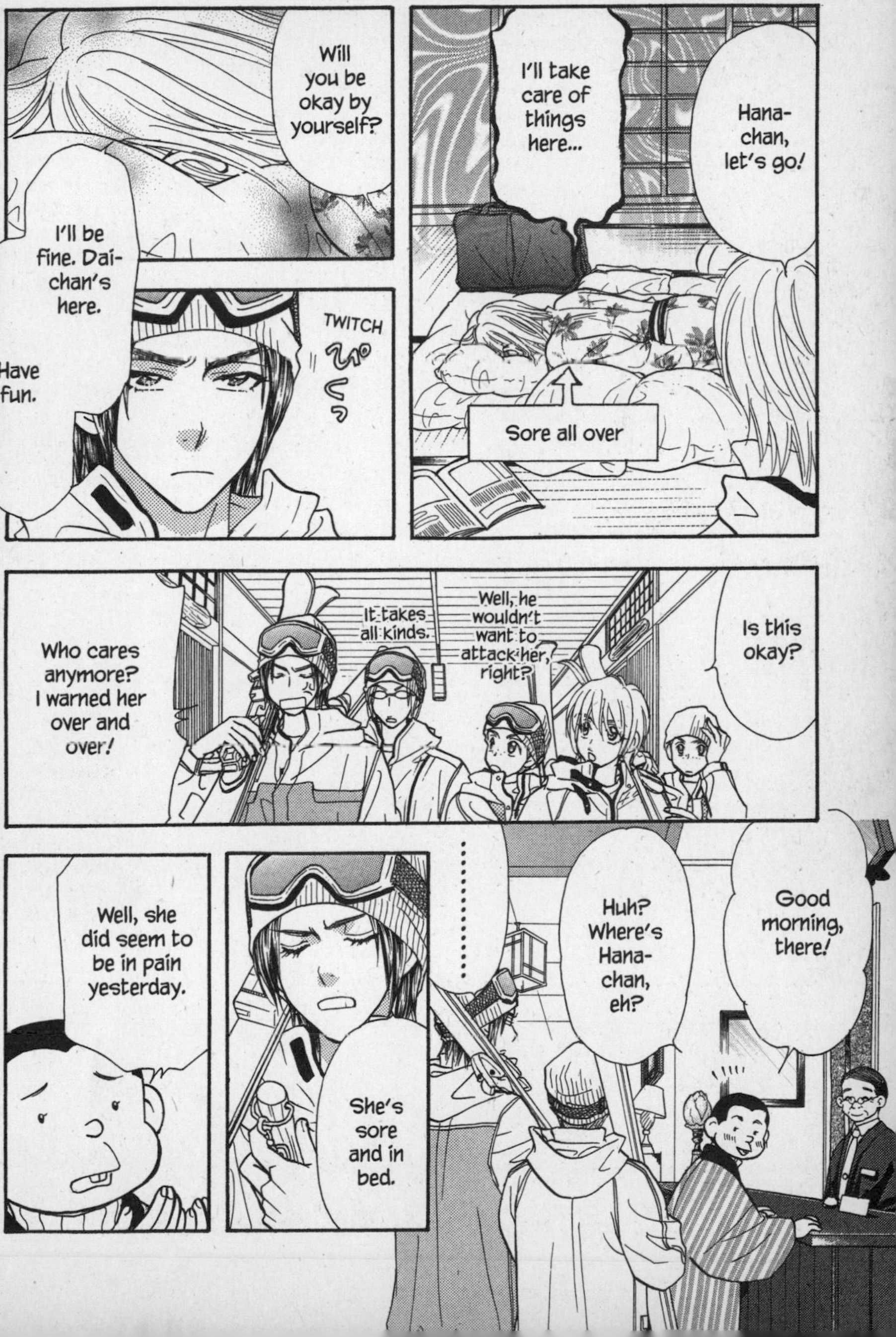
Hana-chan, let's go!
I'll take care of things here...
Sore all over
Will you be okay by yourself?
I'll be fine. Dai-chan's here.
Have fun.
TWITCH
Is this okay?
Well, he wouldn't want to attack her, right?
It takes all kinds.
Who cares anymore? I warned her over and over!
Good morning, there!
Huh? Where's Hana-chan, eh?
......
She's sore and in bed.
Well, she did seem to be in pain yesterday.

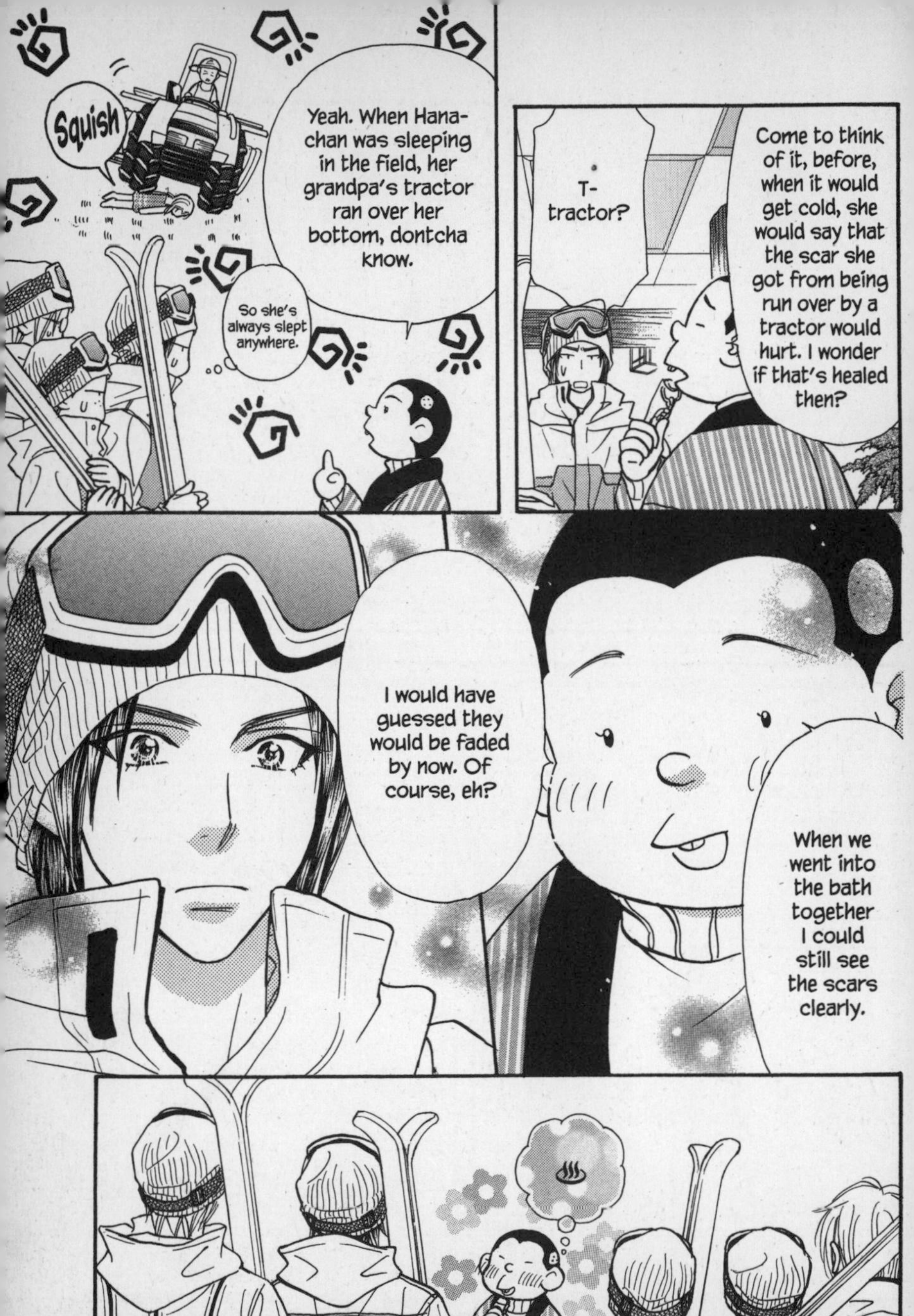
Come to think of it, before, when it would get cold, she would say that the scar she got from being run over by a tractor would hurt. I wonder if that's healed then?
T- tractor?
Yeah. When Hana-chan was sleeping in the field, her grandpa's tractor ran over her bottom, dontcha know.
Squish
So she's always slept anywhere.
When we went into the bath together I could still see the scars clearly.
I would have guessed they would be faded by now. Of course, eh?

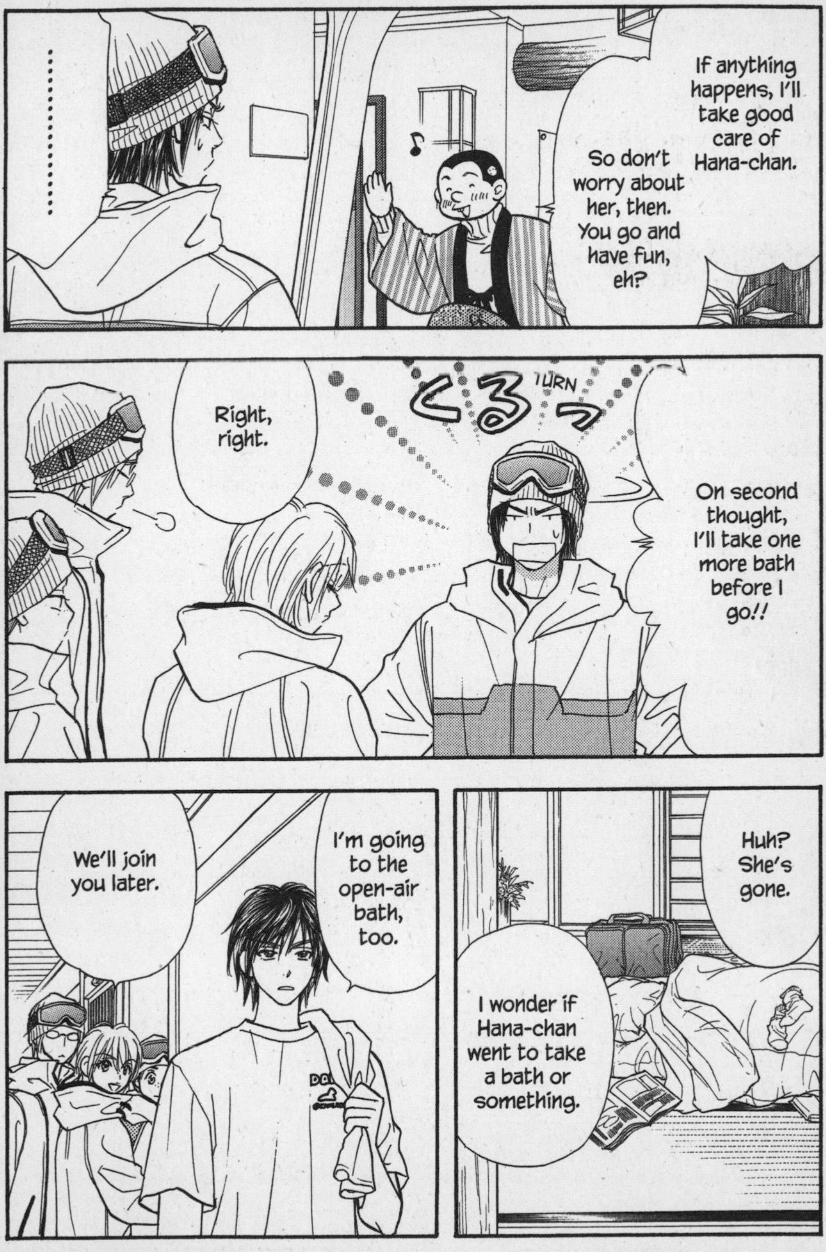
If anything happens, I'll take good care of Hana-chan.
So don't worry about her, then. You go and have fun, eh?
......
On second thought, I'll take one more bath before I go!!
くるっ
TURN
Right, right.
Huh? She's gone.
I wonder if Hana-chan went to take a bath or something.
I'm going to the open-air bath, too.
We'll join you later.

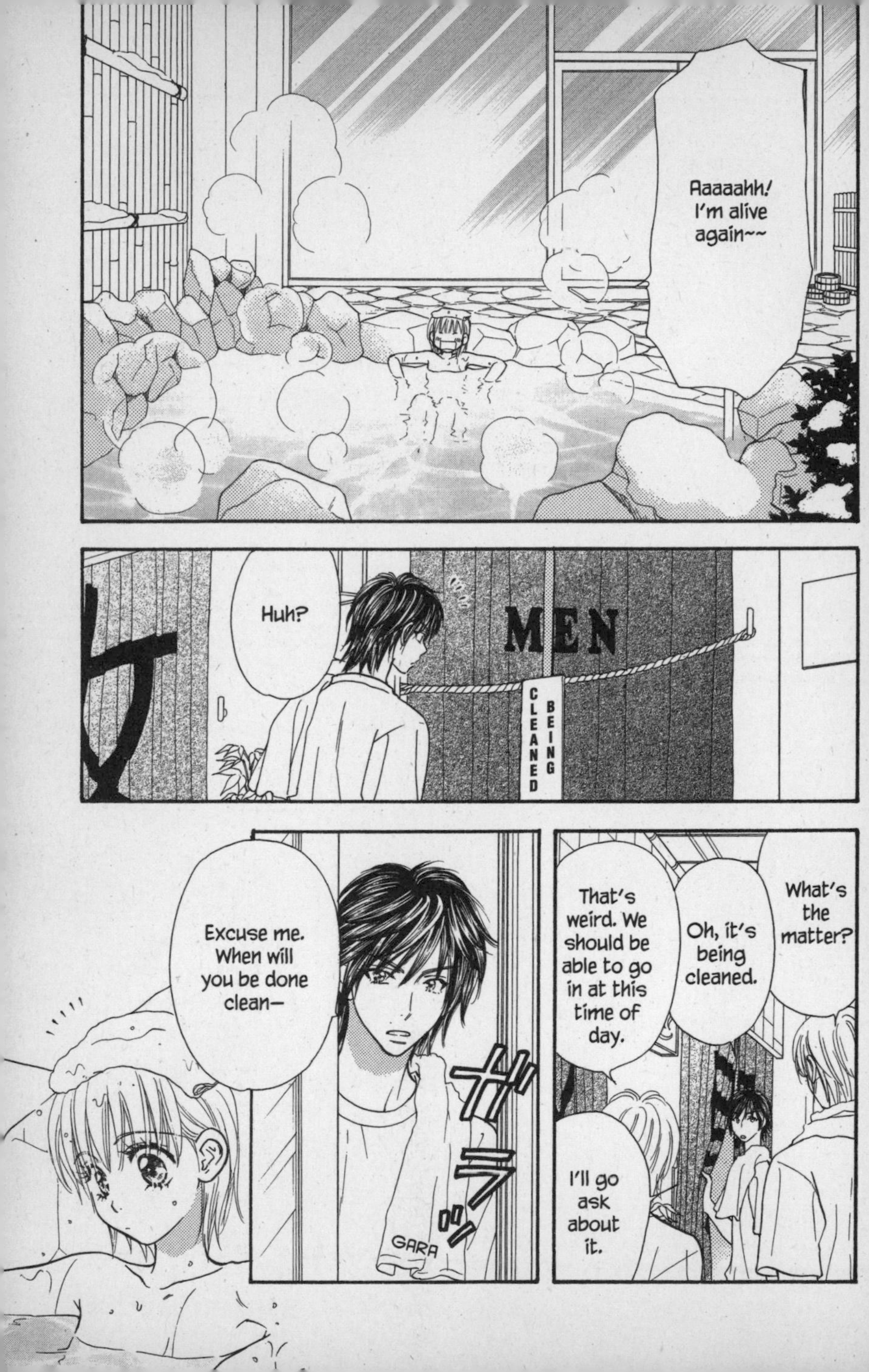

Aaaaahh! I'm alive again~~
Huh?
MEN
BEING CLEANED
What's the matter?
Oh, it's being cleaned.
That's weird. We should be able to go in at this time of day.
I'll go ask about it.
Excuse me. When will you be done clean—
GARA

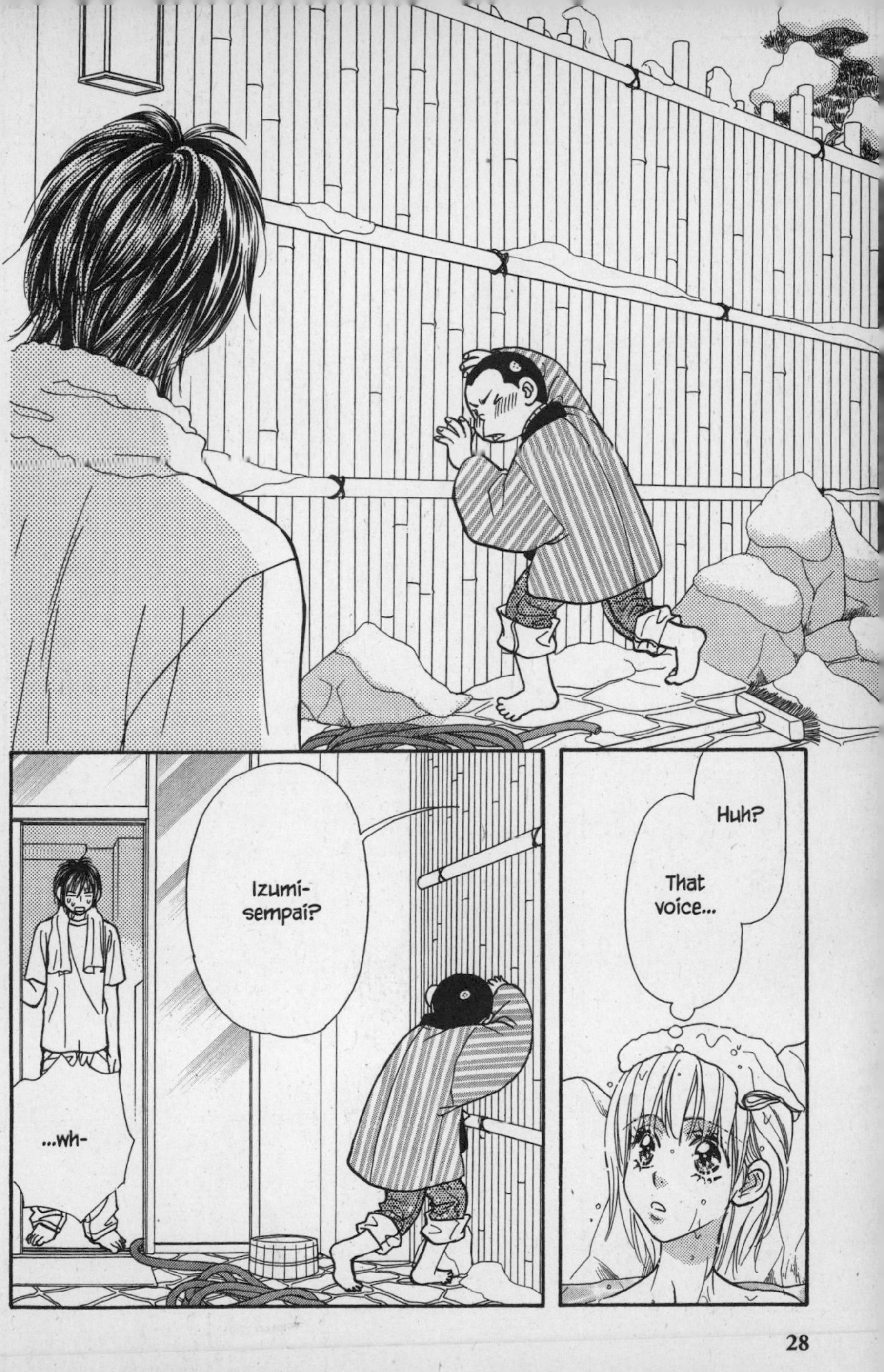
Huh?
That voice...
Izumi-sempai?
...wh-

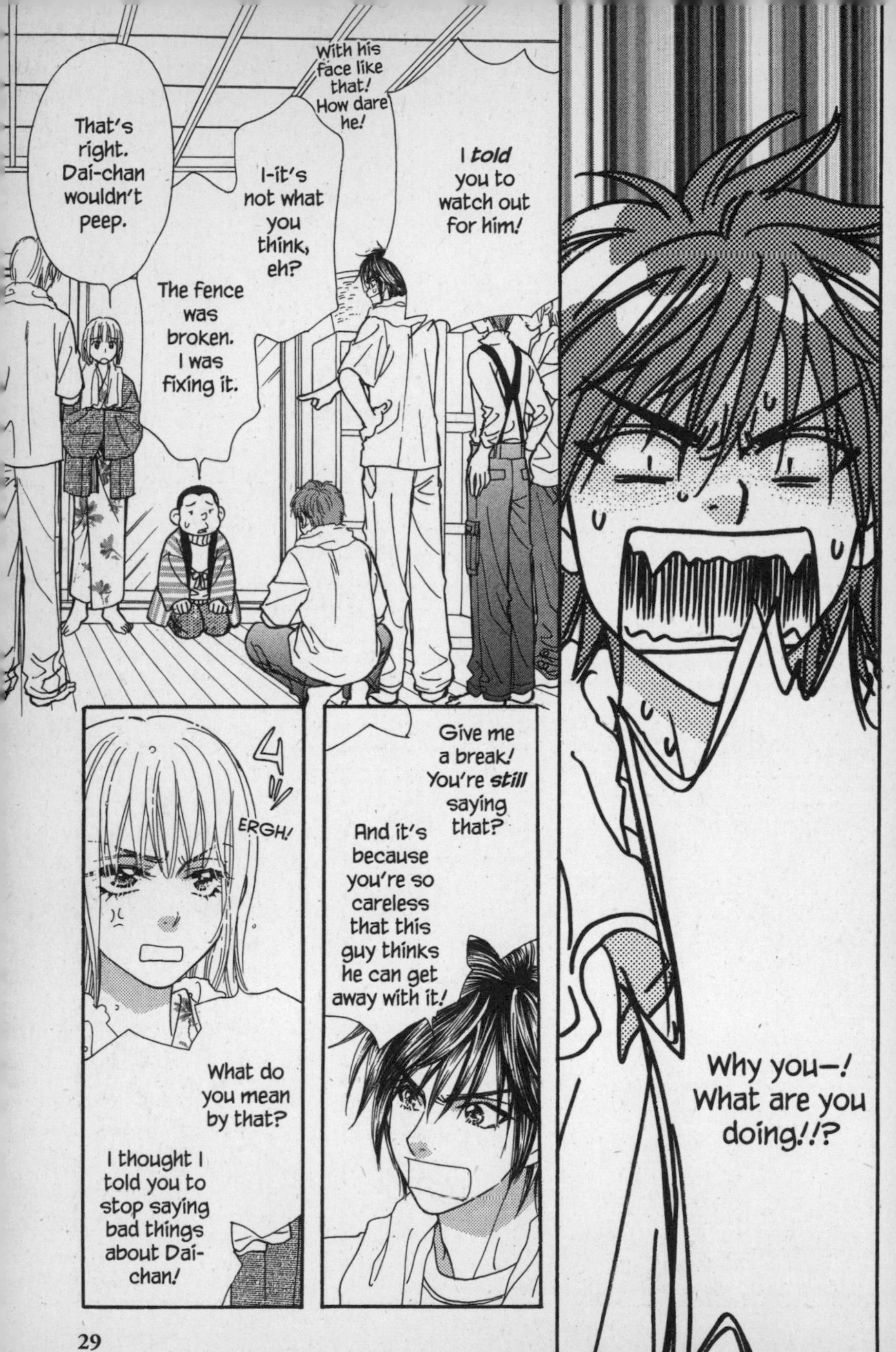

Why you—! What are you doing!!?
With his face like that! How dare he!
I *told* you to watch out for him!
I-it's not what you think, eh?
That's right. Dai-chan wouldn't peep.
The fence was broken. I was fixing it.
Give me a break! You're *still* saying that?
And it's because you're so careless that this guy thinks he can get away with it!
ERGH!
What do you mean by that?
I thought I told you to stop saying bad things about Dai-chan!

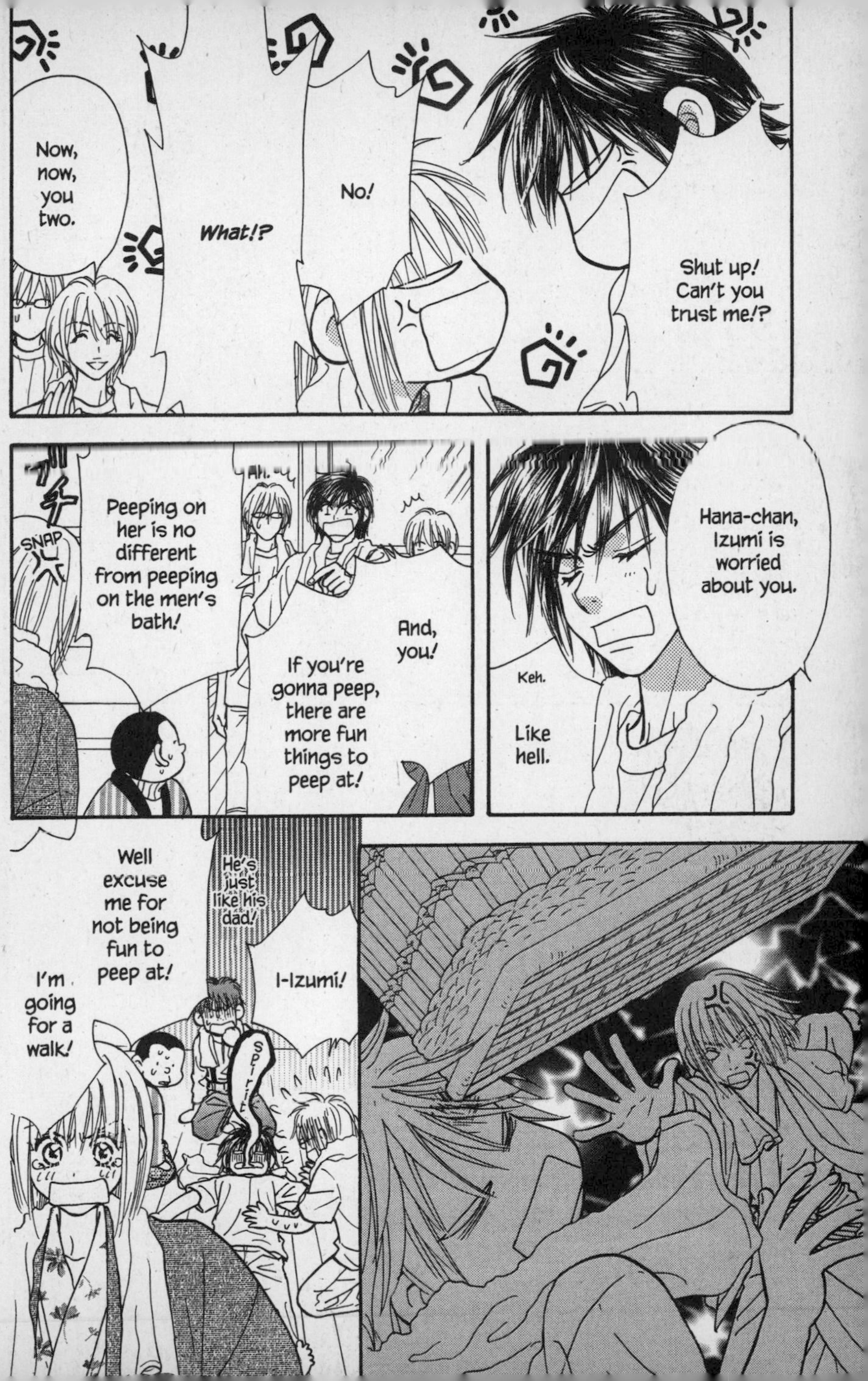
Shut up! Can't you trust me!?
No!
What!?
Now, now, you two.
Hana-chan, Izumi is worried about you.
Keh.
Like hell.
Ah.
SNAP
Peeping on her is no different from peeping on the men's bath!
And, you!
If you're gonna peep, there are more fun things to peep at!
I-Izumi!
He's just like his dad!
Spirit
Well excuse me for not being fun to peep at!
I'm going for a walk!

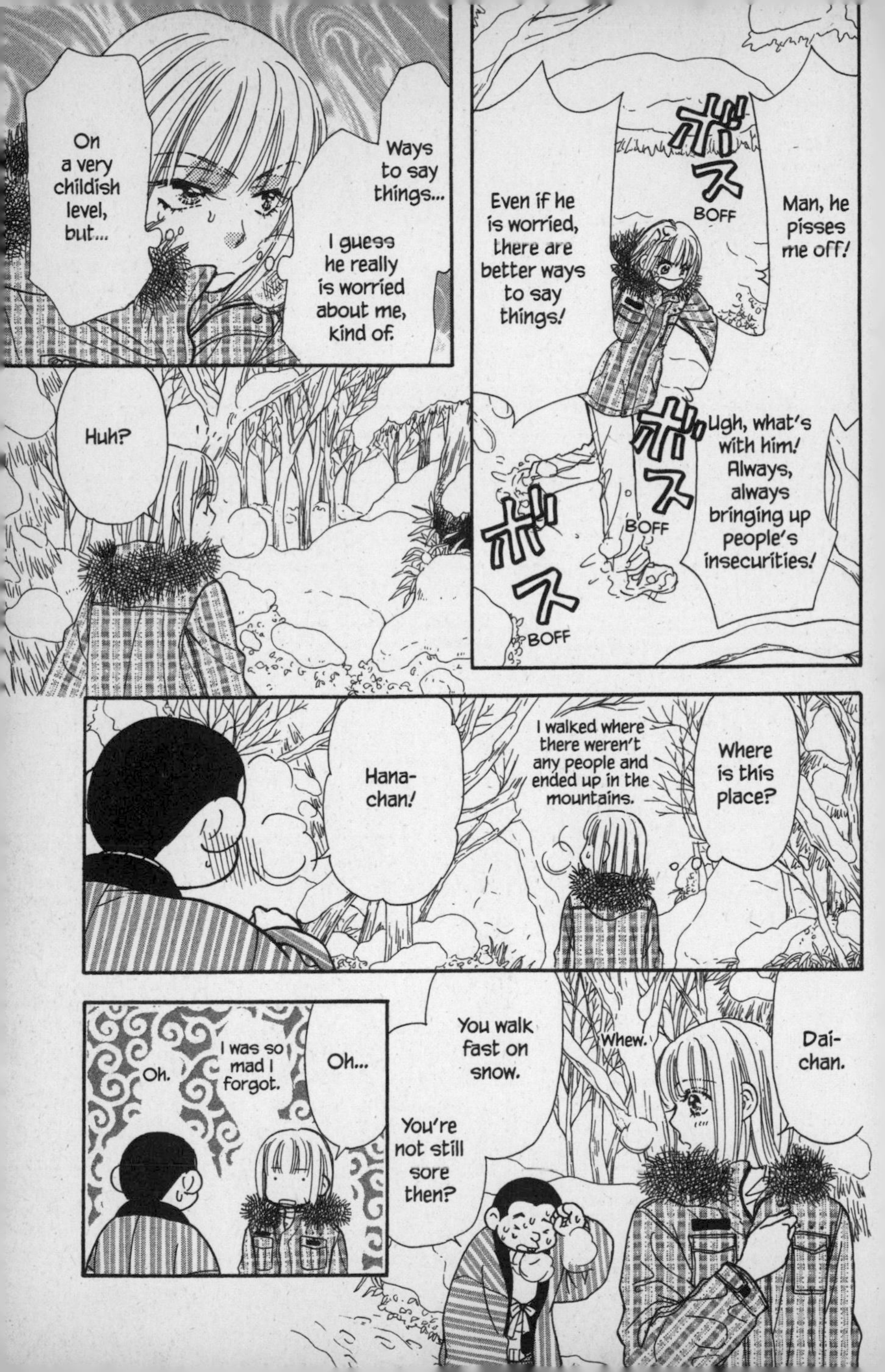
Man, he pisses me off!
ボス
BOFF
Even if he is worried, there are better ways to say things!
Ugh, what's with him! Always, always bringing up people's insecurities!
ボス
BOFF
ボス
BOFF
Ways to say things...
I guess he really is worried about me, kind of.
On a very childish level, but...
Huh?
Where is this place?
I walked where there weren't any people and ended up in the mountains.
Hana-chan!
Dai-chan.
Whew.
You walk fast on snow.
You're not still sore then?
Oh...
I was so mad I forgot.
Oh.

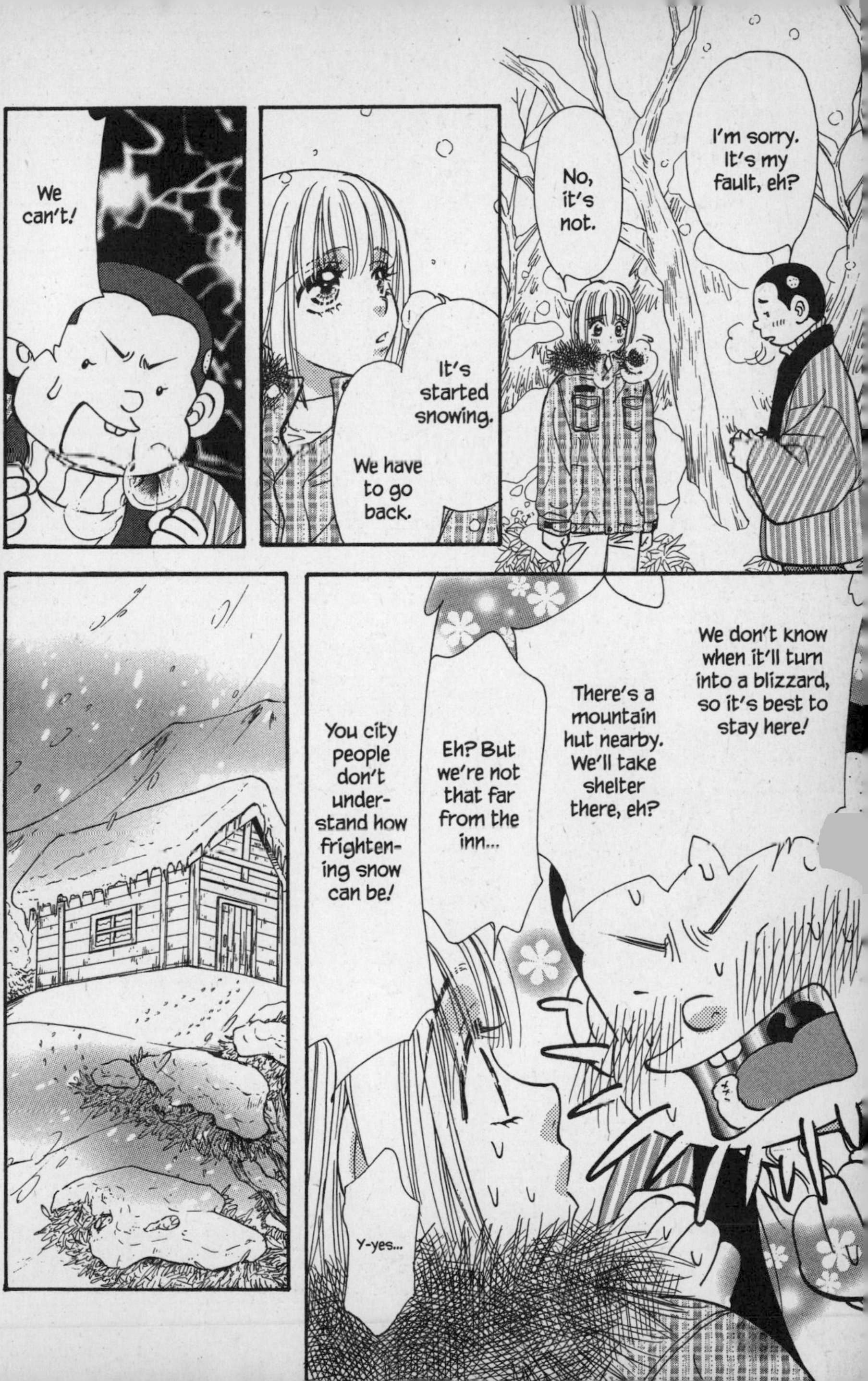
I'm sorry. It's my fault, eh?
No, it's not.
It's started snowing.
We have to go back.
We can't!
We don't know when it'll turn into a blizzard, so it's best to stay here!
There's a mountain hut nearby. We'll take shelter there, eh?
Eh? But we're not that far from the inn...
You city people don't understand how frightening snow can be!
Y-yes...

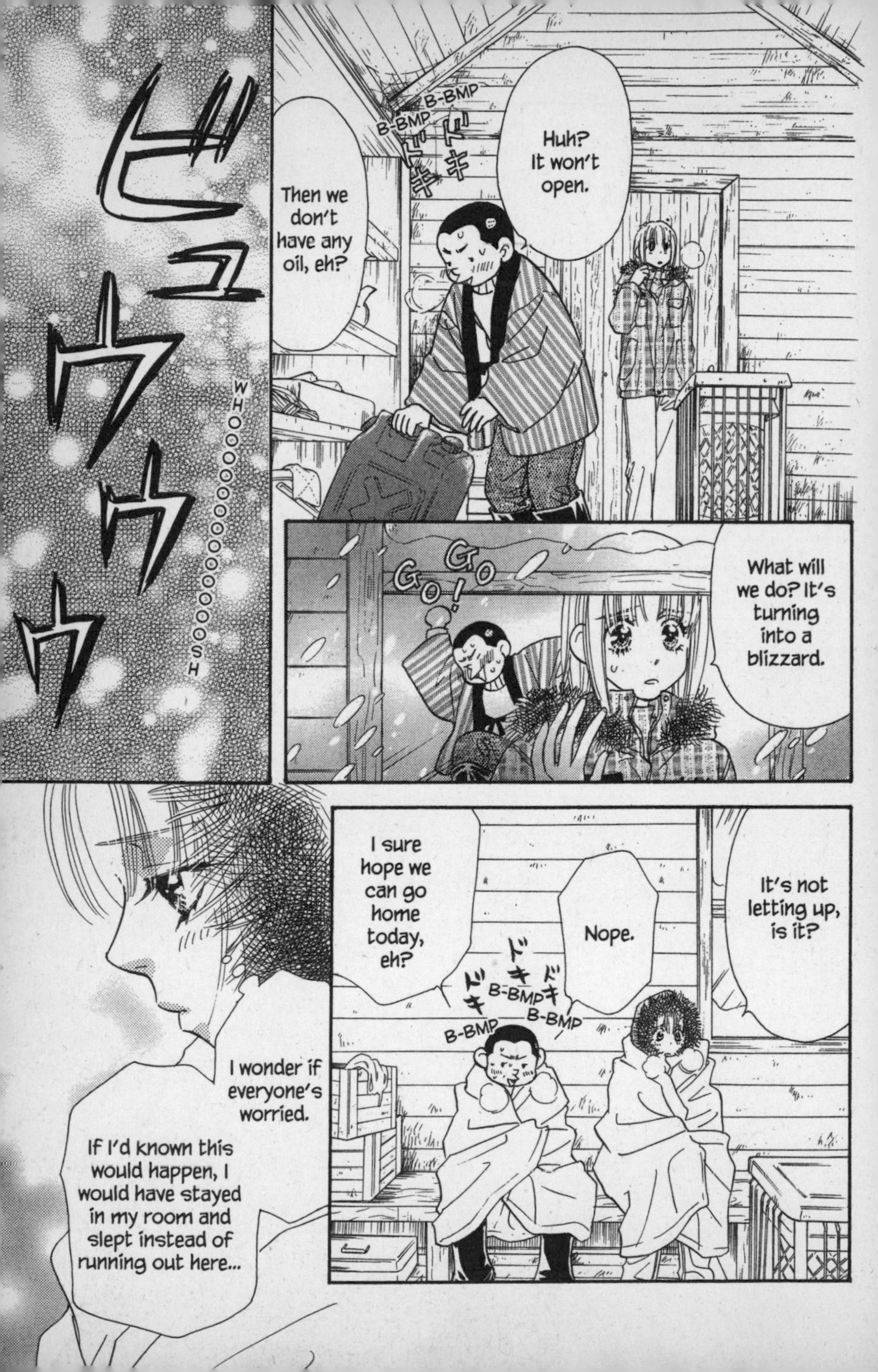
Huh? It won't open.
B-BMP B-BMP
ドキドキ
Then we don't have any oil, eh?
What will we do? It's turning into a blizzard.
GO GO!
ビュウウウウ
WHOOOOOOOOOOOOOOOSH
It's not letting up, is it?
Nope.
ドキドキ
B-BMP B-BMP
ドキドキ
B-BMP
I sure hope we can go home today, eh?
I wonder if everyone's worried.
If I'd known this would happen, I would have stayed in my room and slept instead of running out here...

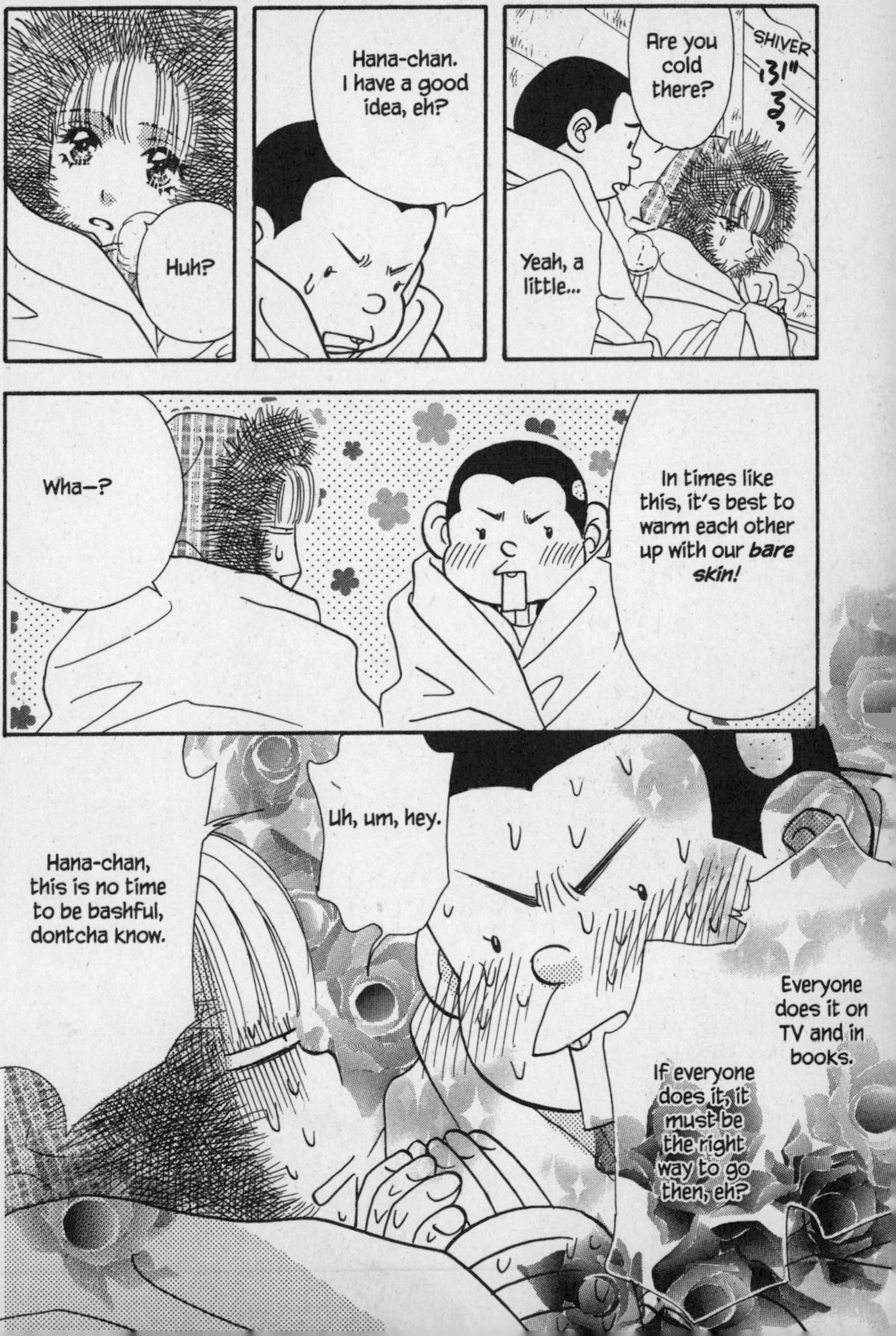
SHIVER
Are you cold there?
Yeah, a little...
Hana-chan. I have a good idea, eh?
Huh?
In times like this, it's best to warm each other up with our *bare skin!*
Wha–?
Everyone does it on TV and in books.
If everyone does it, it must be the right way to go then, eh?
Uh, um, hey.
Hana-chan, this is no time to be bashful, dontcha know.

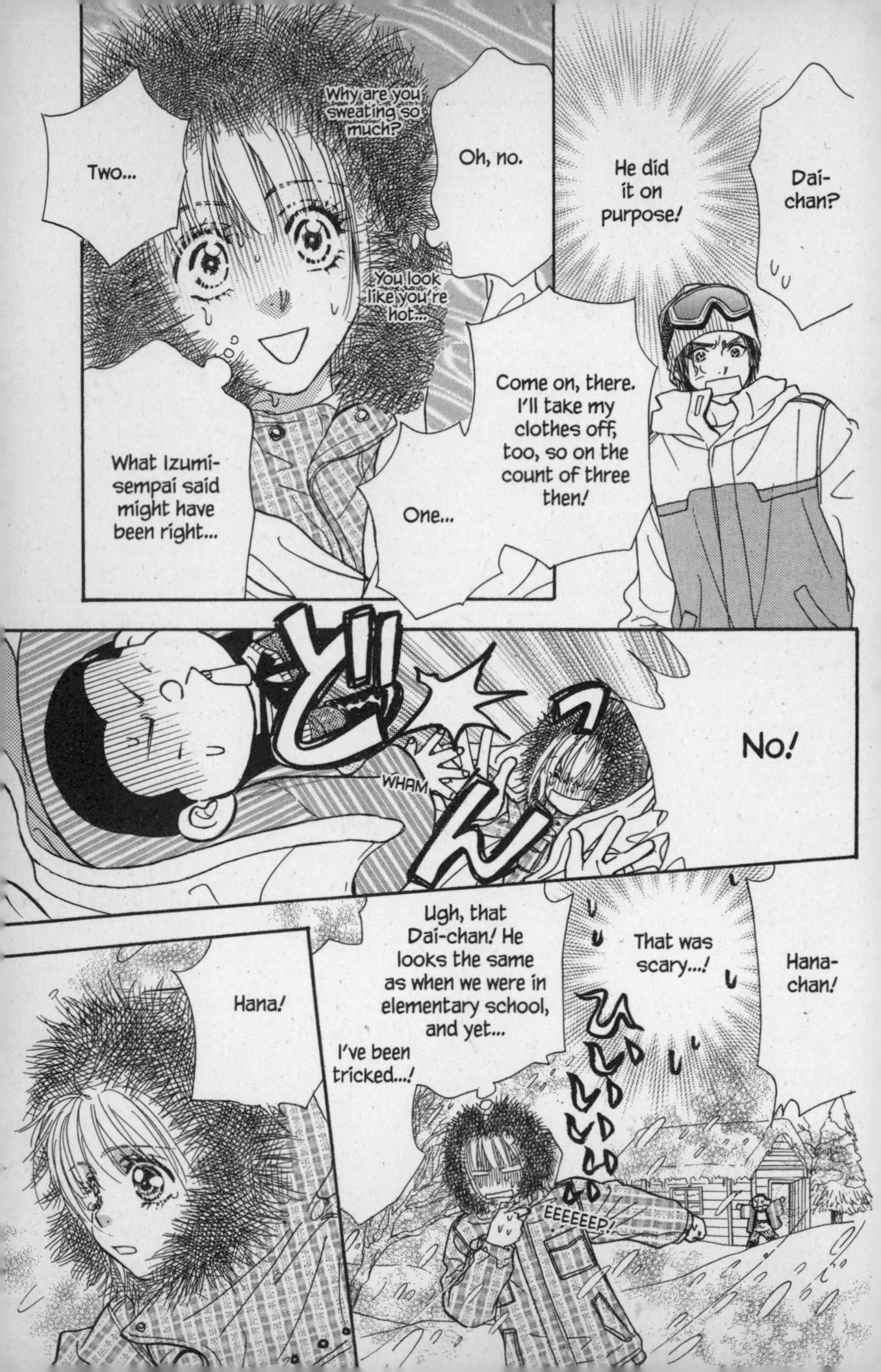
Dai-chan?
He did it on purpose!
Come on, there. I'll take my clothes off, too, so on the count of three then!
Oh, no.
Why are you sweating so much?
You look like you're hot...
One...
What Izumi-sempai said might have been right...
Two...
No!
どん
WHAM
Hana-chan!
That was scary...!
Ugh, that Dai-chan! He looks the same as when we were in elementary school, and yet...
I've been tricked...!
EEEEEEP!
Hana!

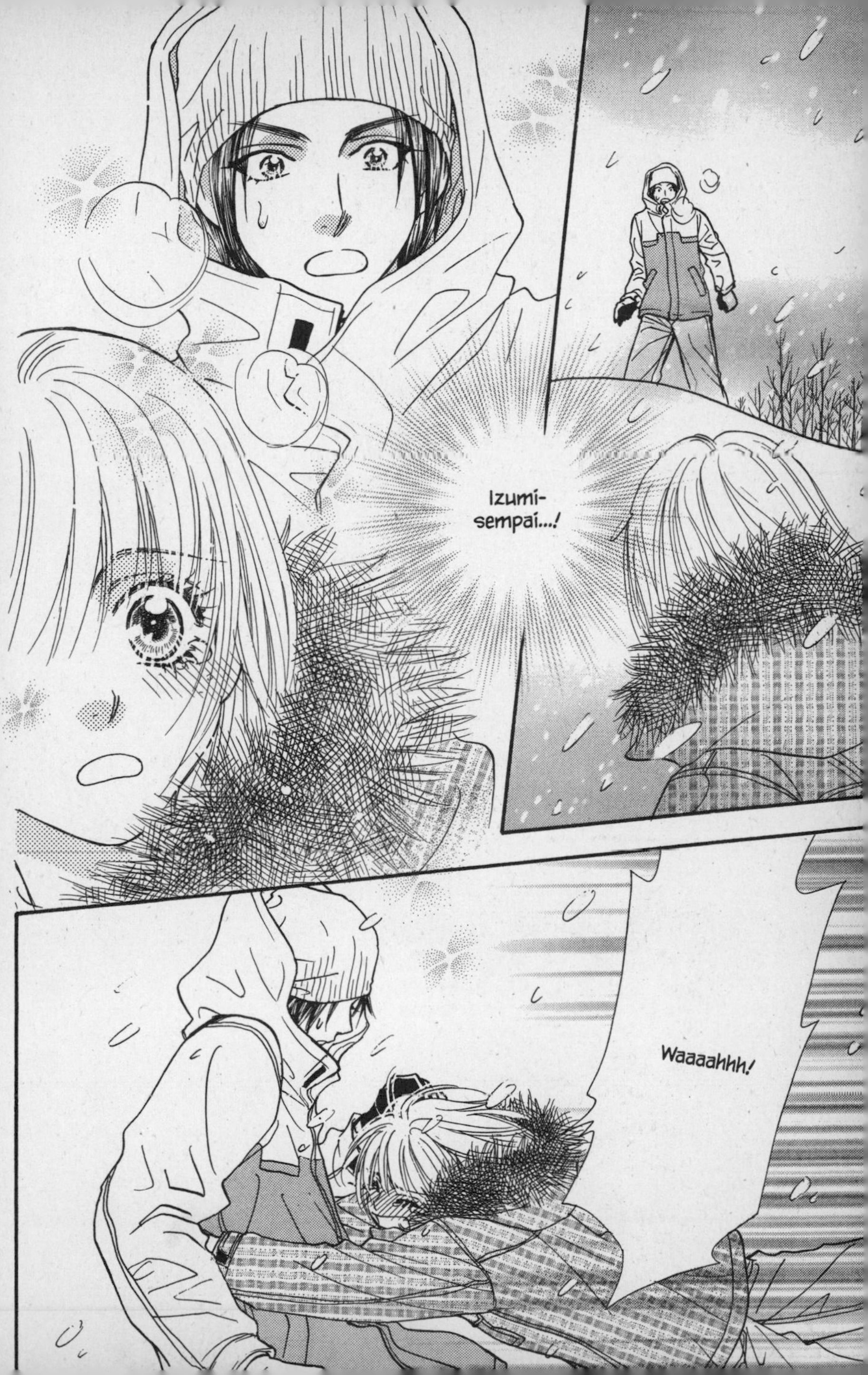
Izumi-
sempai...!
Waaaahhh!

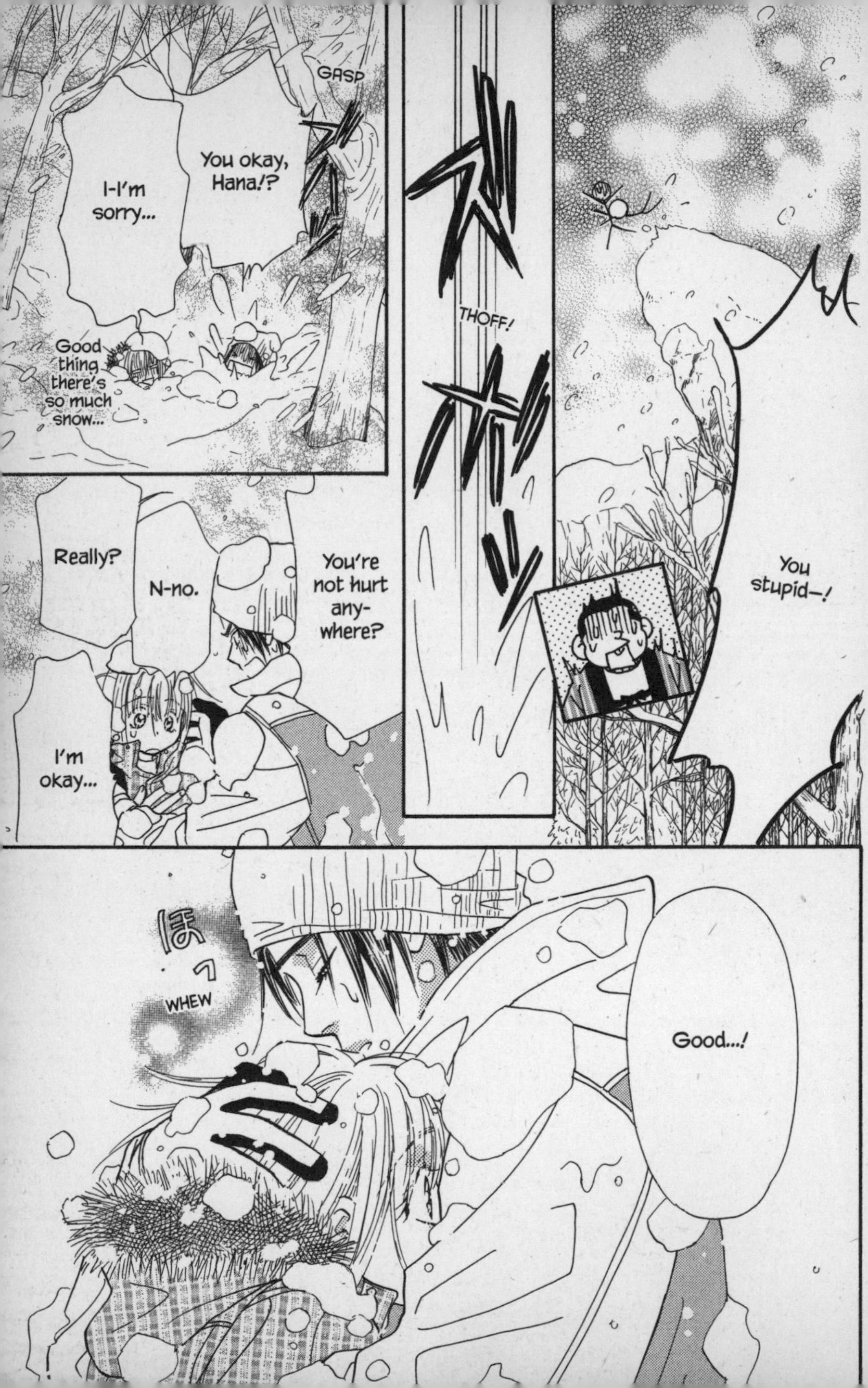
You stupid—!
THOFF!
GASP
You okay, Hana!?
I-I'm sorry...
Good thing there's so much snow...
You're not hurt anywhere?
N-no.
Really?
I'm okay...
Good...!
ほっ
WHEW

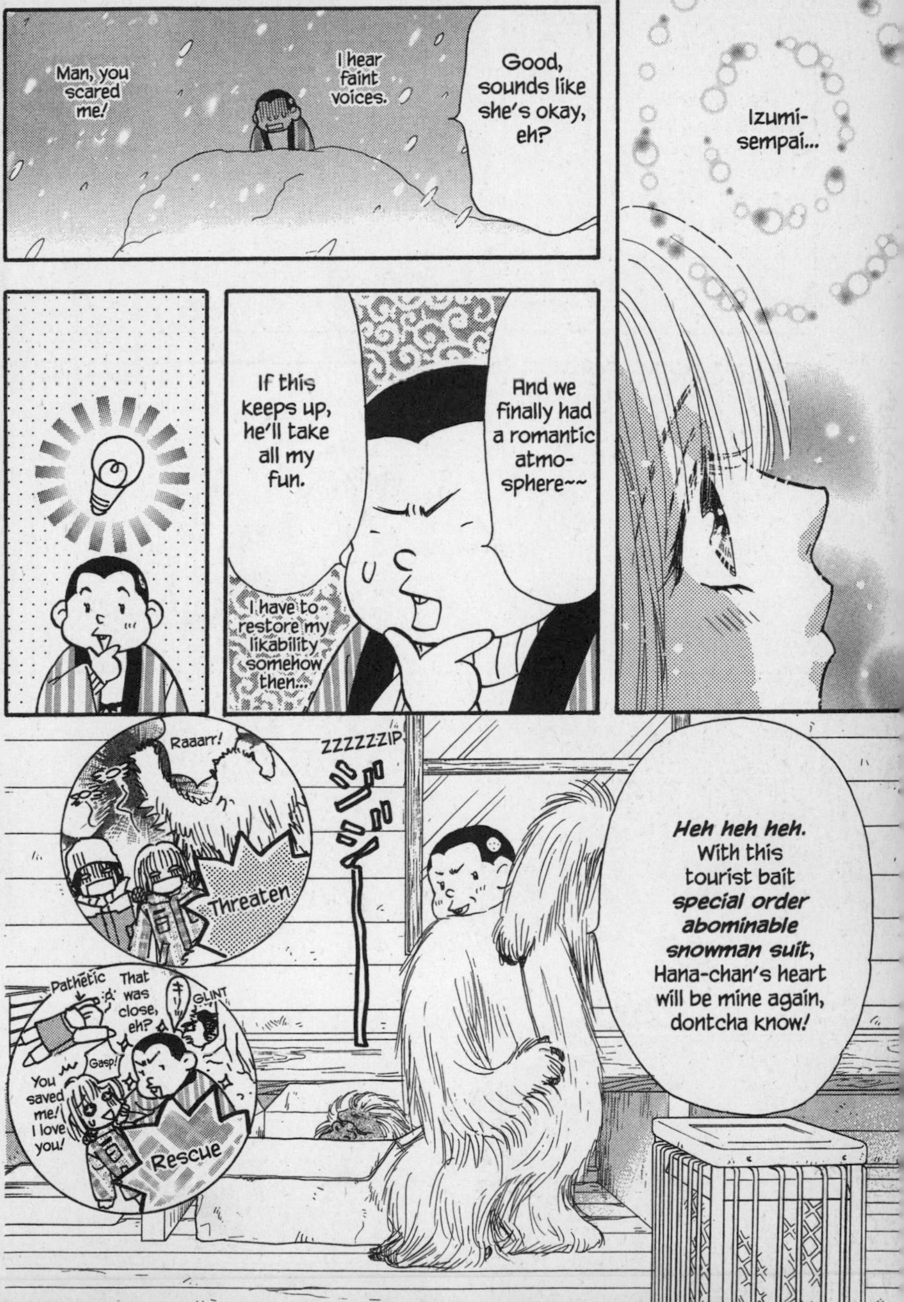
Izumi-sempai...
Good, sounds like she's okay, eh?
I hear faint voices.
Man, you scared me!
And we finally had a romantic atmosphere~~
If this keeps up, he'll take all my fun.
I have to restore my likability somehow then...
Heh heh heh. With this tourist bait *special order abominable snowman suit*, Hana-chan's heart will be mine again, dontcha know!
ZZZZZZIP
Raaarr!
Threaten
GLINT
That was close, eh?
Pathetic
Gasp!
You saved me! I love you!
Rescue

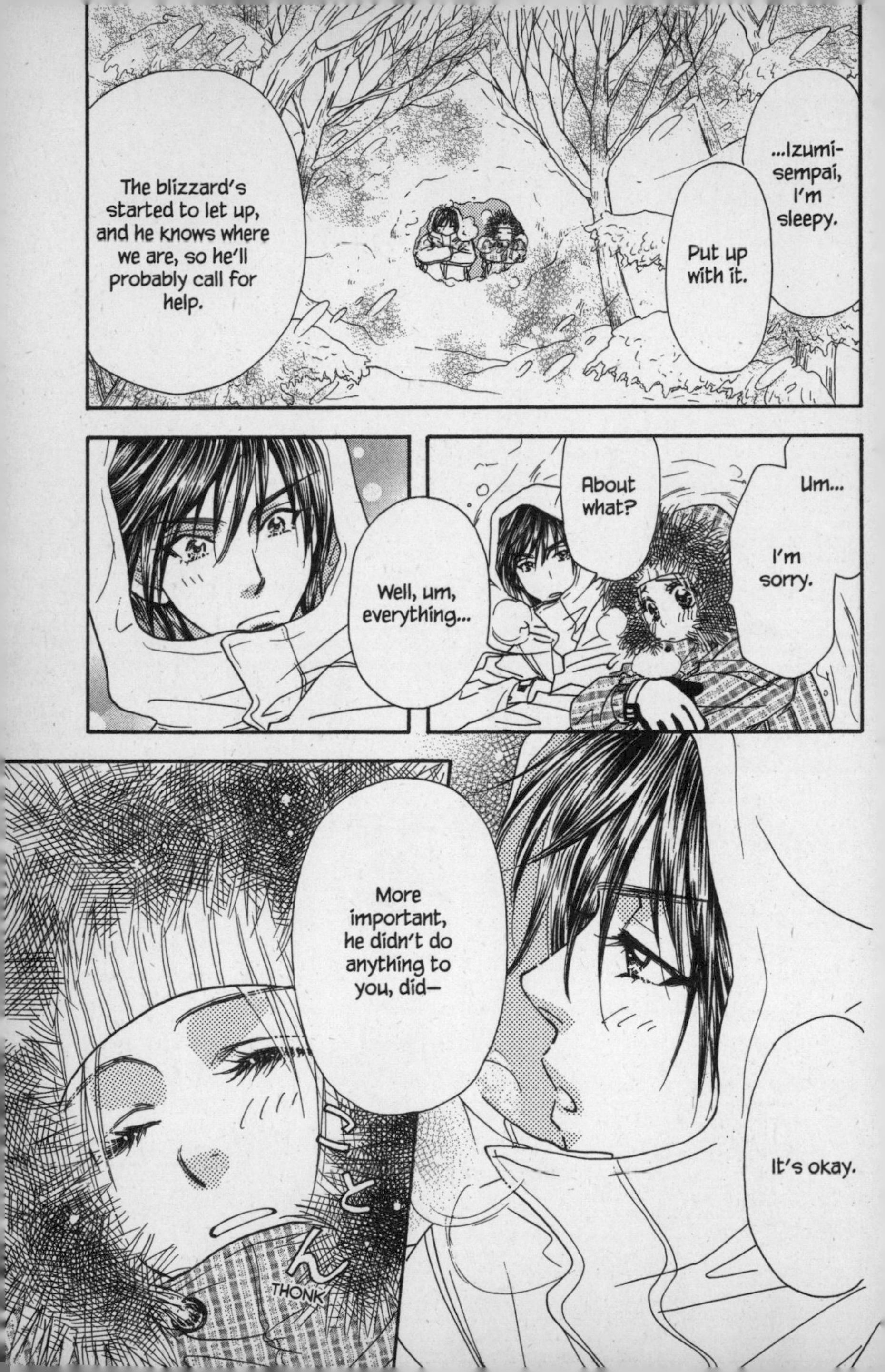
...Izumi-sempai, I'm sleepy.
Put up with it.
The blizzard's started to let up, and he knows where we are, so he'll probably call for help.
Um...
I'm sorry.
About what?
Well, um, everything...
It's okay.
More important, he didn't do anything to you, did—
ことん
THONK

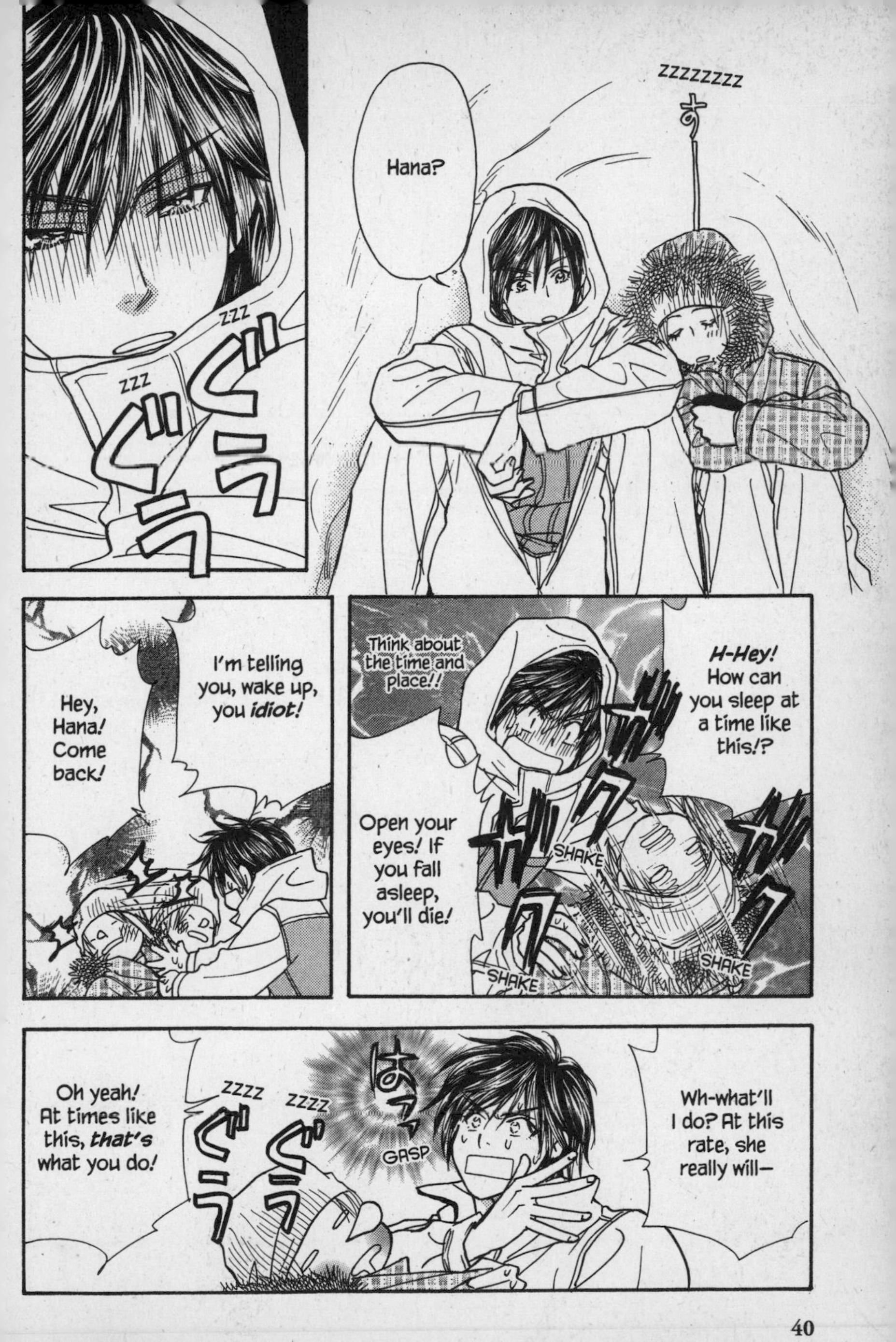
ZZZZZZZZ
Hana?
ZZZ
ZZZ
H-Hey! How can you sleep at a time like this!?
Think about the time and place!!
Open your eyes! If you fall asleep, you'll die!
SHAKE
SHAKE
SHAKE
I'm telling you, wake up, you *idiot!*
Hey, Hana! Come back!
Wh-what'll I do? At this rate, she really will—
GASP
ZZZZ
ZZZZ
Oh yeah! At times like this, ***that's*** what you do!

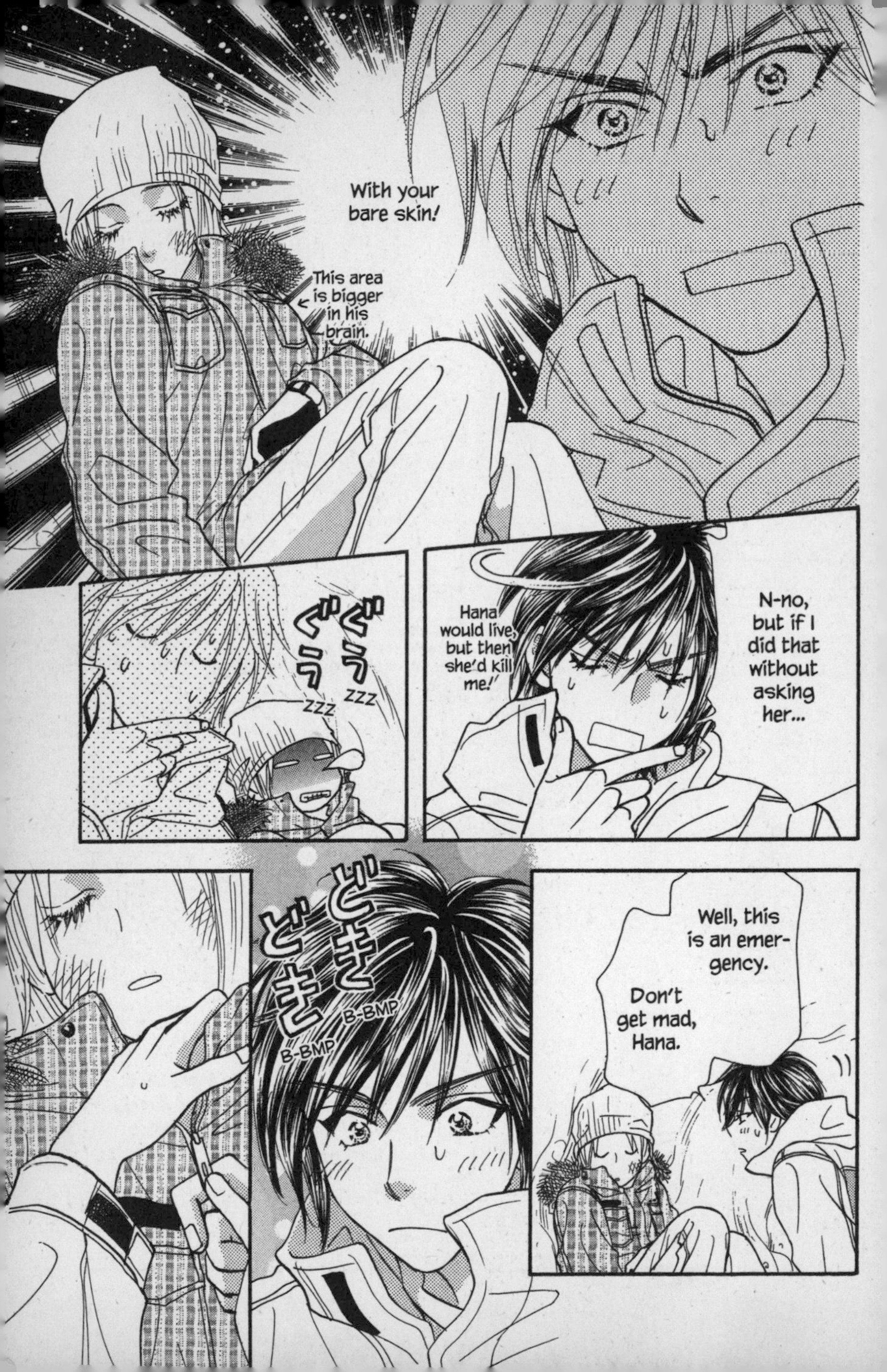
With your bare skin!
This area is bigger in his brain.
N-no, but if I did that without asking her...
Hana would live, but then she'd kill me!
ぐうぐう
ZZZ
ZZZ
Well, this is an emergency.
Don't get mad, Hana.
どきどき
B-BMP
B-BMP

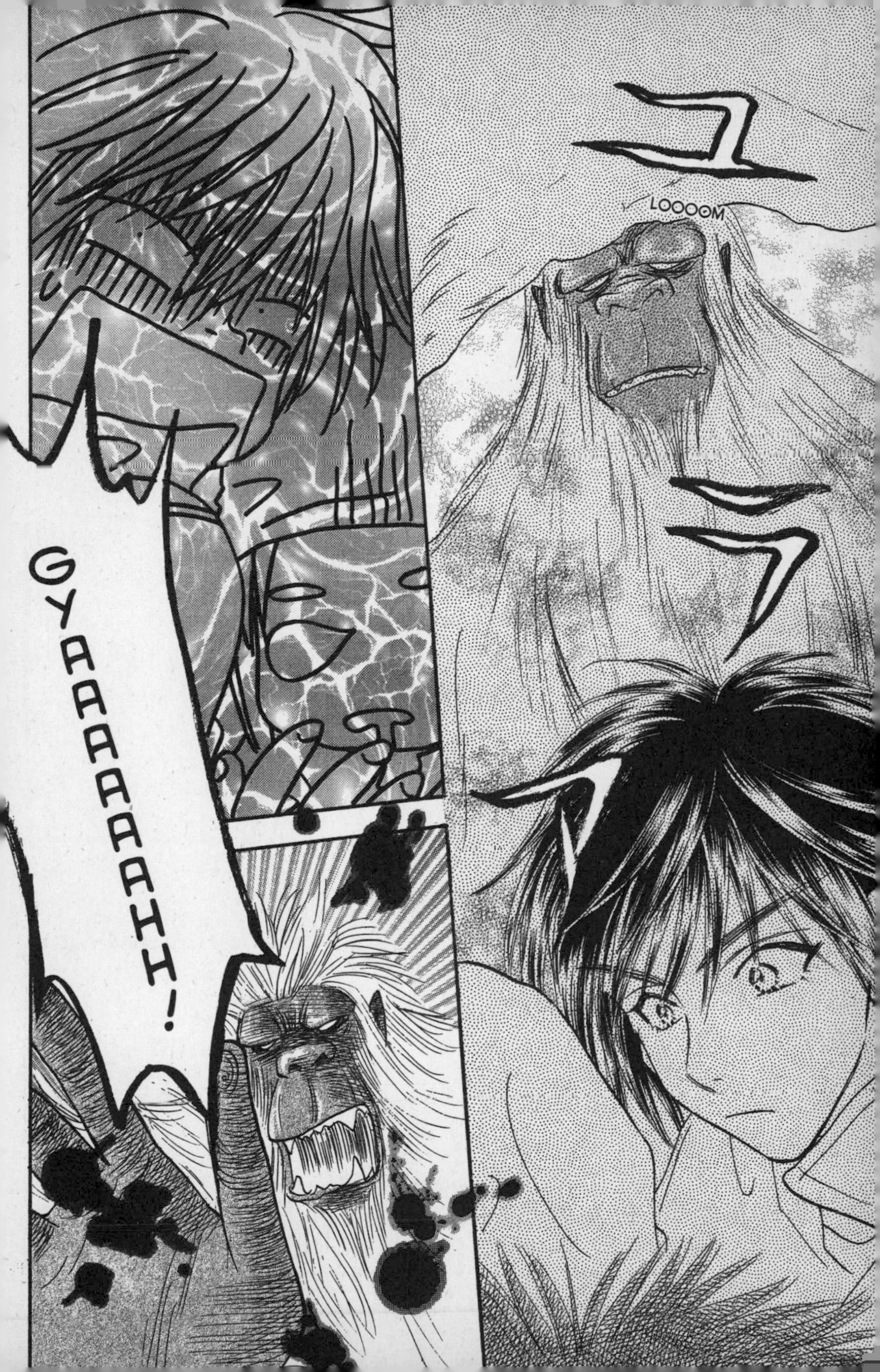
LOOOOM
GYAAAAAAHH!

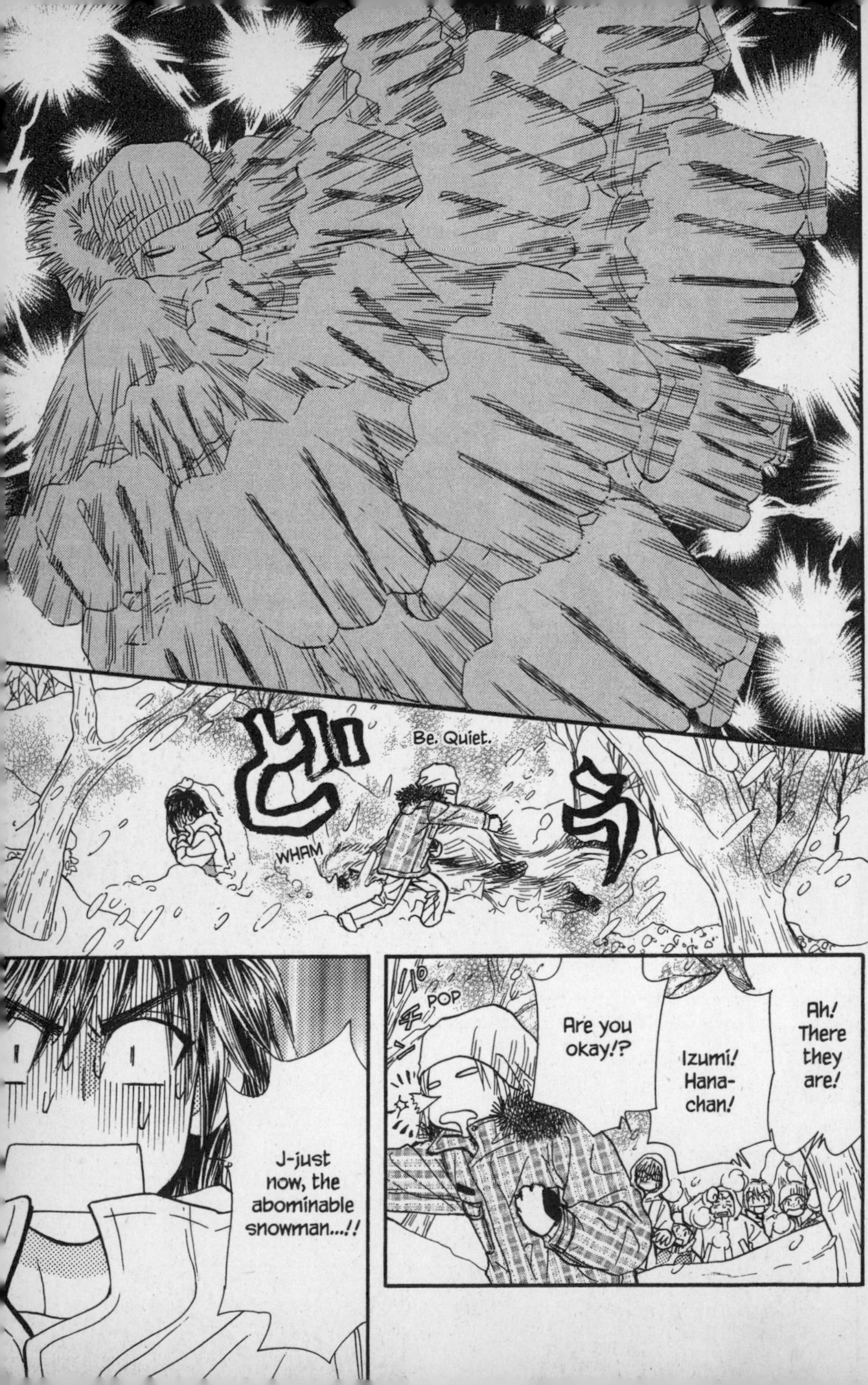
Be. Quiet.
どう
WHAM
Ah! There they are!
Izumi! Hana-chan!
Are you okay!?
POP
J-just now, the abominable snowman...!!

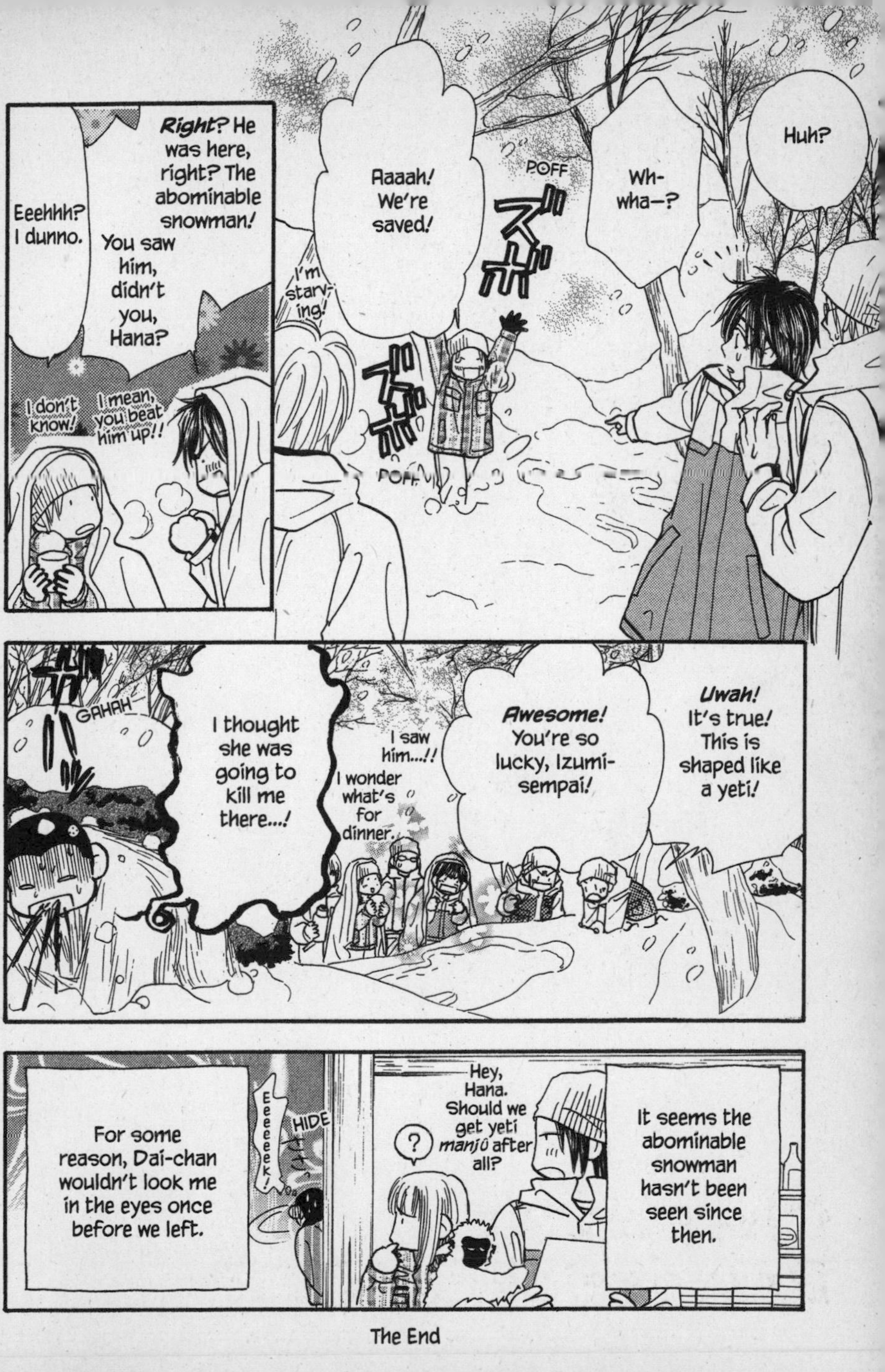
Huh?
Wh-wha–?
POFF
Aaaah! We're saved!
I'm starving!
POFF
Right? He was here, right? The abominable snowman!
You saw him, didn't you, Hana?
Eeehhh? I dunno.
I mean, you beat him up!!
I don't know!
Uwah! It's true! This is shaped like a yeti!
Awesome! You're so lucky, Izumi-sempai!
I saw him...!!
I wonder what's for dinner.
I thought she was going to kill me there...!
GAHAH
It seems the abominable snowman hasn't been seen since then.
Hey, Hana. Should we get yeti manjū after all?
?
HIDE
Eeeeeeek!
For some reason, Dai-chan wouldn't look me in the eyes once before we left.

The End

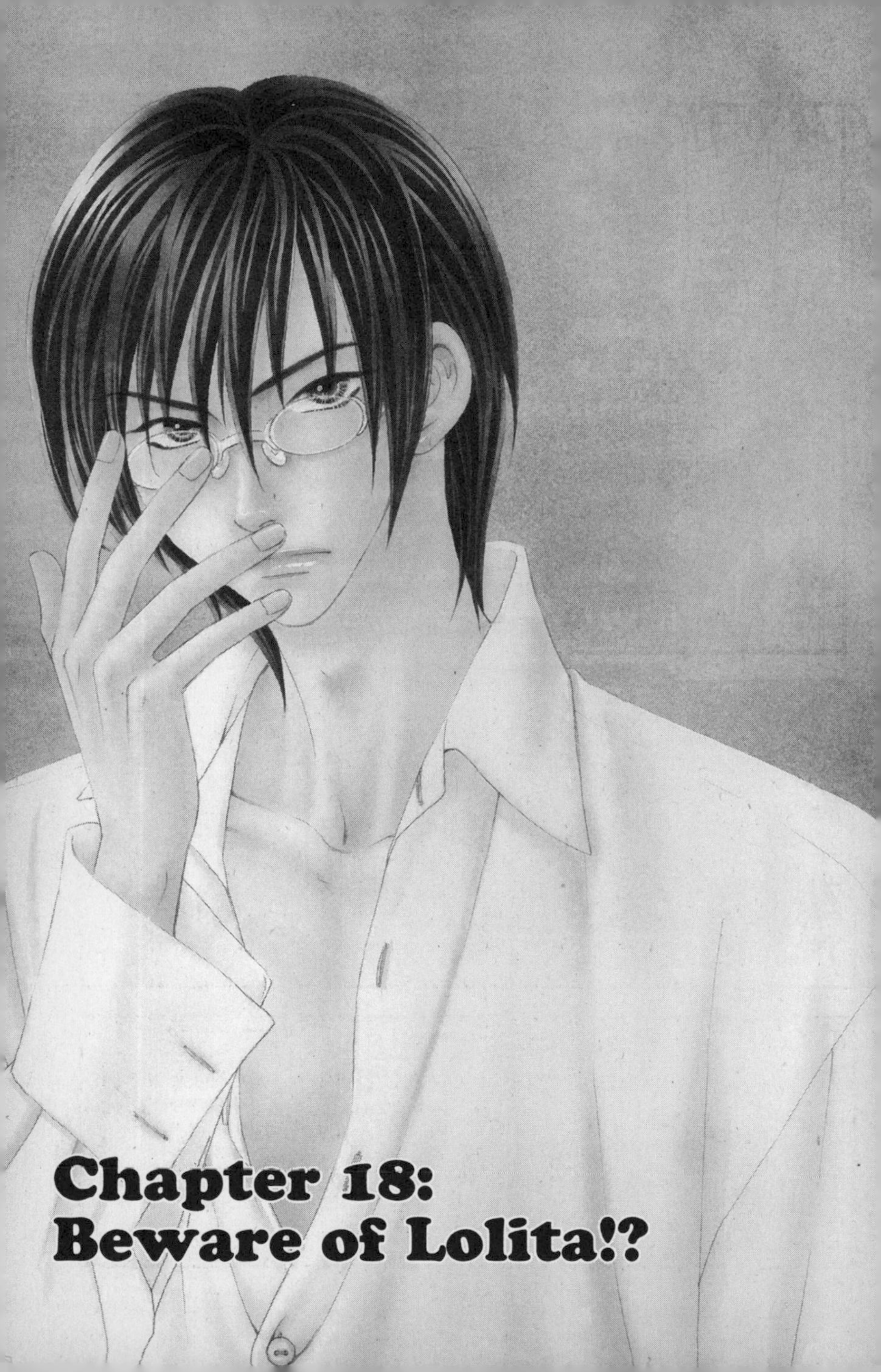

Chapter 18: Beware of Lolita!?

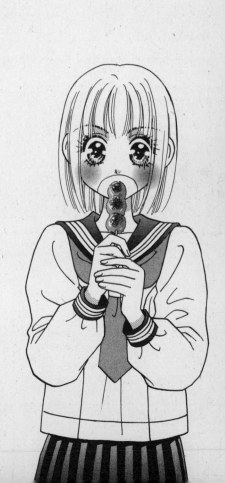

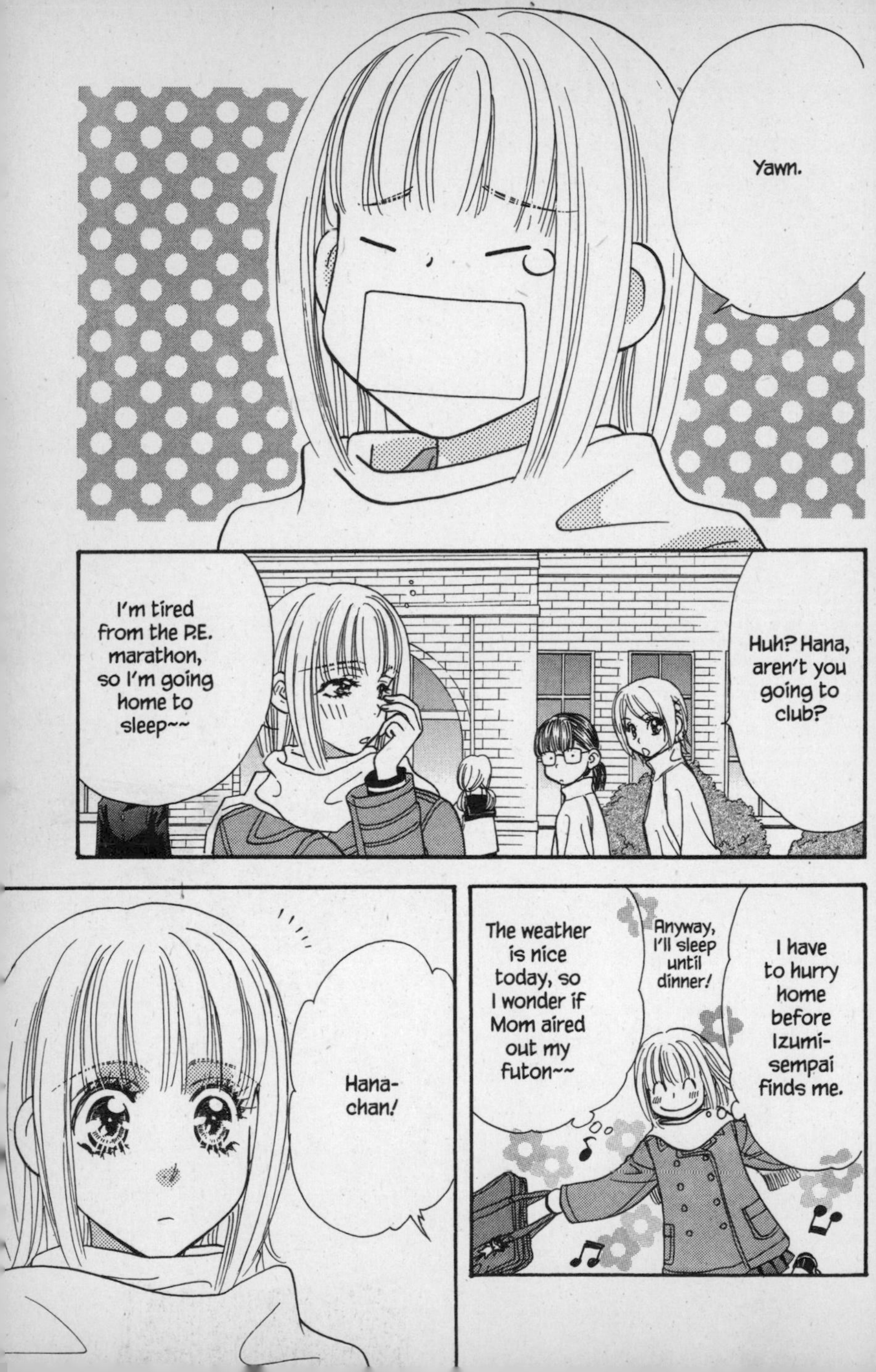
Yawn.
Huh? Hana, aren't you going to club?
I'm tired from the P.E. marathon, so I'm going home to sleep~~
I have to hurry home before Izumi-sempai finds me.
Anyway, I'll sleep until dinner!
The weather is nice today, so I wonder if Mom aired out my futon~~
Hana-chan!

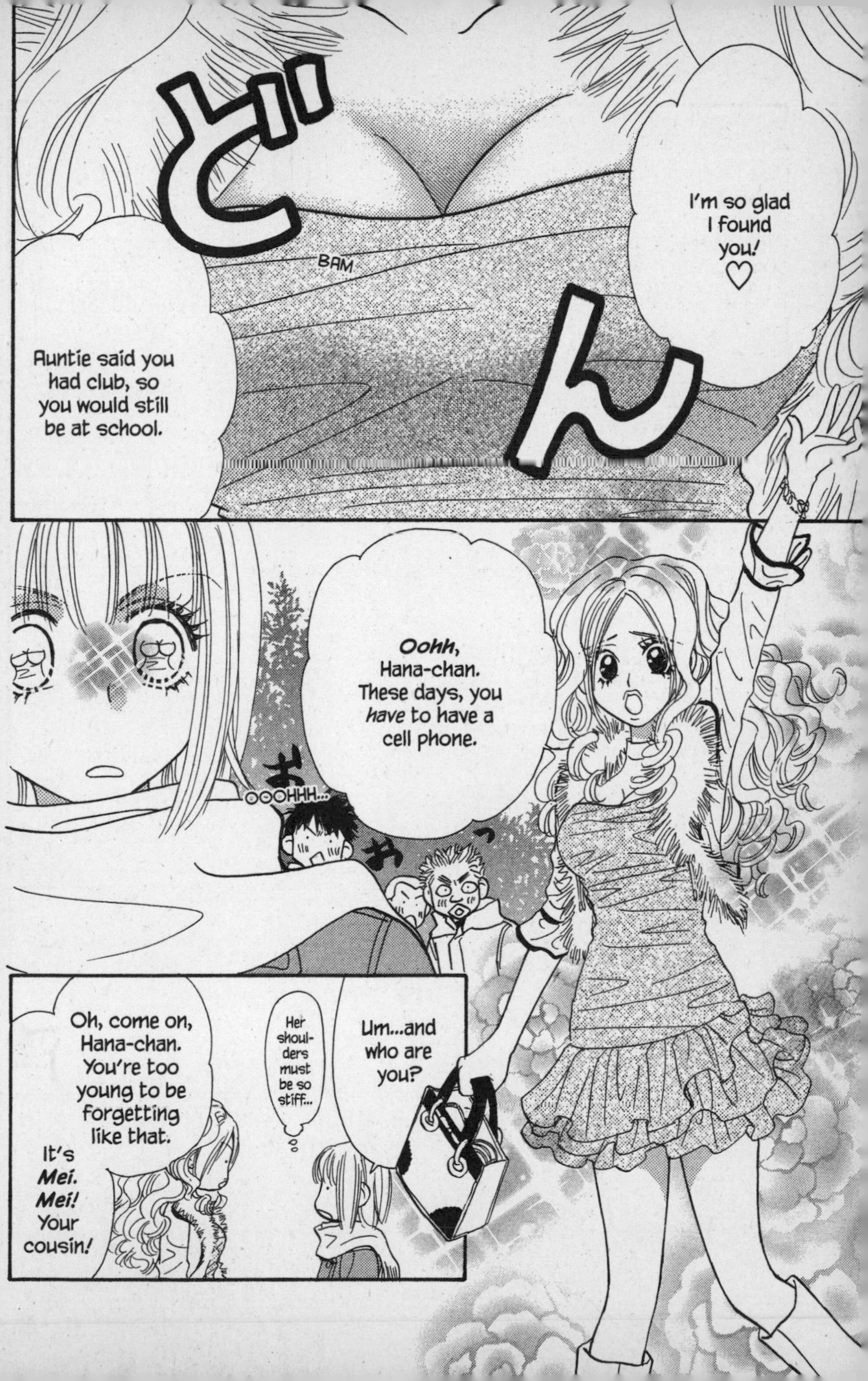

I'm so glad I found you! ♡
どん
BAM
Auntie said you had club, so you would still be at school.
Oohh, Hana-chan. These days, you *have* to have a cell phone.
OOOHHH...
Um...and who are you?
Her shoulders must be so stiff...
Oh, come on, Hana-chan. You're too young to be forgetting like that.
It's *Mei*. *Mei!* Your cousin!

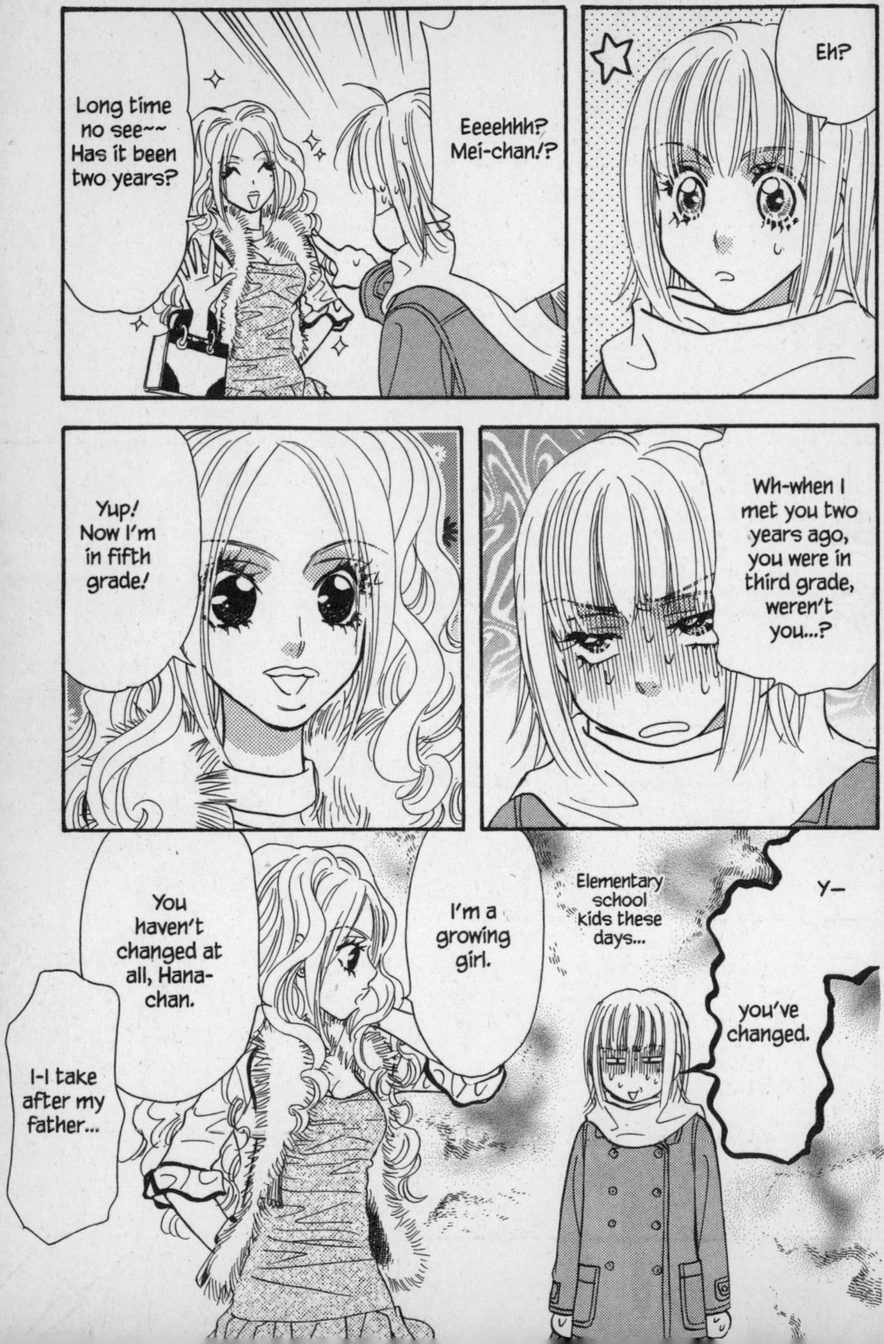
Eh?
Eeeehhh? Mei-chan!?
Long time no see~~ Has it been two years?
Wh-when I met you two years ago, you were in third grade, weren't you...?
Yup! Now I'm in fifth grade!
Y—
you've changed.
Elementary school kids these days...
I'm a growing girl.
You haven't changed at all, Hana-chan.
I-I take after my father...

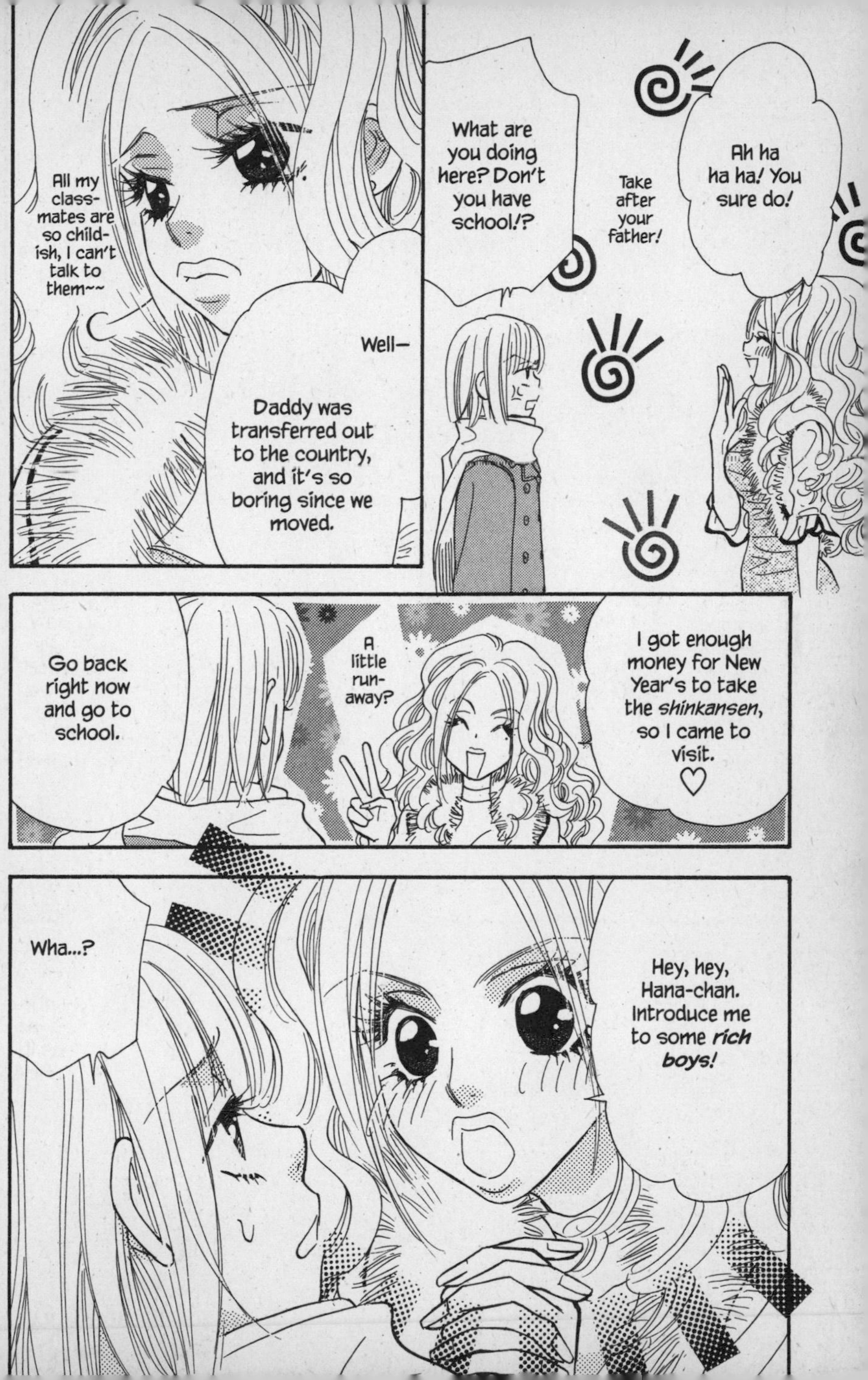
Ah ha ha ha! You sure do!
Take after your father!
What are you doing here? Don't you have school!?
Well—
Daddy was transferred out to the country, and it's so boring since we moved.
All my classmates are so childish, I can't talk to them~~
I got enough money for New Year's to take the *shinkansen*, so I came to visit. ♡
A little runaway?
Go back right now and go to school.
Hey, hey, Hana-chan. Introduce me to some ***rich boys!***
Wha...?

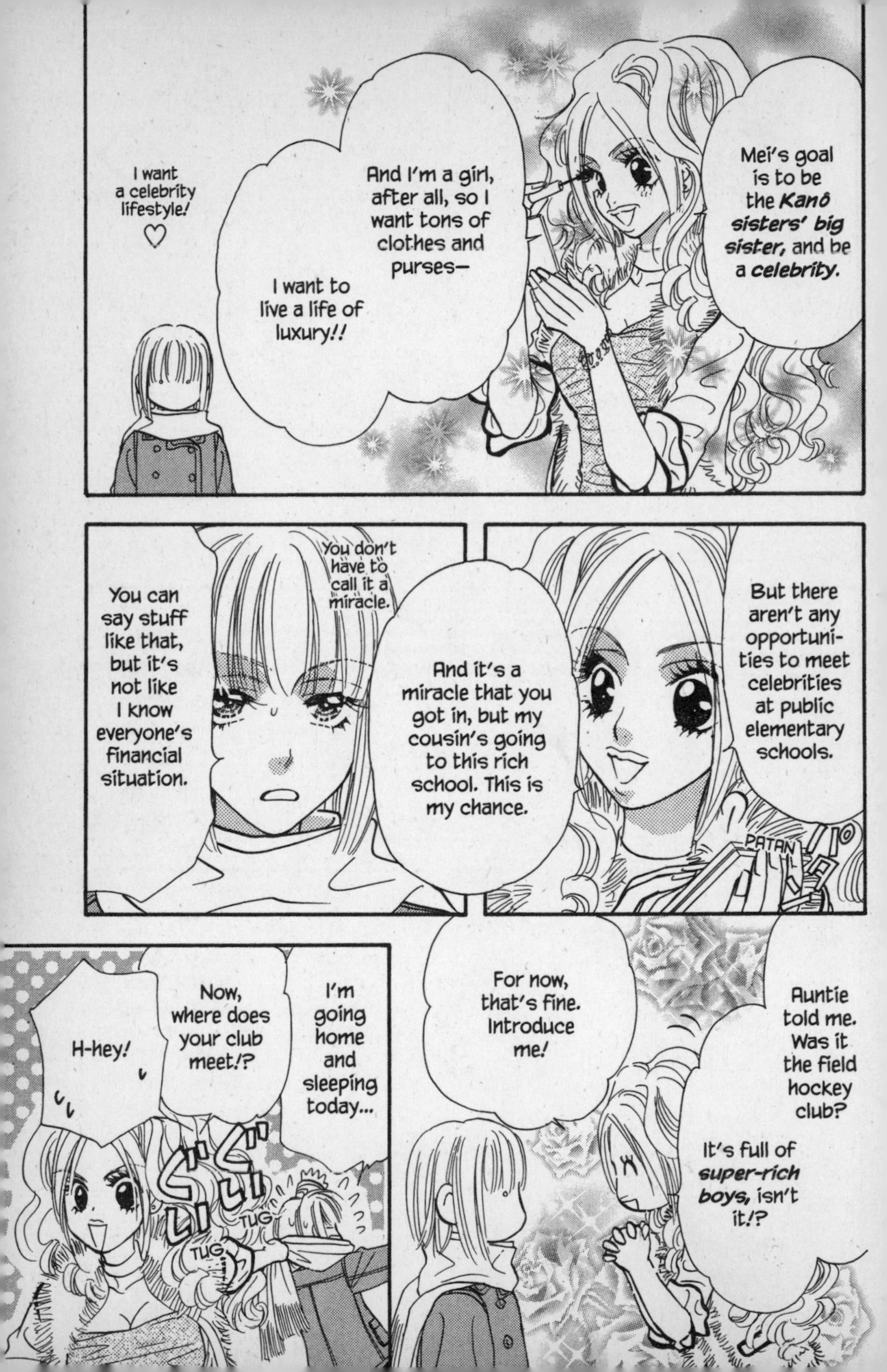
Mei's goal is to be the Kanô sisters' big sister, and be a celebrity.
And I'm a girl, after all, so I want tons of clothes and purses—
I want to live a life of luxury!!
I want a celebrity lifestyle! ♡
But there aren't any opportunities to meet celebrities at public elementary schools.
And it's a miracle that you got in, but my cousin's going to this rich school. This is my chance.
PATAN
You don't have to call it a miracle.
You can say stuff like that, but it's not like I know everyone's financial situation.
Auntie told me. Was it the field hockey club?
It's full of super-rich boys, isn't it!?
For now, that's fine. Introduce me!
I'm going home and sleeping today...
Now, where does your club meet!?
H-hey!
TUG
TUG

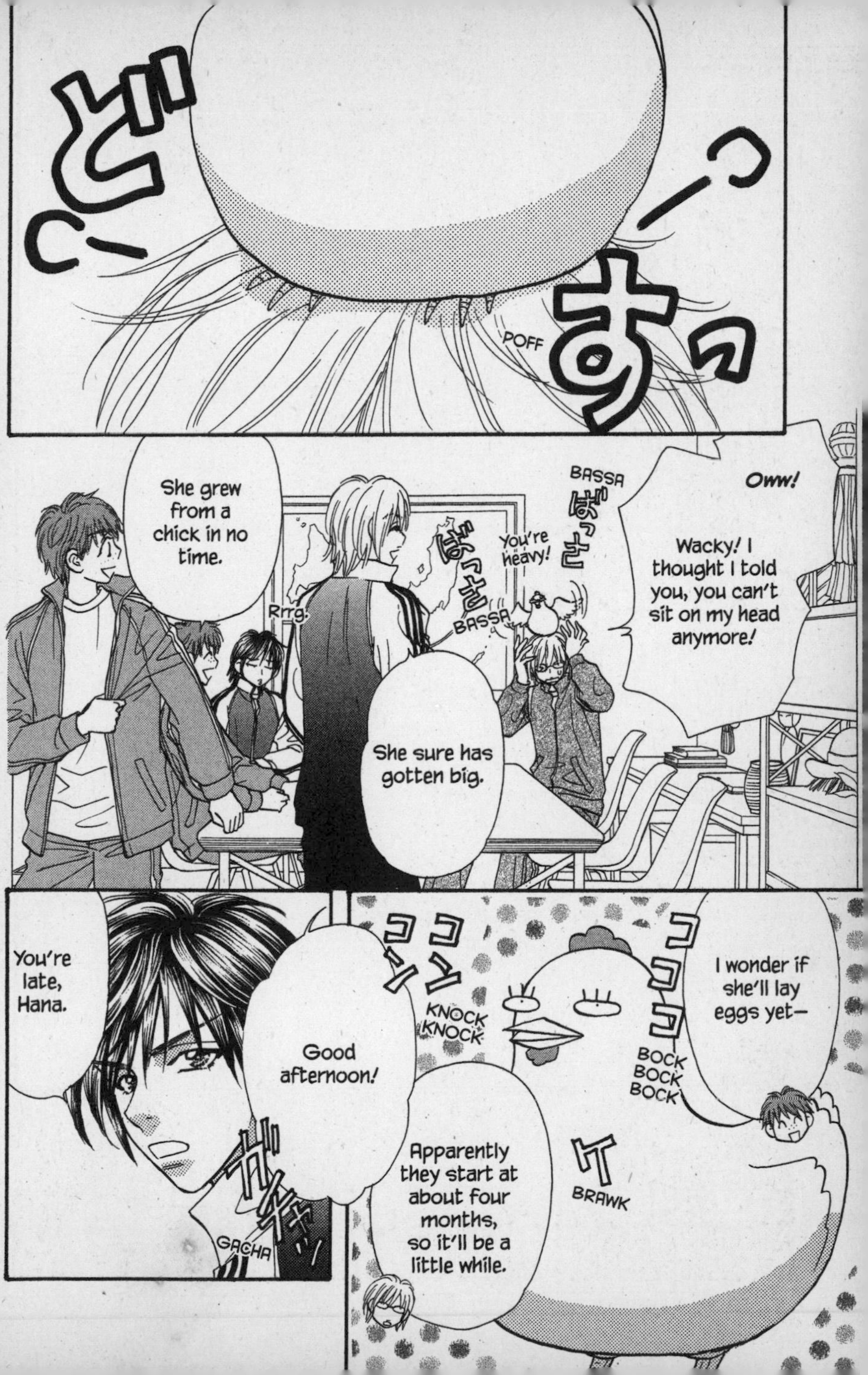
POFF
Oww!
Wacky! I thought I told you, you can't sit on my head anymore!
BASSA
You're heavy!
BASSA
Rrrg.
She sure has gotten big.
She grew from a chick in no time.
I wonder if she'll lay eggs yet—
BOCK BOCK BOCK
KNOCK KNOCK
Good afternoon!
BRAWK
Apparently they start at about four months, so it'll be a little while.
GACHA
You're late, Hana.

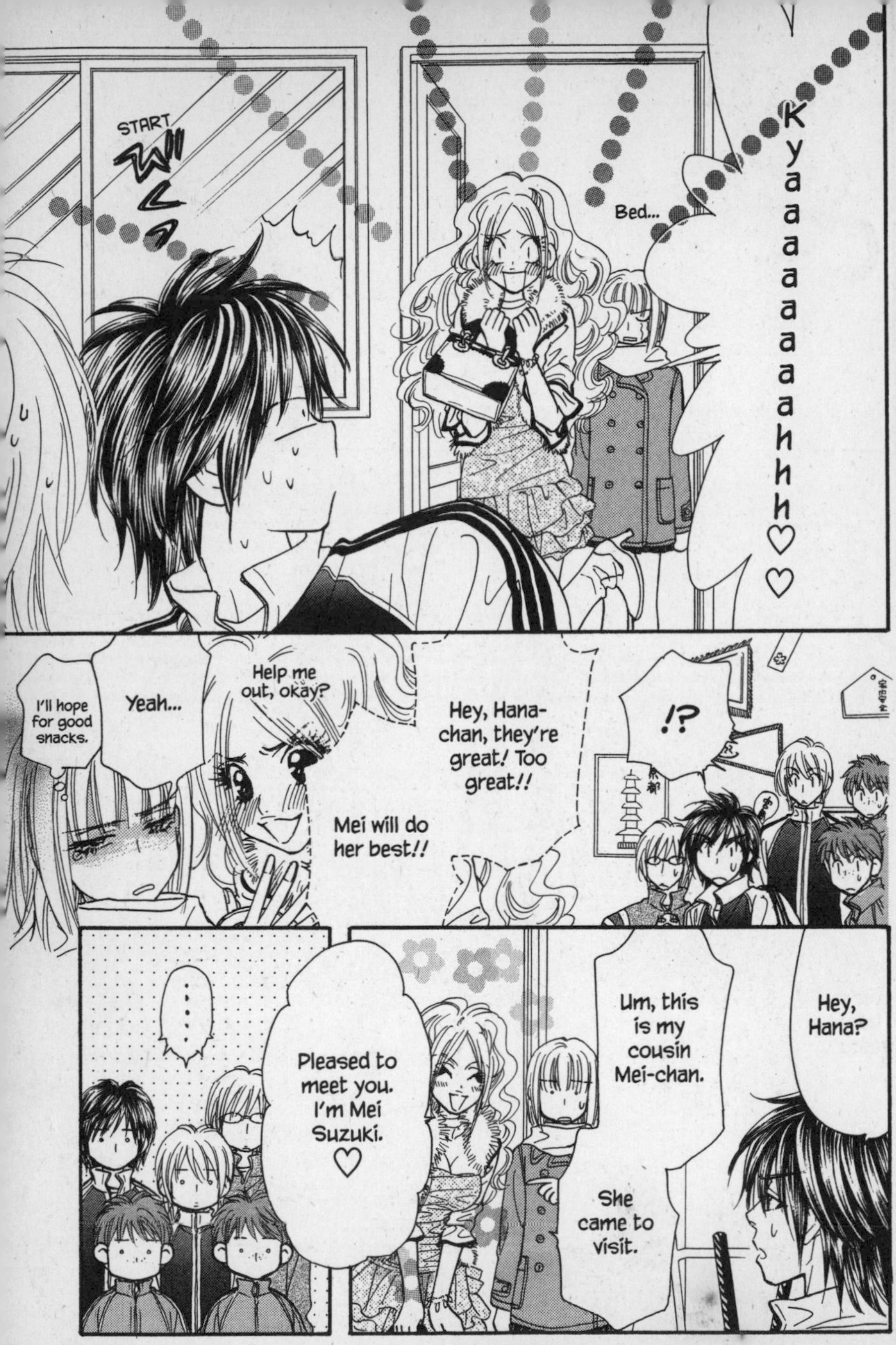
Kyaaaaaaahhh♡♡
Bed...
START
!?
Hey, Hana-chan, they're great! Too great!!
Mei will do her best!!
Help me out, okay?
Yeah...
I'll hope for good snacks.
Hey, Hana?
Um, this is my cousin Mei-chan.
She came to visit.
Pleased to meet you. I'm Mei Suzuki. ♡
...

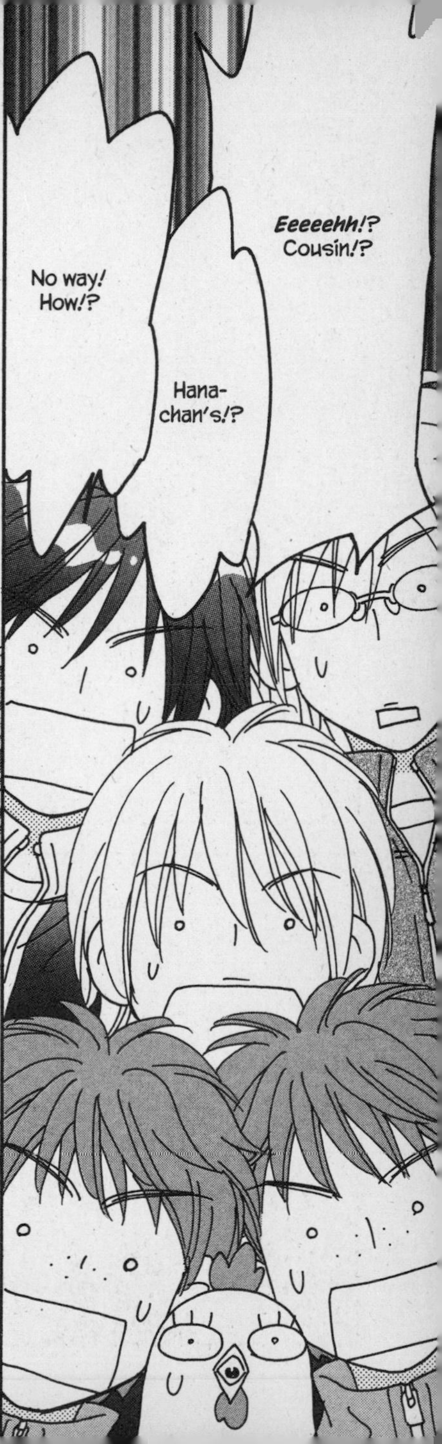
Eeeeehh!? Cousin!?
Hana-chan's!?
No way! How!?

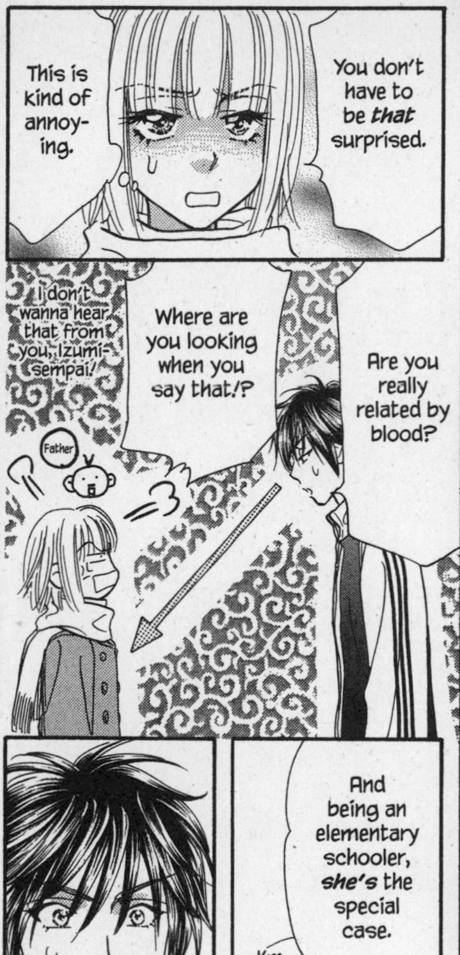
You don't have to be ***that*** surprised.
This is kind of annoy-ing.
Are you really related by blood?
Where are you looking when you say that!?
I don't wanna hear that from you, Izumi-sempai!
Father
And being an elementary schooler, ***she's*** the special case.
I'm normal!
Eh!?

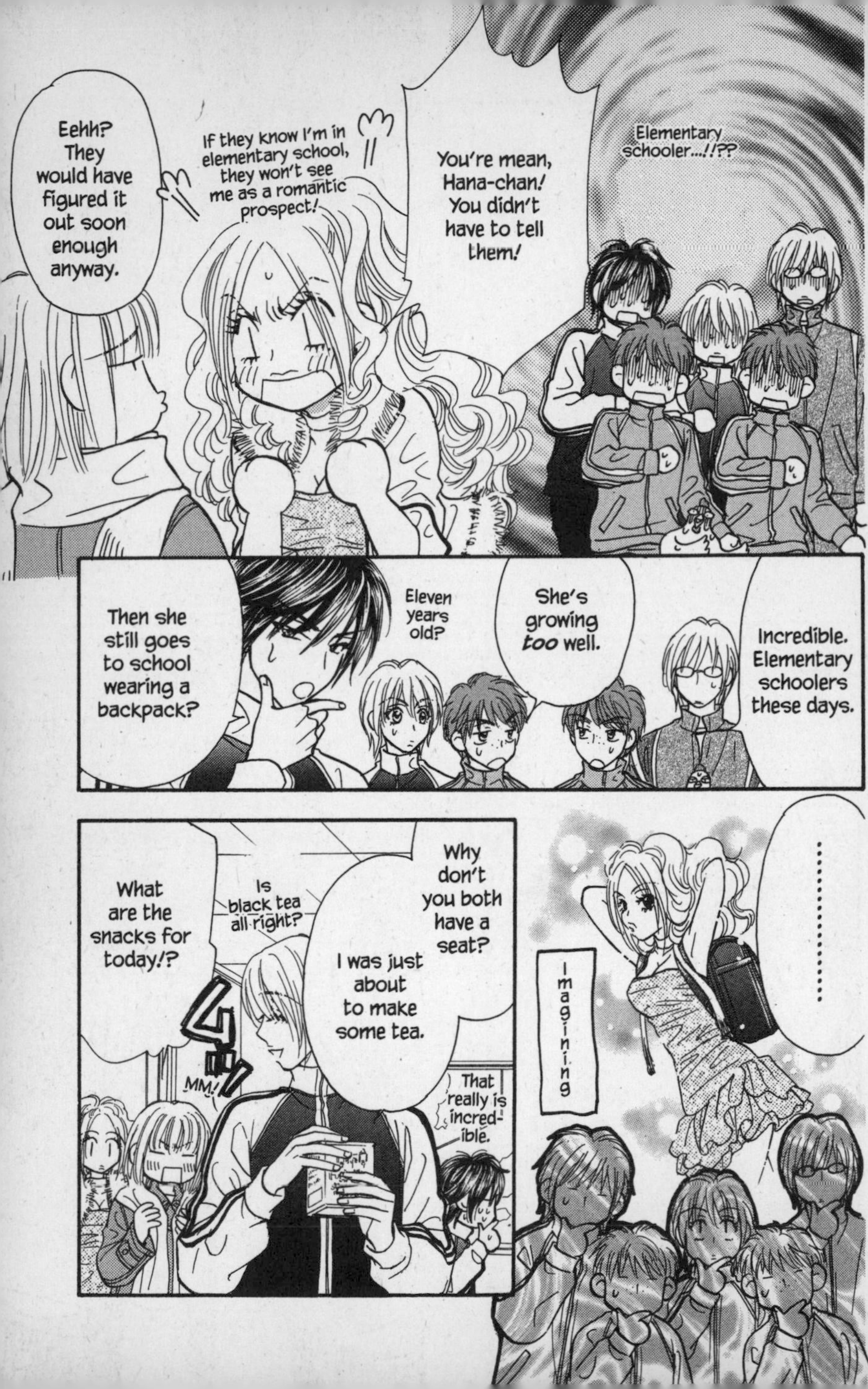
Elementary schooler...!!??
You're mean, Hana-chan! You didn't have to tell them!
If they know I'm in elementary school, they won't see me as a romantic prospect!
Eehh? They would have figured it out soon enough anyway.
Incredible. Elementary schoolers these days.
She's growing *too* well.
Eleven years old?
Then she still goes to school wearing a backpack?
......
Imagining
Why don't you both have a seat?
I was just about to make some tea.
Is black tea all right?
What are the snacks for today!?
That really is incredible.
MM!

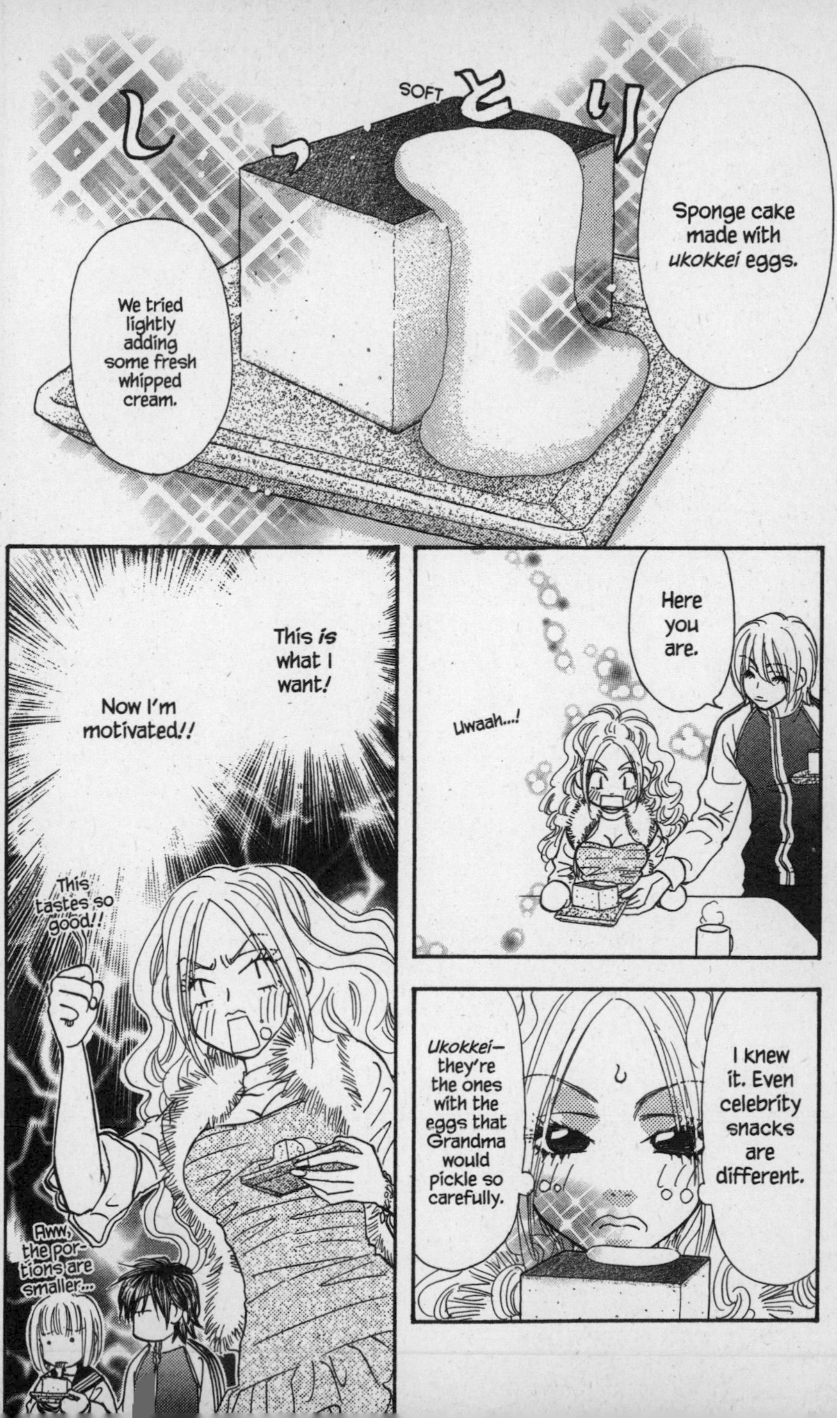
しっとり
SOFT
Sponge cake made with *ukokkei* eggs.
We tried lightly adding some fresh whipped cream.
Here you are.
Uwaah...!
I knew it. Even celebrity snacks are different.
Ukokkei—they're the ones with the eggs that Grandma would pickle so carefully.
This *is* what I want!
Now I'm motivated!!
This tastes so good!!
Aww, the portions are smaller...

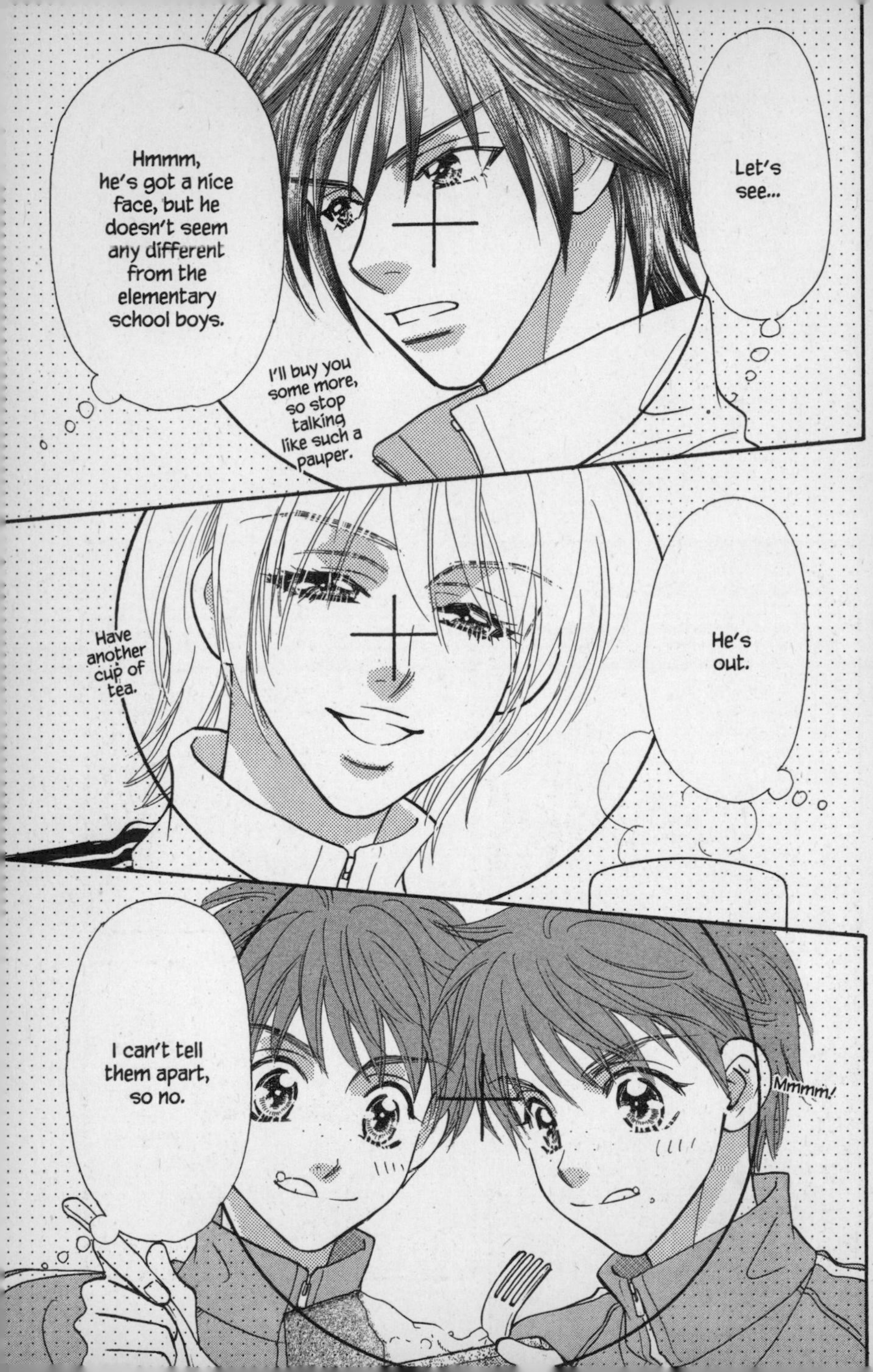
Let's see...
Hmmm, he's got a nice face, but he doesn't seem any different from the elementary school boys.
I'll buy you some more, so stop talking like such a pauper.
He's out.
Have another cup of tea.
Mmmm!
I can't tell them apart, so no.

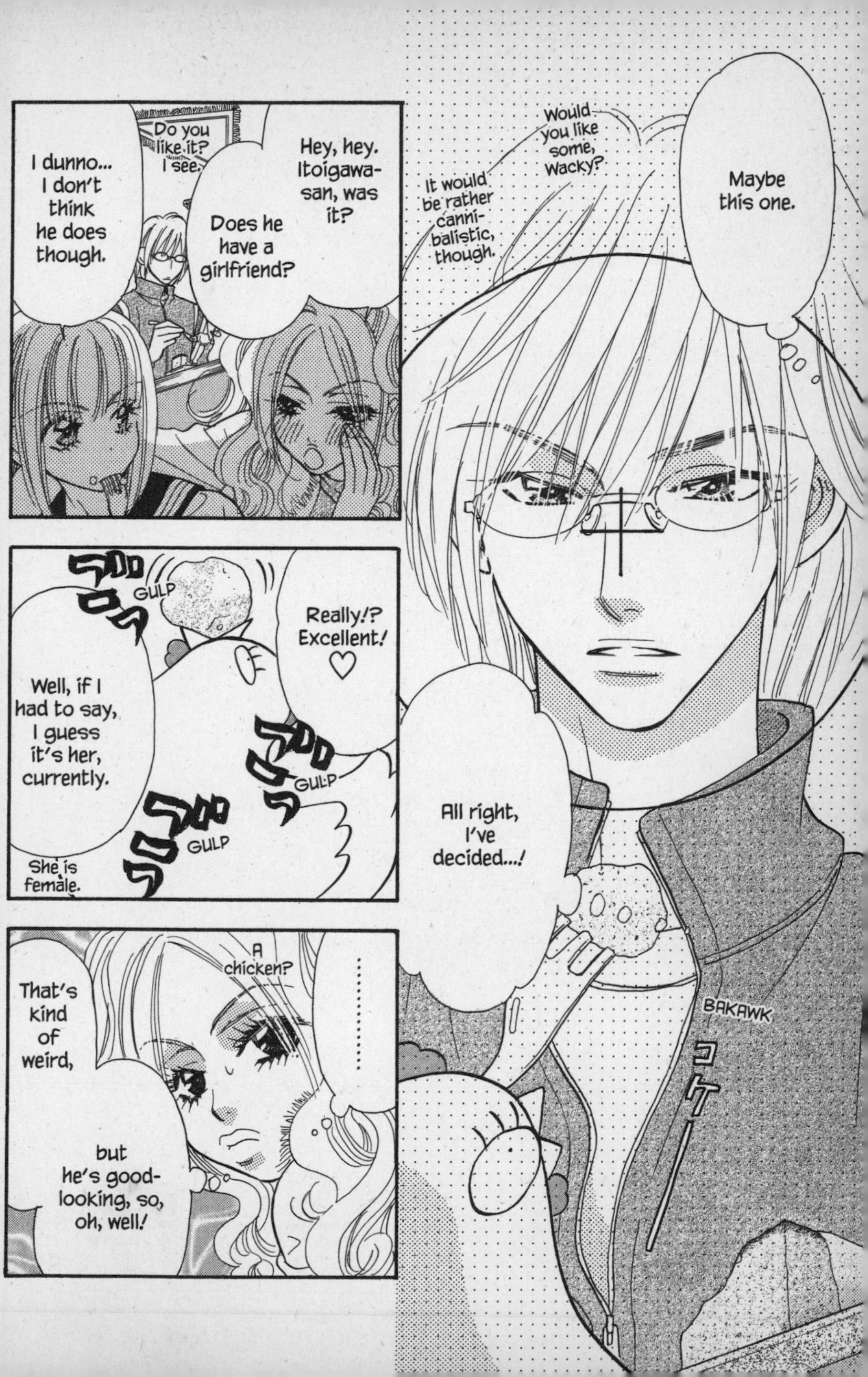
Maybe this one.
Would you like some, Wacky?
It would be rather canni-balistic, though.
All right, I've decided...!
BAKAWK
Hey, hey. Itoigawa-san, was it?
Does he have a girlfriend?
Do you like it? I see.
I dunno... I don't think he does though.
Really!? Excellent! ♡
GULP
GULP
GULP
Well, if I had to say, I guess it's her, currently.
She is female.
......
A chicken?
That's kind of weird,
but he's good-looking, so, oh, well!

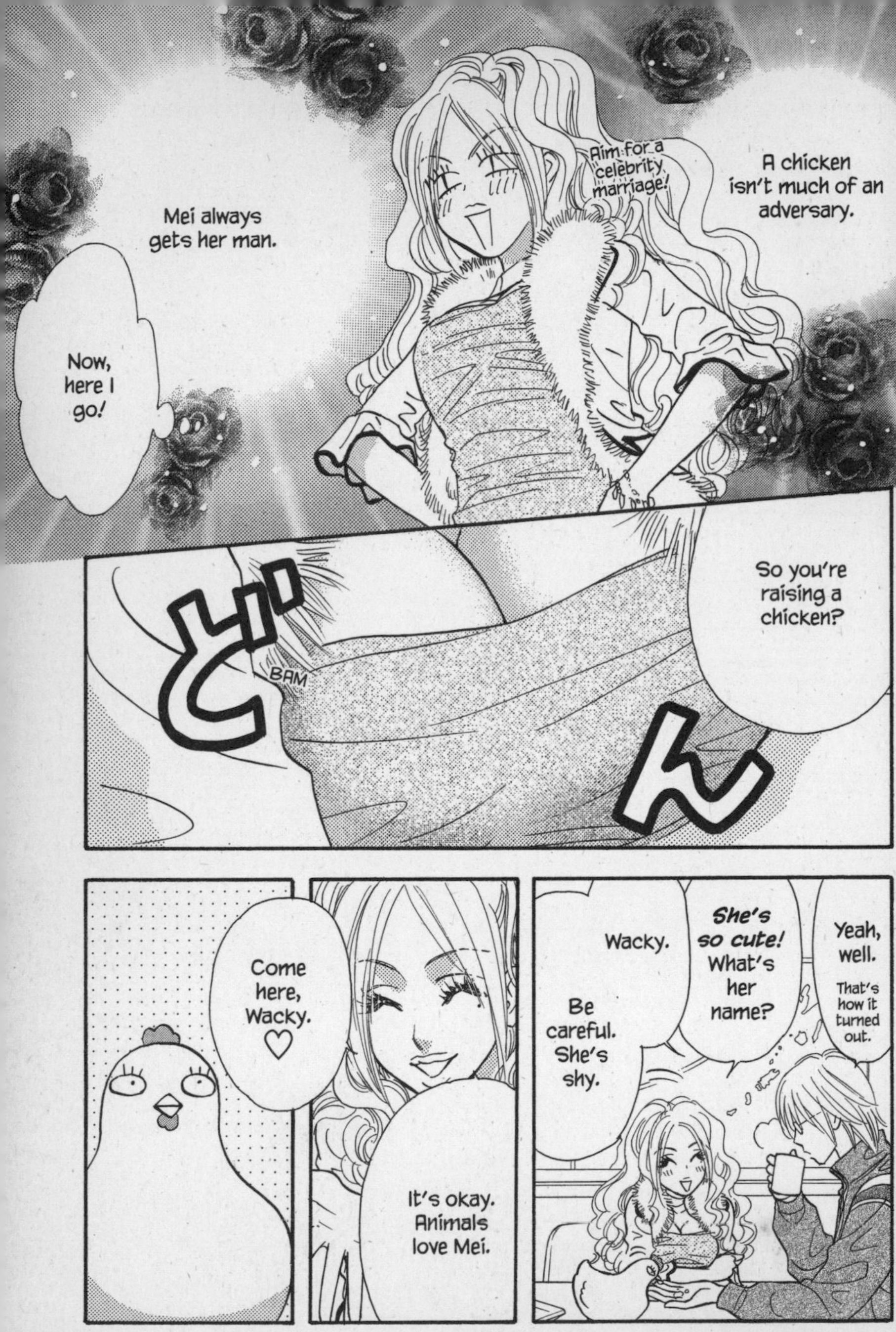
A chicken isn't much of an adversary.
Aim for a celebrity marriage!
Mei always gets her man.
Now, here I go!
So you're raising a chicken?
どん
BAM
Yeah, well.
That's how it turned out.
She's so cute! What's her name?
Wacky.
Be careful. She's shy.
It's okay. Animals love Mei.
Come here, Wacky. ♡

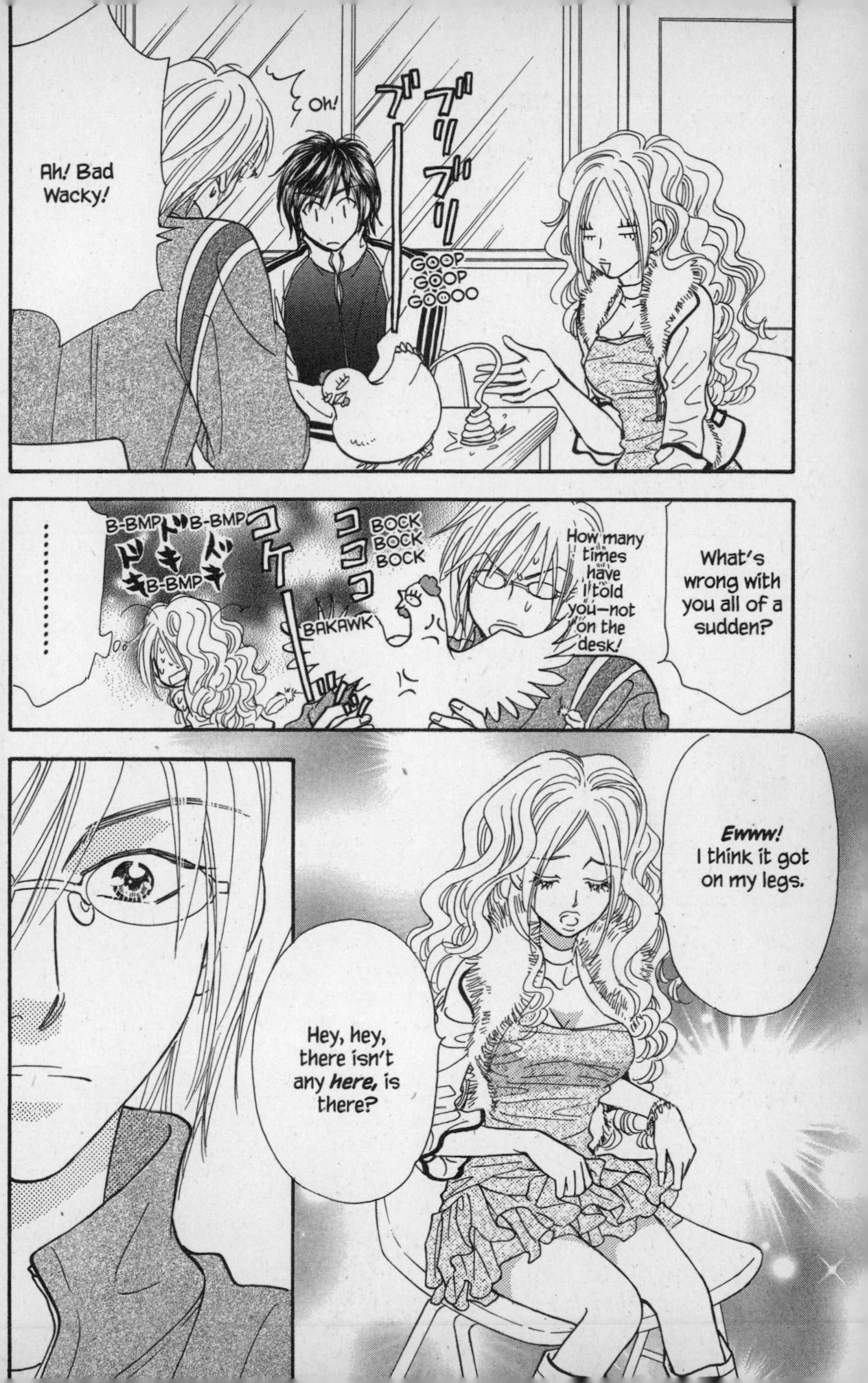

GOOP GOOP GOOOO
Oh!
Ah! Bad Wacky!
What's wrong with you all of a sudden?
How many times have I told you—not on the desk!
コココ BOCK BOCK BOCK
コケー BAKAWK
ドキドキドキ B-BMP B-BMP B-BMP
......
Ewww! I think it got on my legs.
Hey, hey, there isn't any *here*, is there?

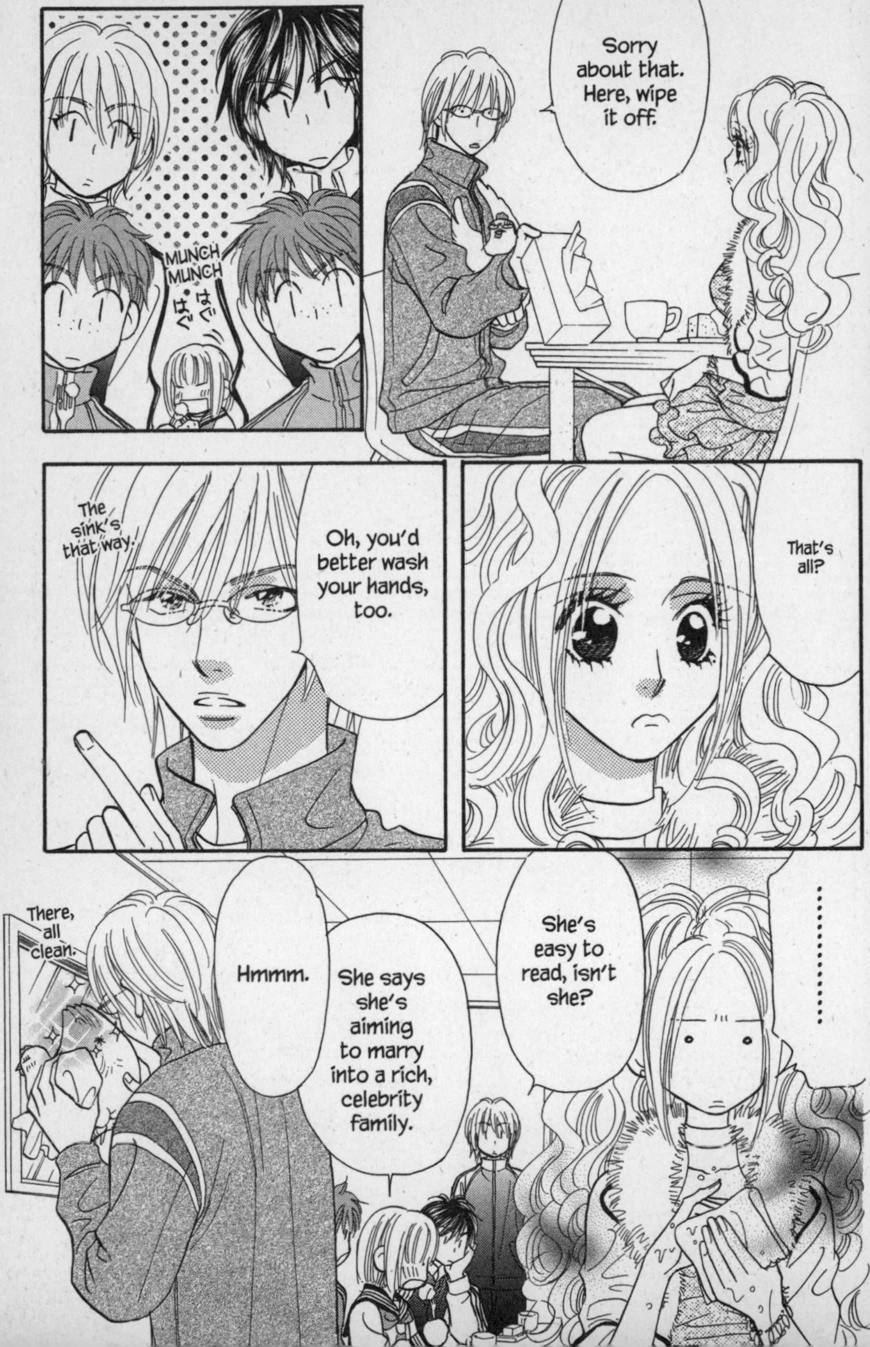
Sorry about that. Here, wipe it off.
MUNCH MUNCH
はぐはぐ
That's all?
Oh, you'd better wash your hands, too.
The sink's that way.
....
She's easy to read, isn't she?
She says she's aiming to marry into a rich, celebrity family.
Hmmm.
There, all clean.

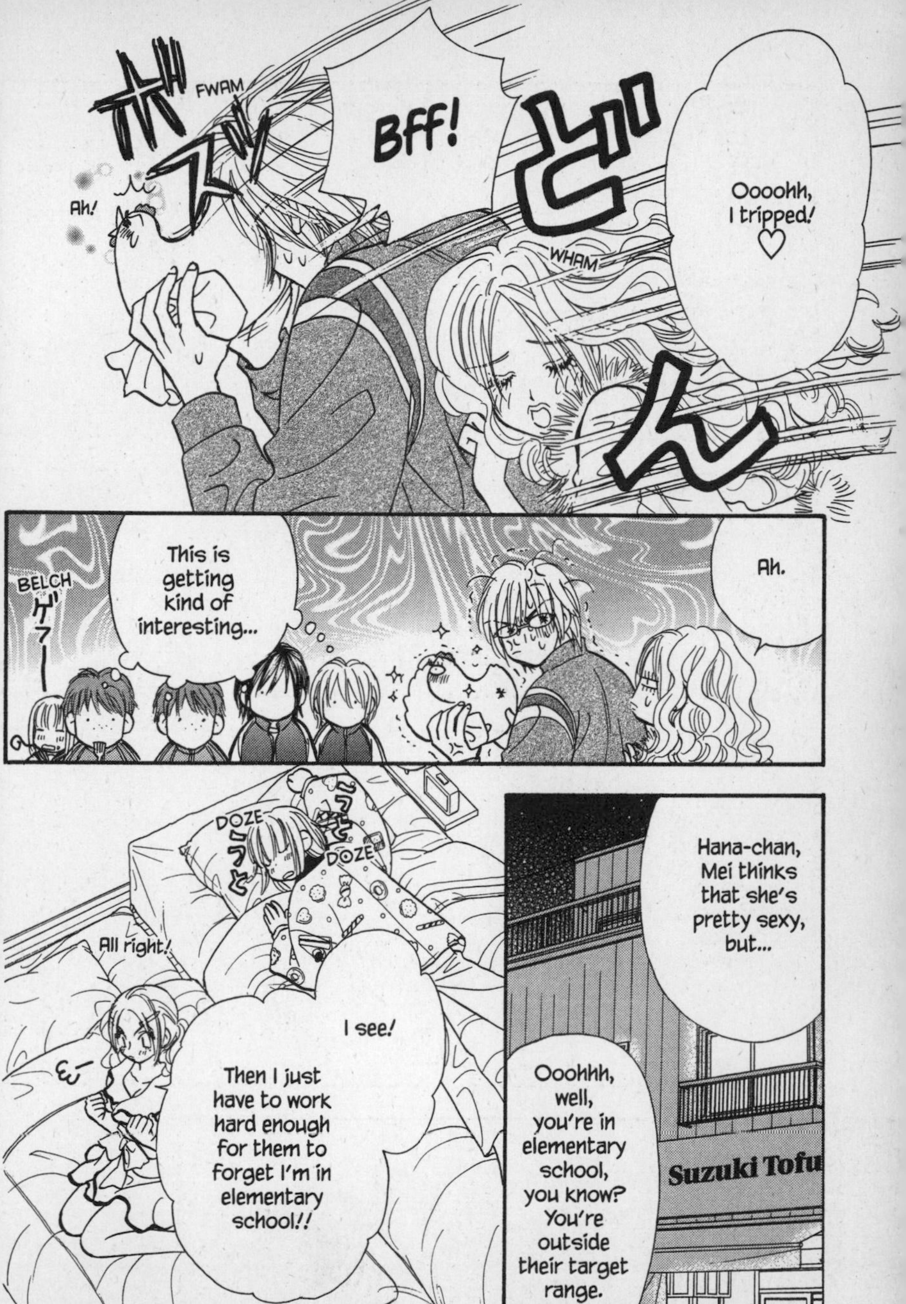
Ooooh, I tripped! ♡
どーん
WHAM
Bff!
FWAM
ボスッ
Ah!
Ah.
This is getting kind of interesting...
BELCH
ゲフー
Hana-chan, Mei thinks that she's pretty sexy, but...
Ooohhh, well, you're in elementary school, you know? You're outside their target range.
Suzuki Tofu
DOZE
DOZE
I see!
Then I just have to work hard enough for them to forget I'm in elementary school!!
All right!

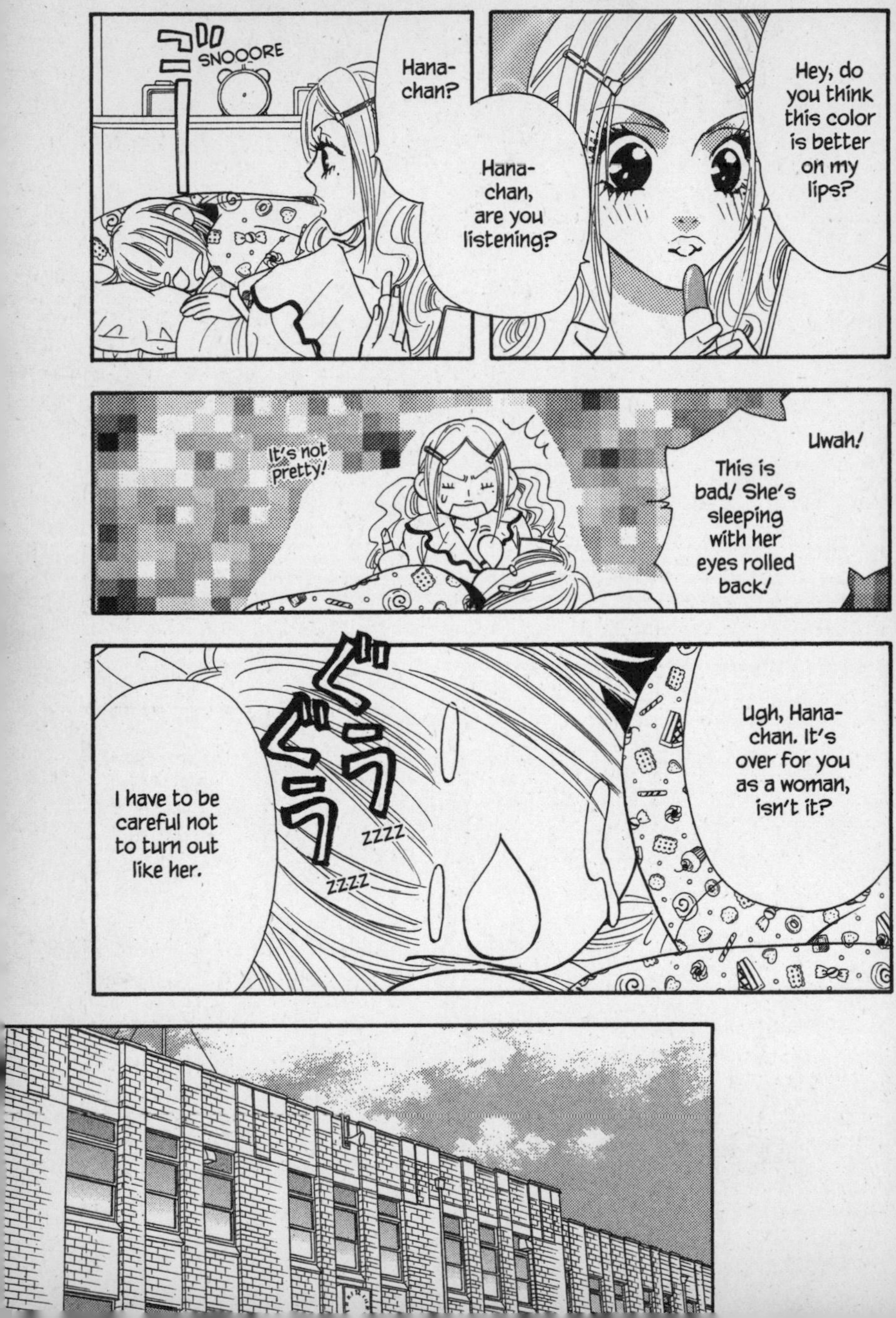
Hey, do you think this color is better on my lips?
Hana-chan?
Hana-chan, are you listening?
SNOOORE
Uwah!
This is bad! She's sleeping with her eyes rolled back!
It's not pretty!
Ugh, Hana-chan. It's over for you as a woman, isn't it?
ぐらぐら
ZZZZ
ZZZZ
I have to be careful not to turn out like her.

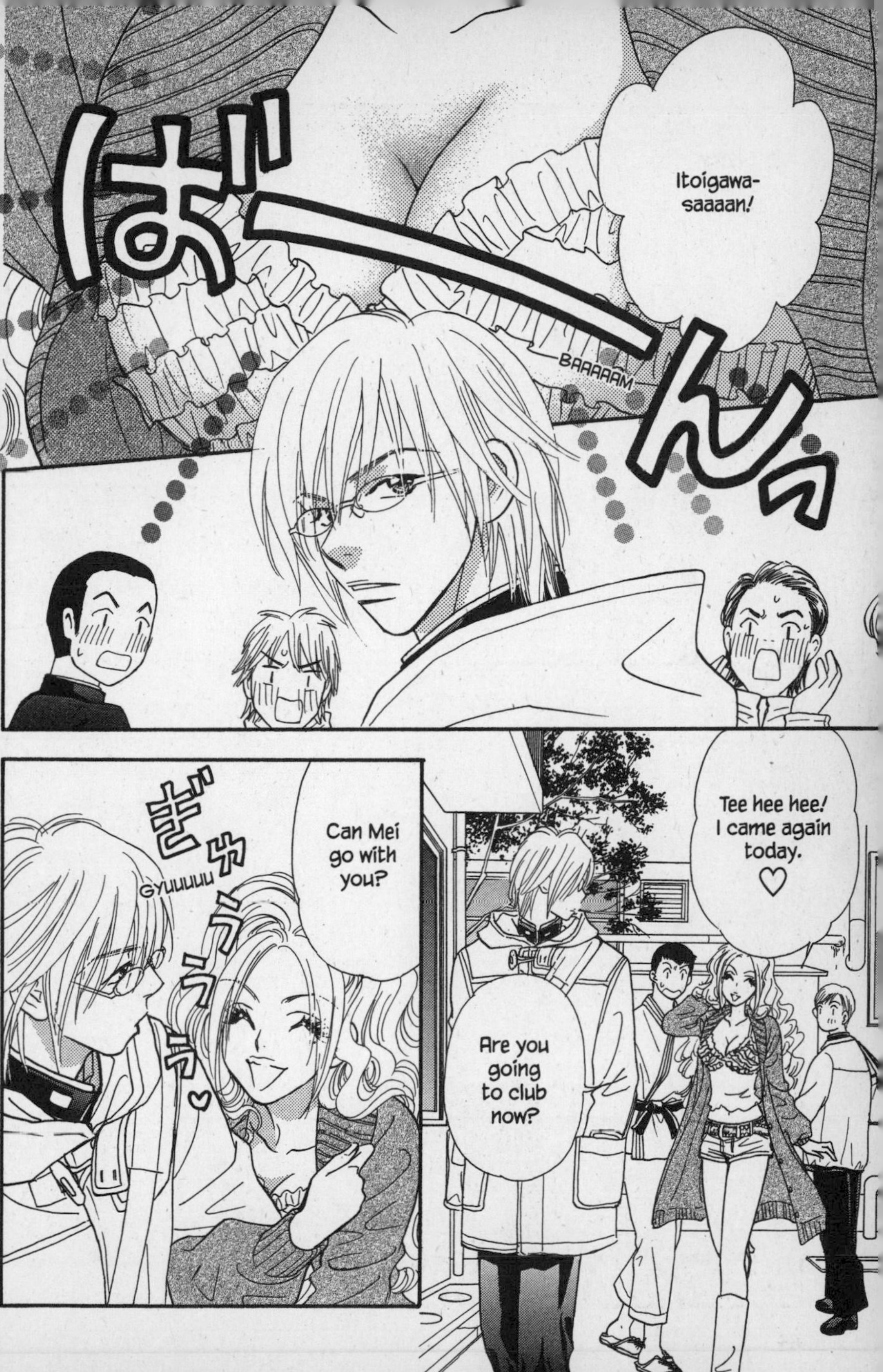
Itoigawa-saaaan!
ばーんっ
BAAAAAM
Tee hee hee! I came again today. ♡
Are you going to club now?
Can Mei go with you?
ぎゅううう
GYUUUUU
♡

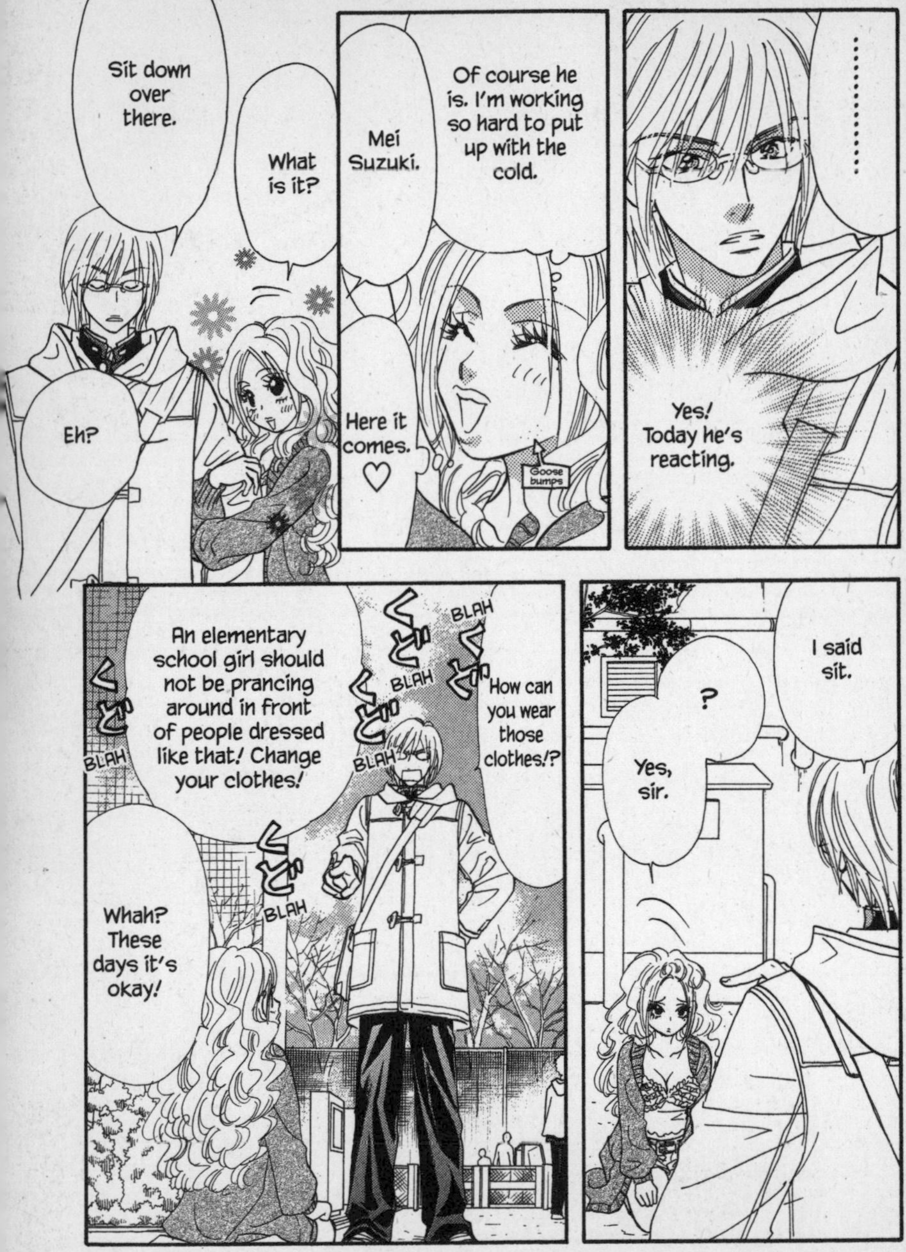
......
Yes! Today he's reacting.
Of course he is. I'm working so hard to put up with the cold.
Mei Suzuki.
Here it comes. ♥
Goose bumps
What is it?
Sit down over there.
Eh?
I said sit.
?
Yes, sir.
BLAH
How can you wear those clothes!?
BLAH
BLAH
An elementary school girl should not be prancing around in front of people dressed like that! Change your clothes!
BLAH
BLAH
Whah? These days it's okay!

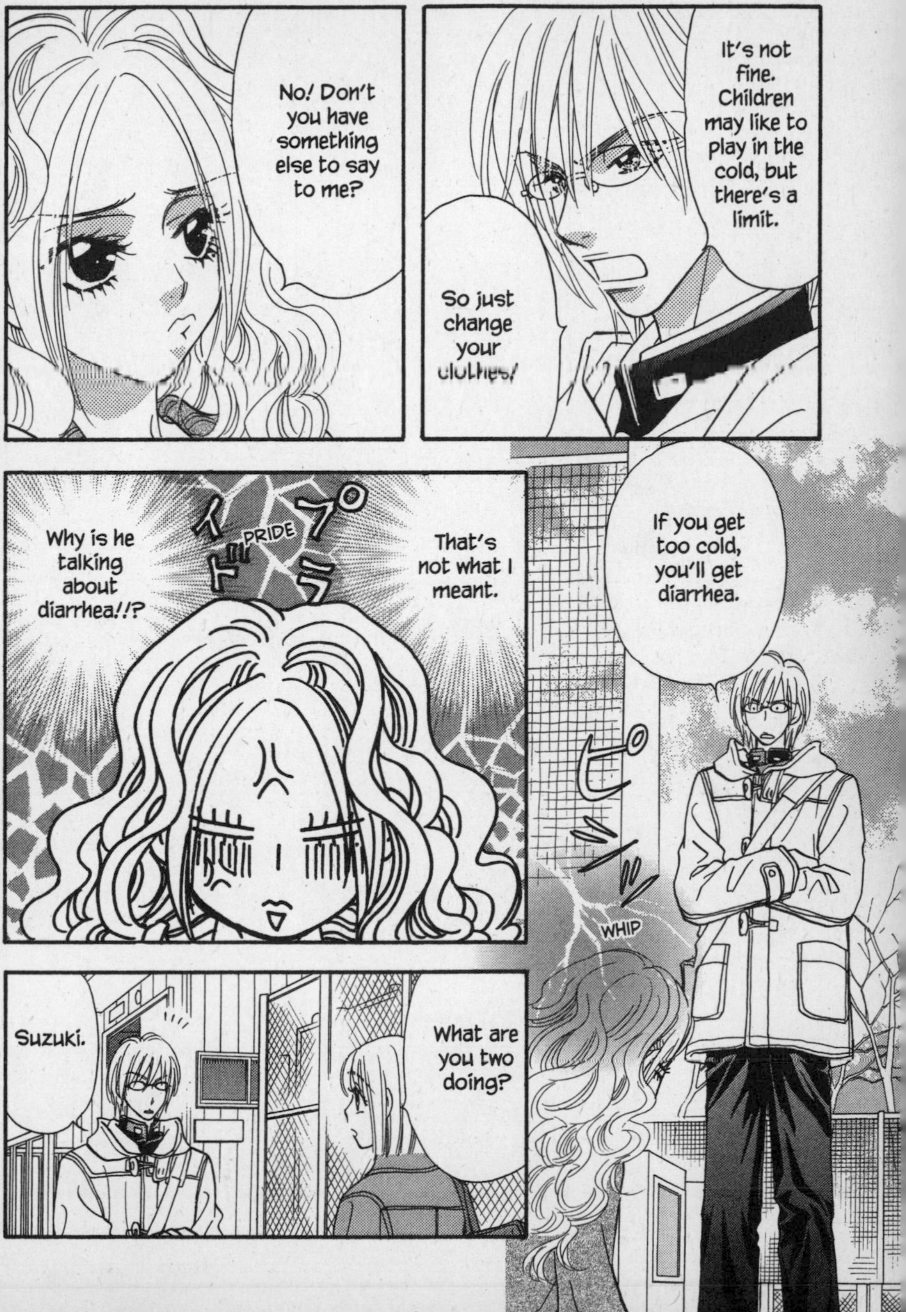
It's not fine. Children may like to play in the cold, but there's a limit.
So just change your clothes!
No! Don't you have something else to say to me?
If you get too cold, you'll get diarrhea.
WHIP
That's not what I meant.
PRIDE
Why is he talking about diarrhea!!?
What are you two doing?
Suzuki.

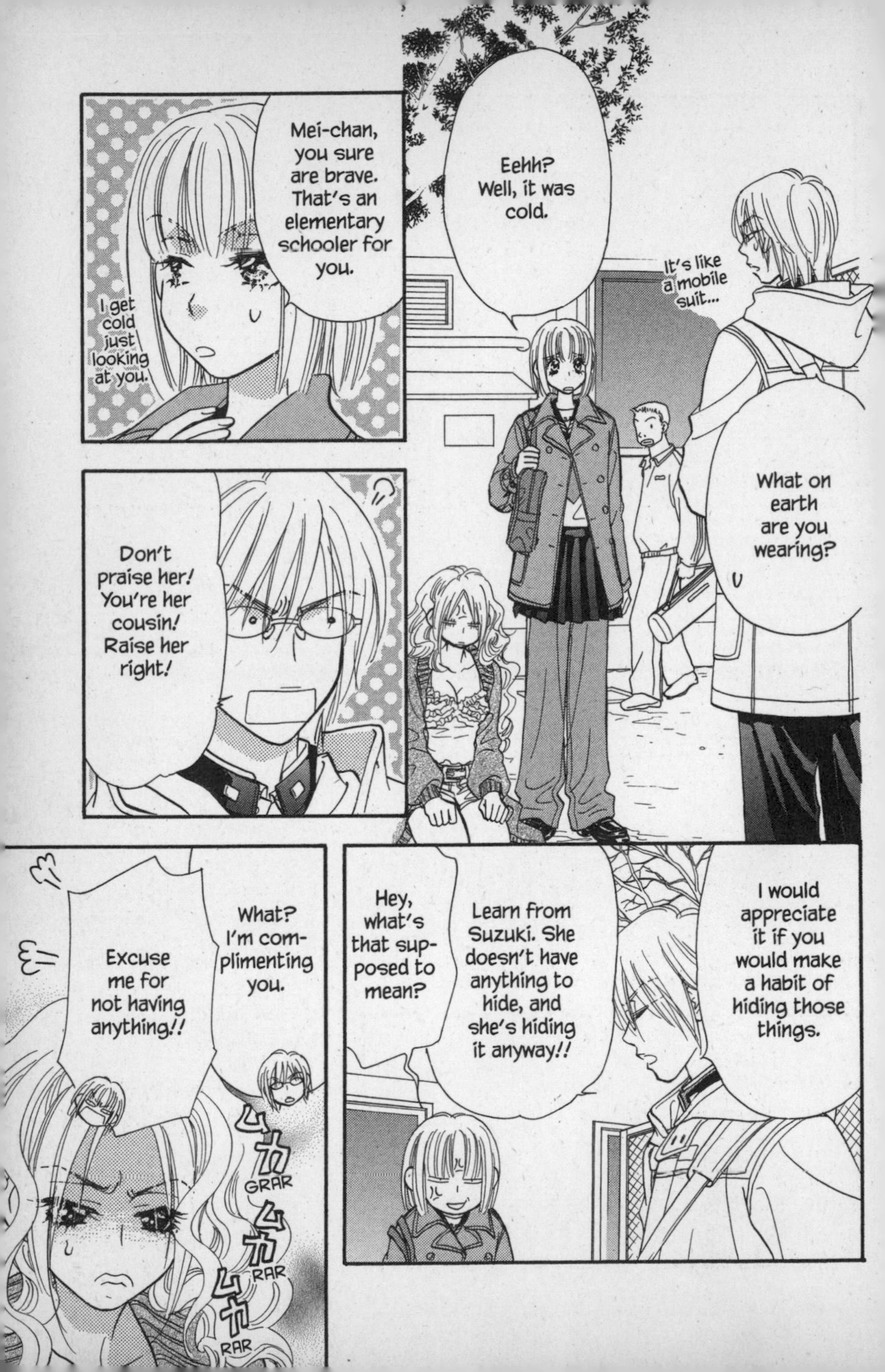
It's like a mobile suit...
What on earth are you wearing?
Eehh? Well, it was cold.
Mei-chan, you sure are brave. That's an elementary schooler for you.
I get cold just looking at you.
Don't praise her! You're her cousin! Raise her right!
I would appreciate it if you would make a habit of hiding those things.
Learn from Suzuki. She doesn't have anything to hide, and she's hiding it anyway!!
Hey, what's that supposed to mean?
What? I'm complimenting you.
Excuse me for not having anything!!
GRAR
RAR
RAR

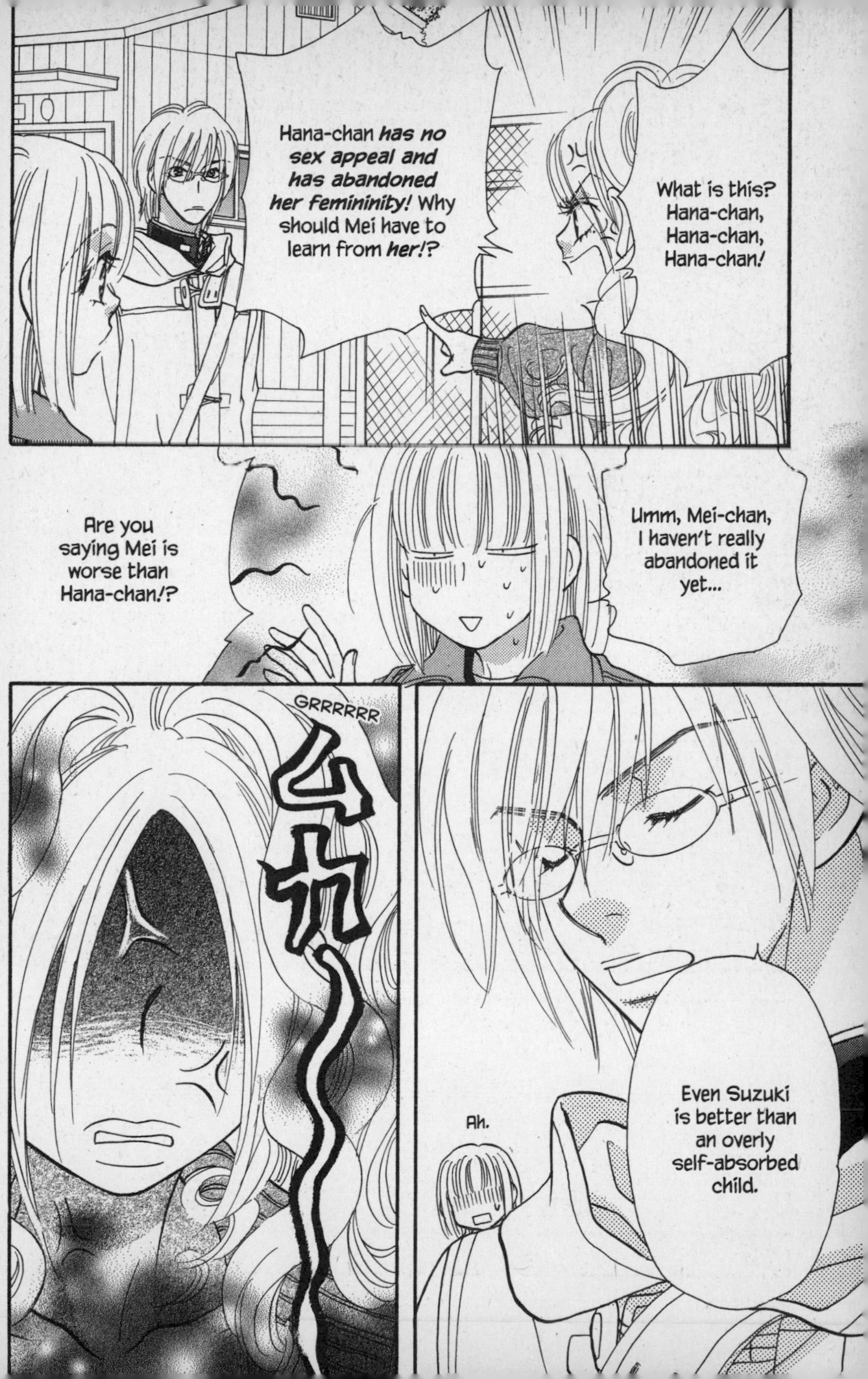
What is this? Hana-chan, Hana-chan, Hana-chan!
Hana-chan has no sex appeal and has abandoned her femininity! Why should Mei have to learn from her!?
Umm, Mei-chan, I haven't really abandoned it yet...
Are you saying Mei is worse than Hana-chan!?
Even Suzuki is better than an overly self-absorbed child.
Ah.
GRRRRRR
ムカ

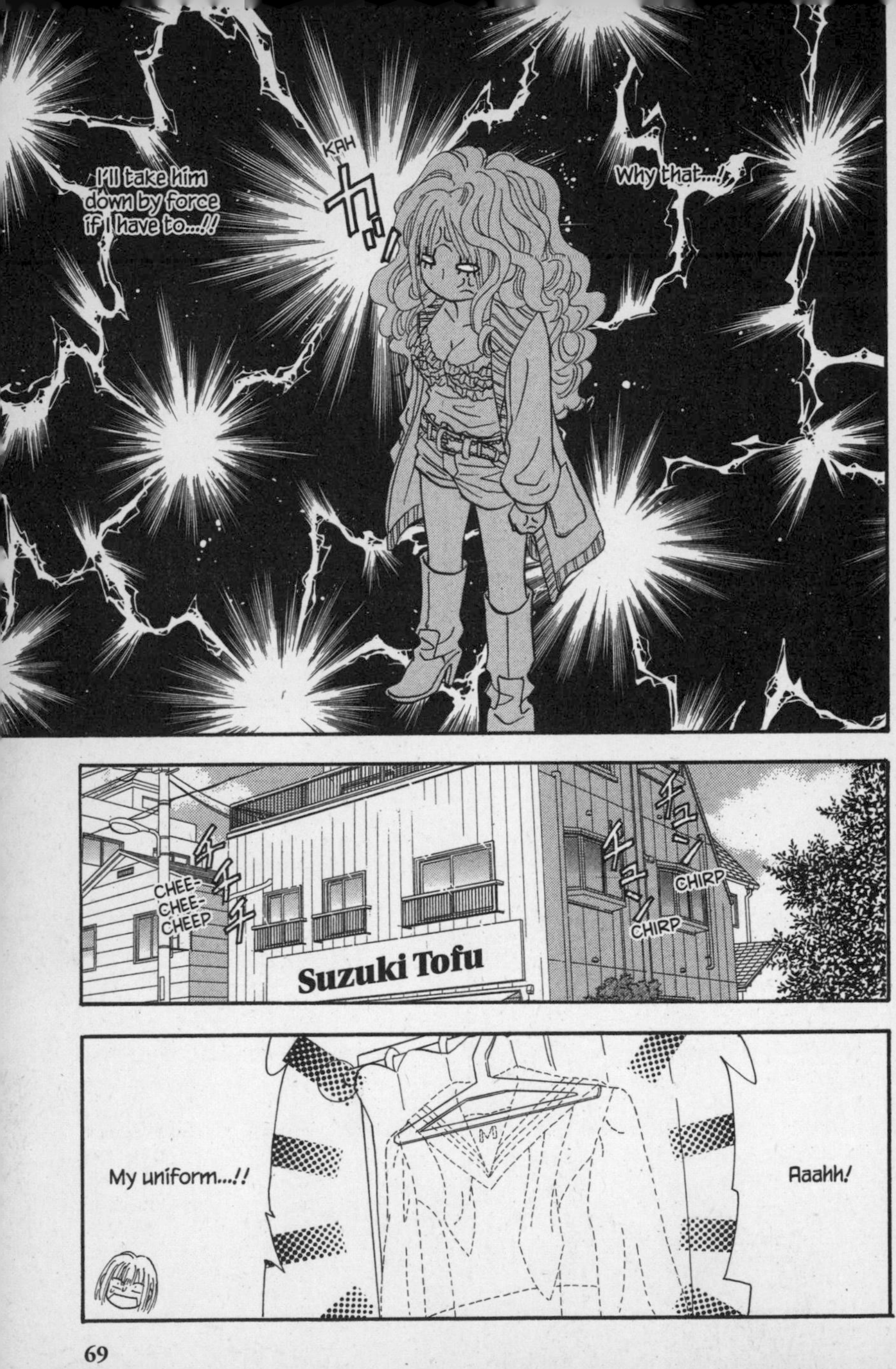
Why that...!
KAH
I'll take him down by force if I have to...!!
CHIRP
CHIRP
CHEE-CHEE-CHEEP
Suzuki Tofu
Aaahh!
My uniform...!!

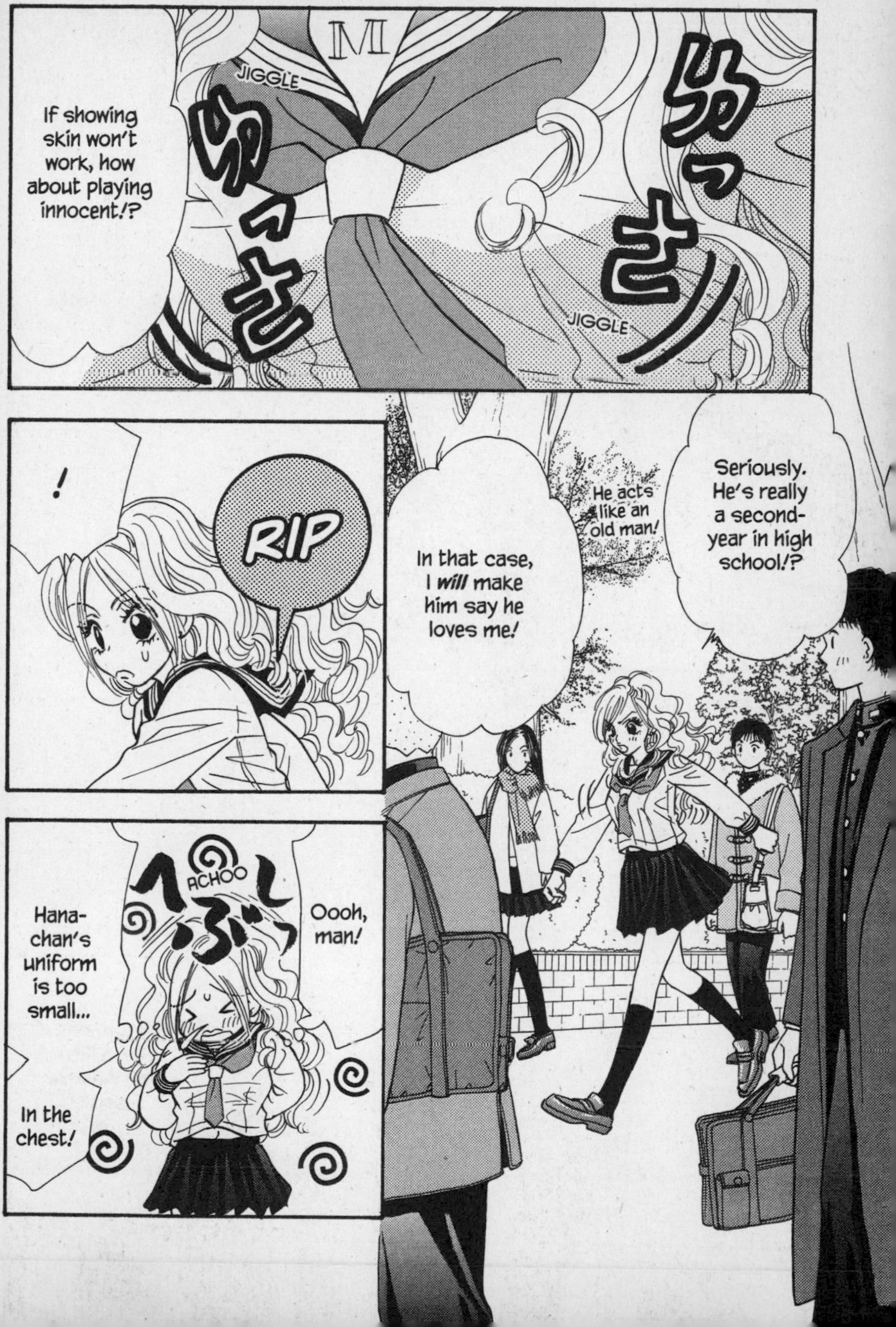
JIGGLE
JIGGLE
If showing skin won't work, how about playing innocent!?
Seriously. He's really a second-year in high school!?
He acts like an old man!
In that case, I *will* make him say he loves me!
RIP
!
ACHOO
Oooh, man!
Hana-chan's uniform is too small...
In the chest!

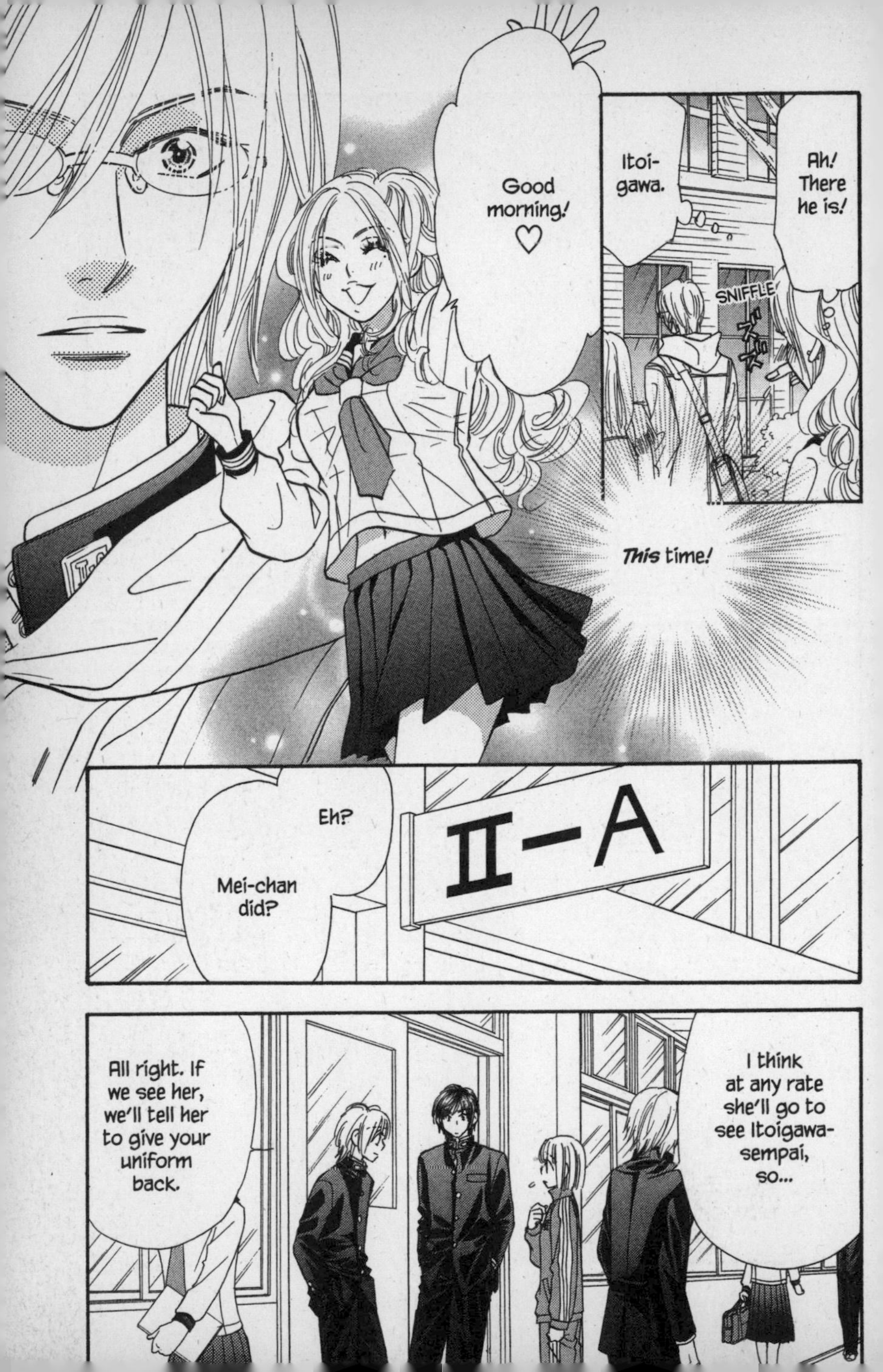
Ah! There he is!
Itoigawa.
SNIFFLE
This time!
Good morning! ♡
II–A
Eh?
Mei-chan did?
I think at any rate she'll go to see Itoigawa-sempai, so...
All right. If we see her, we'll tell her to give your uniform back.

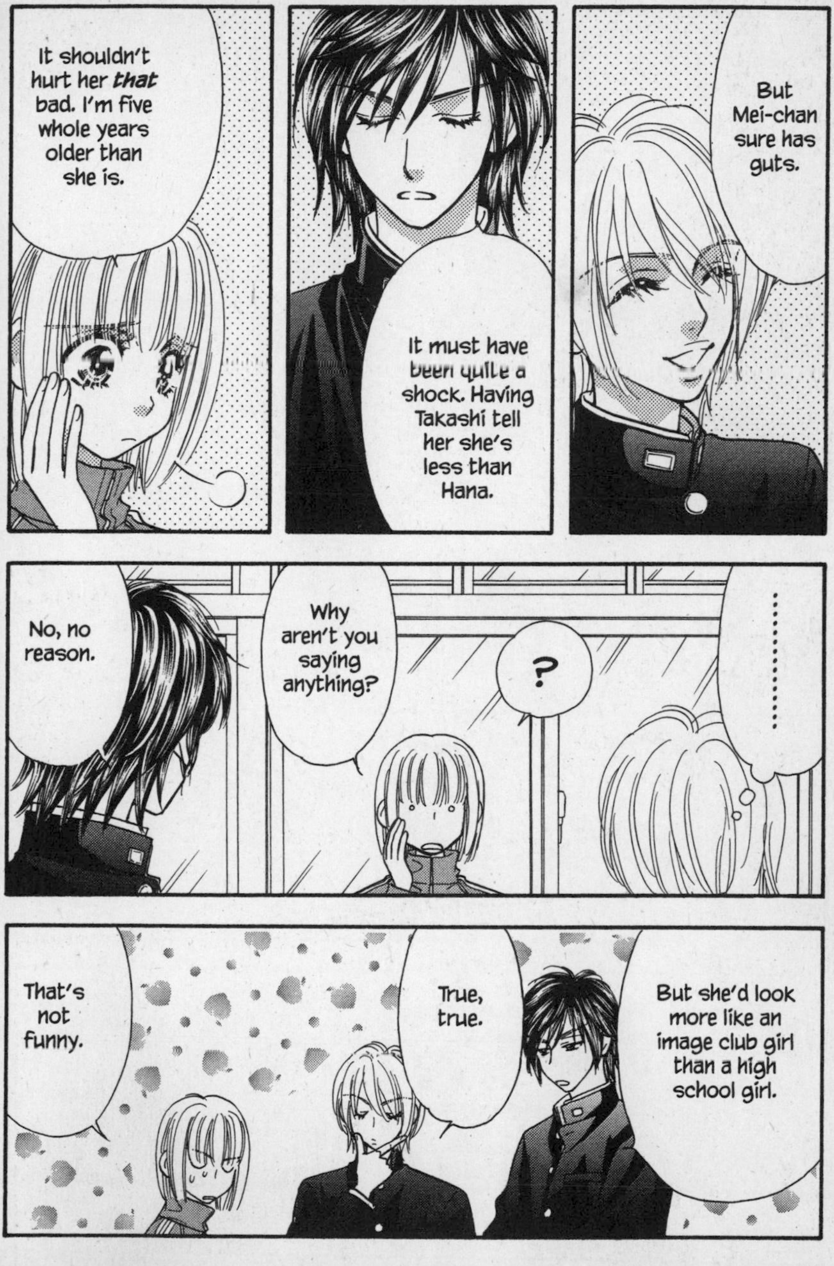
But Mei-chan sure has guts.
It must have been quite a shock. Having Takashi tell her she's less than Hana.
It shouldn't hurt her *that* bad. I'm five whole years older than she is.
....
?
Why aren't you saying anything?
No, no reason.
But she'd look more like an image club girl than a high school girl.
True, true.
That's not funny.

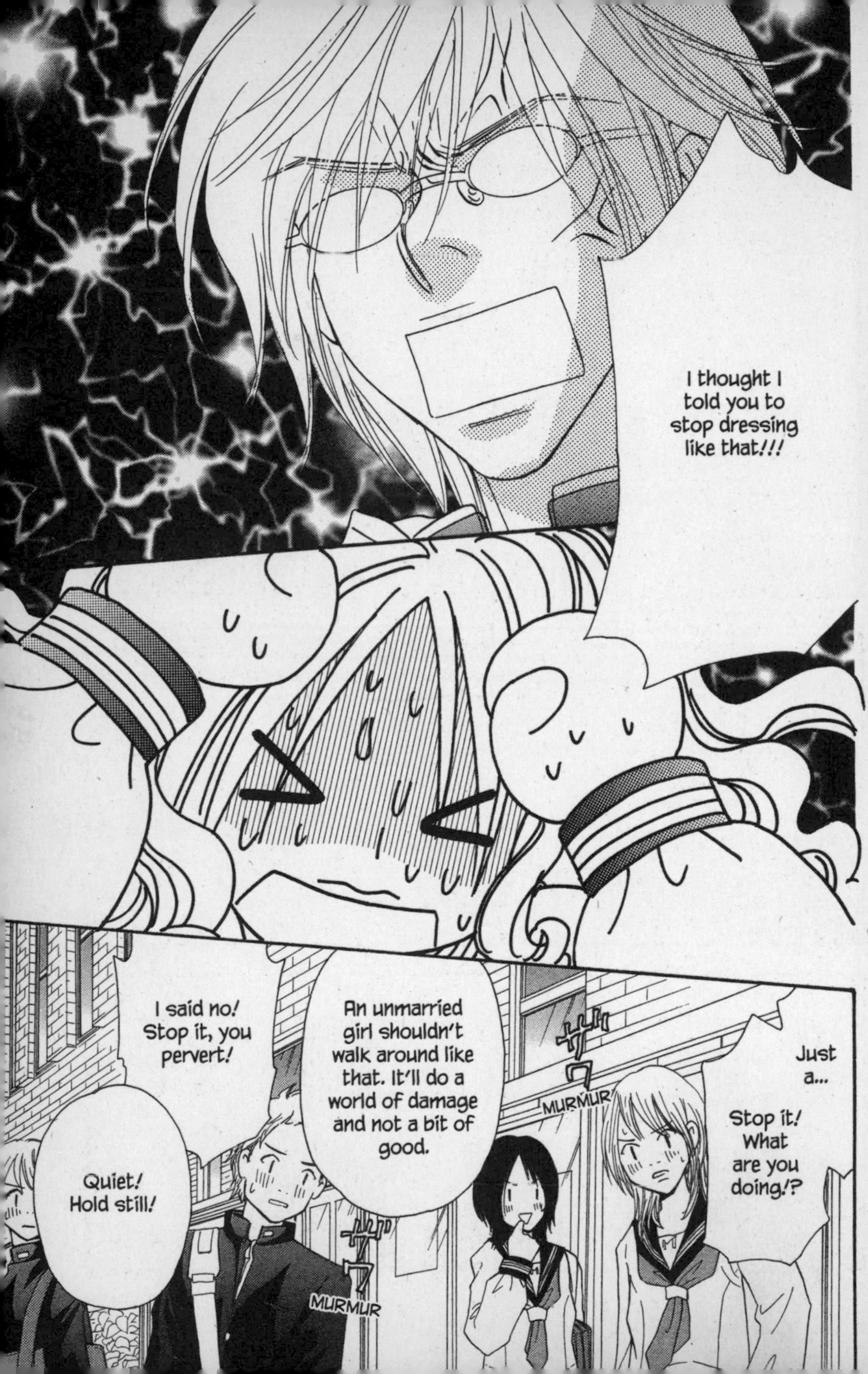
I thought I told you to stop dressing like that!!!
Just a...
Stop it! What are you doing!?
MURMUR
An unmarried girl shouldn't walk around like that. It'll do a world of damage and not a bit of good.
I said no! Stop it, you pervert!
Quiet! Hold still!
MURMUR

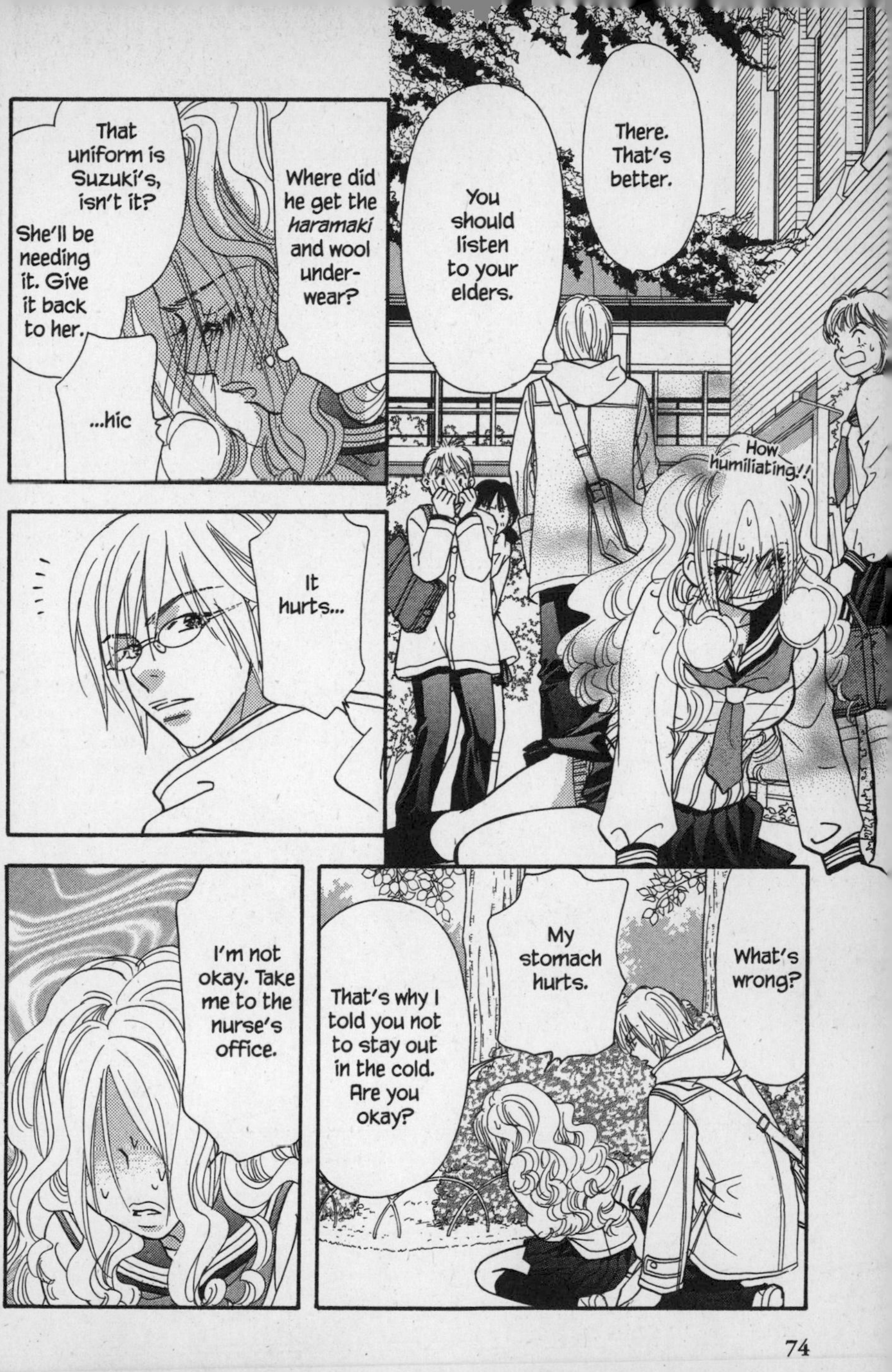
There. That's better.
You should listen to your elders.
How humiliating!!
Where did he get the *haramaki* and wool under-wear?
That uniform is Suzuki's, isn't it?
She'll be needing it. Give it back to her.
...hic
It hurts...
What's wrong?
My stomach hurts.
That's why I told you not to stay out in the cold. Are you okay?
I'm not okay. Take me to the nurse's office.

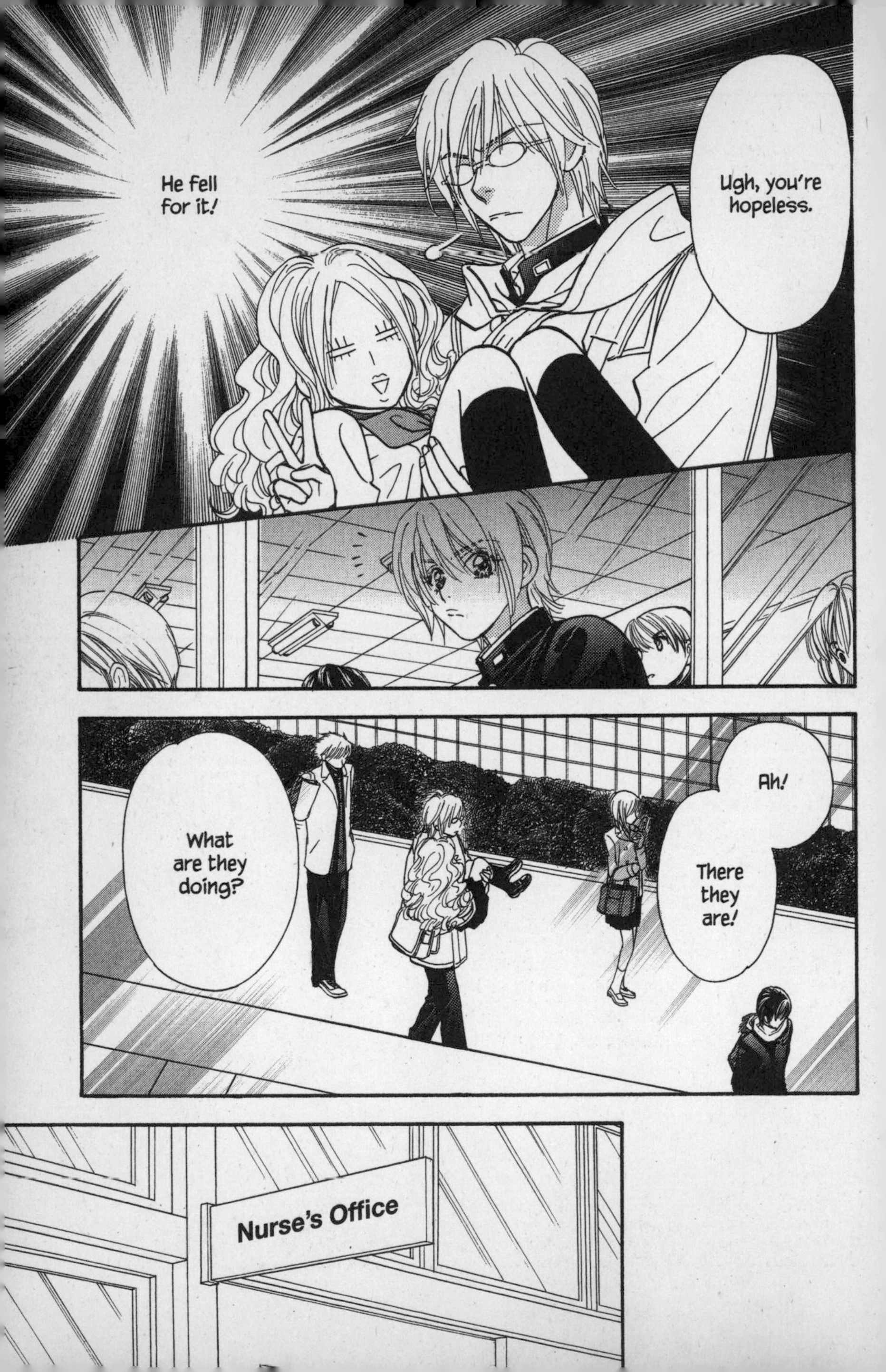
Ugh, you're hopeless.
He fell for it!
Ah!
There they are!
What are they doing?
Nurse's Office

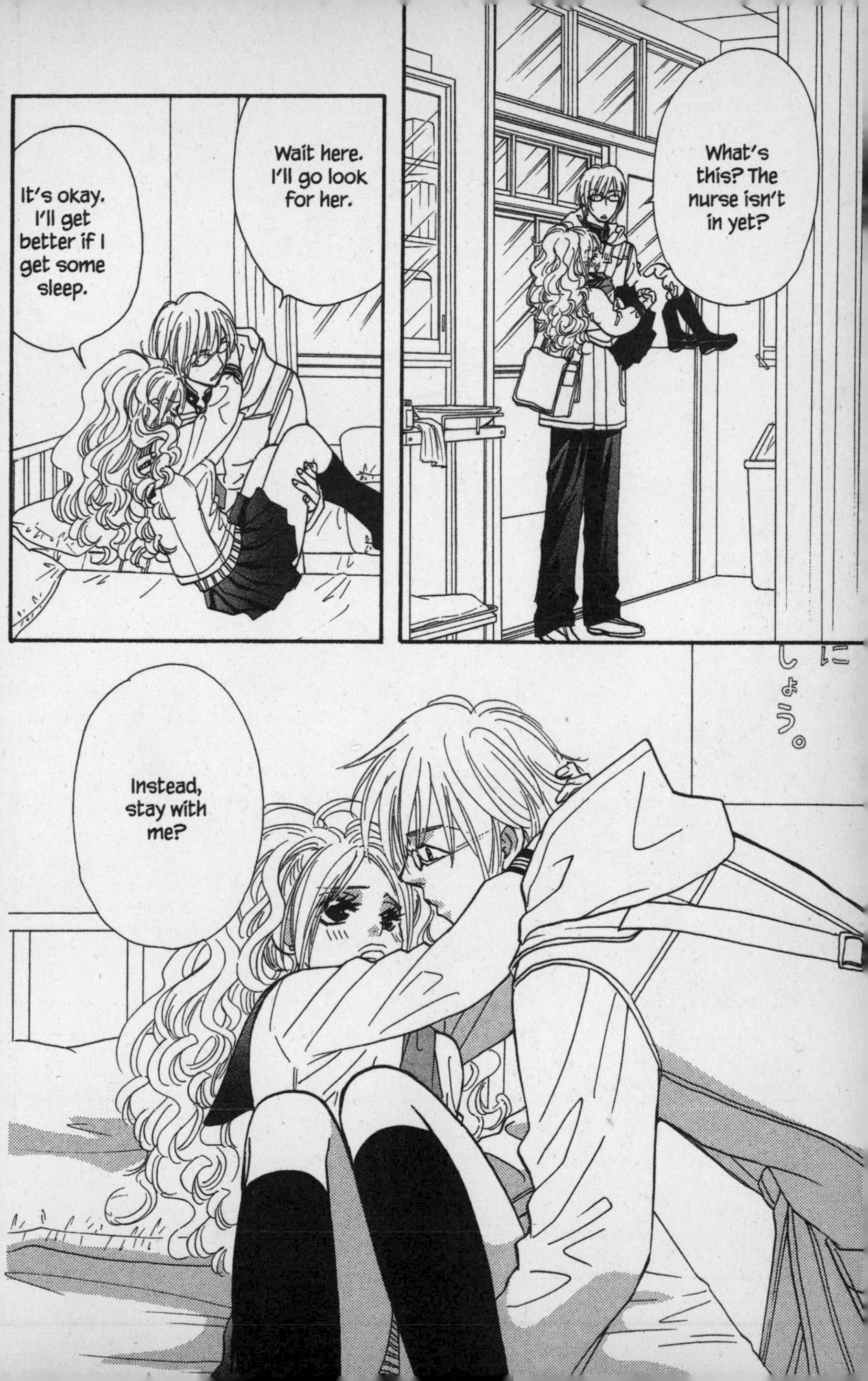
What's this? The nurse isn't in yet?
Wait here. I'll go look for her.
It's okay. I'll get better if I get some sleep.
にしよう。
Instead, stay with me?

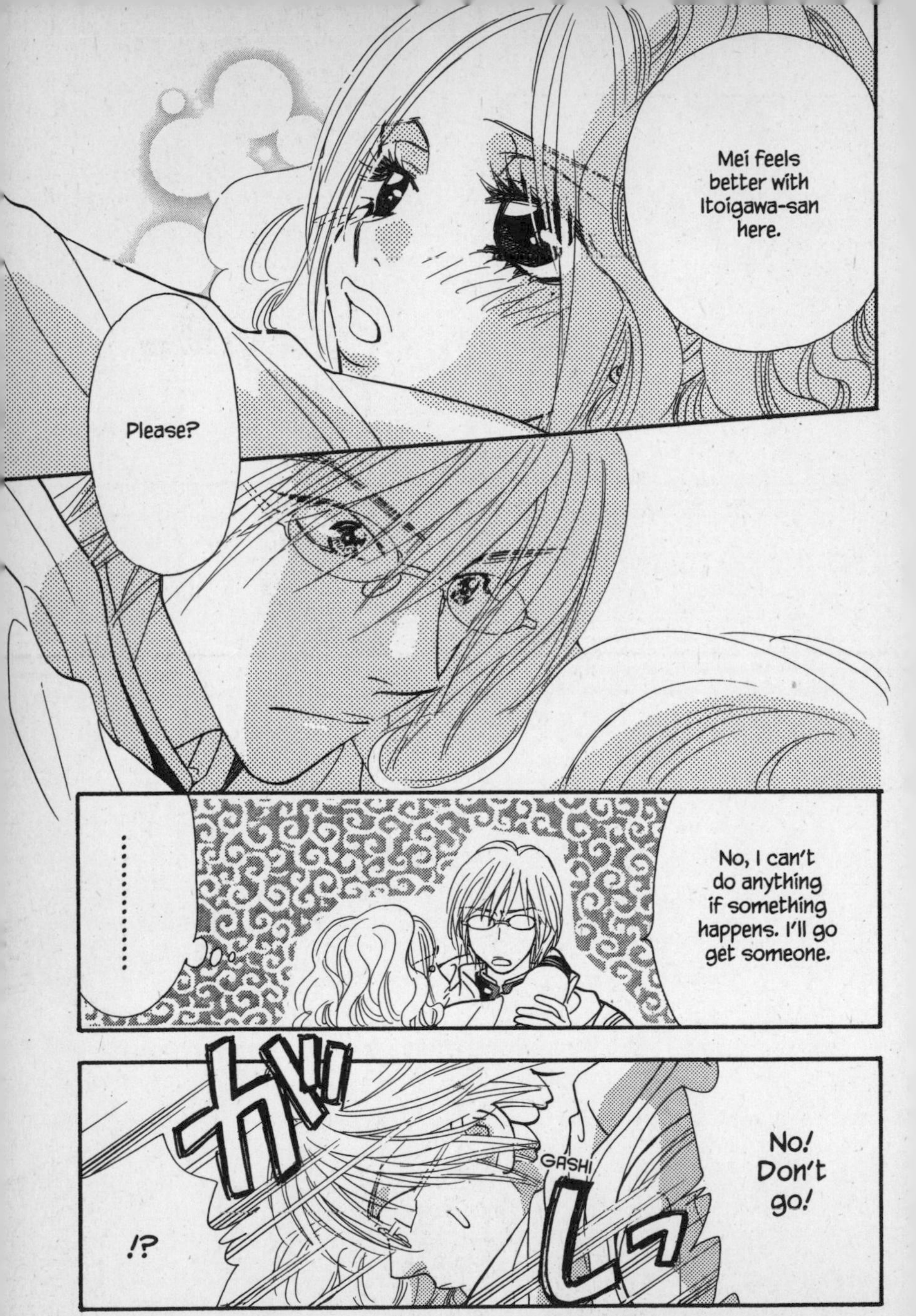
Mei feels better with Itoigawa-san here.
Please?
No, I can't do anything if something happens. I'll go get someone.
....
No! Don't go!
GASHI
!?

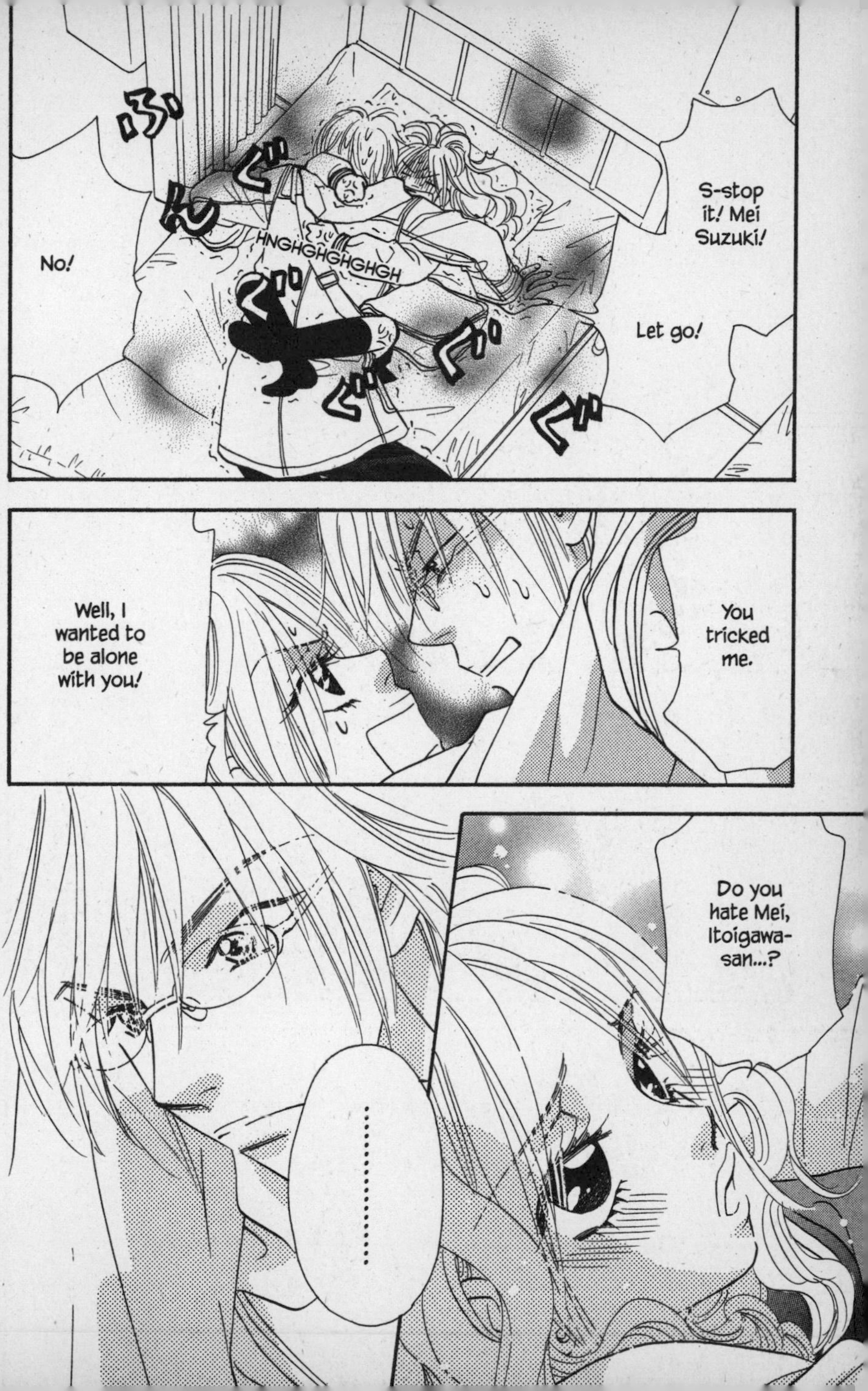
S-stop it! Mei Suzuki!
Let go!
HNGHGHGHGHGH
No!
You tricked me.
Well, I wanted to be alone with you!
Do you hate Mei, Itoigawa-san...?
....

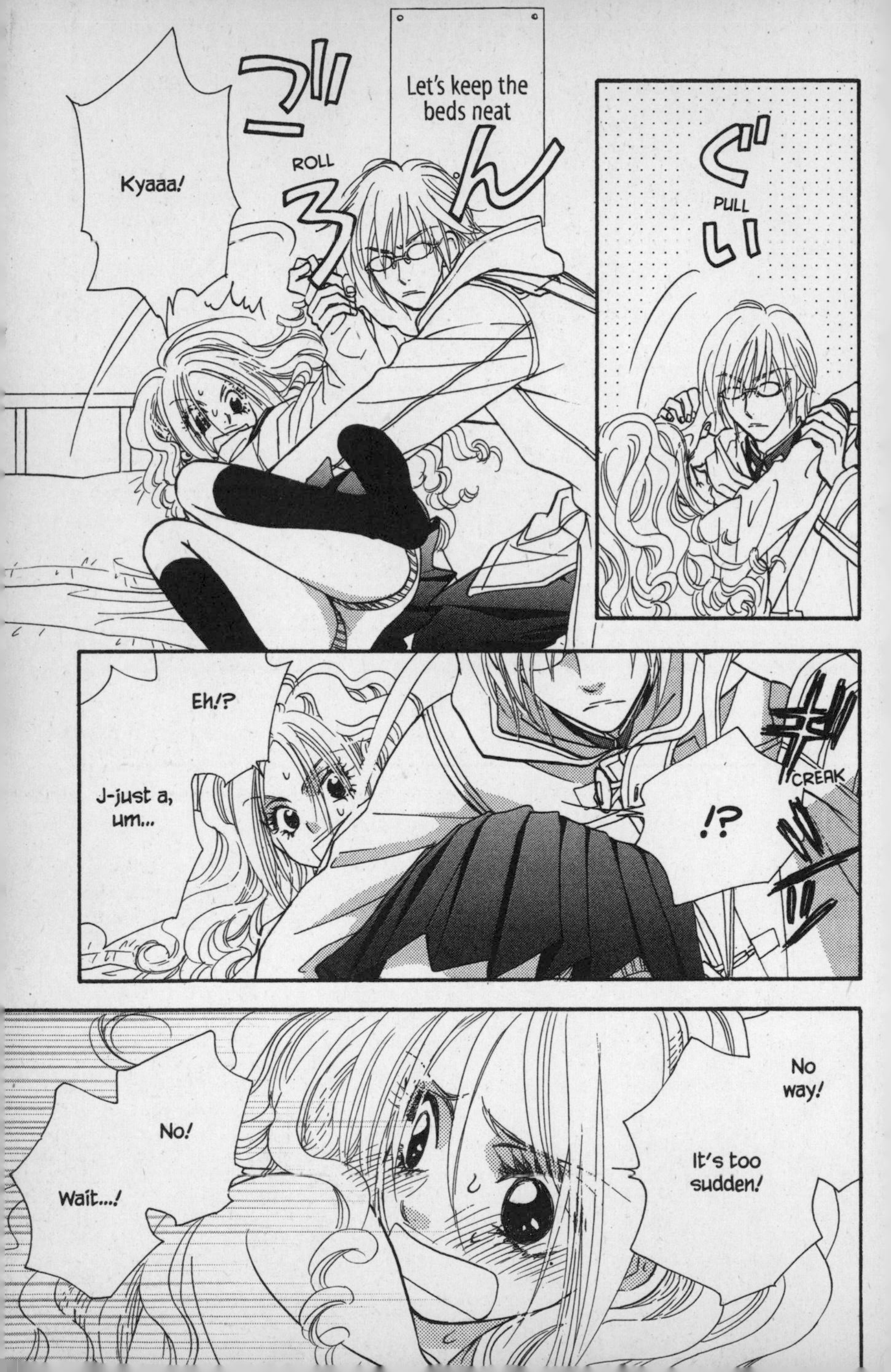
ぐい
PULL
Let's keep the beds neat
ごろん
ROLL
Kyaaa!
ギシ
CREAK
!?
Eh!?
J-just a, um...
No way!
It's too sudden!
No!
Wait...!

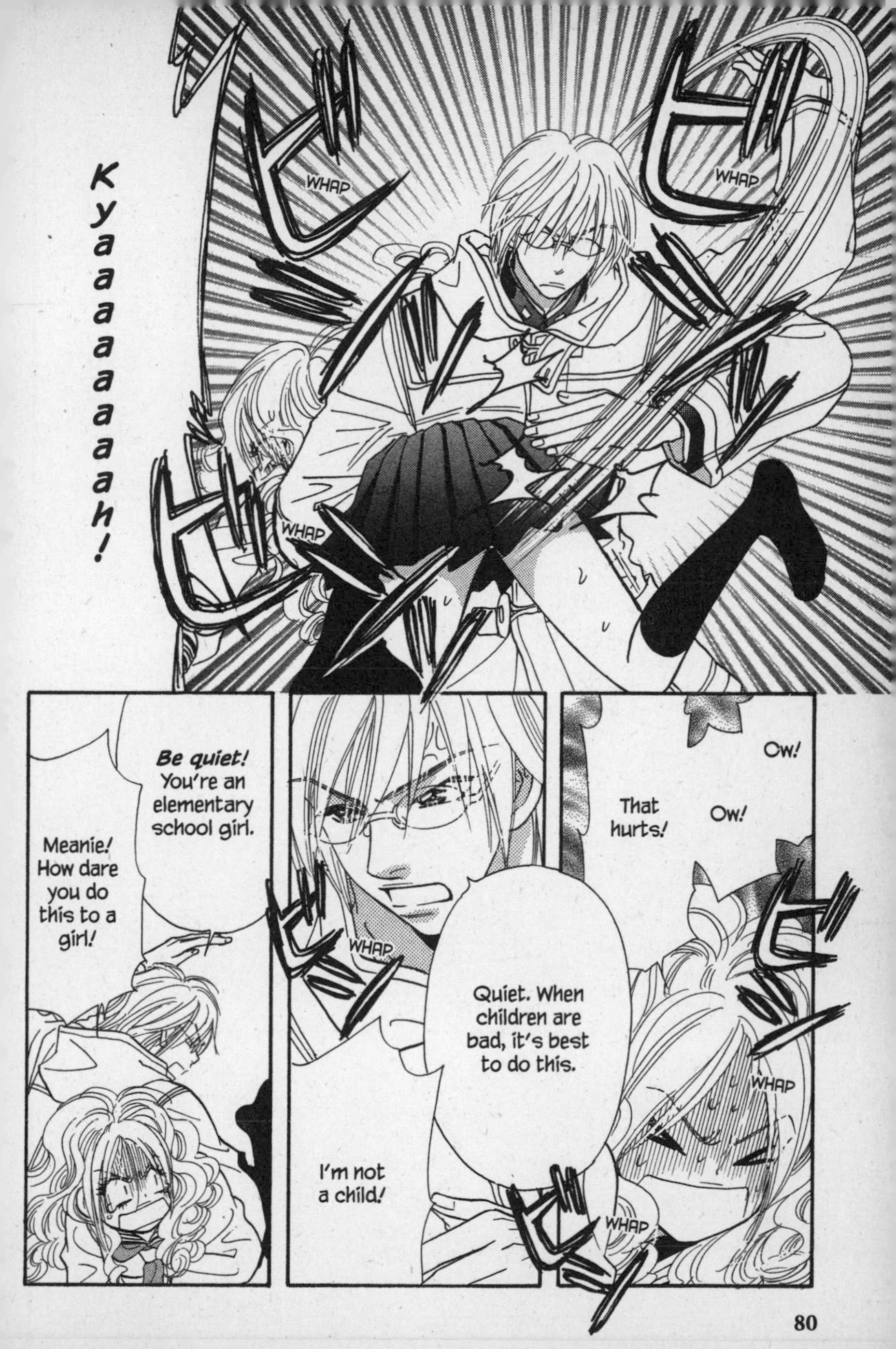
WHAP
WHAP
Kyaaaaaaaaaah!
WHAP
Ow!
That hurts!
Ow!
WHAP
WHAP
WHAP
Quiet. When children are bad, it's best to do this.
I'm not a child!
Be quiet! You're an elementary school girl.
Meanie! How dare you do this to a girl!

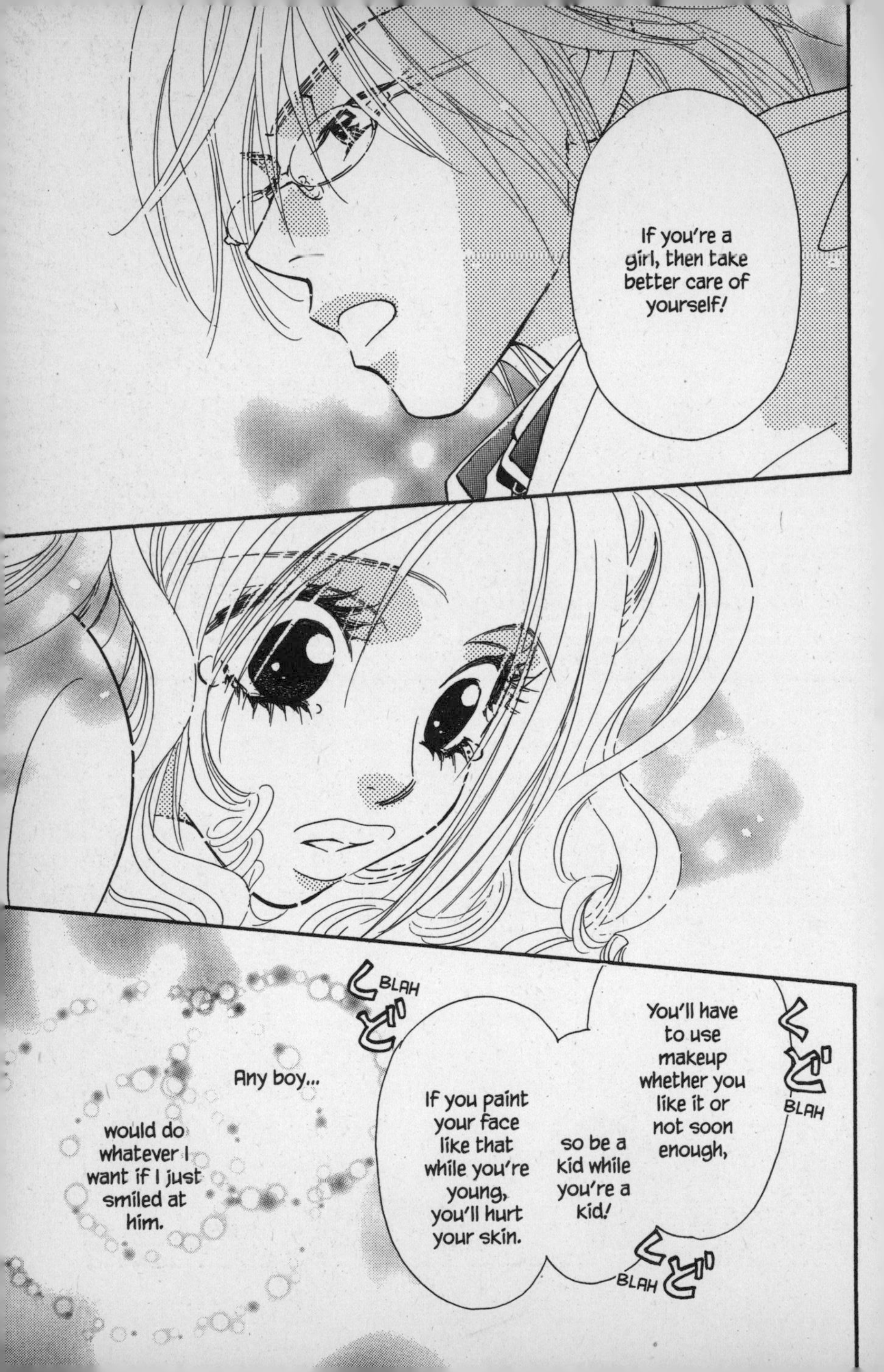
If you're a girl, then take better care of yourself!
BLAH
You'll have to use makeup whether you like it or not soon enough,
so be a kid while you're a kid!
BLAH
If you paint your face like that while you're young, you'll hurt your skin.
BLAH
Any boy...
would do whatever I want if I just smiled at him.

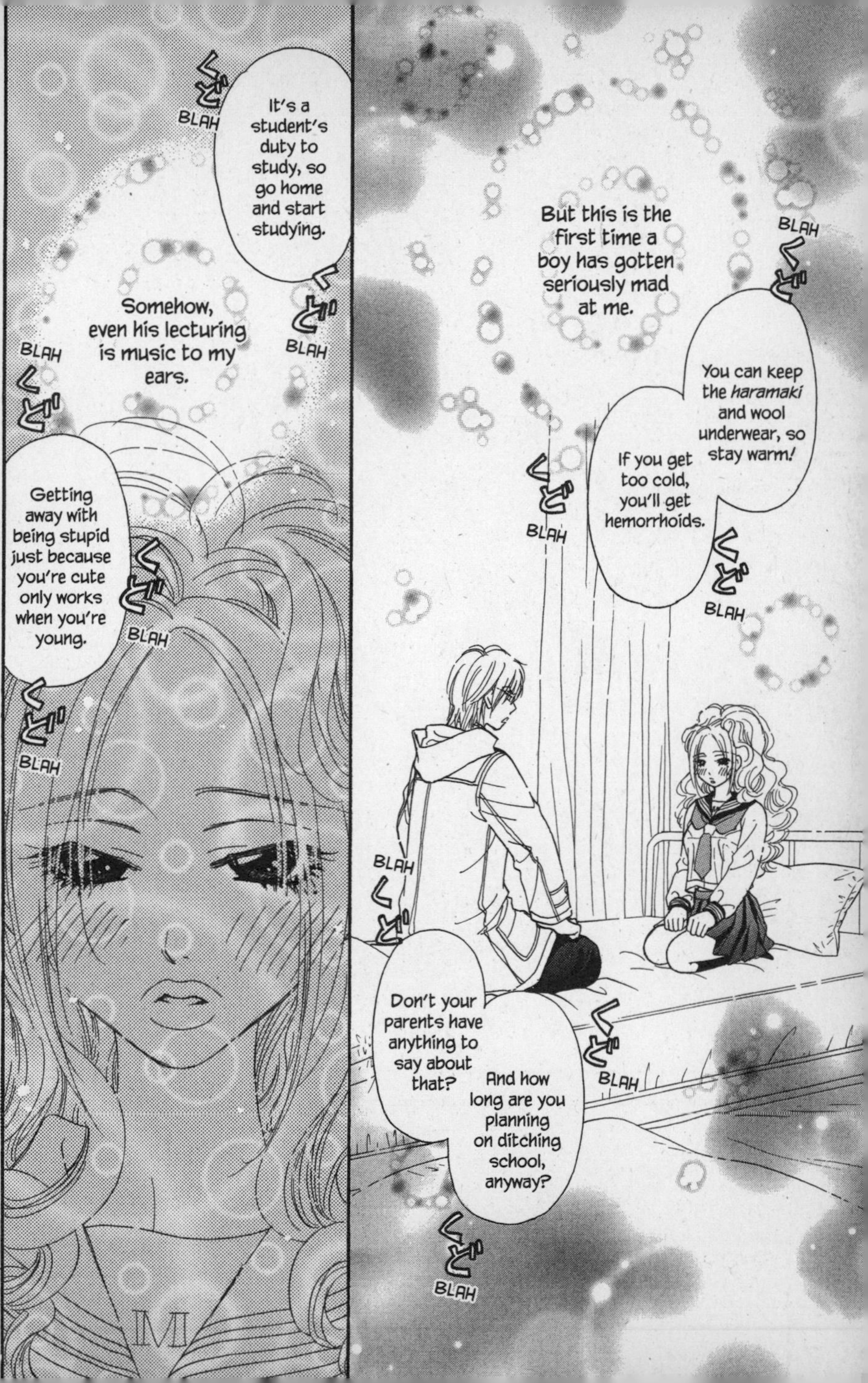
But this is the first time a boy has gotten seriously mad at me.
BLAH
You can keep the *haramaki* and wool underwear, so stay warm!
BLAH
If you get too cold, you'll get hemorrhoids.
BLAH
BLAH
Don't your parents have anything to say about that?
And how long are you planning on ditching school, anyway?
BLAH
BLAH
BLAH
It's a student's duty to study, so go home and start studying.
BLAH
Somehow, even his lecturing is music to my ears.
BLAH
Getting away with being stupid just because you're cute only works when you're young.
BLAH
BLAH

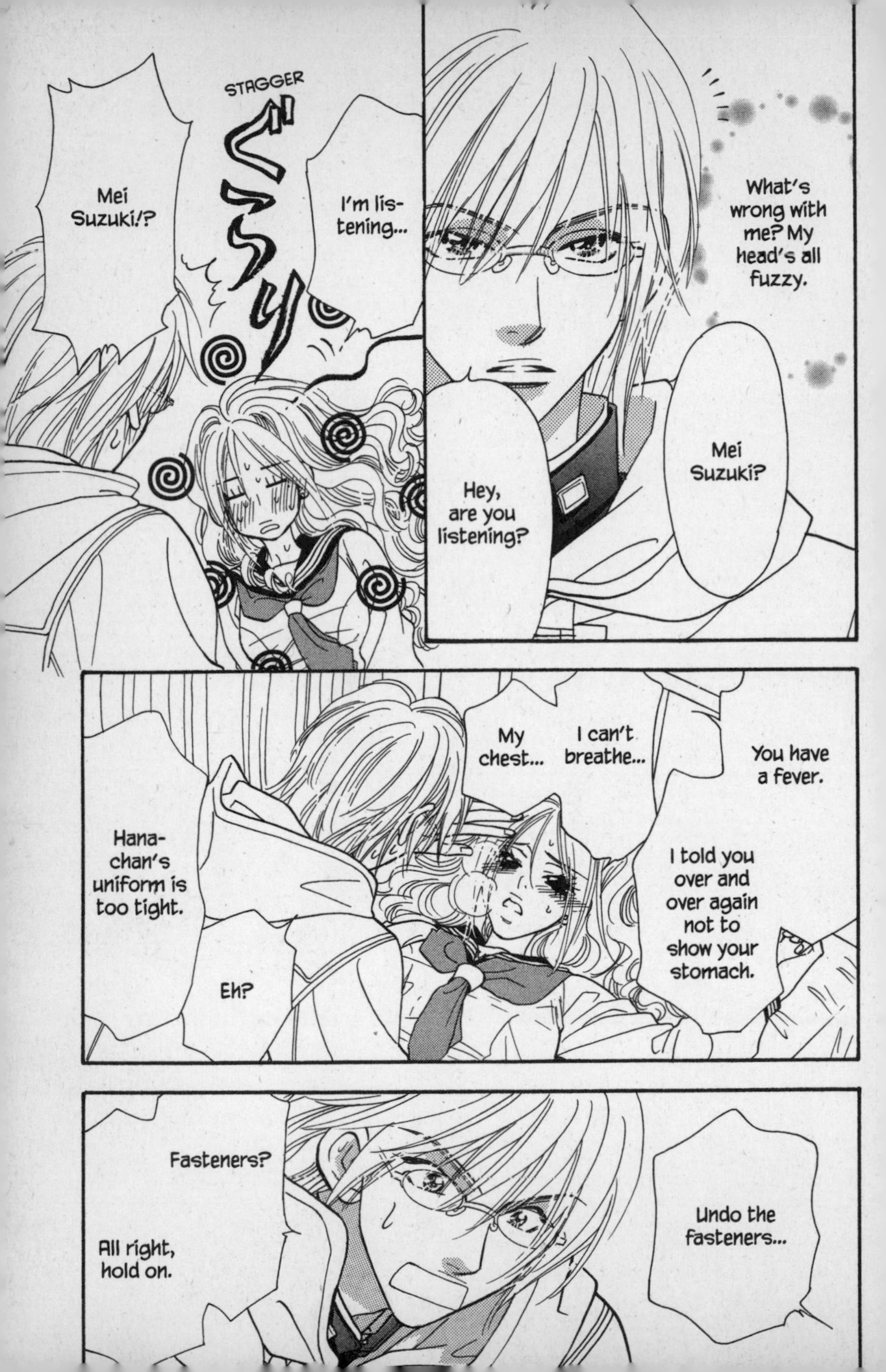
What's wrong with me? My head's all fuzzy.
Mei Suzuki?
Hey, are you listening?
I'm listening...
STAGGER
ぐらり
Mei Suzuki!?
You have a fever.
I told you over and over again not to show your stomach.
I can't breathe...
My chest...
Hana-chan's uniform is too tight.
Eh?
Undo the fasteners...
Fasteners?
All right, hold on.

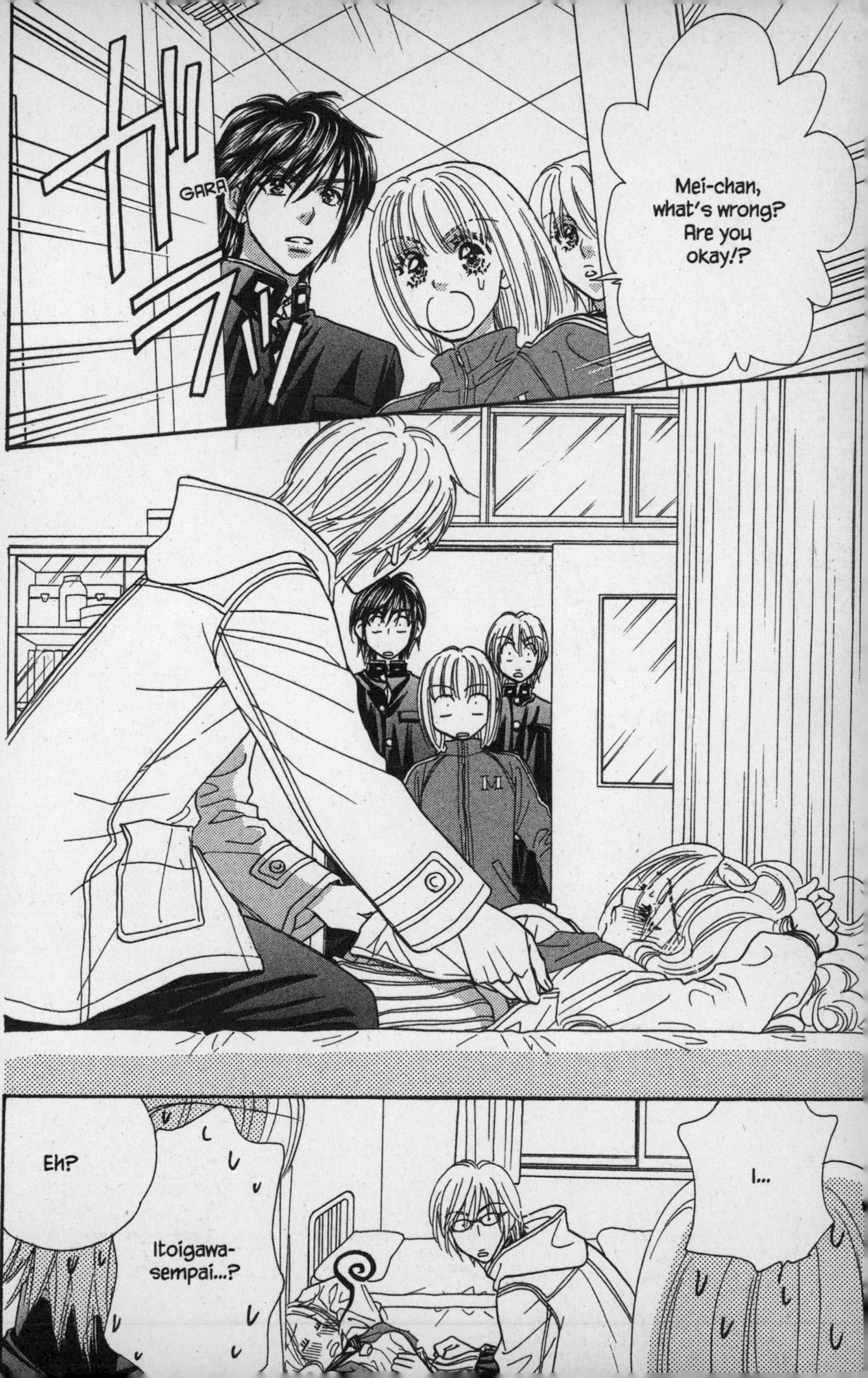
Mei-chan, what's wrong? Are you okay!?
GARA
I...
Eh?
Itoigawa-sempai...?

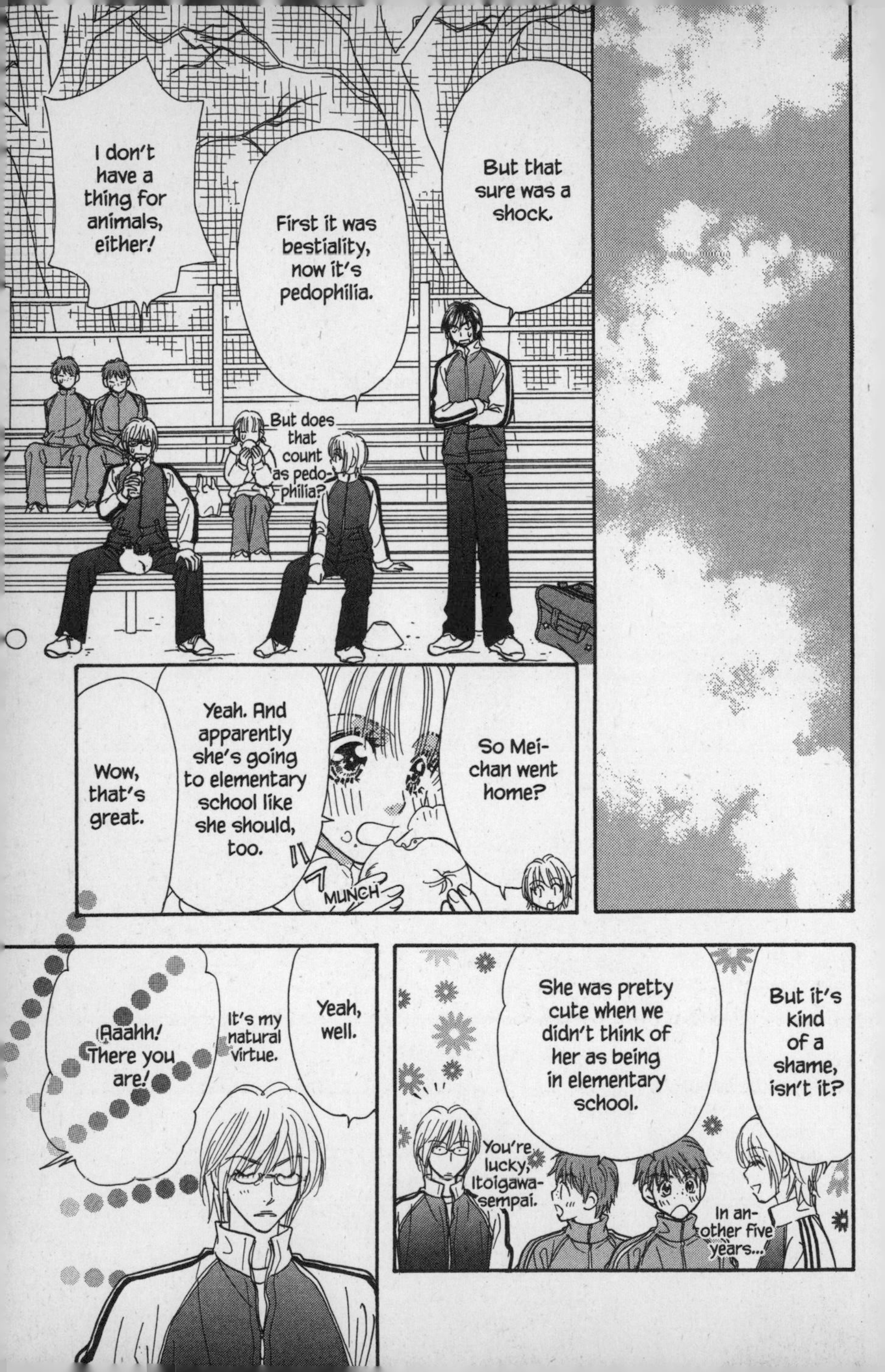
But that sure was a shock.
First it was bestiality, now it's pedophilia.
I don't have a thing for animals, either!
But does that count as pedo-philia?
So Mei-chan went home?
Yeah. And apparently she's going to elementary school like she should, too.
Wow, that's great.
MUNCH
But it's kind of a shame, isn't it?
She was pretty cute when we didn't think of her as being in elementary school.
In an-other five years...
You're lucky, Itoigawa-sempai.
Yeah, well.
It's my natural virtue.
Aaahh! There you are!

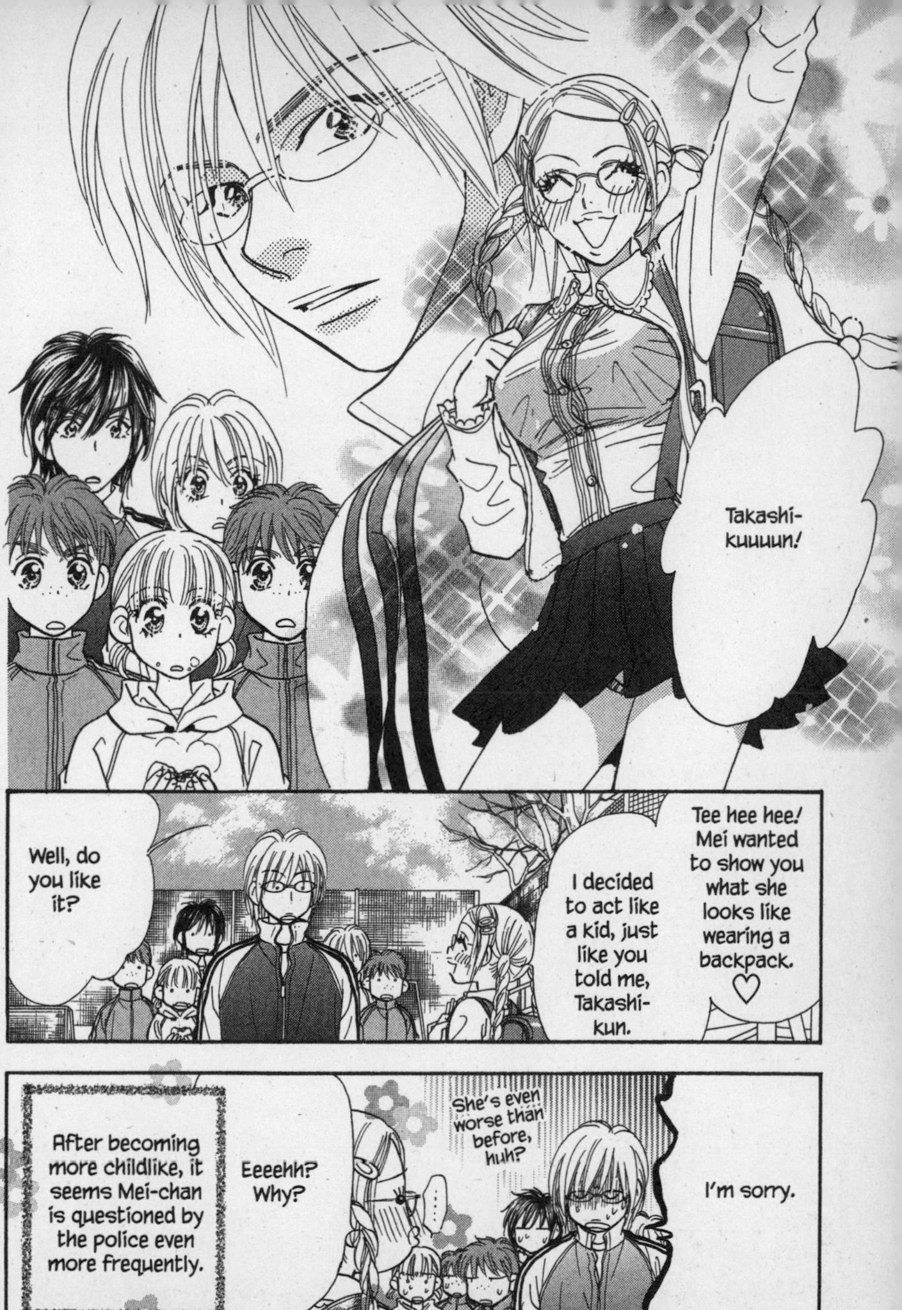
Takashi-kuuuun!
Tee hee hee! Mei wanted to show you what she looks like wearing a backpack. ♡
I decided to act like a kid, just like you told me, Takashi-kun.
Well, do you like it?
I'm sorry.
She's even worse than before, huh?
. . .
Eeeehh? Why?
After becoming more childlike, it seems Mei-chan is questioned by the police even more frequently.

The End

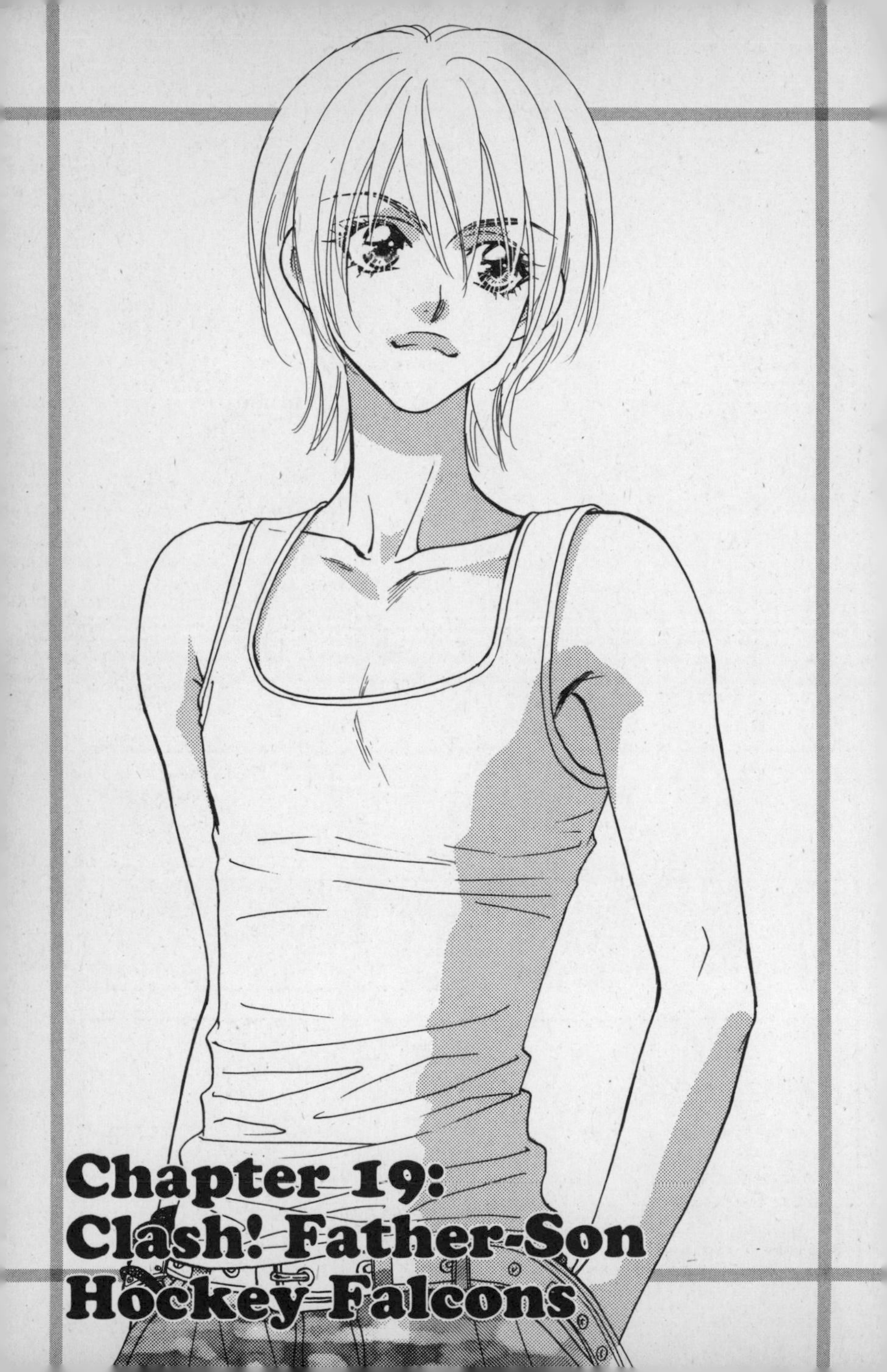

Chapter 19: Clash! Father-Son Hockey Falcons

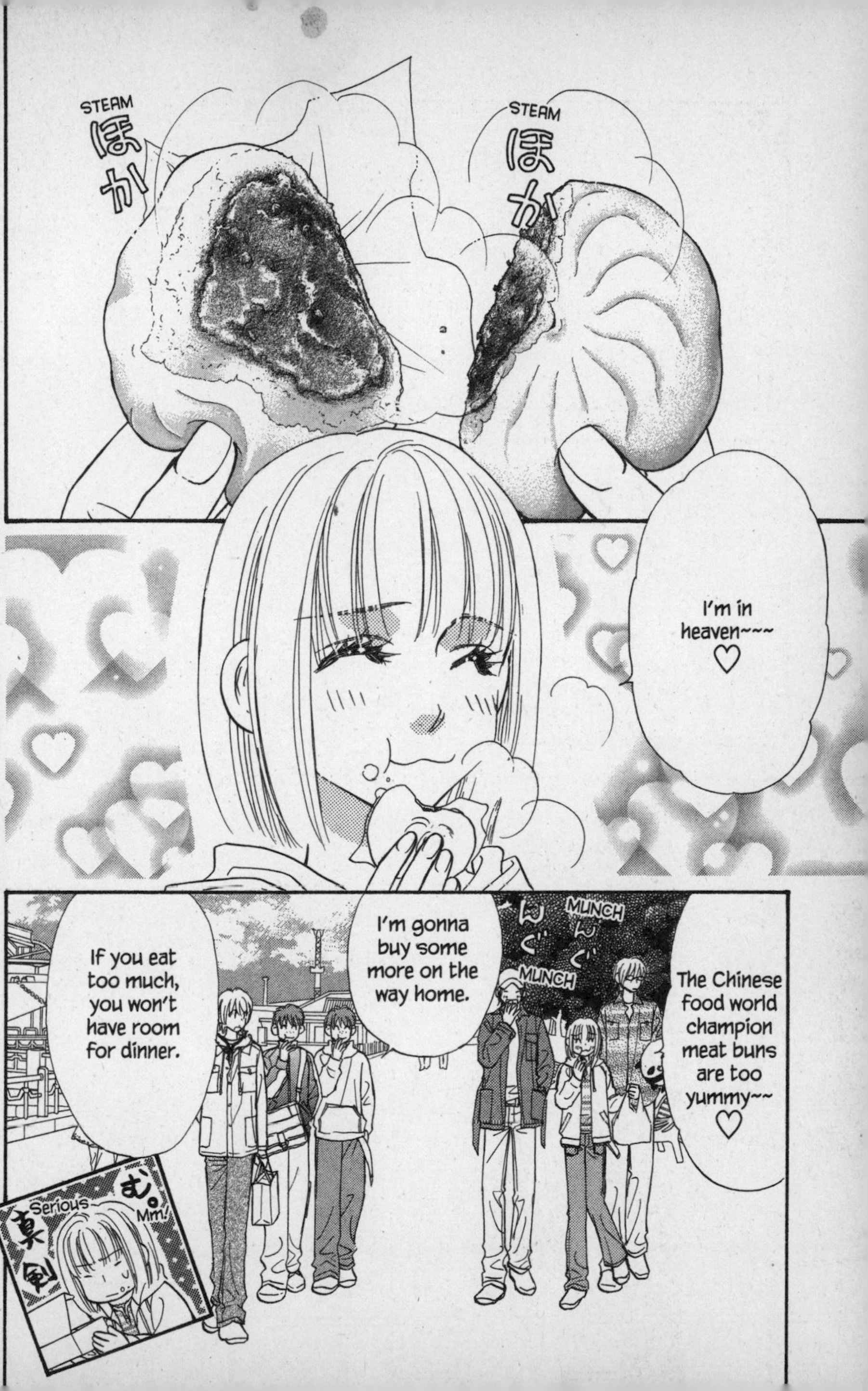
STEAM
ほか
STEAM
ほか
I'm in heaven~~~ ♡
The Chinese food world champion meat buns are too yummy~~ ♡
MUNCH
んぐ
MUNCH
んぐ
I'm gonna buy some more on the way home.
If you eat too much, you won't have room for dinner.
む。
Mm!
真剣
Serious

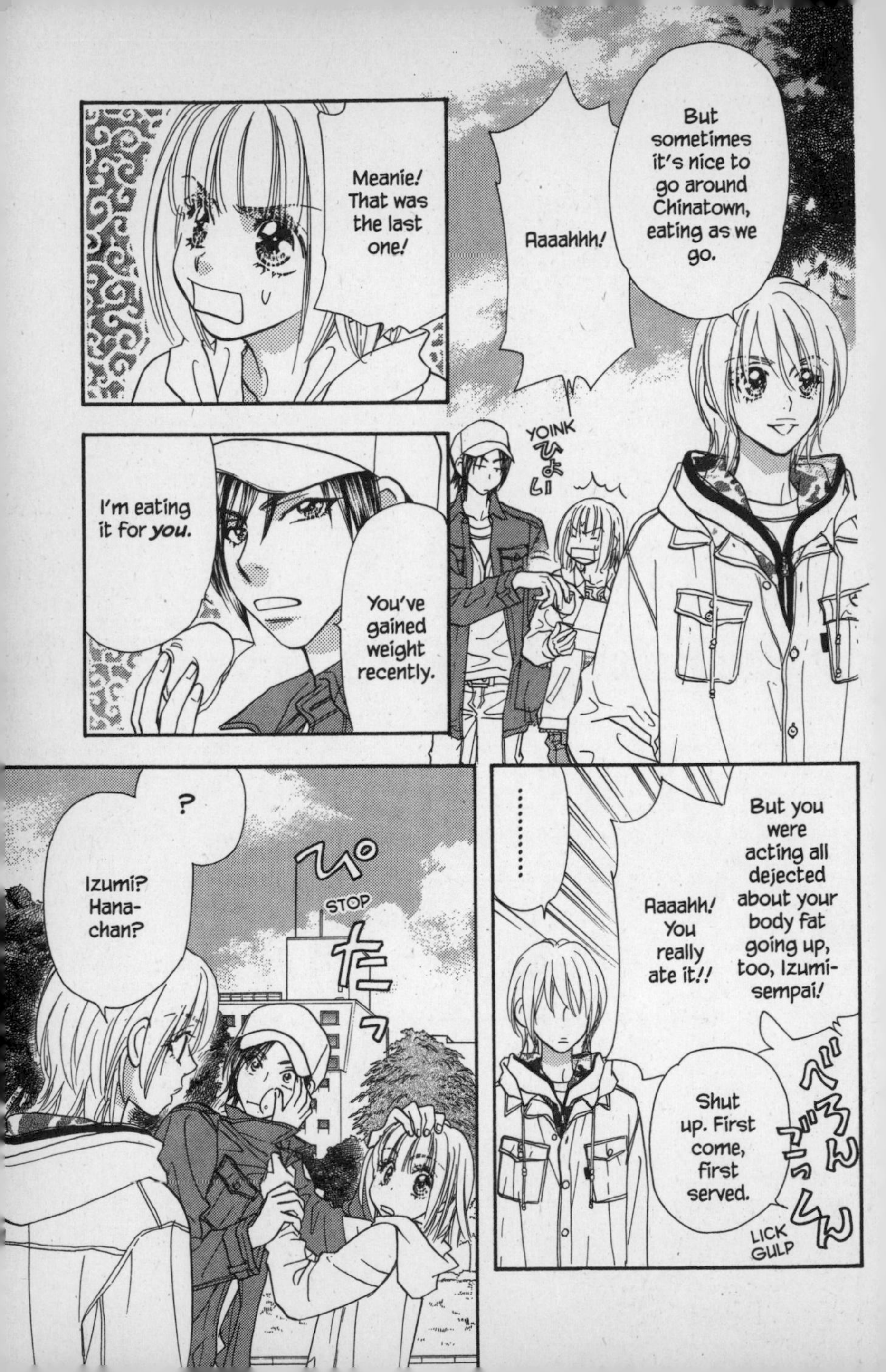

But sometimes it's nice to go around Chinatown, eating as we go.
Aaaahhh!
YOINK
ひょい
Meanie! That was the last one!
I'm eating it for *you*.
You've gained weight recently.
......
But you were acting all dejected about your body fat going up, too, Izumi-sempai!
Aaaahh! You really ate it!!
Shut up. First come, first served.
ぺろん
ごっくん
LICK
GULP
?
Izumi? Hana-chan?
ぴ
STOP
たっ

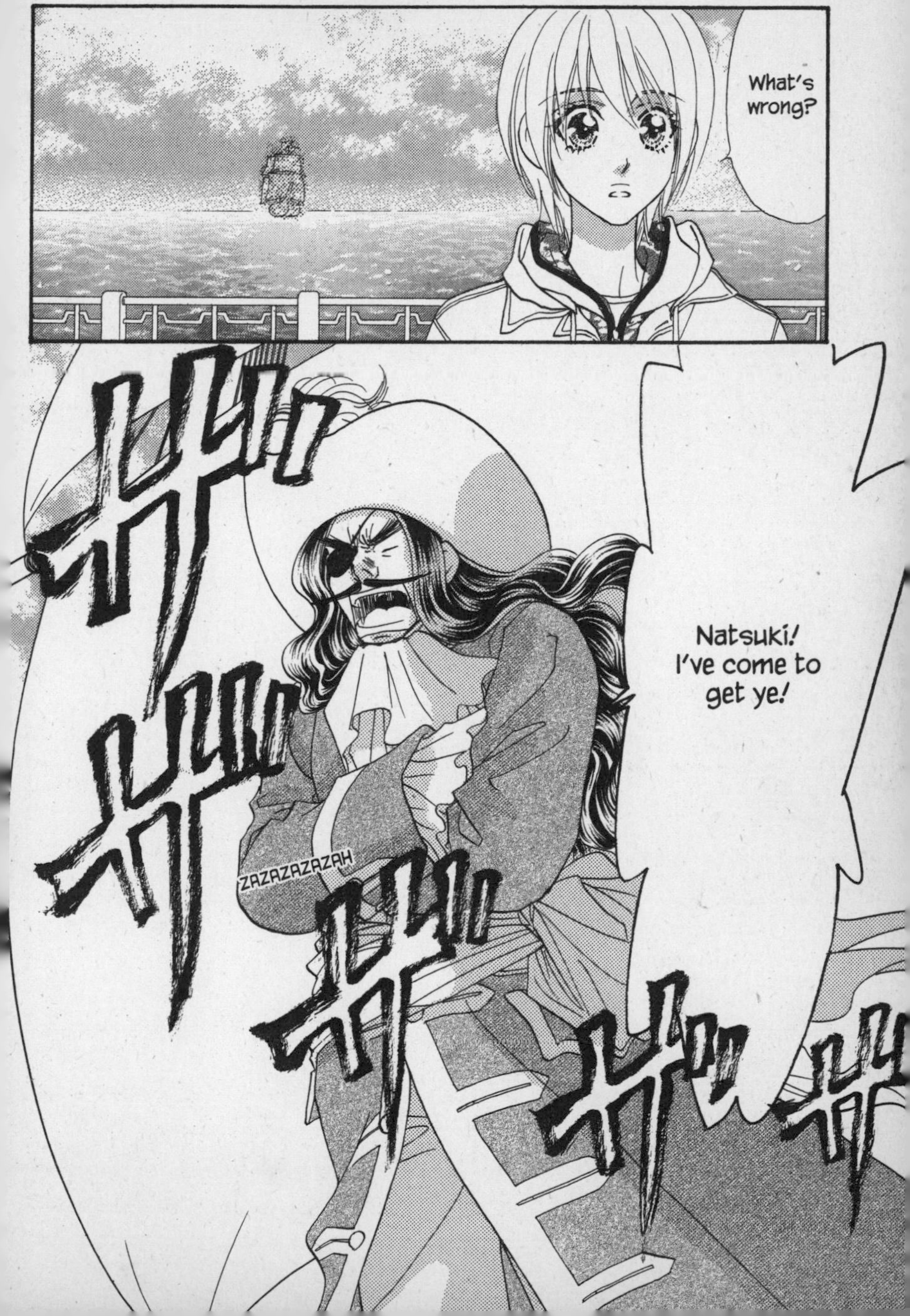
What's wrong?
Natsuki! I've come to get ye!
ZAZAZAZAZAH

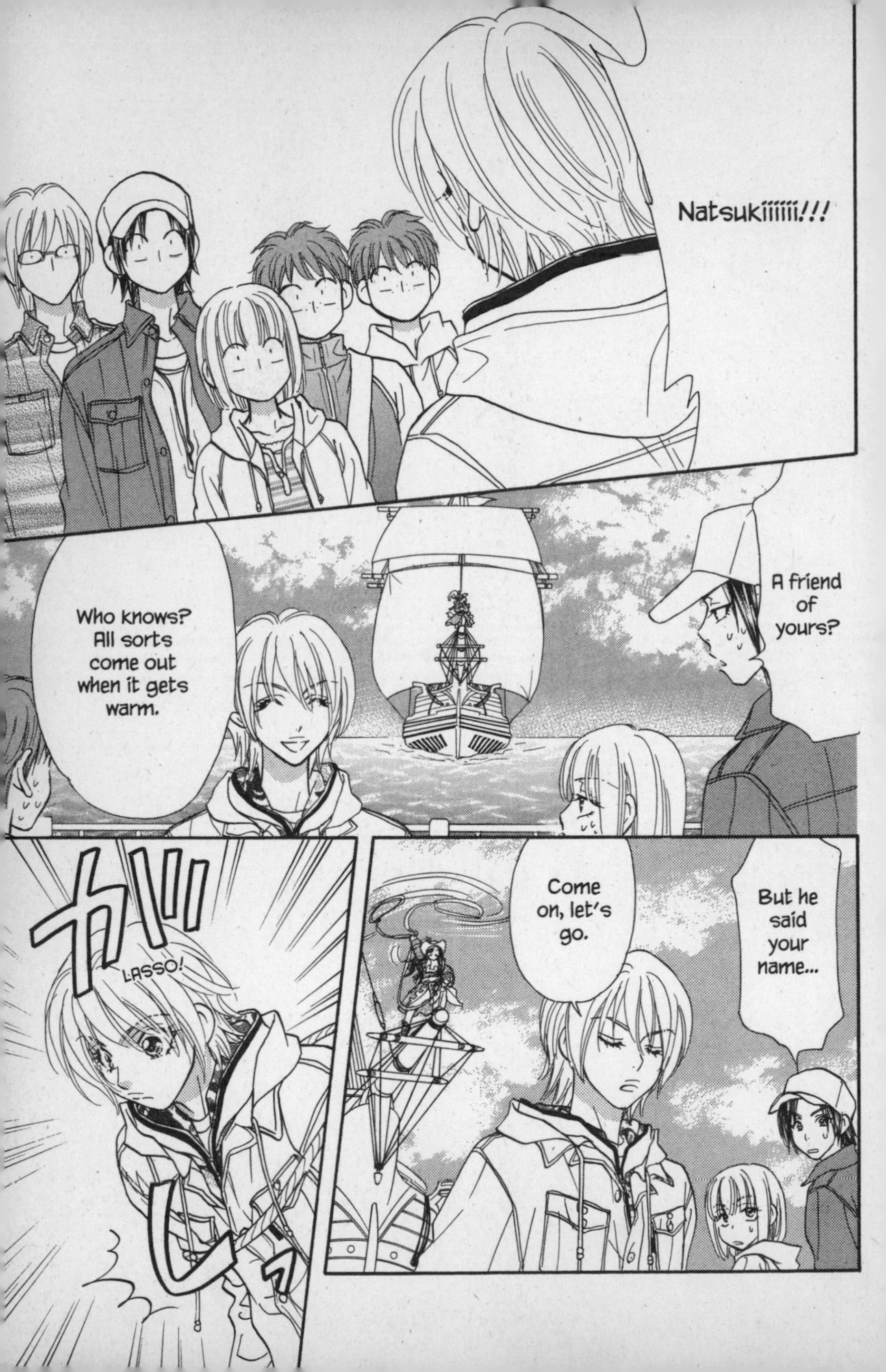
Natsukiiiiii!!!
A friend of yours?
Who knows? All sorts come out when it gets warm.
But he said your name...
Come on, let's go.
LASSO!

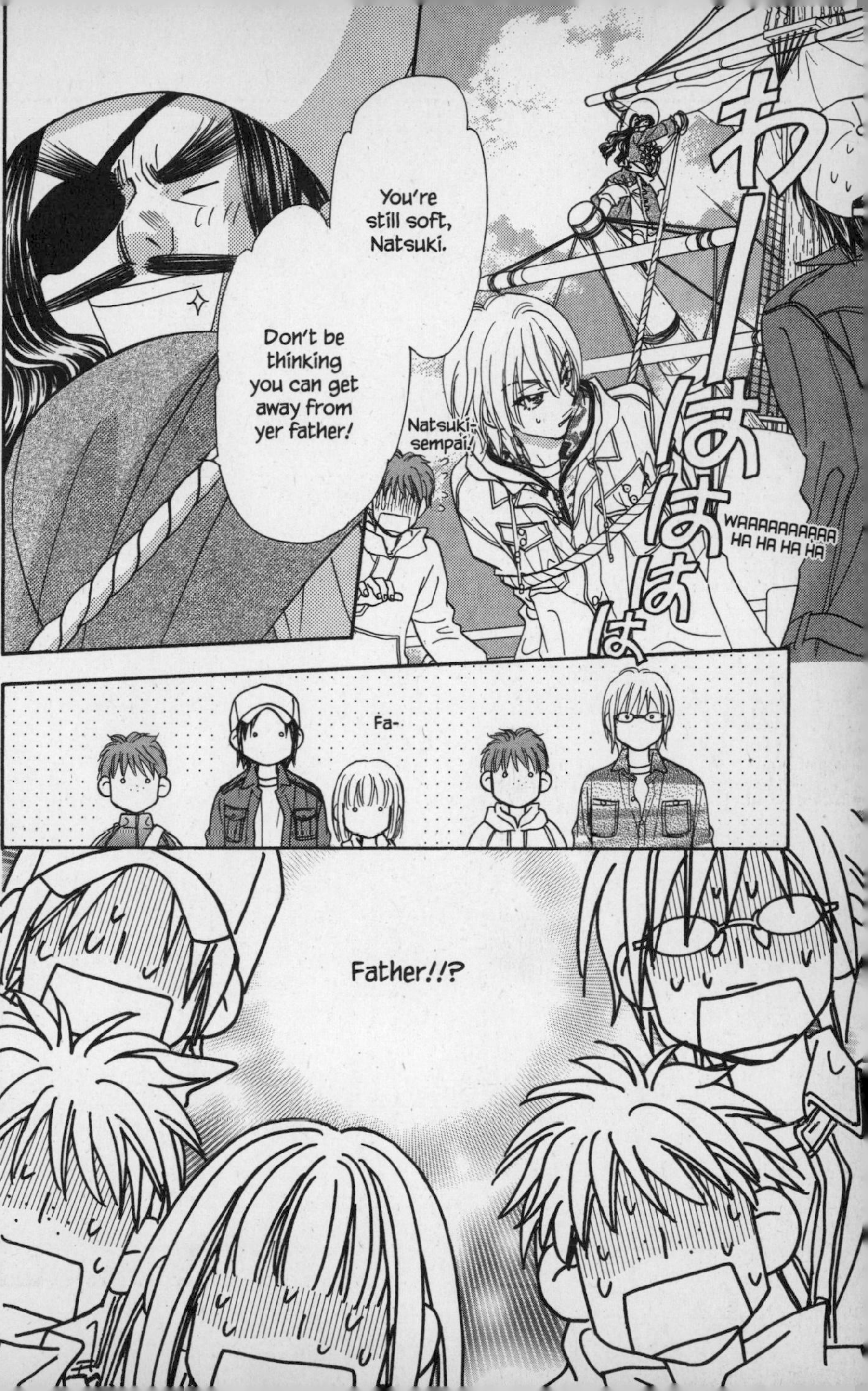
わーはははは
WAAAAAAAAAA HA HA HA HA
Natsuki-sempai!
You're still soft, Natsuki.
Don't be thinking you can get away from yer father!
Fa-
Father!!?

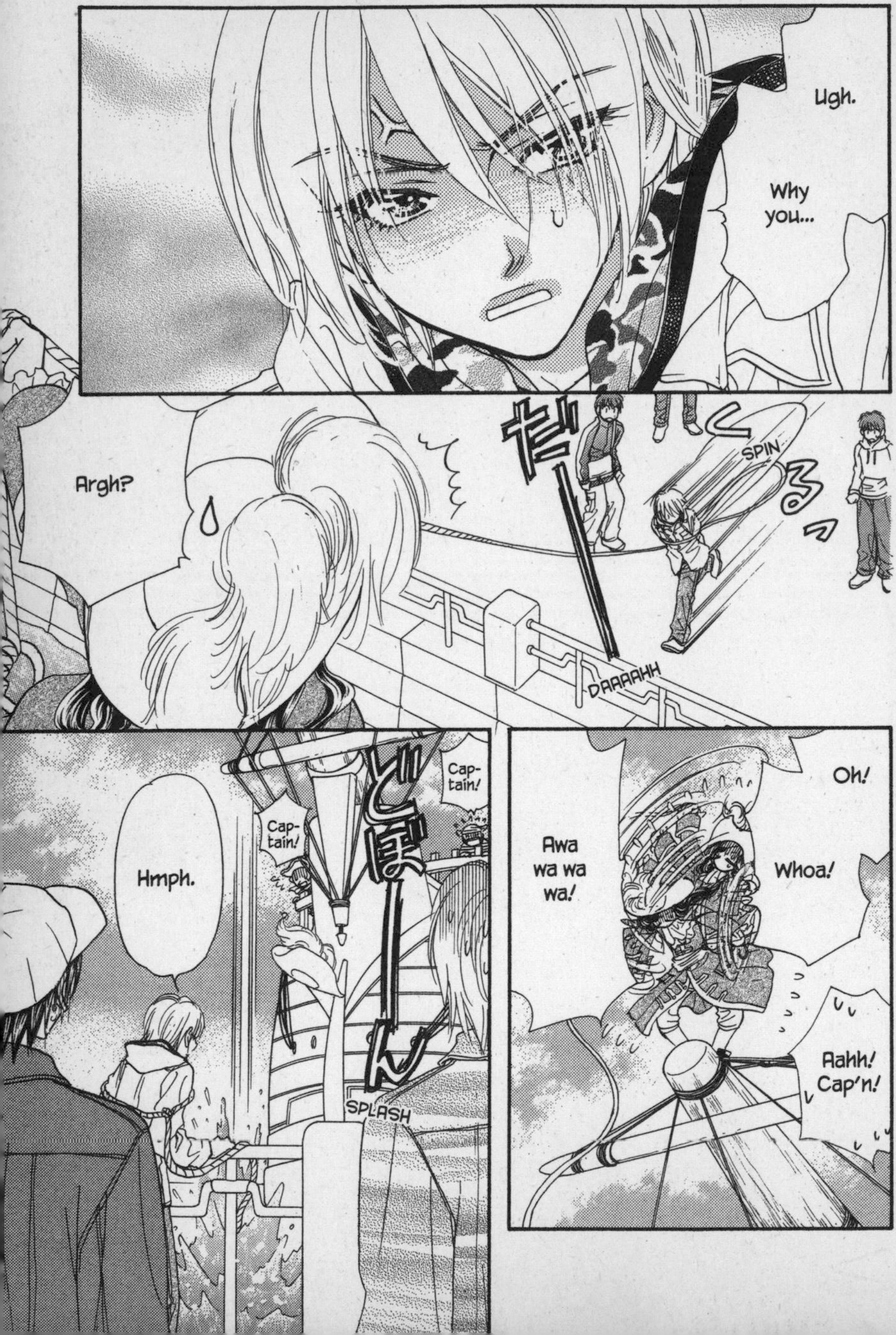
Ugh.
Why you...
SPIN
DAAAAAHH
Argh?
Oh!
Whoa!
Awa wa wa wa!
Aahh! Cap'n!
Cap-tain!
Cap-tain!
Hmph.
どぼーん
SPLASH

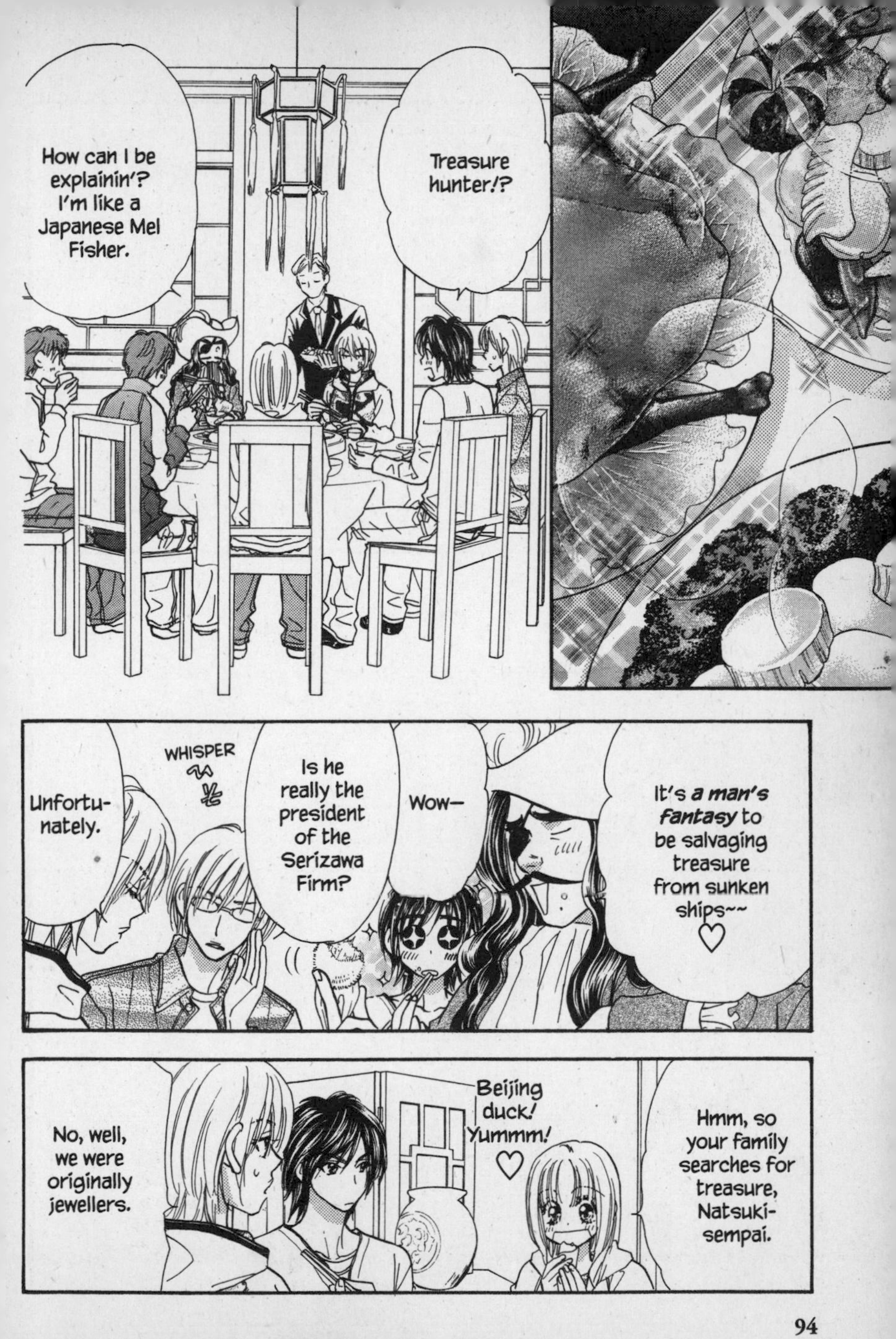
Treasure hunter!?
How can I be explainin'? I'm like a Japanese Mel Fisher.
It's ***a man's fantasy*** to be salvaging treasure from sunken ships~~ ♡
Wow—
Is he really the president of the Serizawa Firm?
WHISPER
Unfortunately.
Hmm, so your family searches for treasure, Natsuki-sempai.
Beijing duck! Yummm! ♡
No, well, we were originally jewellers.

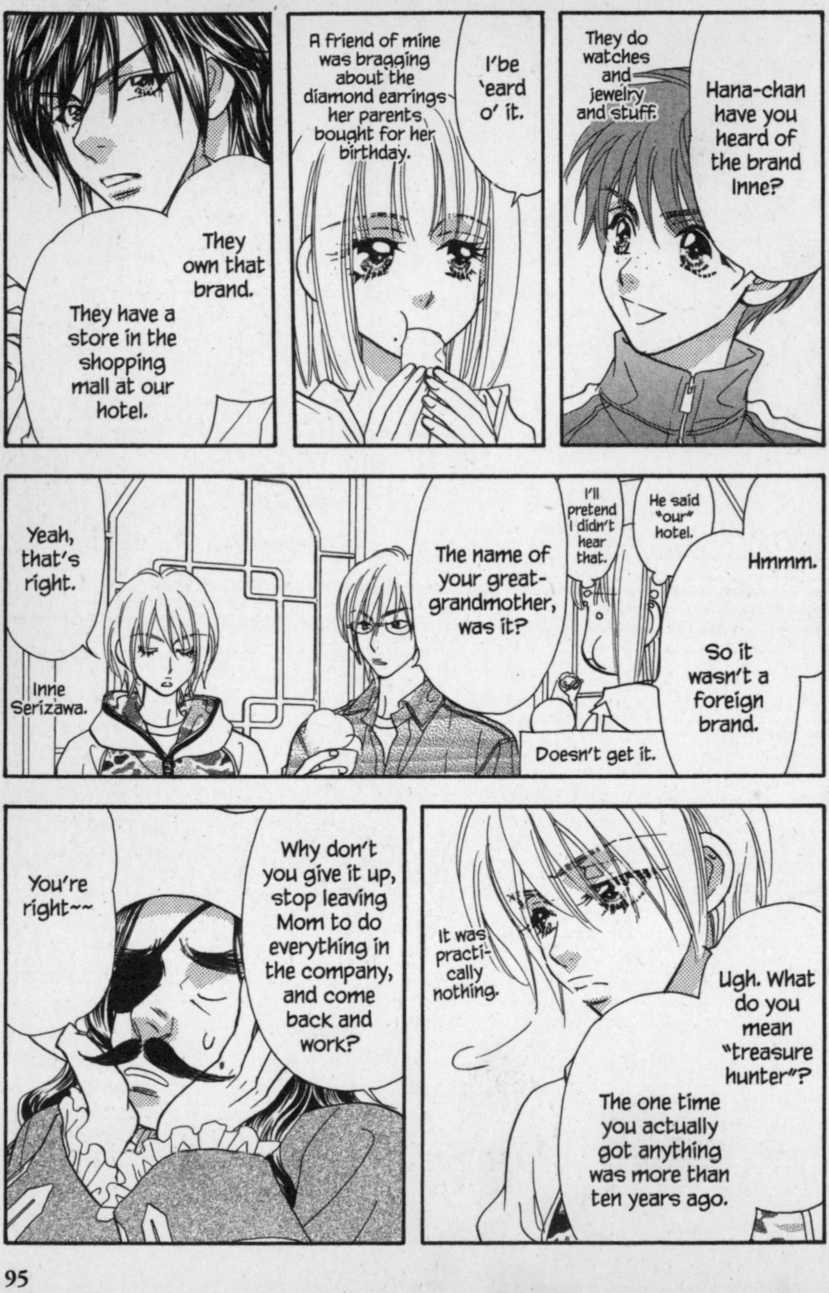
Hana-chan have you heard of the brand Inne?
They do watches and jewelry and stuff.
I'be 'eard o' it.
A friend of mine was bragging about the diamond earrings her parents bought for her birthday.
They own that brand.
They have a store in the shopping mall at our hotel.
Hmmm.
He said "our" hotel.
I'll pretend I didn't hear that.
So it wasn't a foreign brand.
The name of your great-grandmother, was it?
Doesn't get it.
Yeah, that's right.
Inne Serizawa.
Ugh. What do you mean "treasure hunter"?
The one time you actually got anything was more than ten years ago.
It was practi-cally nothing.
Why don't you give it up, stop leaving Mom to do everything in the company, and come back and work?
You're right~~

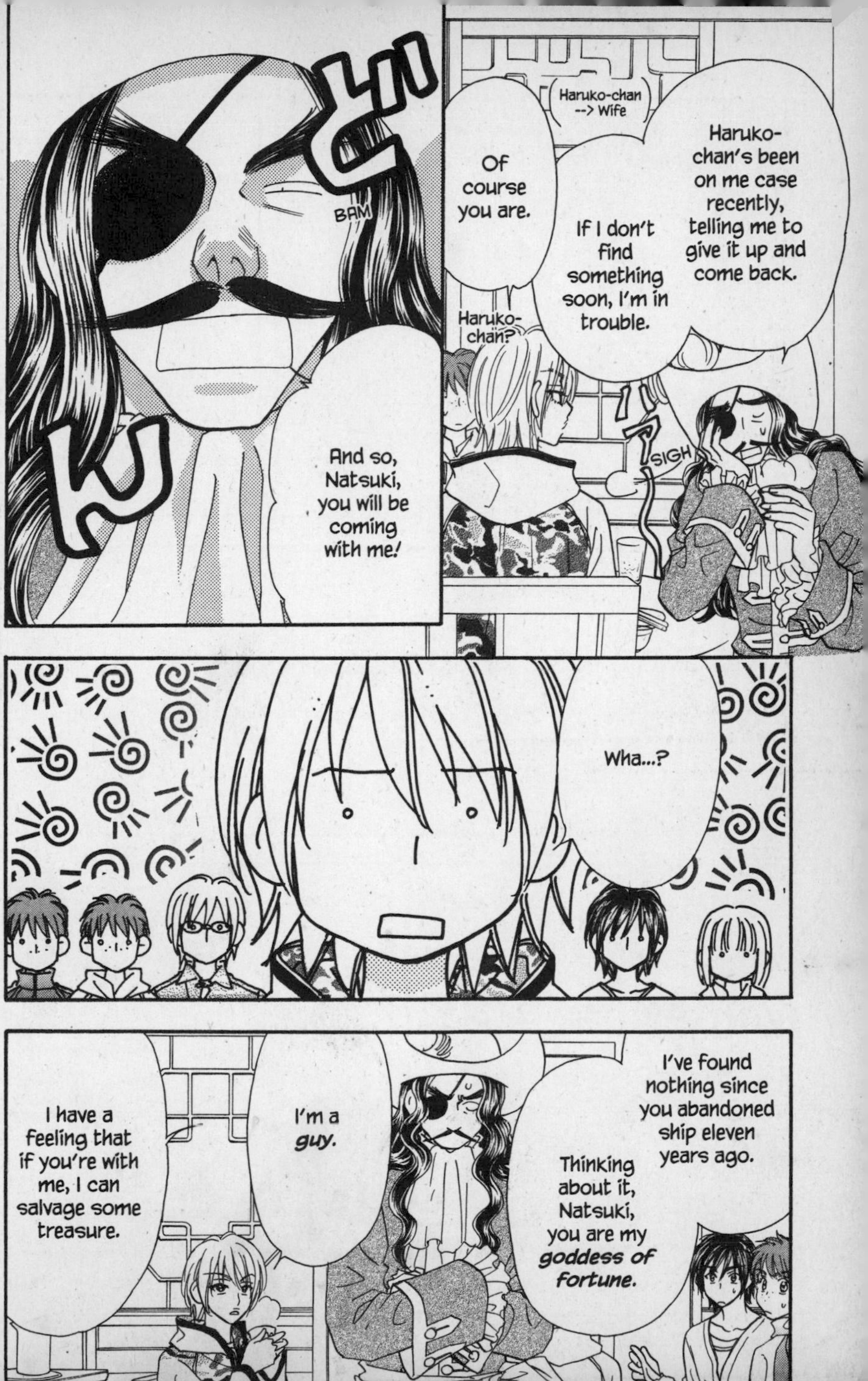

Haruko-chan's been on me case recently, telling me to give it up and come back.
Haruko-chan --> Wife
If I don't find something soon, I'm in trouble.
Of course you are.
Haruko-chan?
SIGH
BAM
And so, Natsuki, you will be coming with me!
Wha...?
I've found nothing since you abandoned ship eleven years ago.
Thinking about it, Natsuki, you are my *goddess of fortune*.
I'm a *guy*.
I have a feeling that if you're with me, I can salvage some treasure.

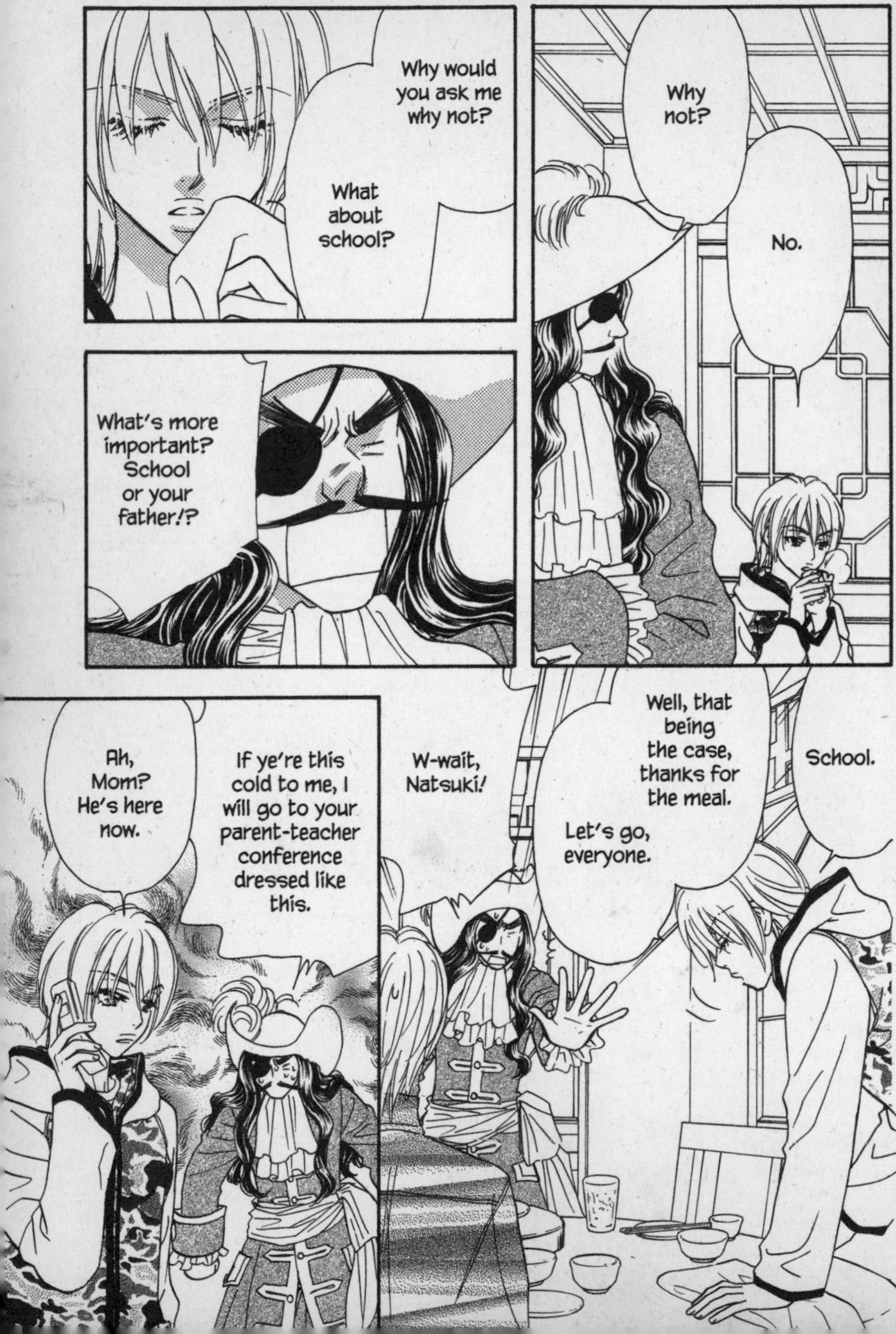
Why not?
No.
Why would you ask me why not?
What about school?
What's more important? School or your father!?
School.
Well, that being the case, thanks for the meal.
Let's go, everyone.
W-wait, Natsuki!
If ye're this cold to me, I will go to your parent-teacher conference dressed like this.
Ah, Mom? He's here now.

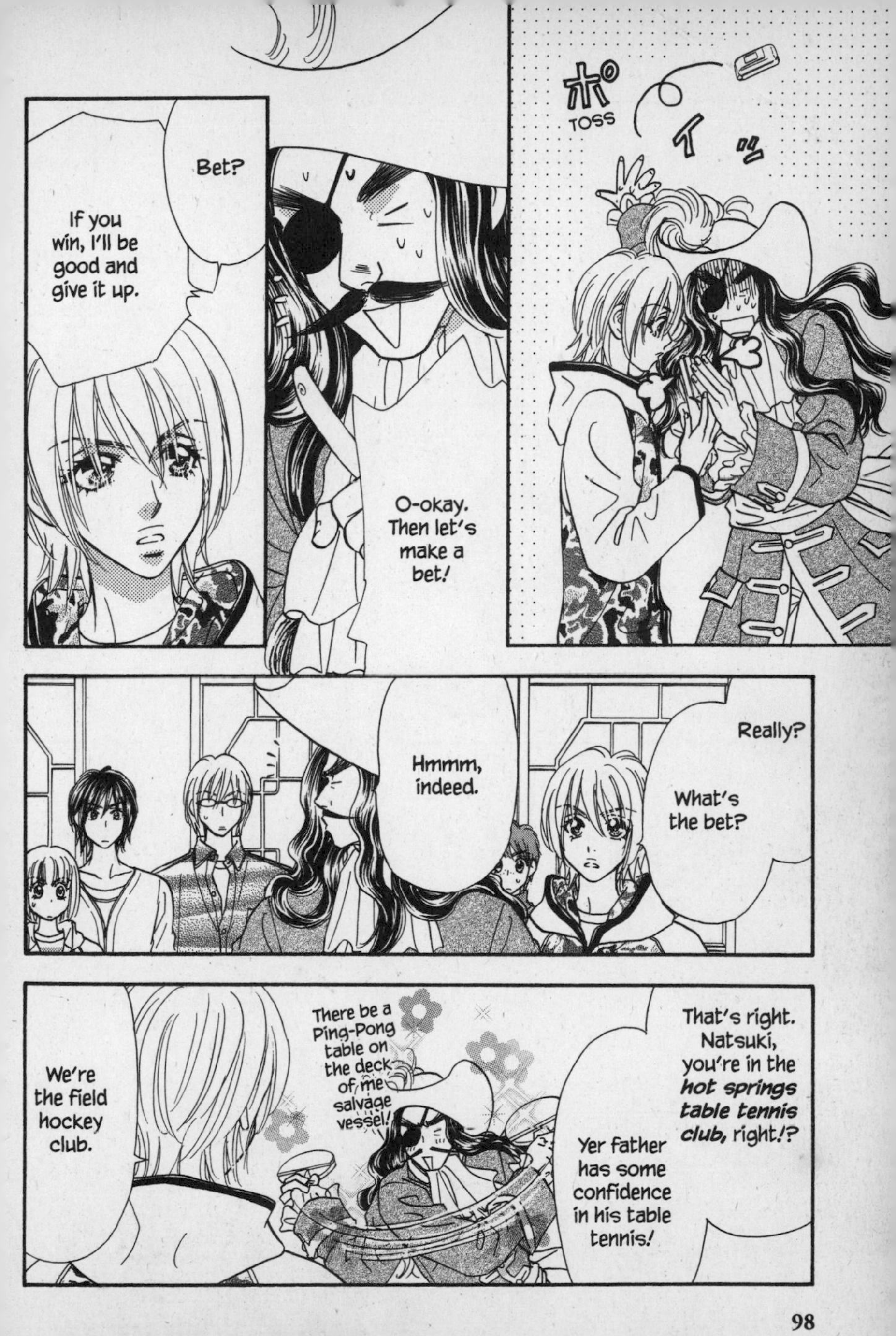
ポイッ
TOSS
O-okay. Then let's make a bet!
Bet?
If you win, I'll be good and give it up.
Really?
What's the bet?
Hmmm, indeed.
That's right. Natsuki, you're in the ***hot springs table tennis club,*** right!?
Yer father has some confidence in his table tennis!
There be a Ping-Pong table on the deck of me salvage vessel!
We're the field hockey club.

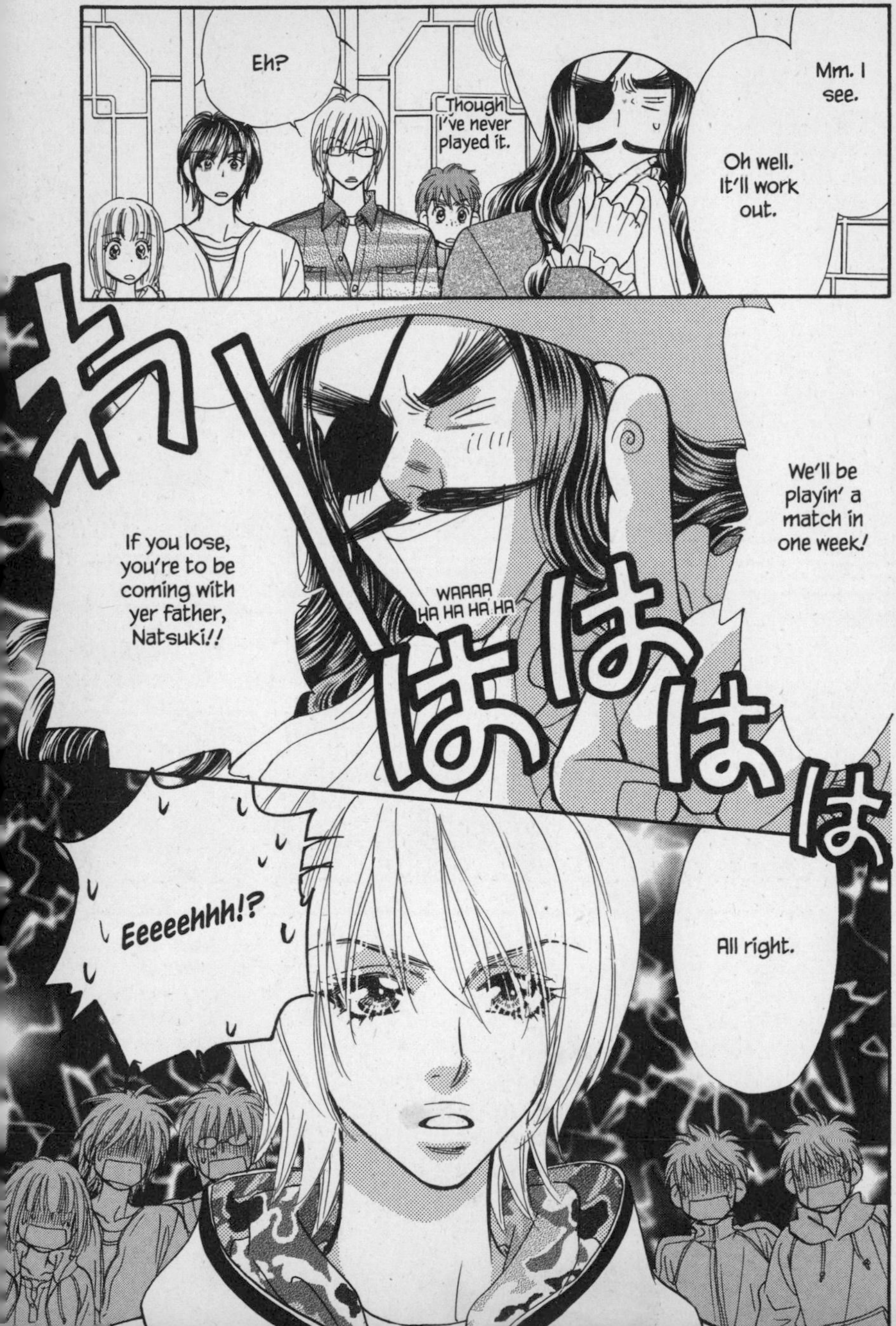

Mm. I see.
Oh well. It'll work out.
Though I've never played it.
Eh?
We'll be playin' a match in one week!
わーはははは
WAAAA HA HA HA HA
If you lose, you're to be coming with yer father, Natsuki!!
All right.
Eeeeehhh!?

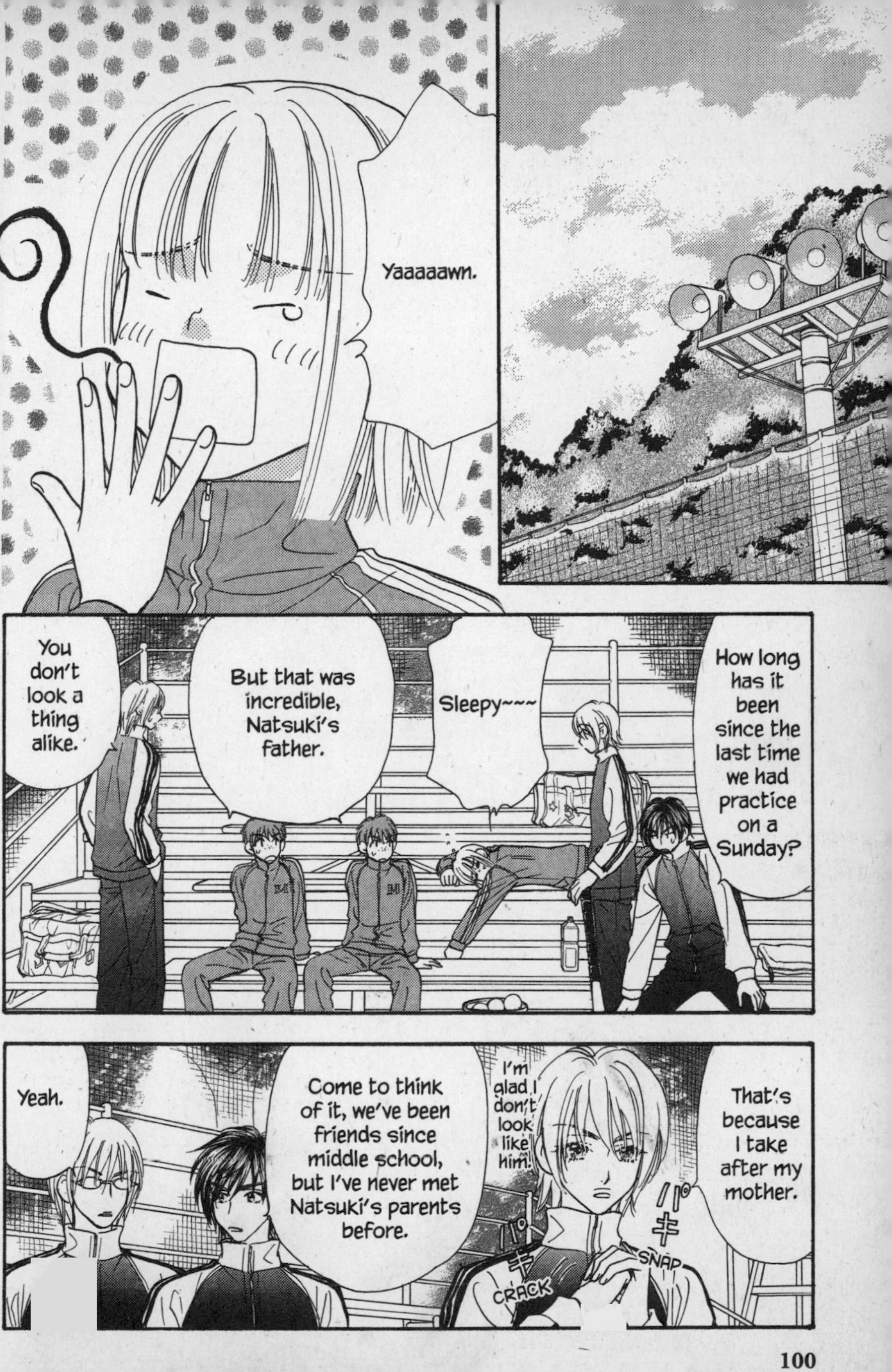

Yaaaaawn.
How long has it been since the last time we had practice on a Sunday?
Sleepy~~~
But that was incredible, Natsuki's father.
You don't look a thing alike.
That's because I take after my mother.
パキ
SNAP
I'm glad I don't look like him.
パキ
CRACK
Come to think of it, we've been friends since middle school, but I've never met Natsuki's parents before.
Yeah.

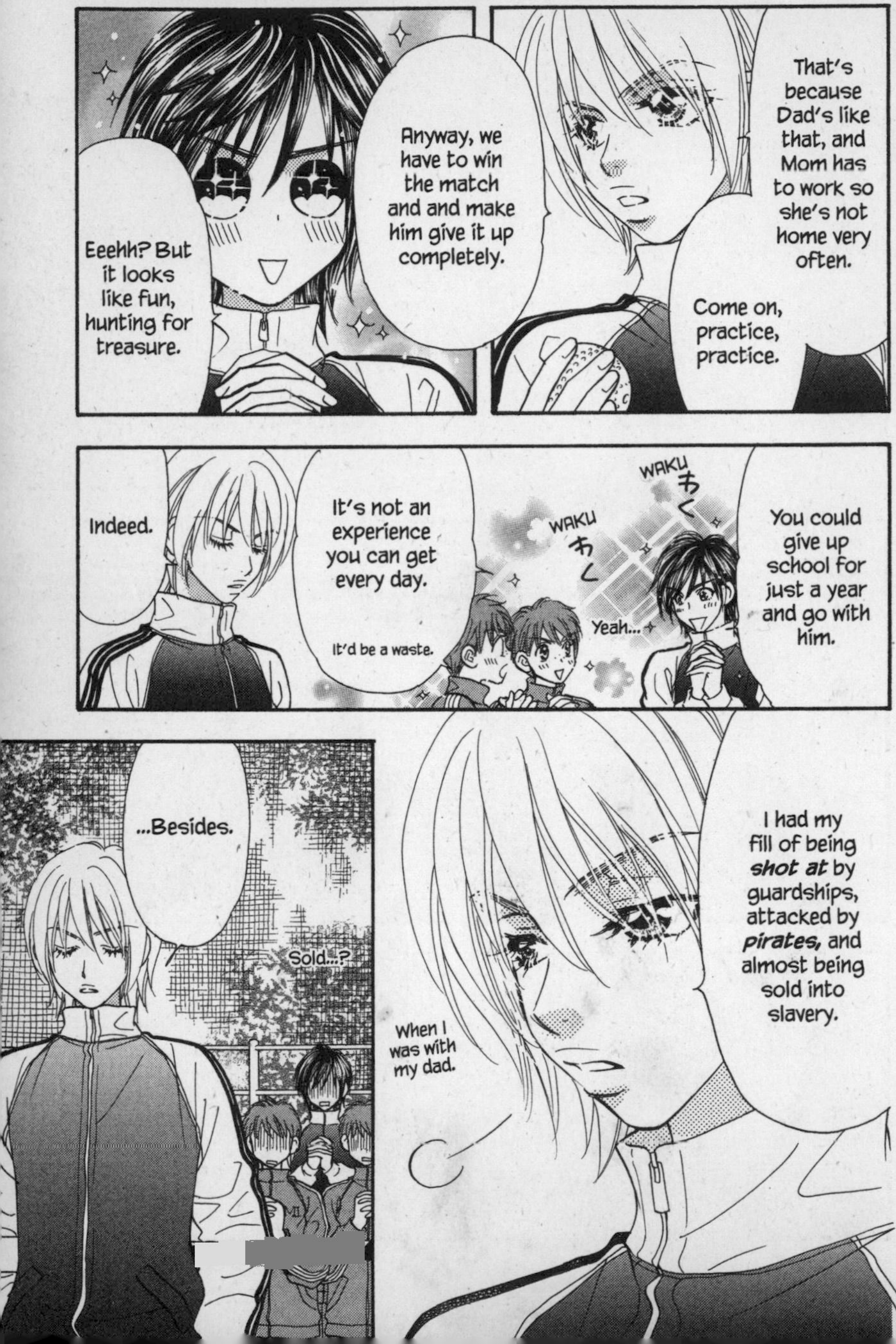
That's because Dad's like that, and Mom has to work so she's not home very often.
Come on, practice, practice.
Anyway, we have to win the match and and make him give it up completely.
Eeehh? But it looks like fun, hunting for treasure.
You could give up school for just a year and go with him.
WAKU
WAKU
Yeah...
It's not an experience you can get every day.
It'd be a waste.
Indeed.
I had my fill of being ***shot at*** by guardships, attacked by ***pirates,*** and almost being sold into slavery.
When I was with my dad.
...Besides.
Sold...?

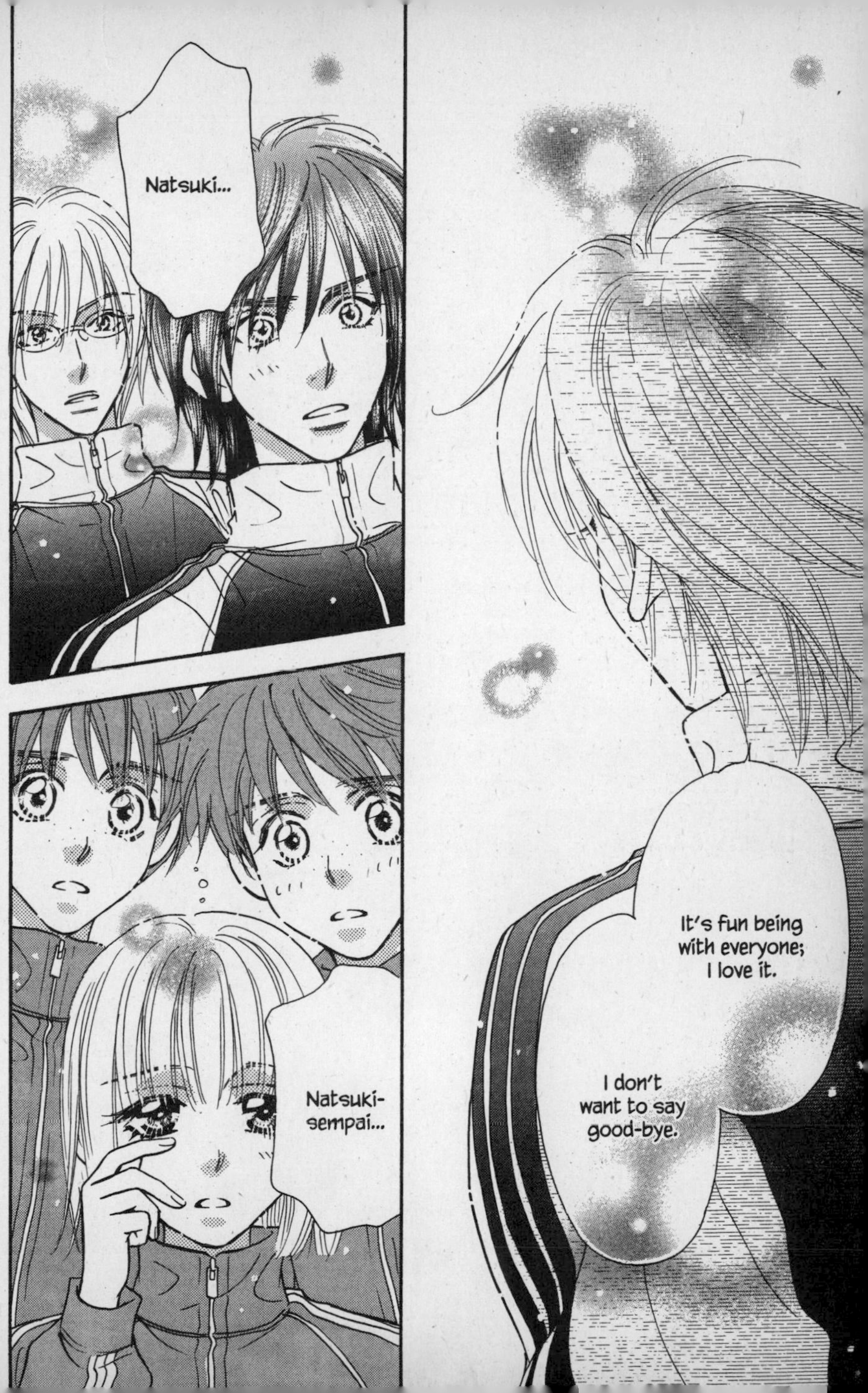
It's fun being with everyone; I love it.
I don't want to say good-bye.
Natsuki...
Natsuki-sempai...

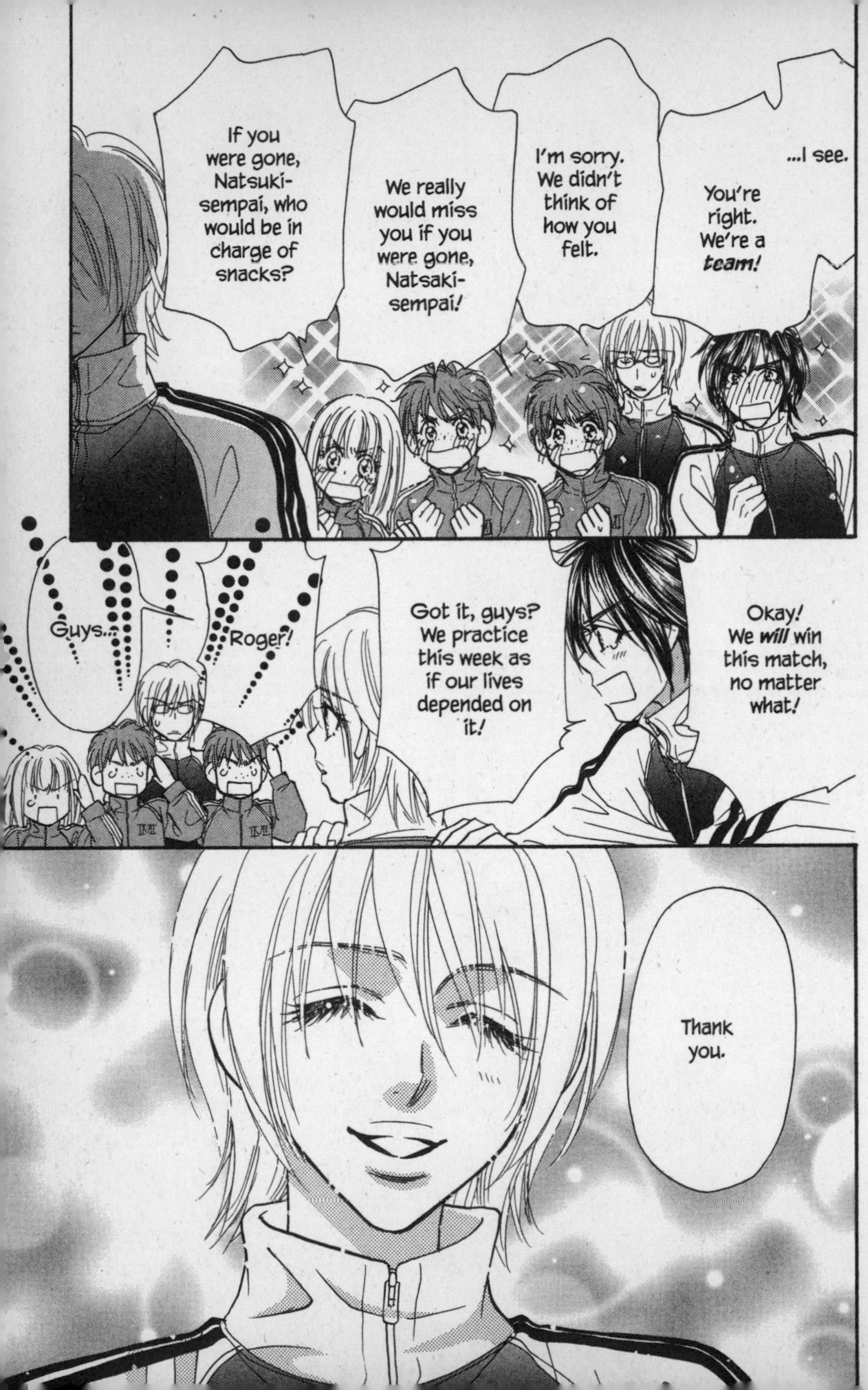
...I see. You're right. We're a *team!*
I'm sorry. We didn't think of how you felt.
We really would miss you if you were gone, Natsaki-sempai!
If you were gone, Natsuki-sempai, who would be in charge of snacks?
Okay! We *will* win this match, no matter what!
Got it, guys? We practice this week as if our lives depended on it!
Roger!
Guys...
Thank you.

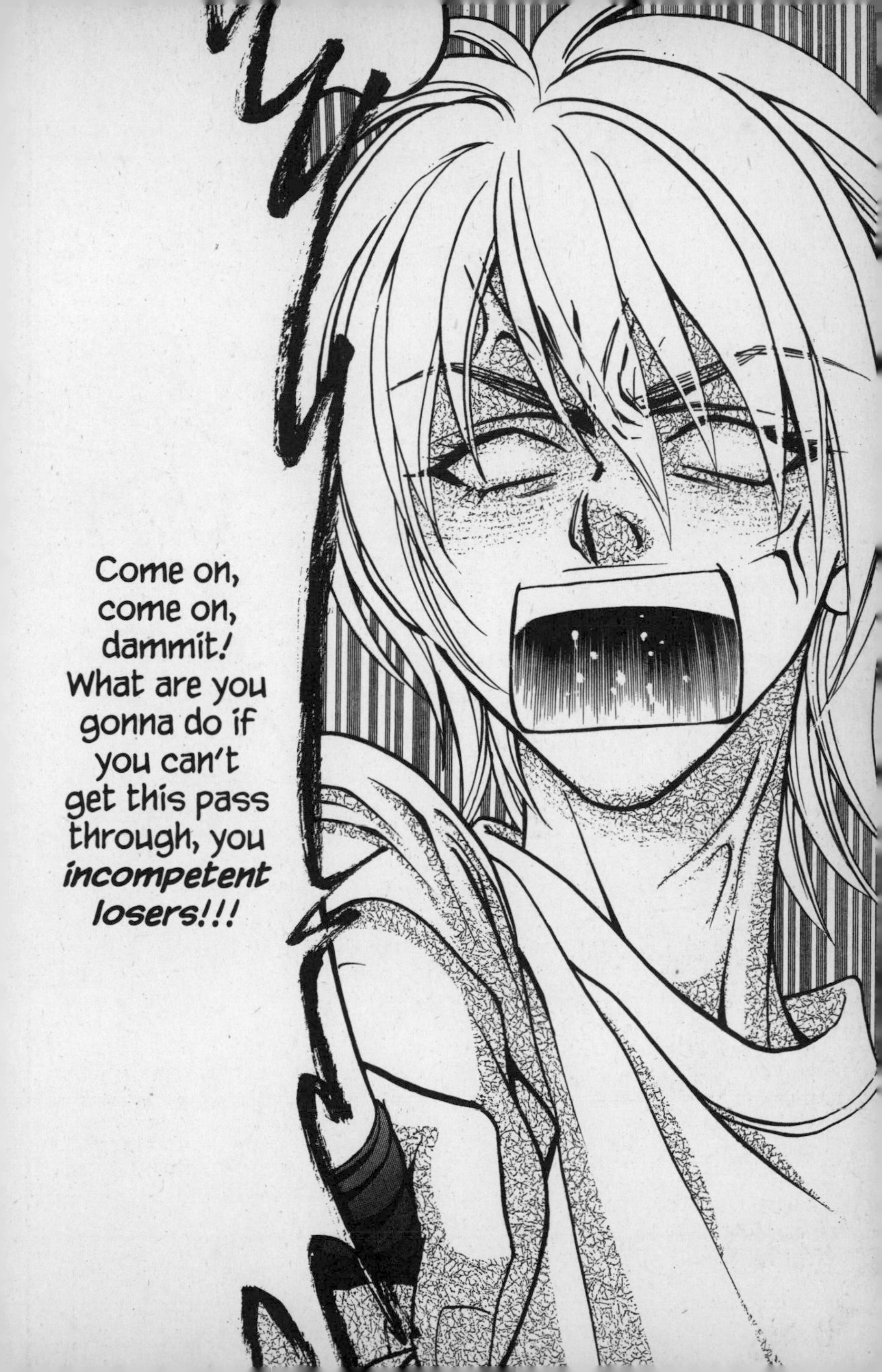
Come on, come on, dammit! What are you gonna do if you can't get this pass through, you *incompetent losers!!!*

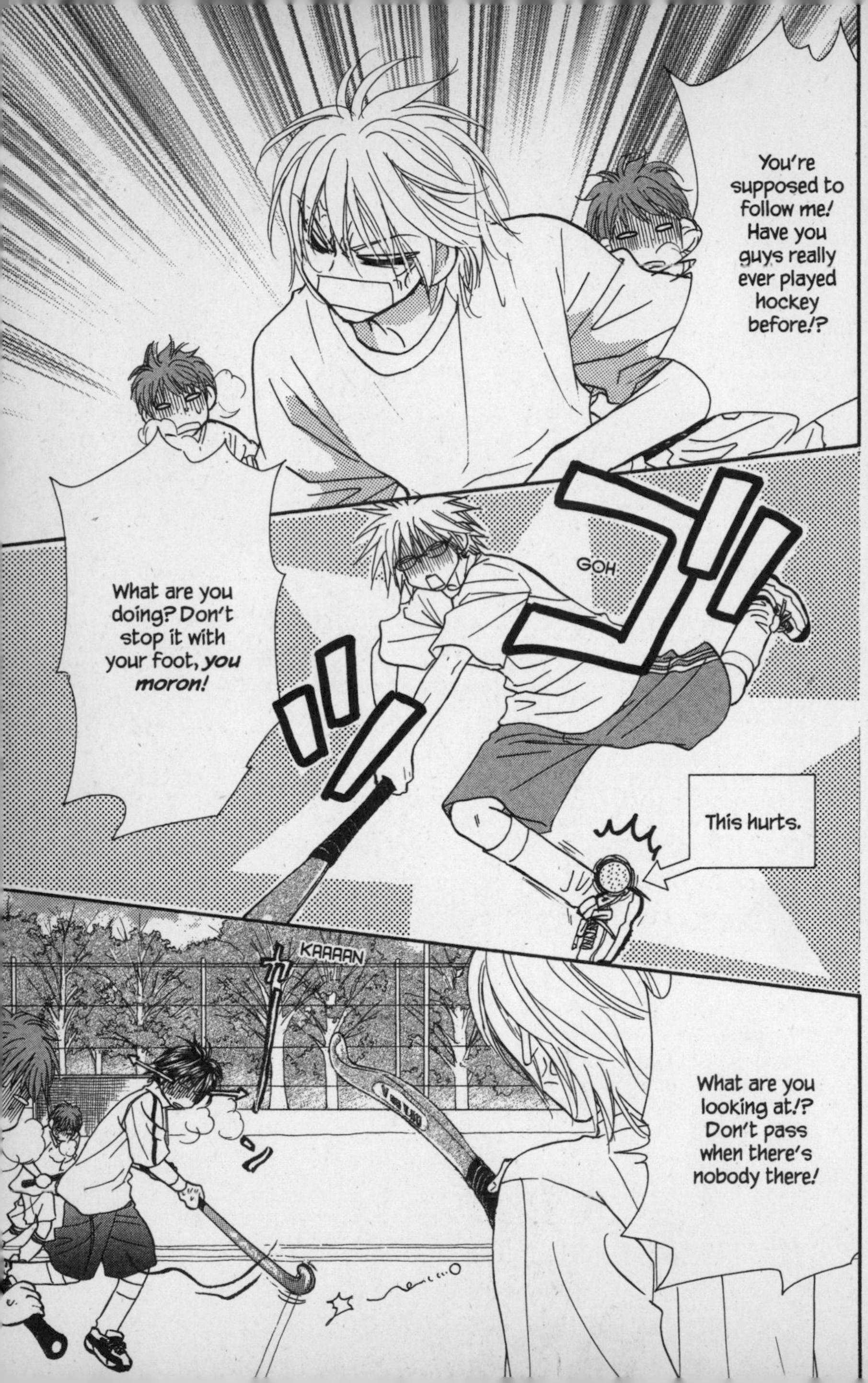
You're supposed to follow me! Have you guys really ever played hockey before!?
What are you doing? Don't stop it with your foot, *you moron!*
GOH
This hurts.
KAAAAN
What are you looking at!? Don't pass when there's nobody there!

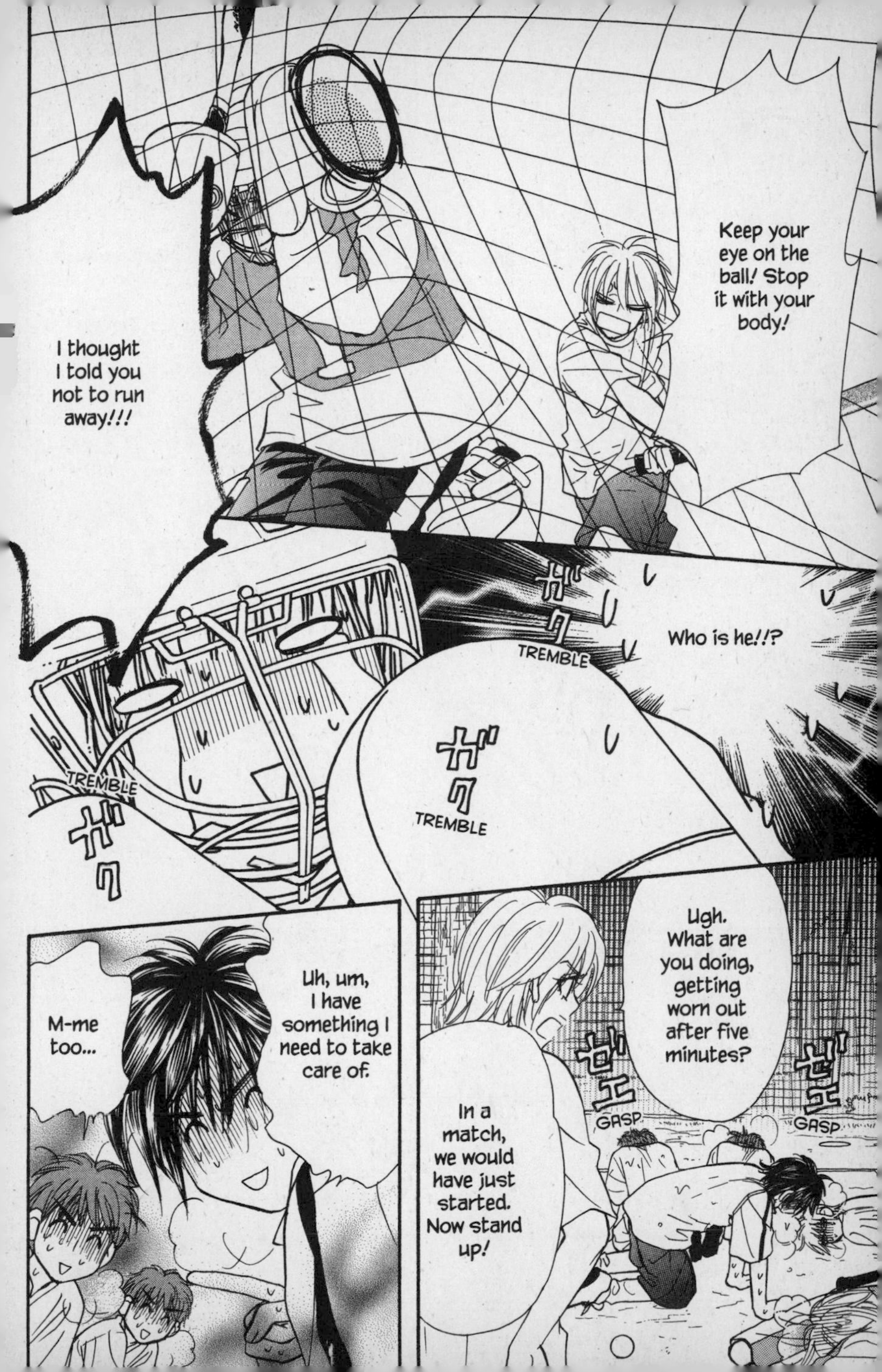
Keep your eye on the ball! Stop it with your body!
I thought I told you not to run away!!!
ガク
TREMBLE
Who is he!!?
ガク
TREMBLE
ガク
TREMBLE
Ugh. What are you doing, getting worn out after five minutes?
ゼェ
GASP
ゼェ
GASP
In a match, we would have just started. Now stand up!
Uh, um, I have something I need to take care of.
M-me too...

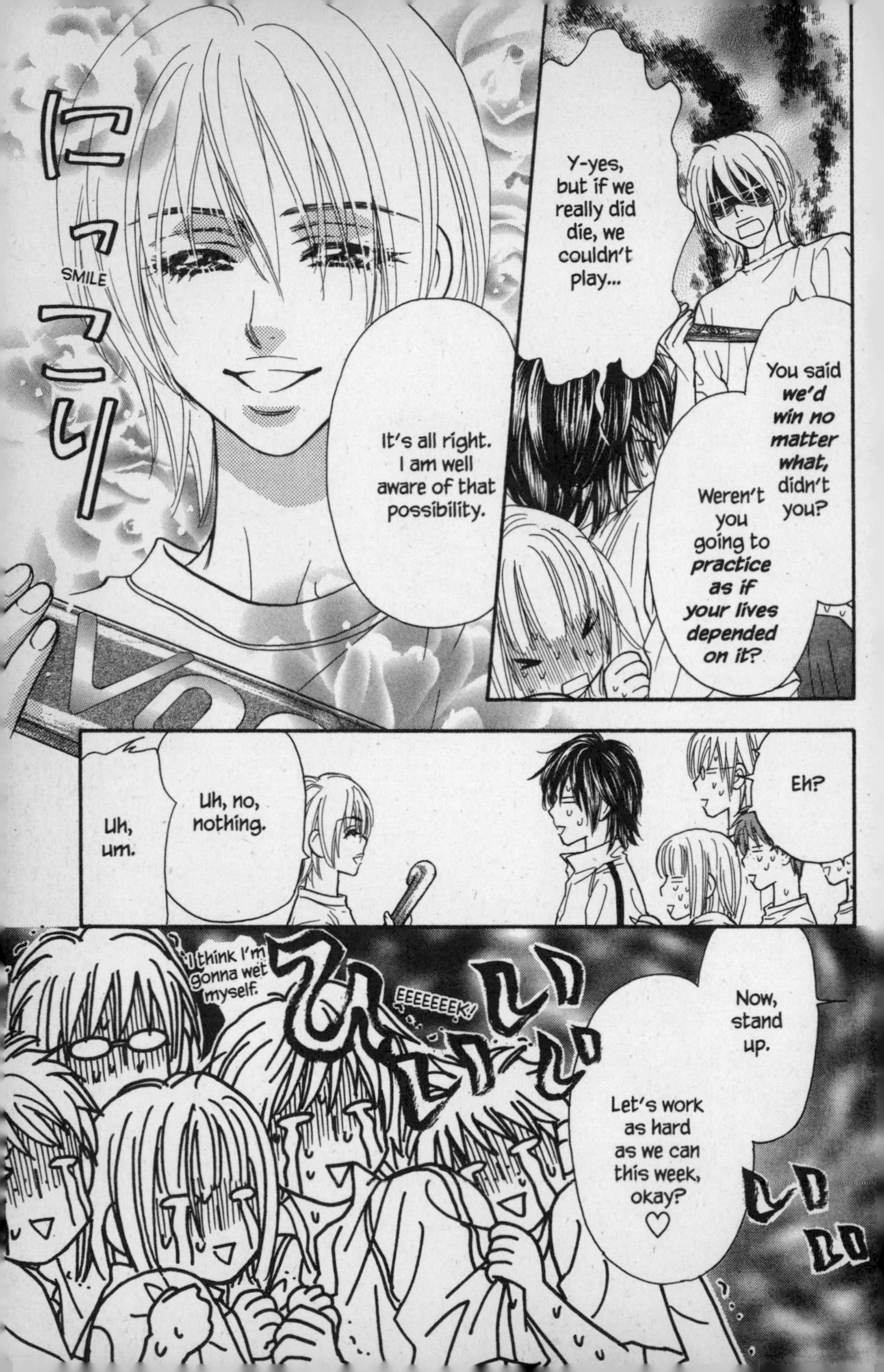
Y-yes, but if we really did die, we couldn't play...
You said we'd win no matter what, didn't you?
Weren't you going to practice as if your lives depended on it?
SMILE
It's all right. I am well aware of that possibility.
Eh?
Uh, no, nothing.
Uh, um.
Now, stand up.
Let's work as hard as we can this week, okay? ♡
EEEEEEEK!
I think I'm gonna wet myself.

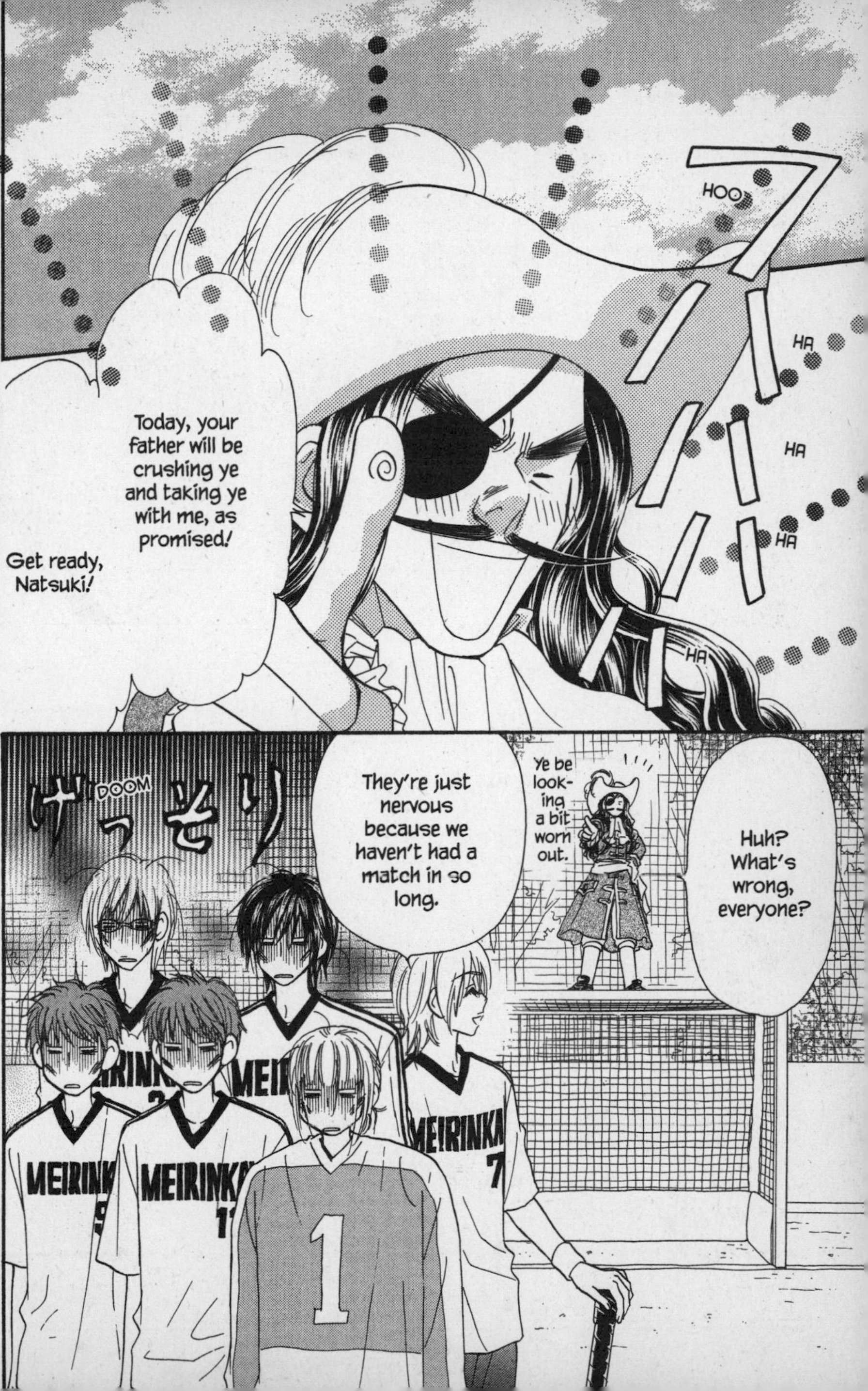
HOO
HA
HA
HA
HA
Today, your father will be crushing ye and taking ye with me, as promised!
Get ready, Natsuki!
Huh? What's wrong, everyone?
Ye be looking a bit worn out.
They're just nervous because we haven't had a match in so long.
げっそり
DOOM
MEIRINKA
7
1

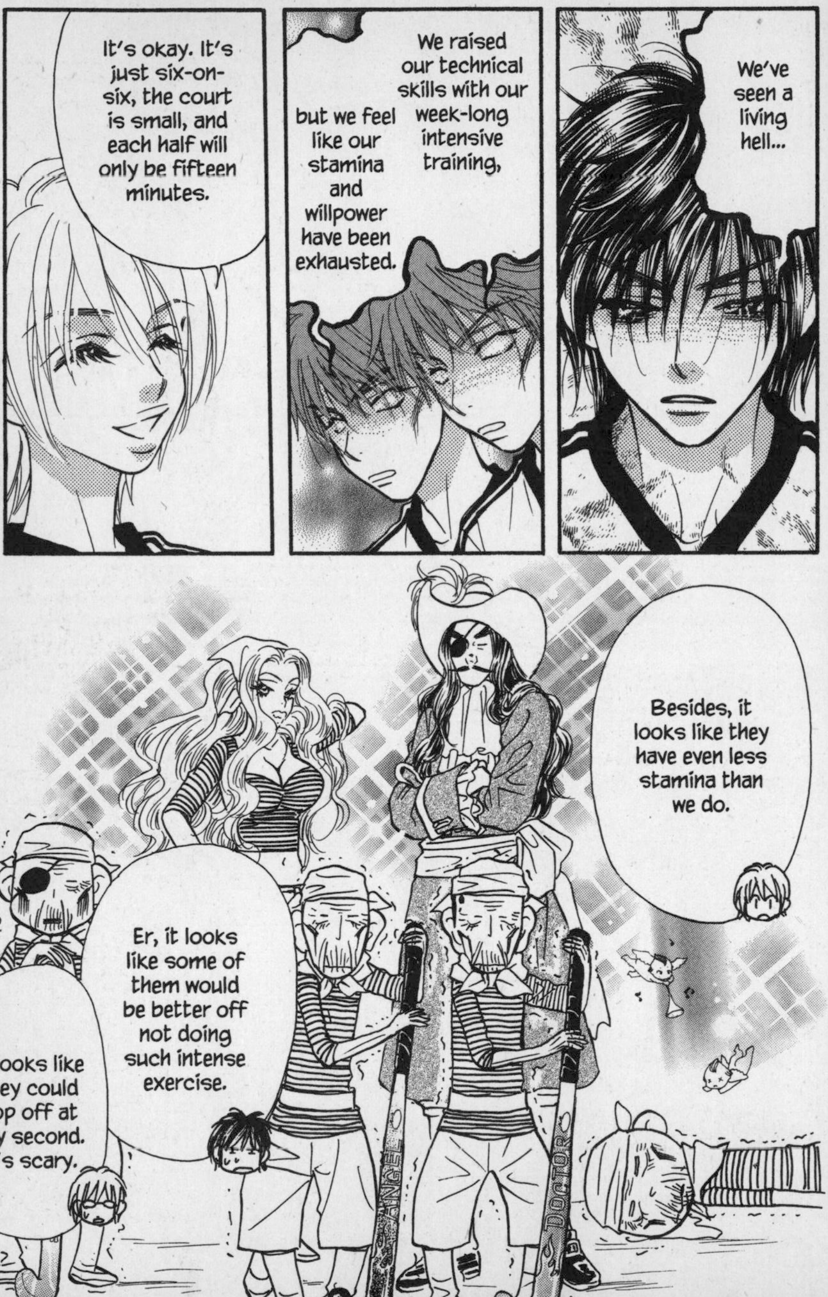
We've seen a living hell...
We raised our technical skills with our week-long intensive training,
but we feel like our stamina and willpower have been exhausted.
It's okay. It's just six-on-six, the court is small, and each half will only be fifteen minutes.
Besides, it looks like they have even less stamina than we do.
Er, it looks like some of them would be better off not doing such intense exercise.
It looks like they could pop off at any second. It's scary.
ANGEL
DOCTOR

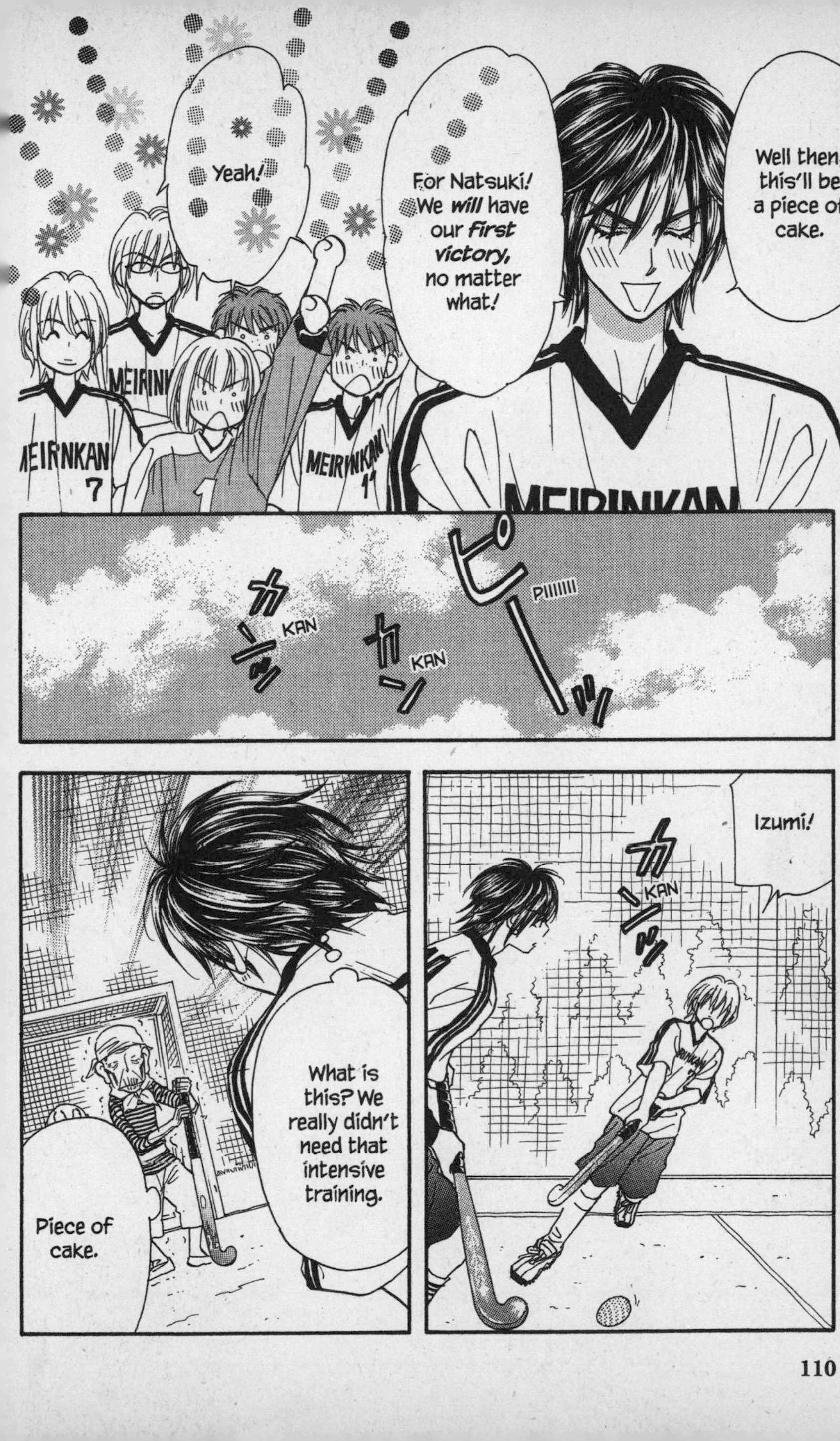
Well then, this'll be a piece of cake.
For Natsuki! We *will* have our *first victory,* no matter what!
Yeah!
MEIRINKAN
PIIIIII
KAN
KAN
Izumi!
KAN
What is this? We really didn't need that intensive training.
Piece of cake.

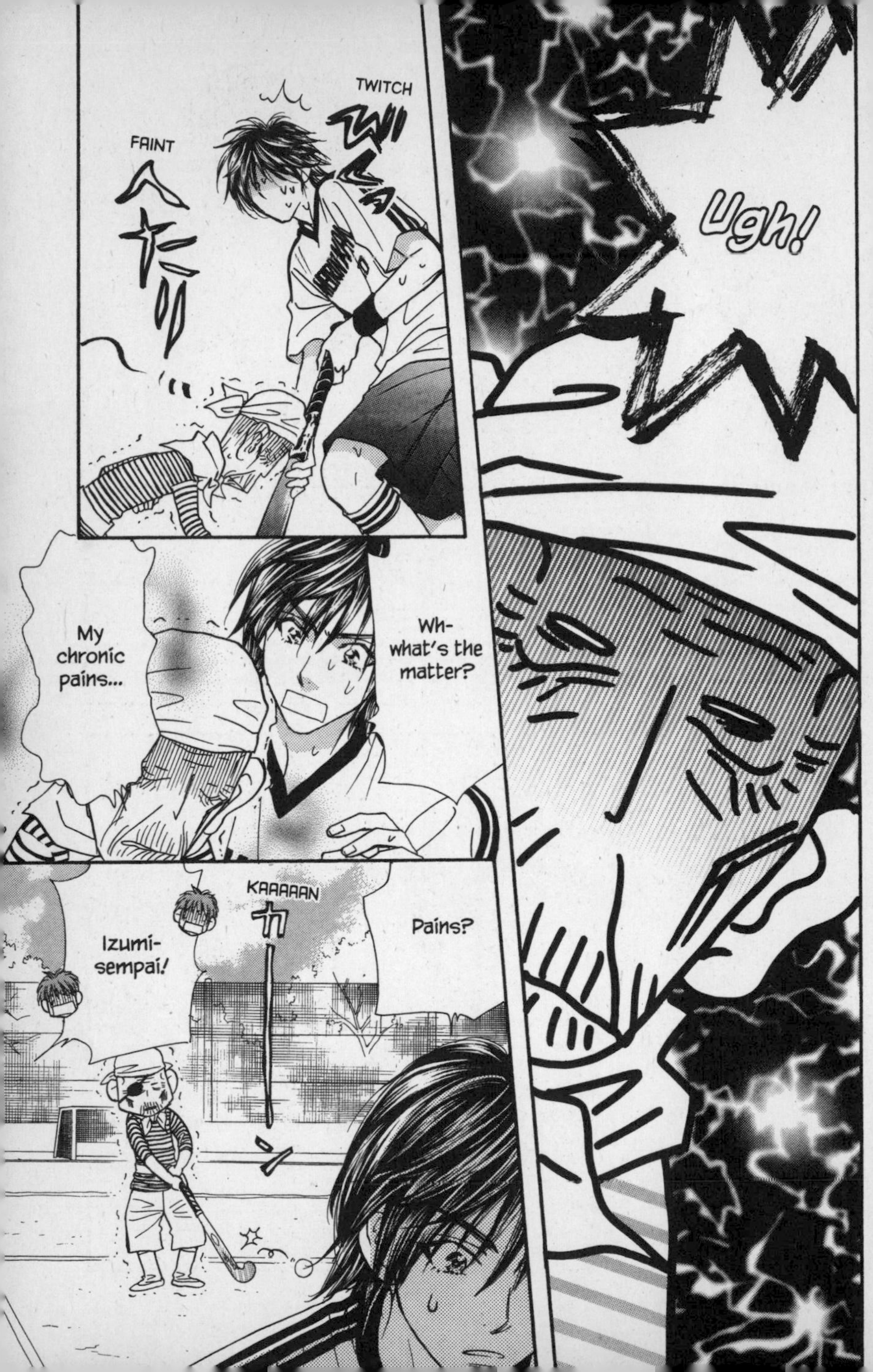
Ugh!
TWITCH
FAINT
Wh- what's the matter?
My chronic pains...
KAAAAAAN
Pains?
Izumi-sempai!

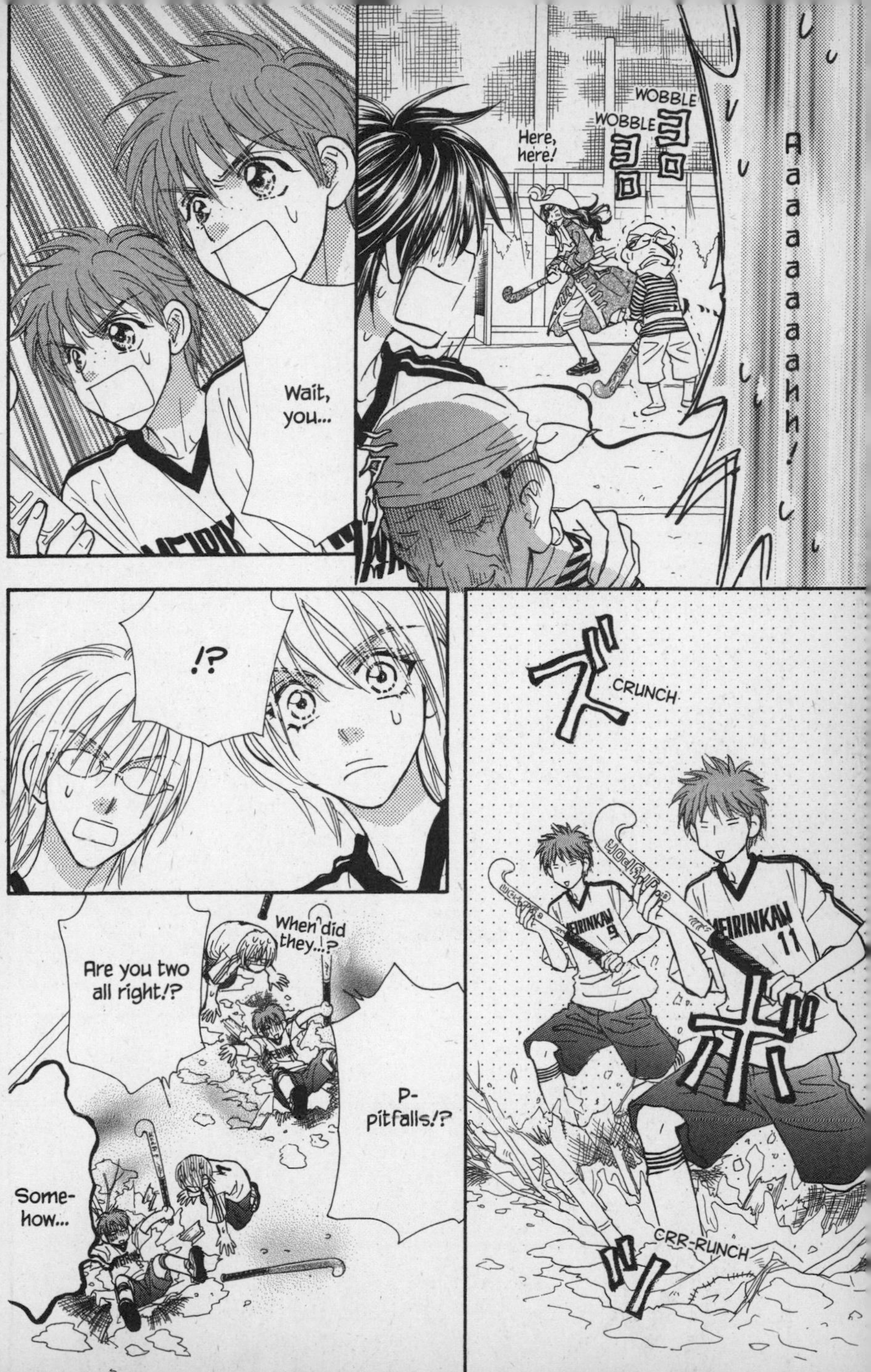

Aaaaaaaahh!
WOBBLE
WOBBLE
Here, here!
Wait, you...
CRUNCH
CRR-RUNCH
!?
When did they...!?
Are you two all right!?
P-pitfalls!?
Some-how...

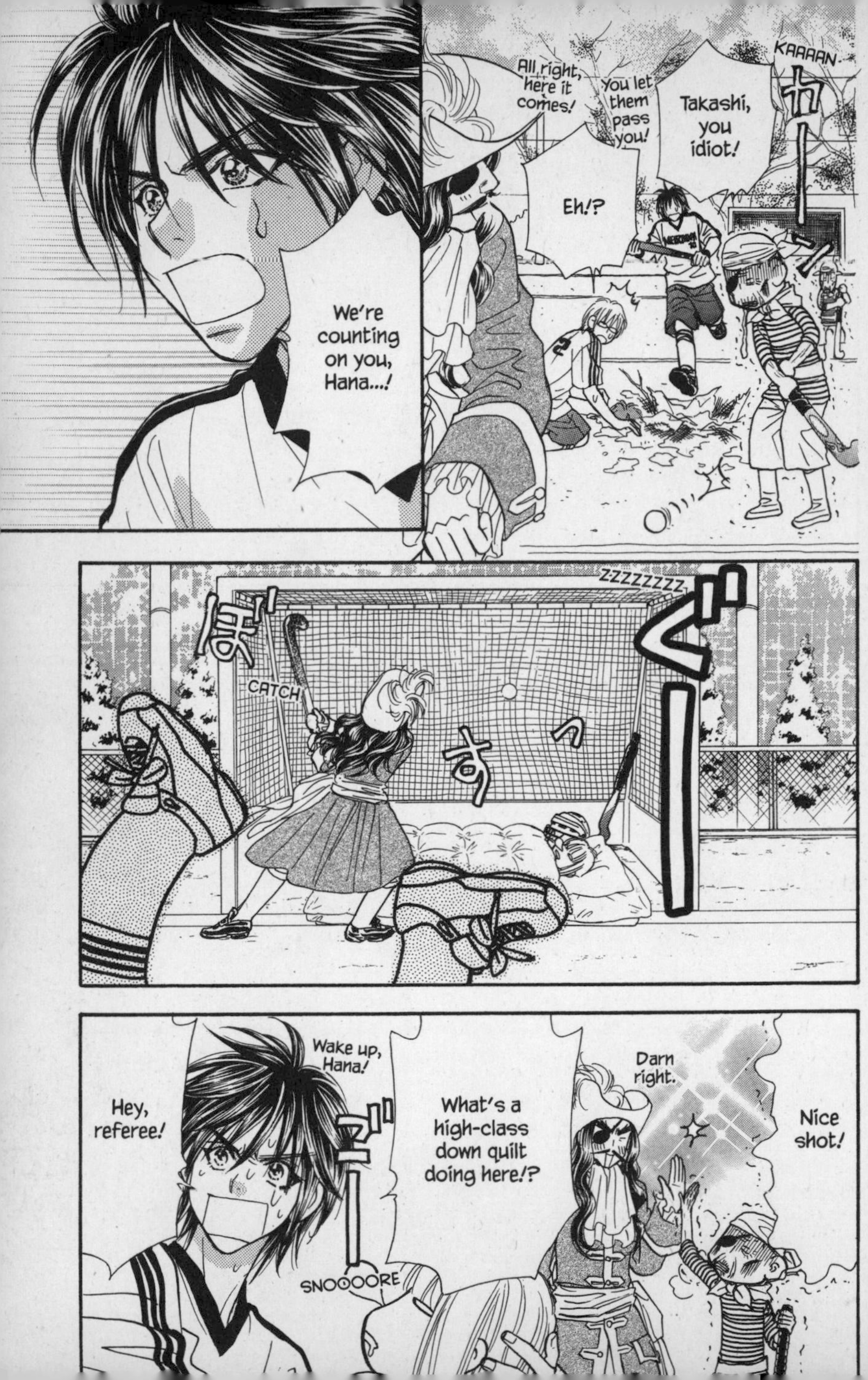
KAAAAN
Takashi, you idiot!
You let them pass you!
All right, here it comes!
Eh!?
We're counting on you, Hana...!
ZZZZZZZZ
CATCH
Nice shot!
Darn right.
What's a high-class down quilt doing here!?
Wake up, Hana!
Hey, referee!
SNOOOORE

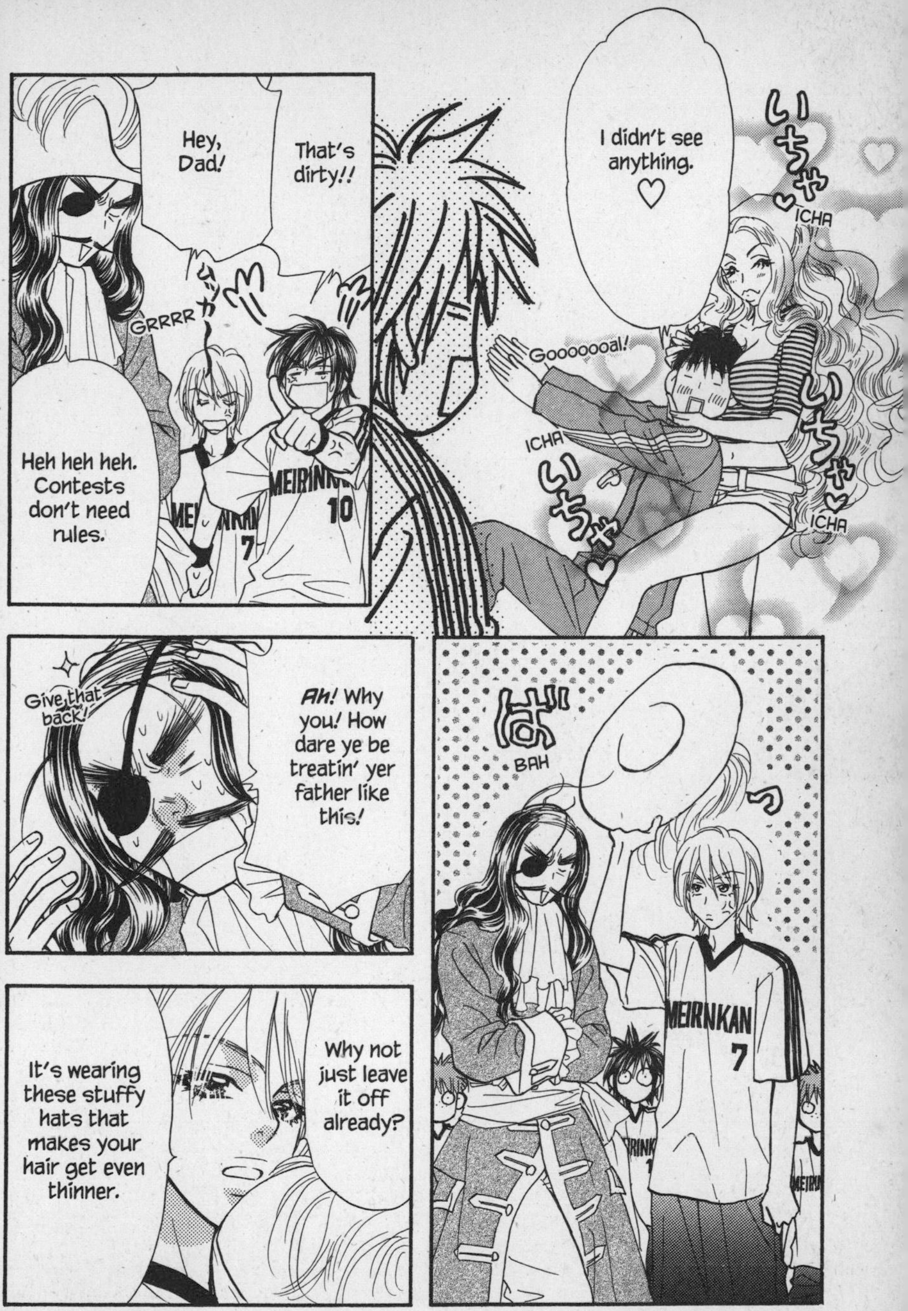
I didn't see anything. ♡
いちゃ♡ ICHA
いちゃ♡ ICHA
Gooooooal!
ICHA いちゃ♡
Hey, Dad!
That's dirty!!
ムッカ GRRRR
Heh heh heh. Contests don't need rules.
ば BAH
Ah! Why you! How dare ye be treatin' yer father like this!
Give that back!
Why not just leave it off already?
It's wearing these stuffy hats that makes your hair get even thinner.

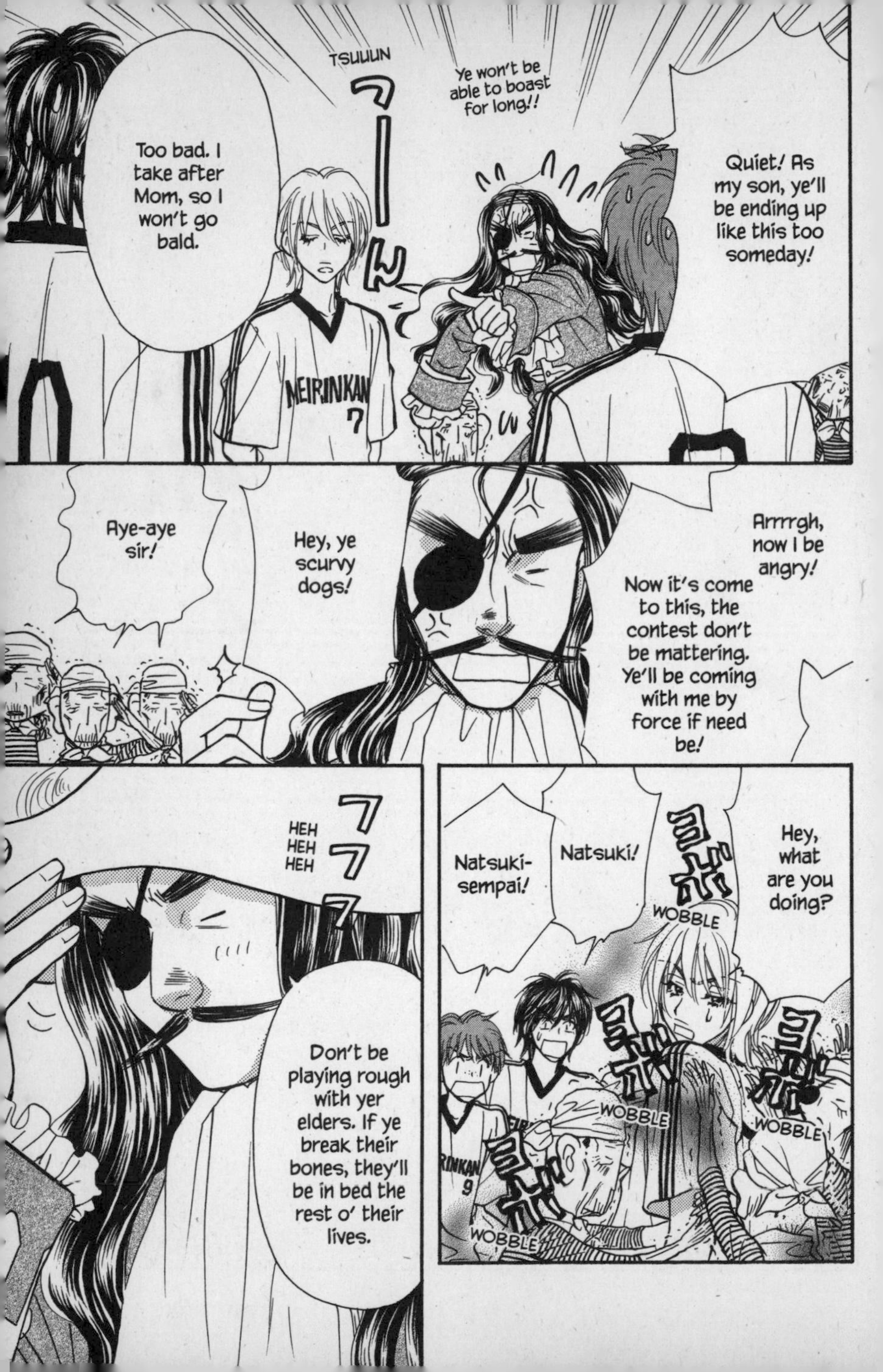
Quiet! As my son, ye'll be ending up like this too someday!
Ye won't be able to boast for long!!
TSUUUN
Too bad. I take after Mom, so I won't go bald.
Arrrrgh, now I be angry!
Now it's come to this, the contest don't be mattering. Ye'll be coming with me by force if need be!
Hey, ye scurvy dogs!
Aye-aye sir!
Hey, what are you doing?
WOBBLE
Natsuki!
Natsuki-sempai!
WOBBLE
WOBBLE
WOBBLE
HEH HEH HEH
Don't be playing rough with yer elders. If ye break their bones, they'll be in bed the rest o' their lives.

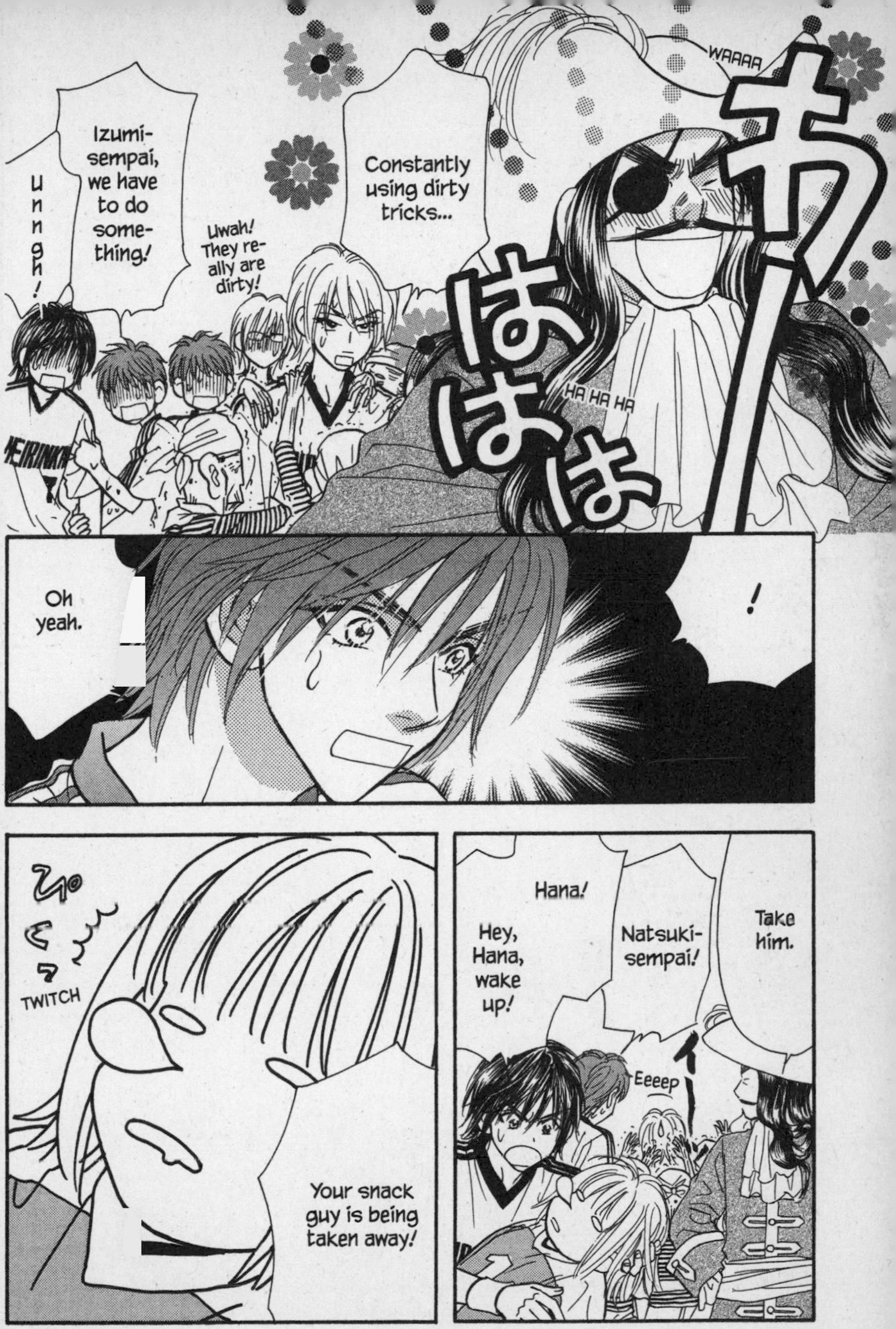
WAAAA
オウ
Constantly using dirty tricks...
ははは
HA HA HA
Uwah! They really are dirty!
Izumi-sempai, we have to do something!
Unnngh!
!
Oh yeah.
Take him.
Natsuki-sempai!
Hana!
Hey, Hana, wake up!
Eeeep
Your snack guy is being taken away!
ぴくっ
TWITCH

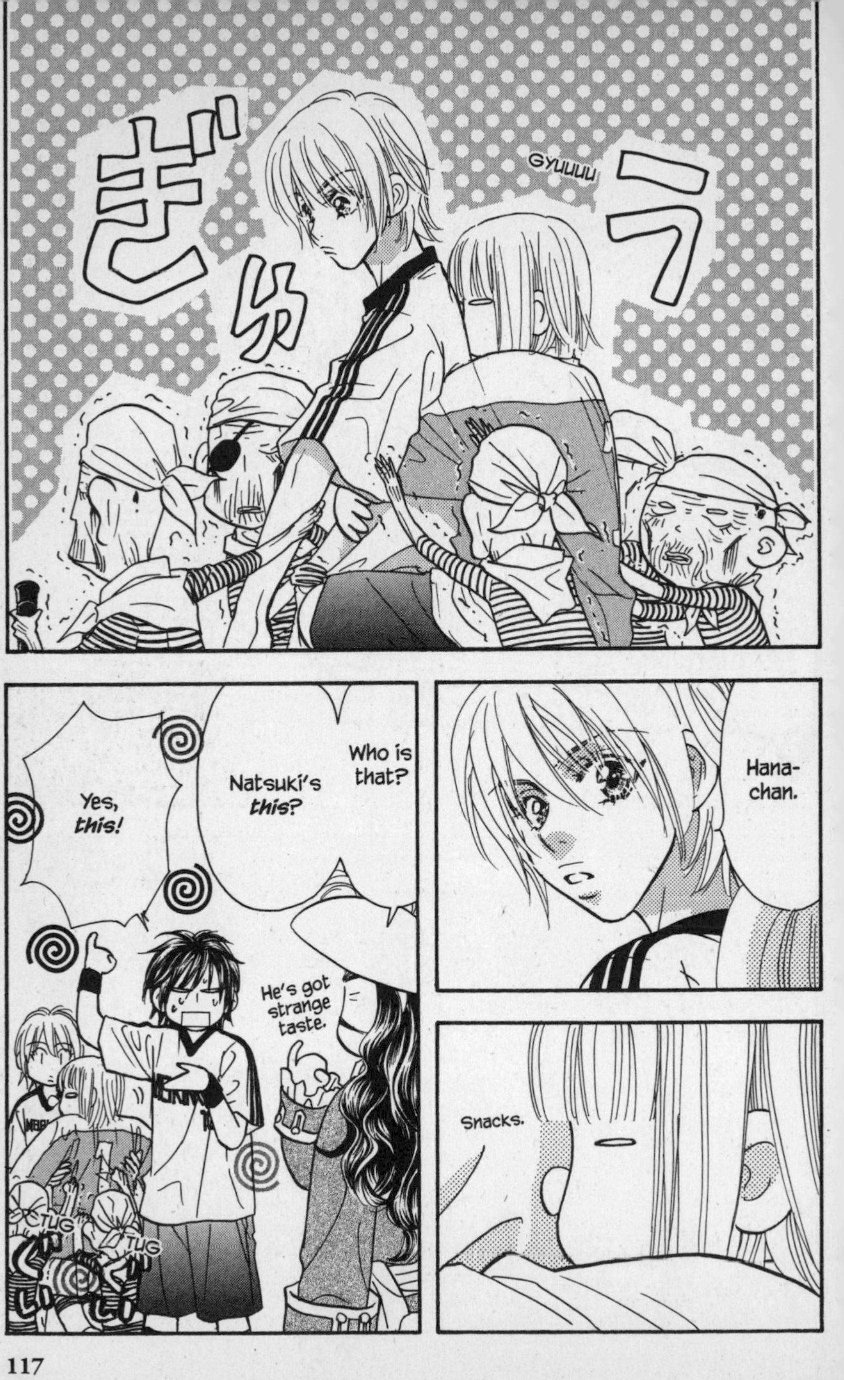
ぎゅう
GYUUUU
Hana-chan.
Snacks.
Who is that?
Natsuki's *this*?
Yes, *this*!
He's got strange taste.
TUG
TUG

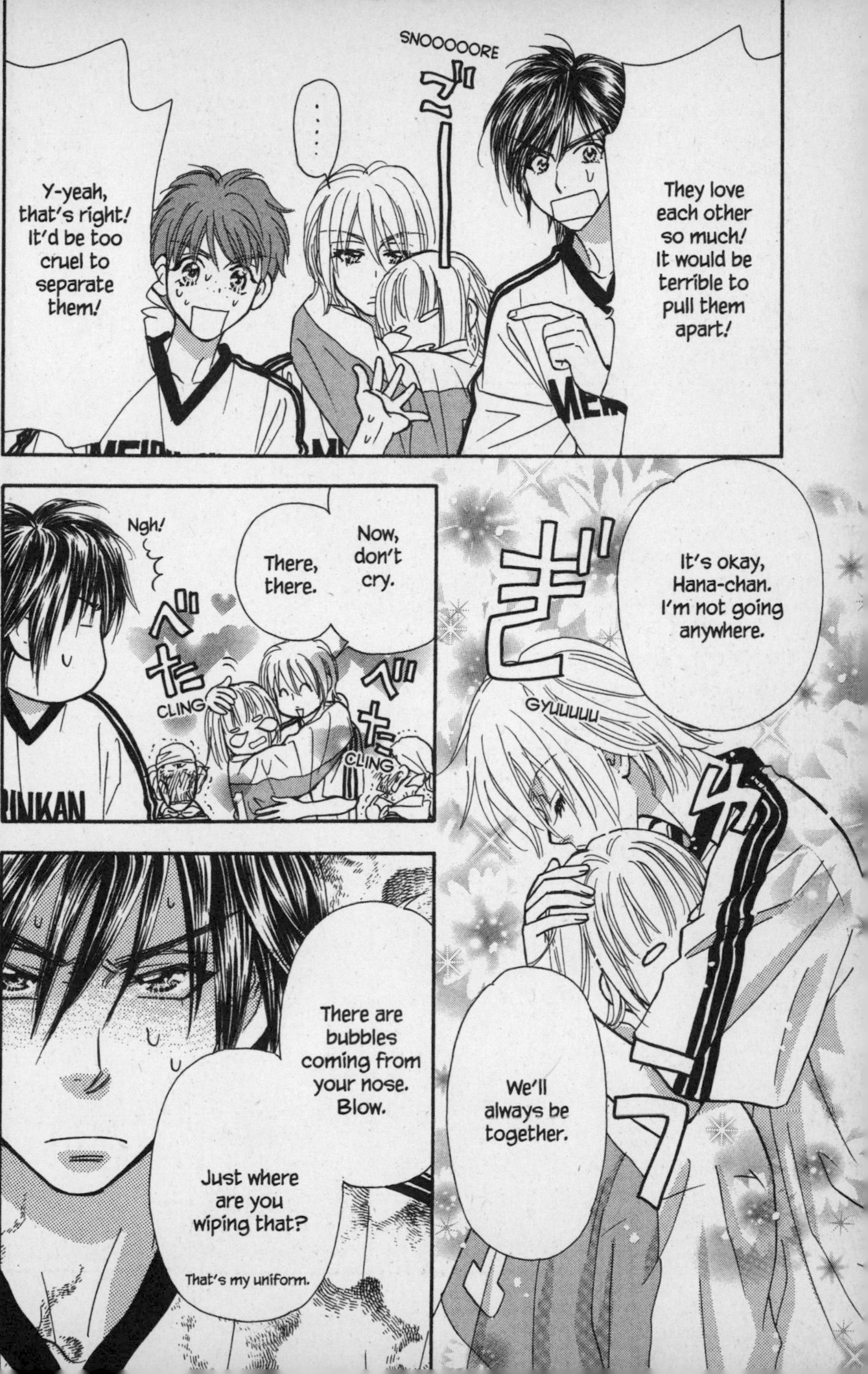
SNOOOOORE
They love each other so much! It would be terrible to pull them apart!
......
Y-yeah, that's right! It'd be too cruel to separate them!
It's okay, Hana-chan. I'm not going anywhere.
GYUUUUU
We'll always be together.
Now, don't cry.
There, there.
Ngh!
CLING
CLING
There are bubbles coming from your nose. Blow.
Just where are you wiping that?
That's my uniform.

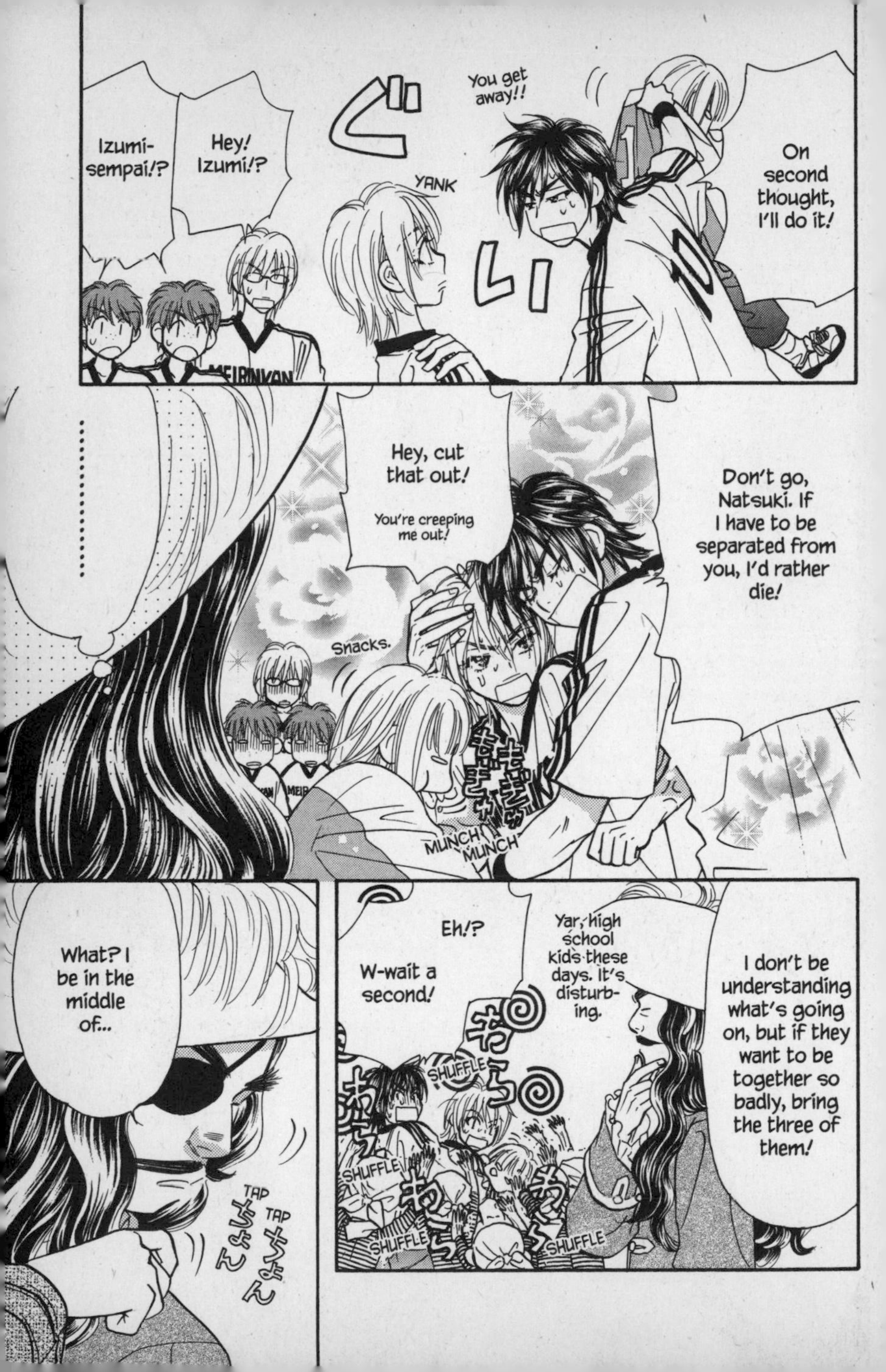
On second thought, I'll do it!
You get away!!
ぐい
YANK
Hey! Izumi!?
Izumi-sempai!?
Don't go, Natsuki. If I have to be separated from you, I'd rather die!
Hey, cut that out!
You're creeping me out!
Snacks.
MUNCH MUNCH
......
I don't be understanding what's going on, but if they want to be together so badly, bring the three of them!
Yar, high school kids these days. It's disturbing.
Eh!?
W-wait a second!
SHUFFLE
SHUFFLE
SHUFFLE
SHUFFLE
What? I be in the middle of...
TAP TAP
ちょんちょん

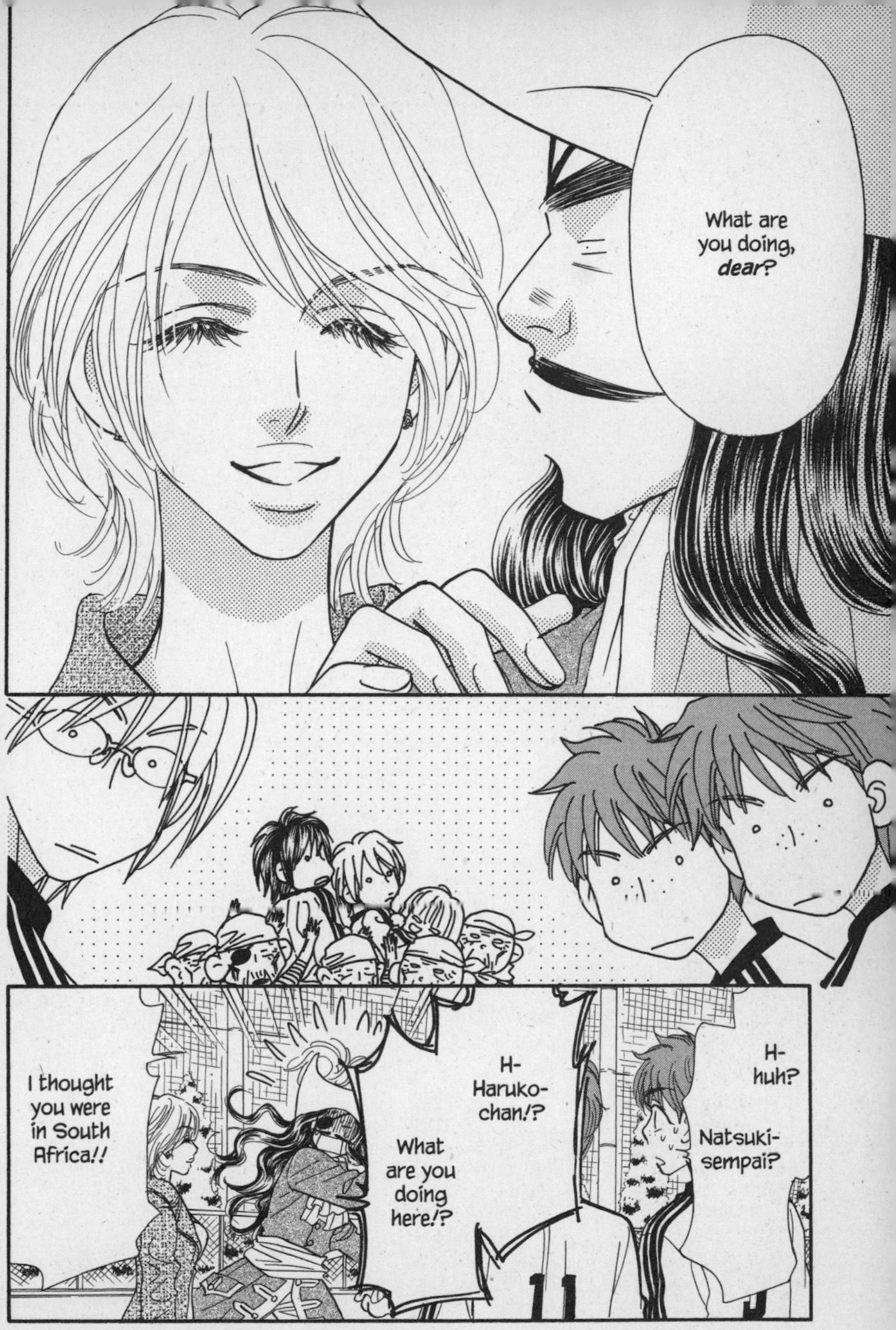
What are you doing, *dear*?
H- huh?
Natsuki-sempai?
H- Haruko-chan!?
What are you doing here!?
I thought you were in South Africa!!

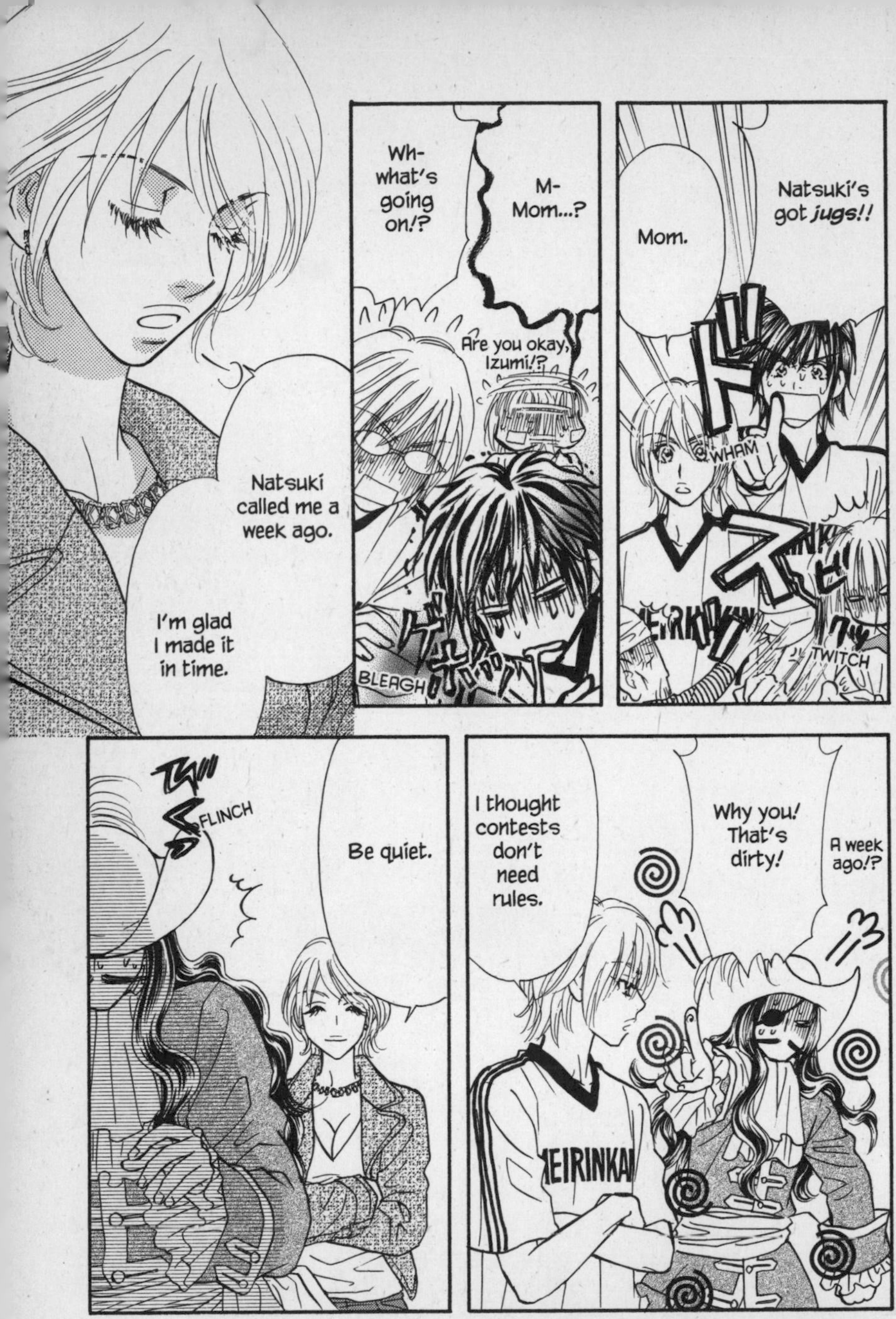
Natsuki's got *jugs!!*
Mom.
WHAM
TWITCH
M-Mom...?
Wh-what's going on!?
Are you okay, Izumi!?
BLEAGH
Natsuki called me a week ago.
I'm glad I made it in time.
A week ago!?
Why you! That's dirty!
I thought contests don't need rules.
Be quiet.
FLINCH

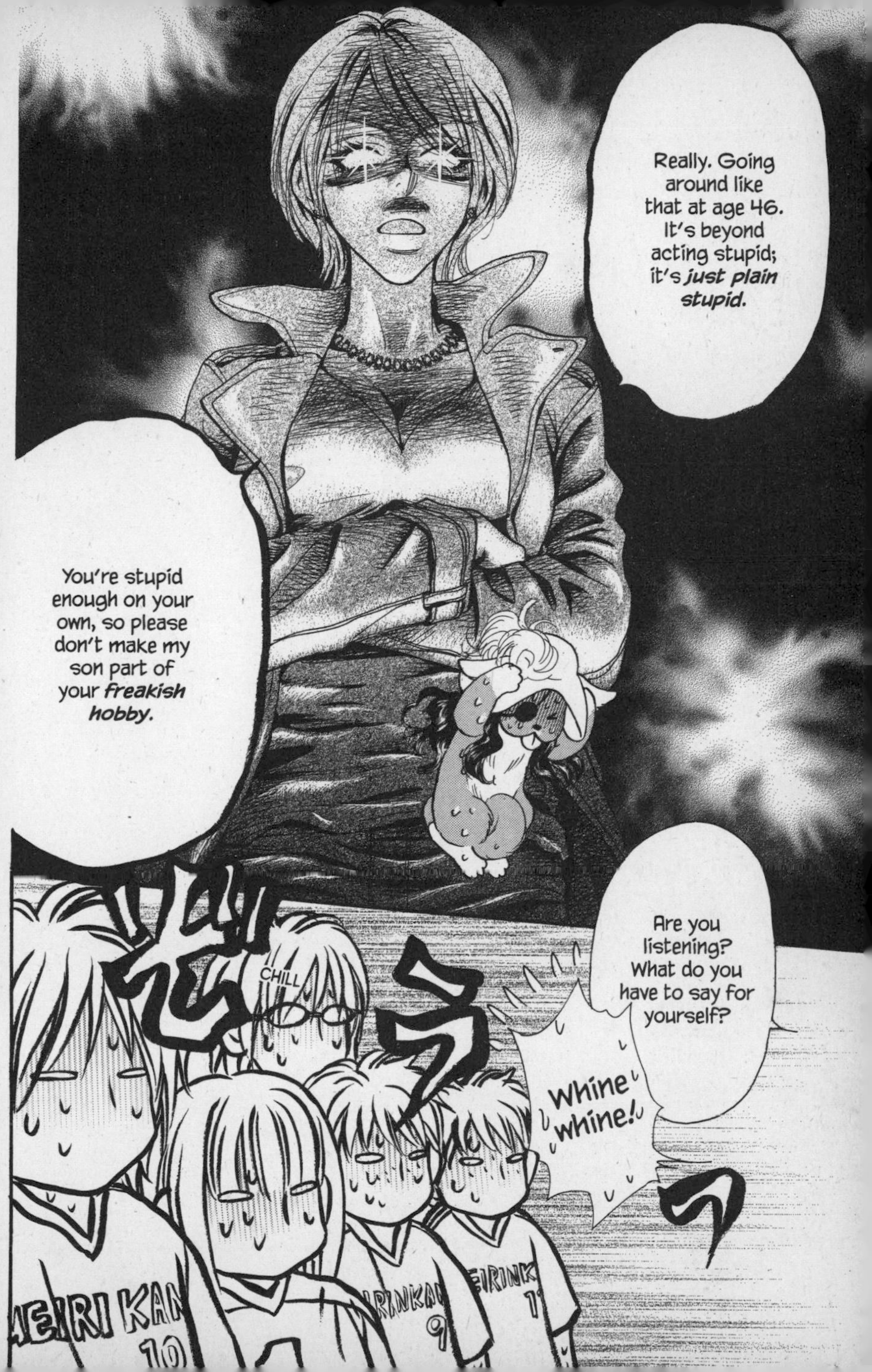
Really. Going around like that at age 46. It's beyond acting stupid; it's ***just plain stupid.***
You're stupid enough on your own, so please don't make my son part of your ***freakish hobby.***
Are you listening? What do you have to say for yourself?
Whine whine!
CHILL
EIRI KAN
10
IRINKAN
9
EIRINK
11

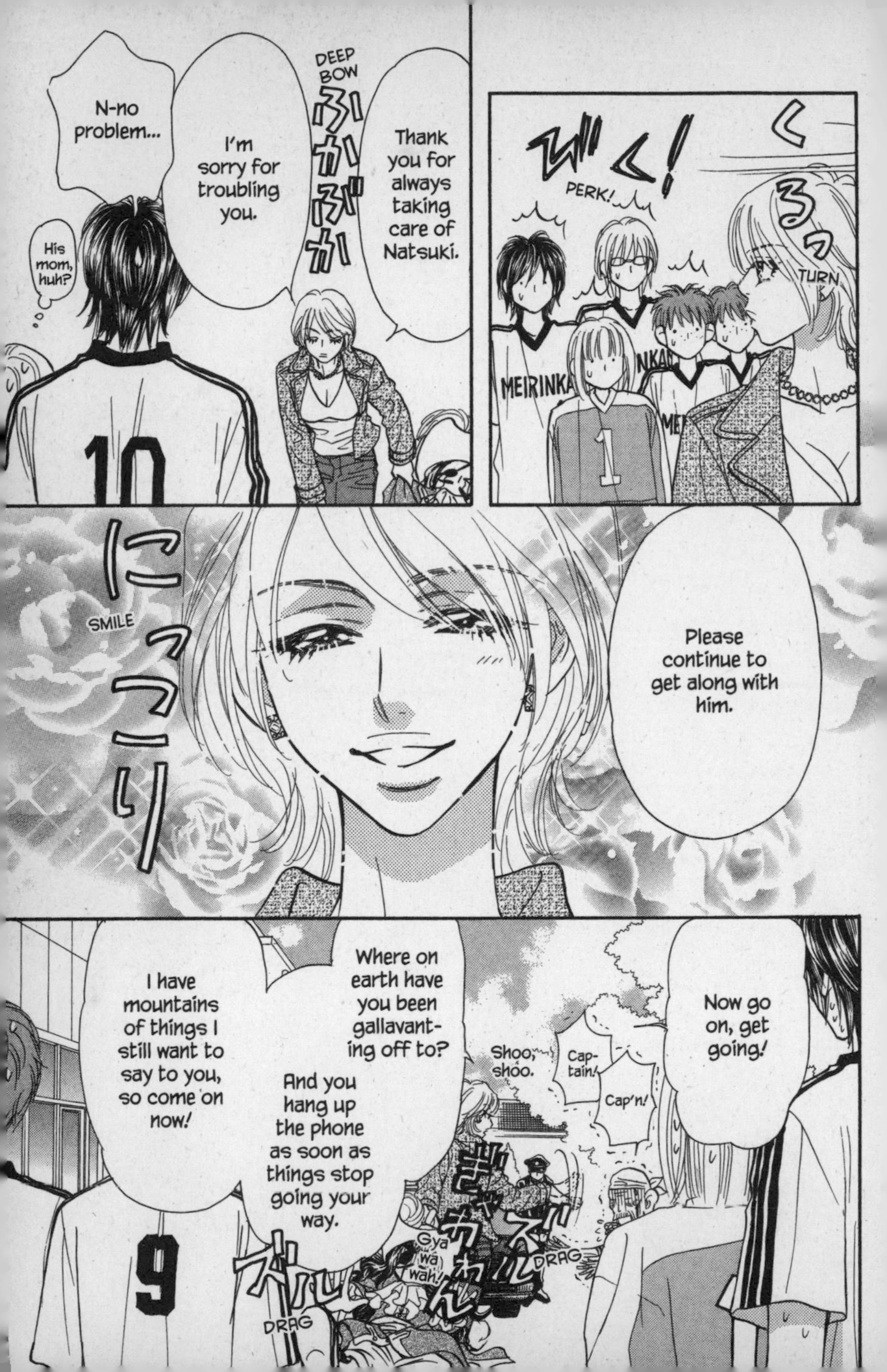
TURN
PERK!
Thank you for always taking care of Natsuki.
DEEP BOW
I'm sorry for troubling you.
N-no problem...
His mom, huh?
Please continue to get along with him.
にっこり
SMILE
Now go on, get going!
Cap'n!
Cap-tain!
Shoo, shoo.
DRAG
Gya wa wah!
Where on earth have you been gallavant-ing off to?
And you hang up the phone as soon as things stop going your way.
I have mountains of things I still want to say to you, so come on now!
DRAG

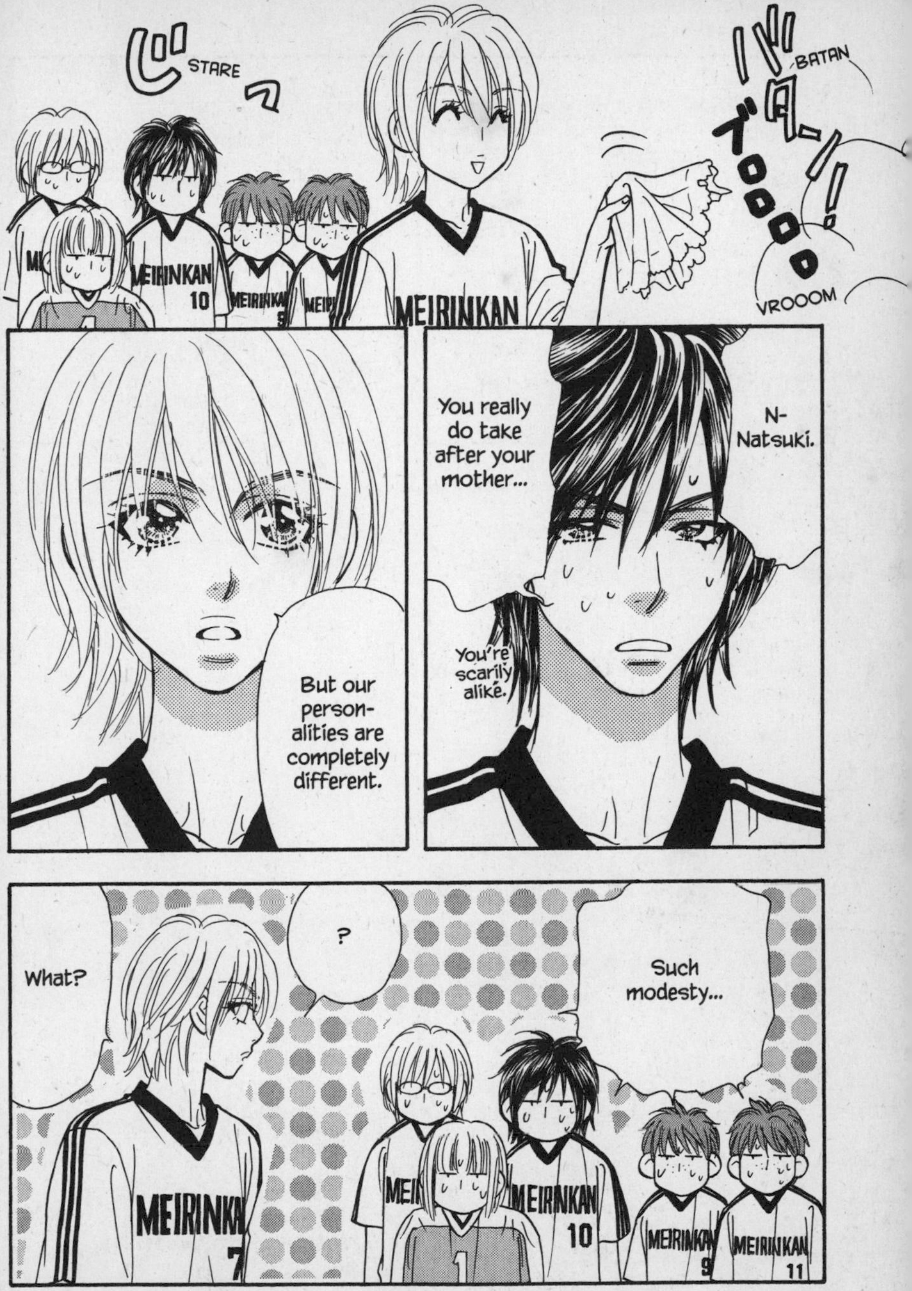
BATAN
VROOOM
STARE
N-Natsuki.
You really do take after your mother...
You're scarily alike.
But our personalities are completely different.
Such modesty...
?
What?

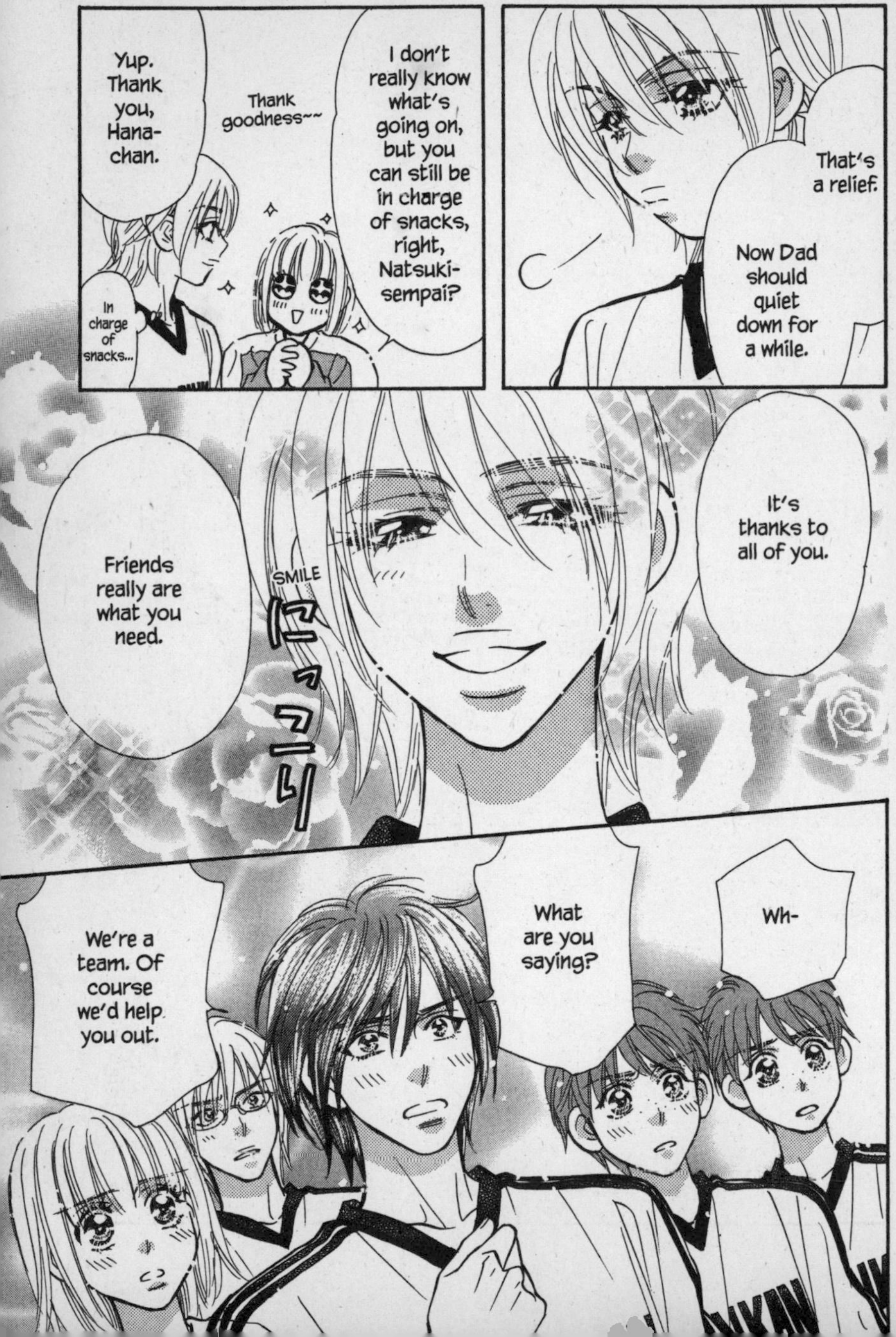
That's a relief.
Now Dad should quiet down for a while.
I don't really know what's going on, but you can still be in charge of snacks, right, Natsuki-sempai?
Thank goodness~~
Yup. Thank you, Hana-chan.
In charge of snacks...
It's thanks to all of you.
SMILE
Friends really are what you need.
Wh-
What are you saying?
We're a team. Of course we'd help you out.

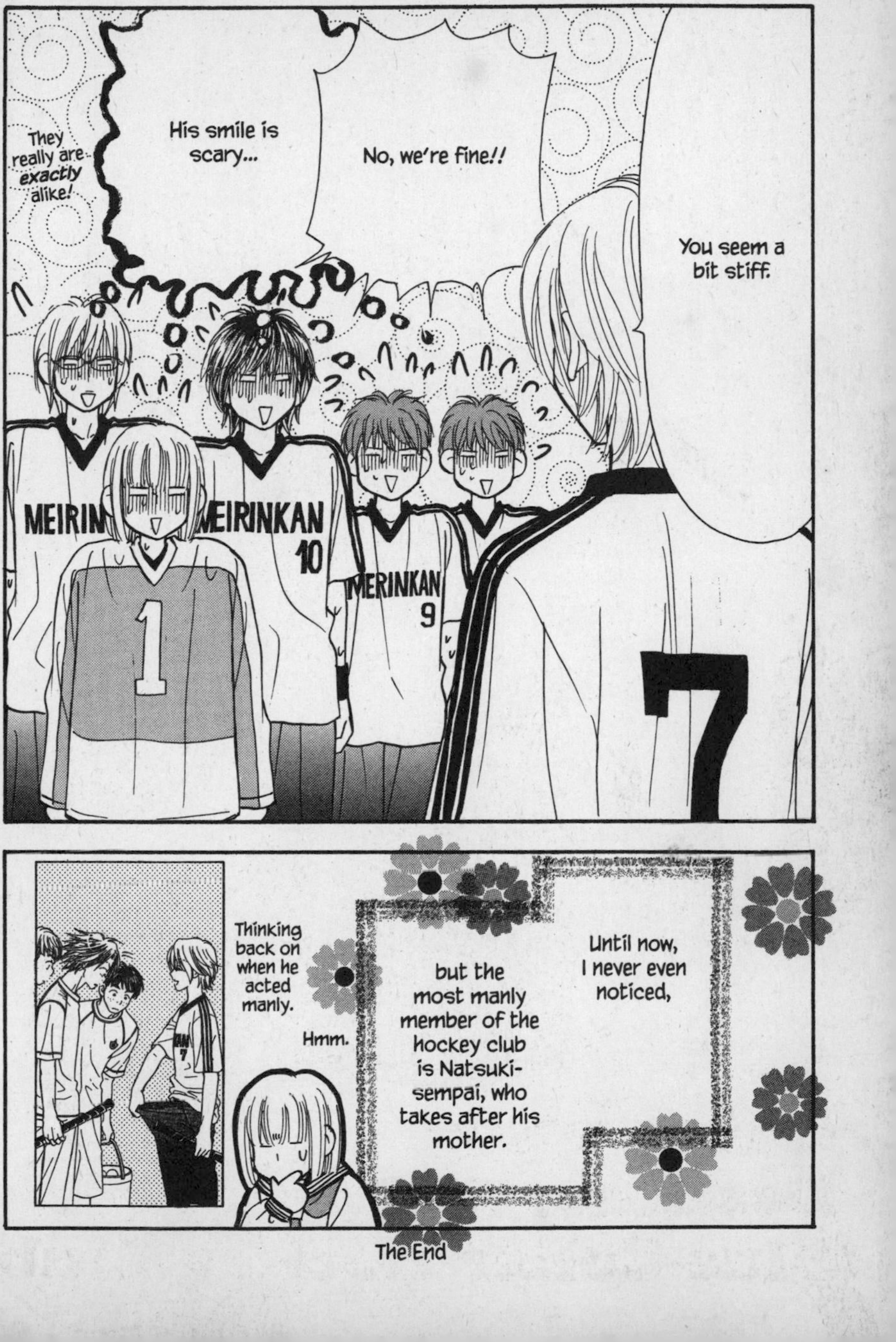
You seem a bit stiff.
No, we're fine!!
His smile is scary...
They really are *exactly* alike!
MEIRINKAN 10
MEIRIN
MERINKAN 9
Until now, I never even noticed,
but the most manly member of the hockey club is Natsuki-sempai, who takes after his mother.
Hmm.
Thinking back on when he acted manly.

The End

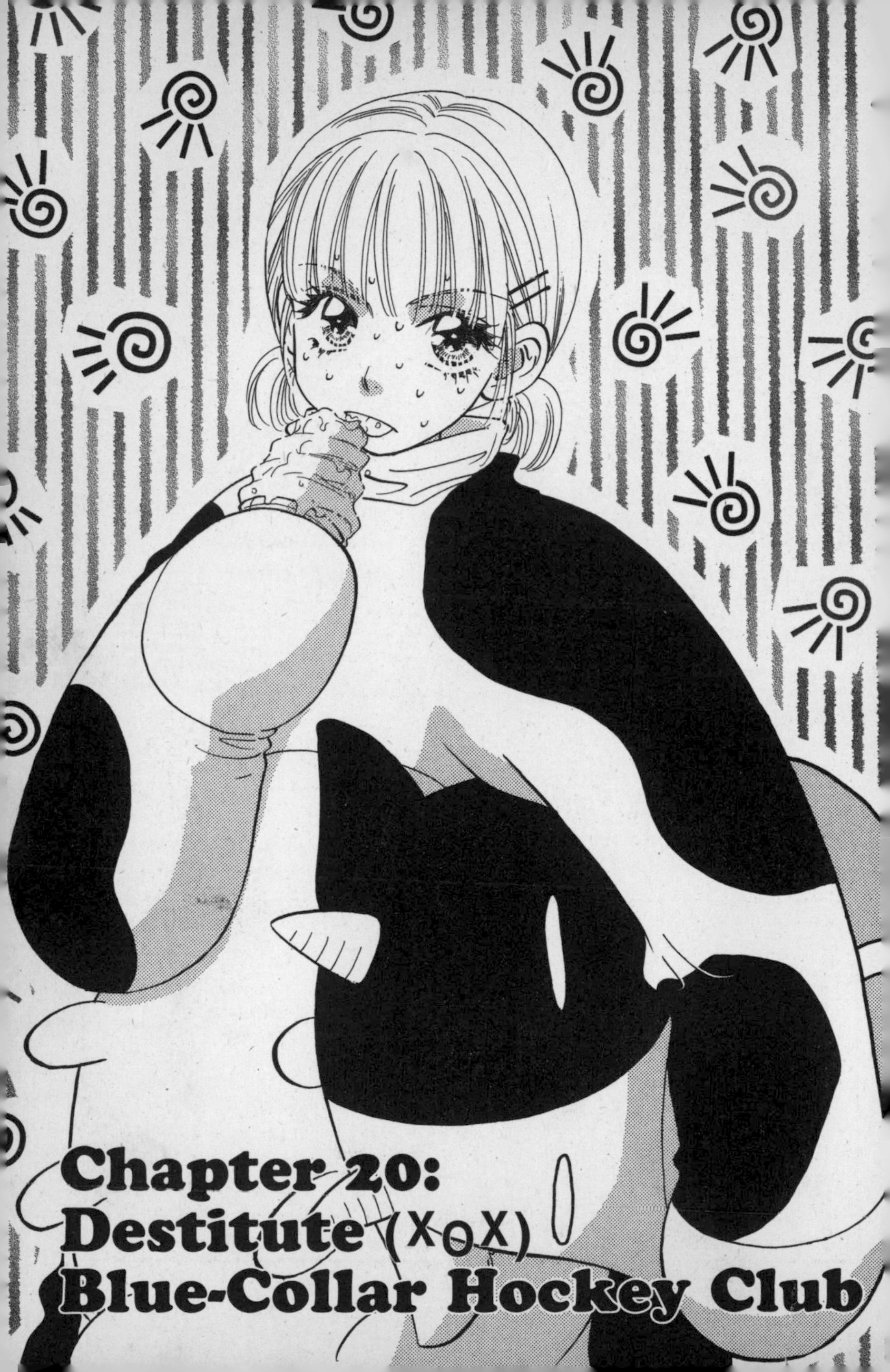
Chapter 20:
Destitute (X_OX)
Blue-Collar Hockey Club

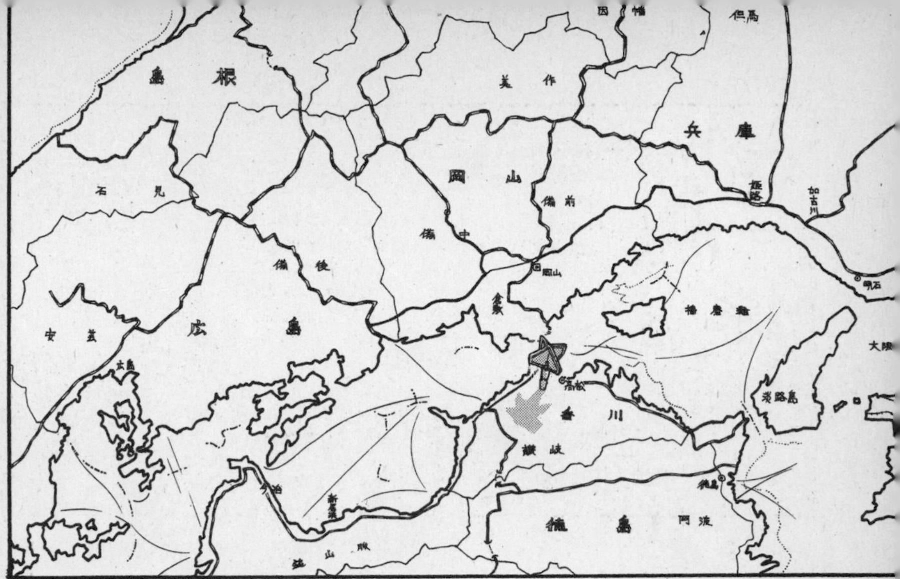
島根
美作
但馬
兵庫
岡山
備前
備中
備後
石見
姫路
加古川
明石
広島
安芸
播磨灘
淡路島
大阪
香川
讃岐
徳島
阿波
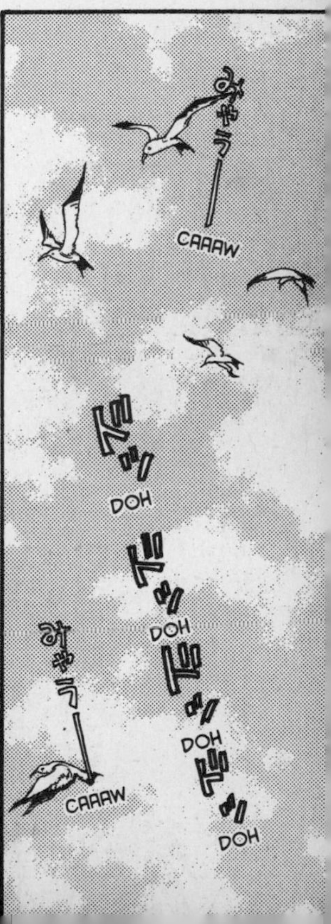
CAAAW
DOH
DOH
DOH
DOH
CAAAW
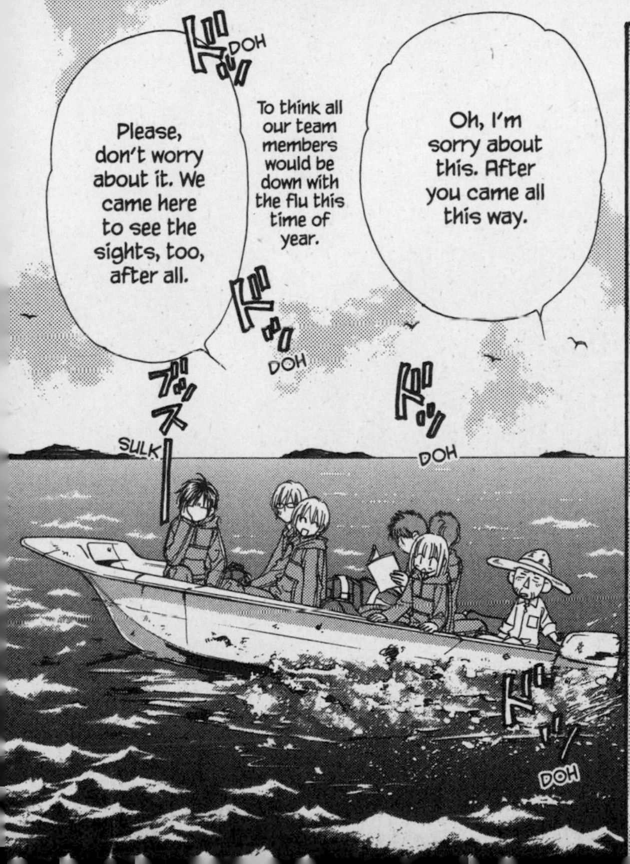
Oh, I'm sorry about this. After you came all this way.
To think all our team members would be down with the flu this time of year.
DOH
Please, don't worry about it. We came here to see the sights, too, after all.
DOH
DOH
SULK
DOH

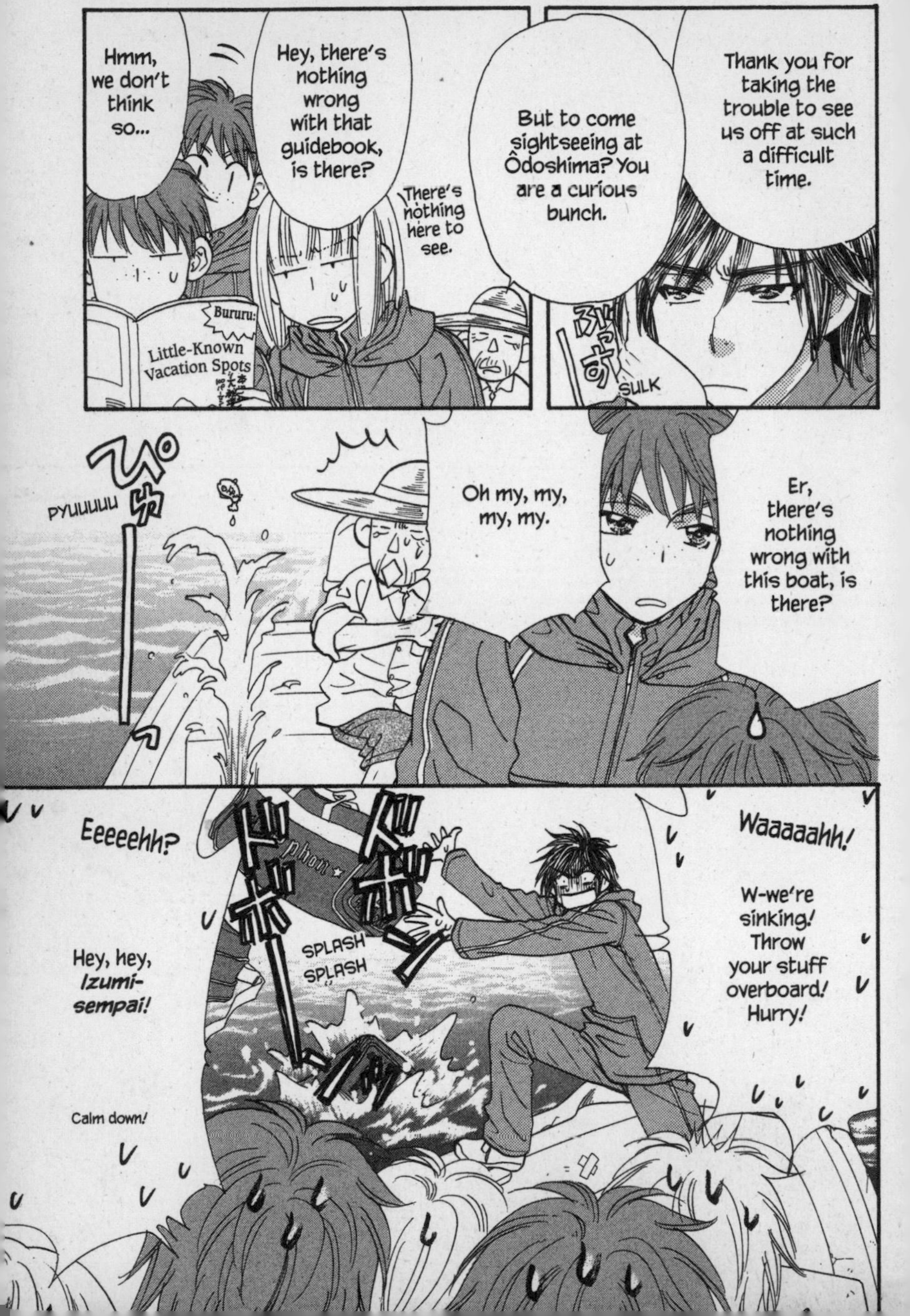
Thank you for taking the trouble to see us off at such a difficult time.
But to come sightseeing at Ôdoshima? You are a curious bunch.
SULK
Hey, there's nothing wrong with that guidebook, is there?
There's nothing here to see.
Hmm, we don't think so...
Bururu:
Little-Known Vacation Spots
Er, there's nothing wrong with this boat, is there?
Oh my, my, my, my.
PYUUUUU
Waaaaahh!
W-we're sinking! Throw your stuff overboard! Hurry!
SPLASH SPLASH
Eeeeehh?
Hey, hey, *Izumi-sempai!*
Calm down!

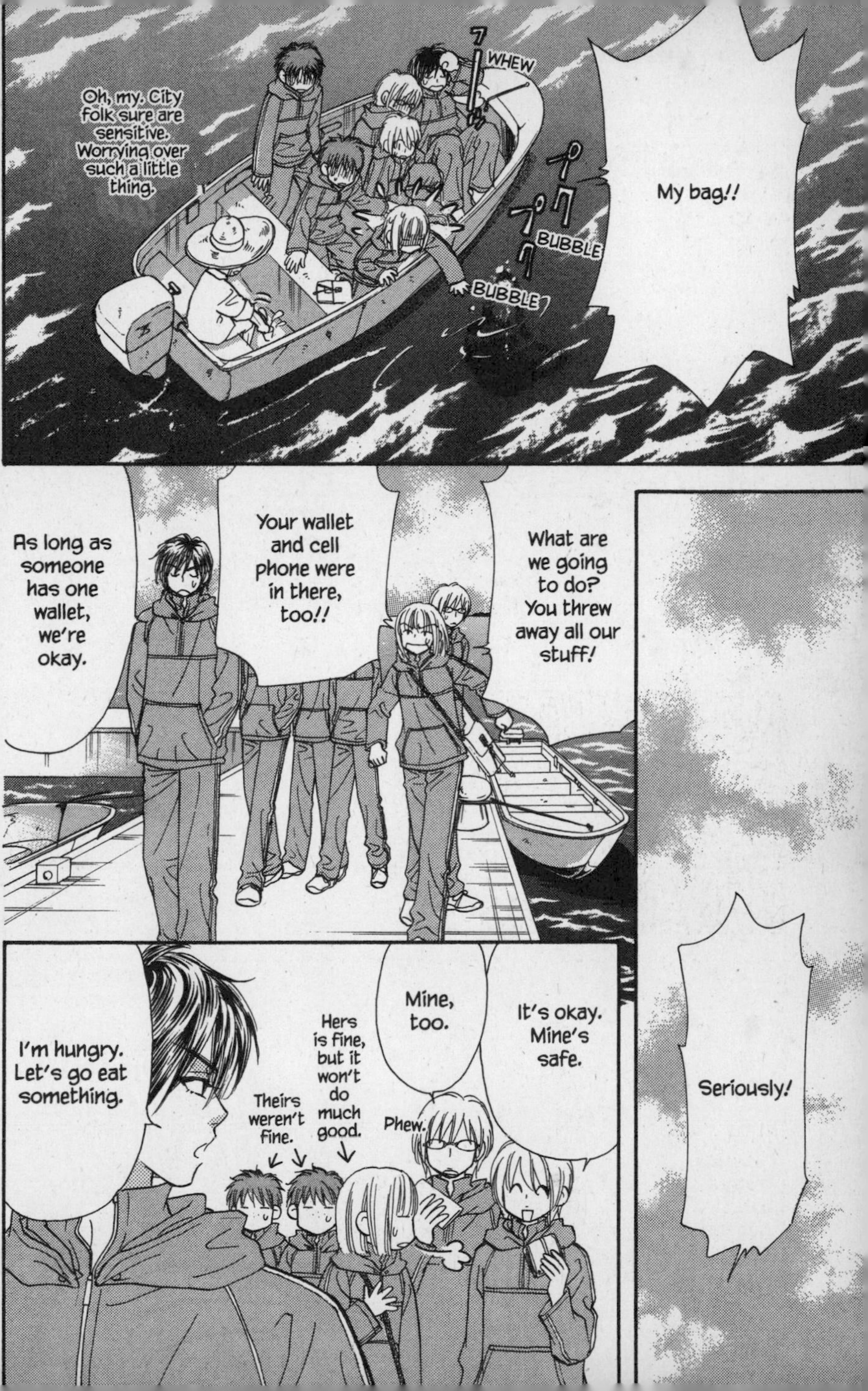
My bag!!
WHEW
BUBBLE
BUBBLE
Oh, my. City folk sure are sensitive. Worrying over such a little thing.
Seriously!
What are we going to do? You threw away all our stuff!
Your wallet and cell phone were in there, too!!
As long as someone has one wallet, we're okay.
It's okay. Mine's safe.
Mine, too.
Phew.
Hers is fine, but it won't do much good.
Theirs weren't fine.
I'm hungry. Let's go eat something.

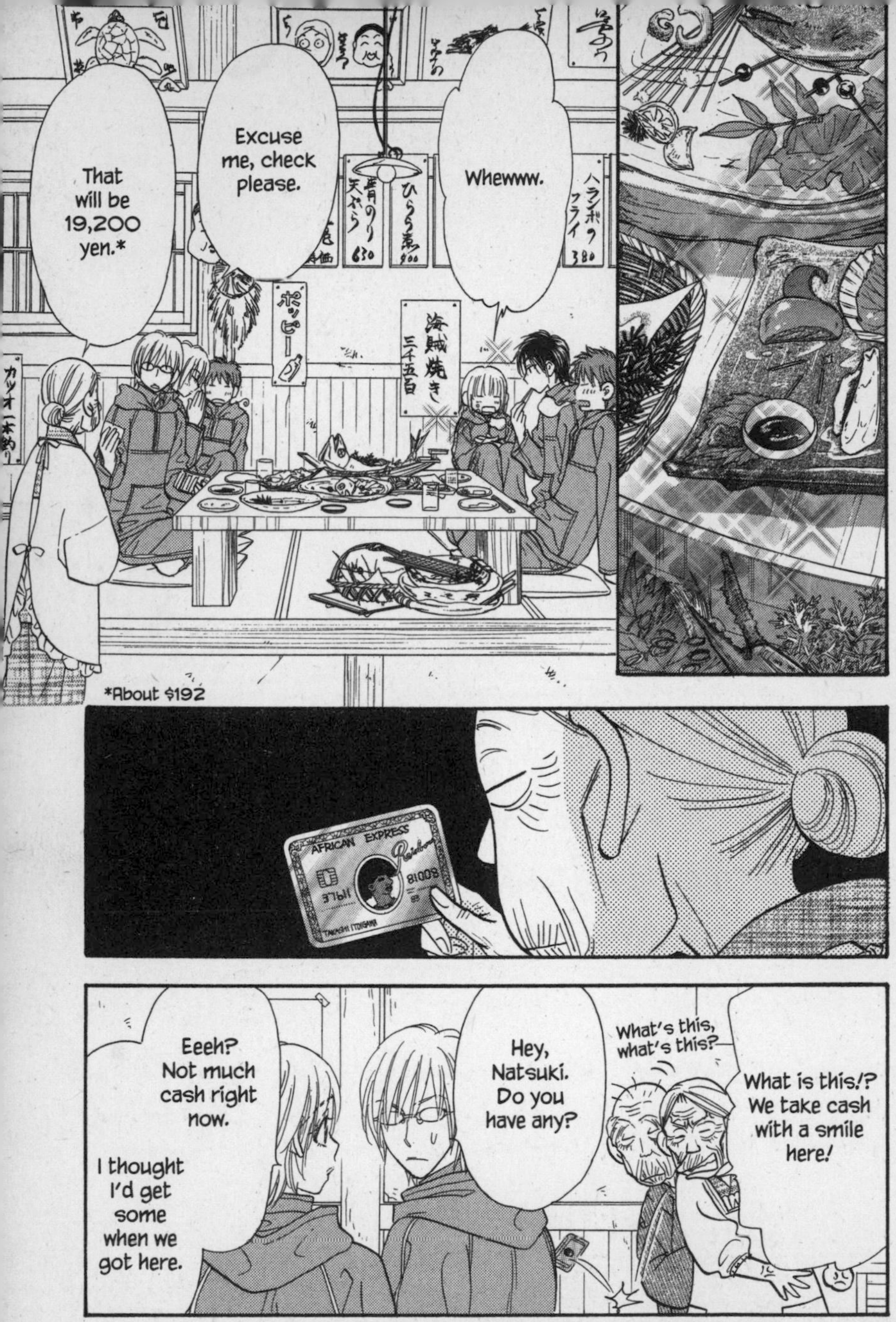
Whewww.
Excuse me, check please.
That will be 19,200 yen.*
*About $192
AFRICAN EXPRESS
What is this!? We take cash with a smile here!
What's this, what's this?
Hey, Natsuki. Do you have any?
Eeeh? Not much cash right now.
I thought I'd get some when we got here.

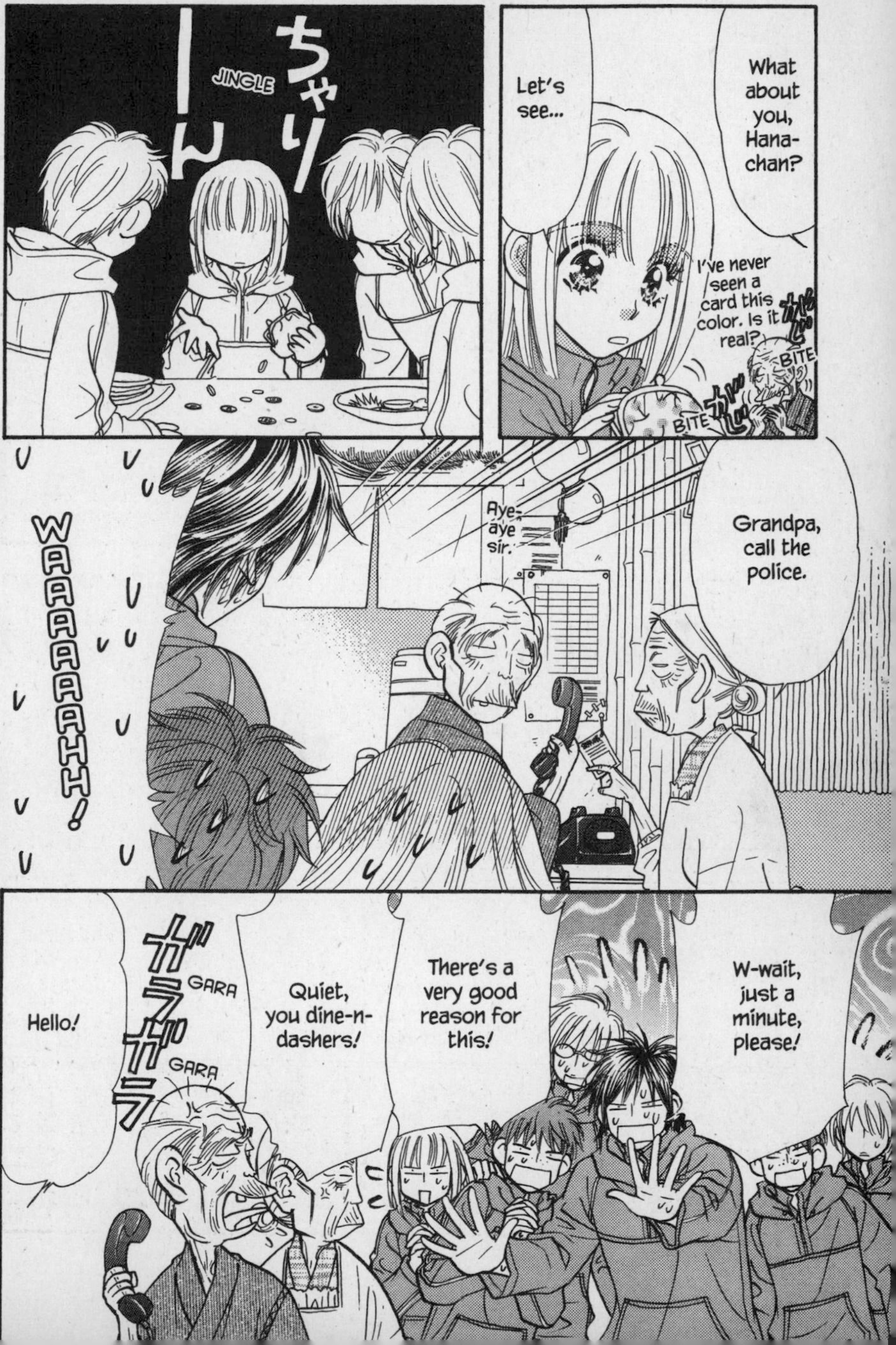
What about you, Hana-chan?
Let's see...
I've never seen a card this color. Is it real?
BITE
BITE
ちゃりーん
JINGLE
Grandpa, call the police.
Aye-aye sir.
WAAAAAAAAHH!
W-wait, just a minute, please!
There's a very good reason for this!
Quiet, you dine-n-dashers!
ガラガラ
GARA
GARA
Hello!

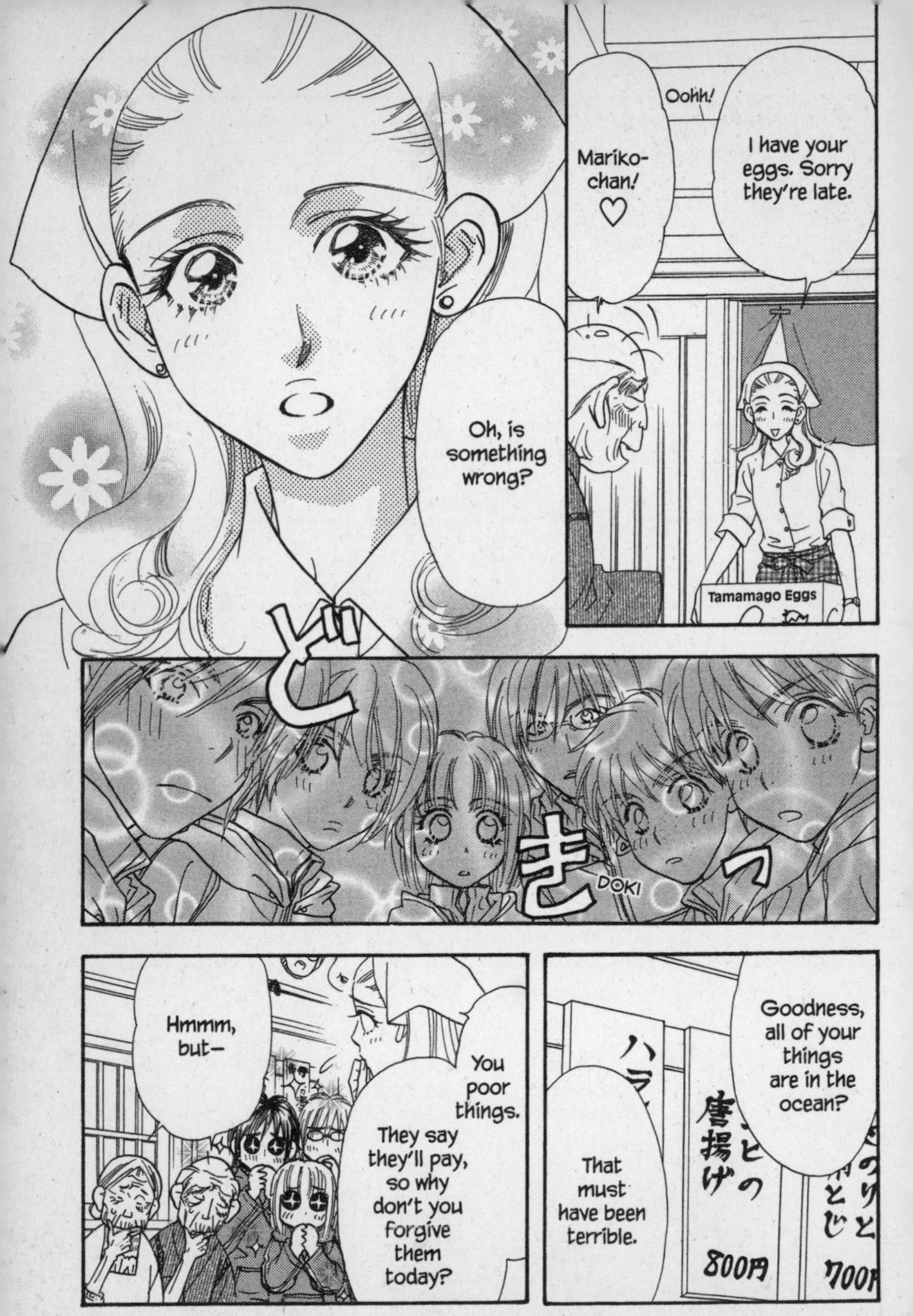
I have your eggs. Sorry they're late.
Oohh!
Mariko-chan! ♡
Tamamago Eggs
Oh, is something wrong?
どきっ
DOKI
Goodness, all of your things are in the ocean?
That must have been terrible.
唐揚げ
800円
You poor things.
They say they'll pay, so why don't you forgive them today?
Hmmm, but–

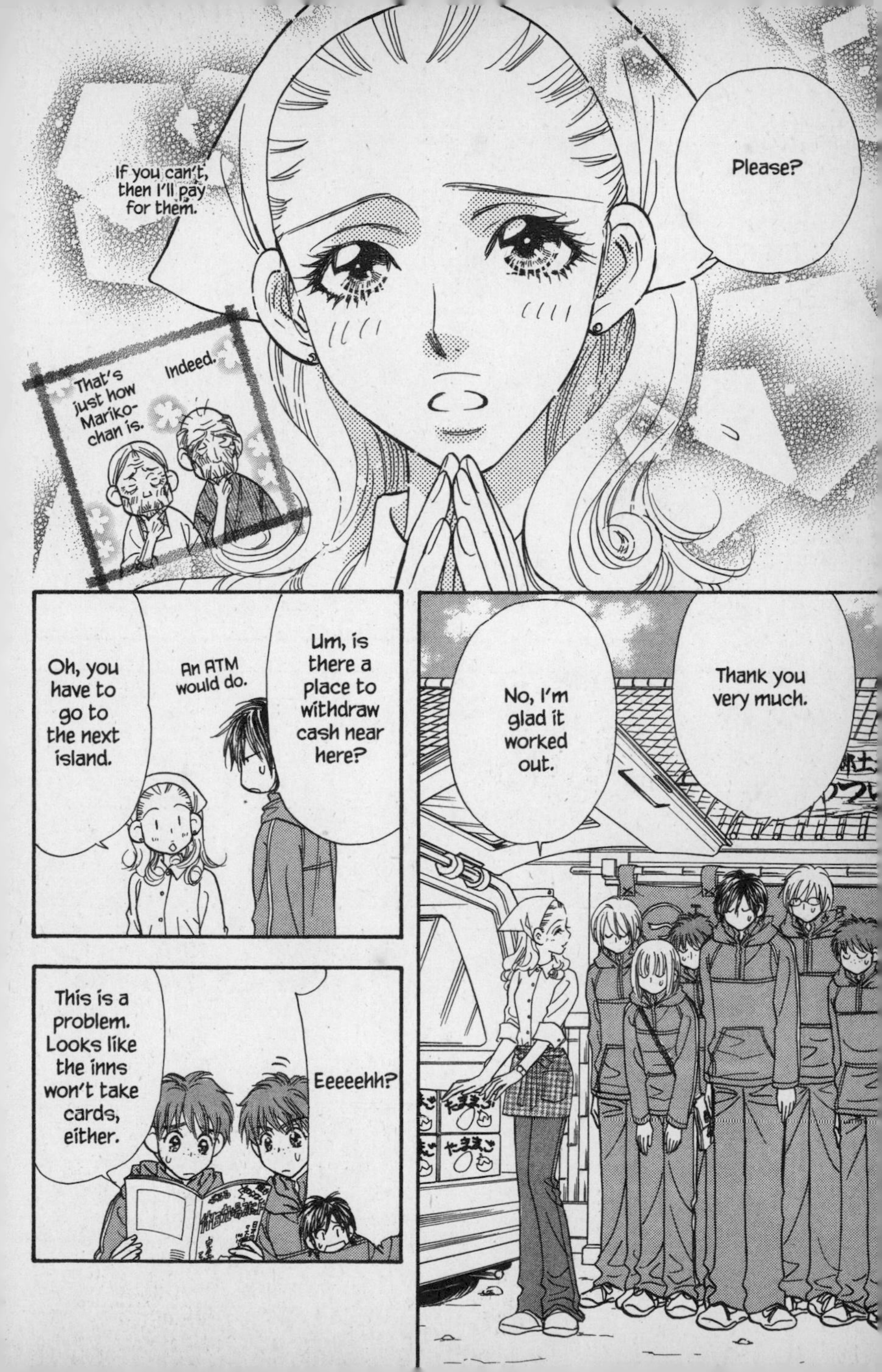
Please?
If you can't, then I'll pay for them.
That's just how Mariko-chan is.
Indeed.
Thank you very much.
No, I'm glad it worked out.
Um, is there a place to withdraw cash near here?
An ATM would do.
Oh, you have to go to the next island.
Eeeeehh?
This is a problem. Looks like the inns won't take cards, either.

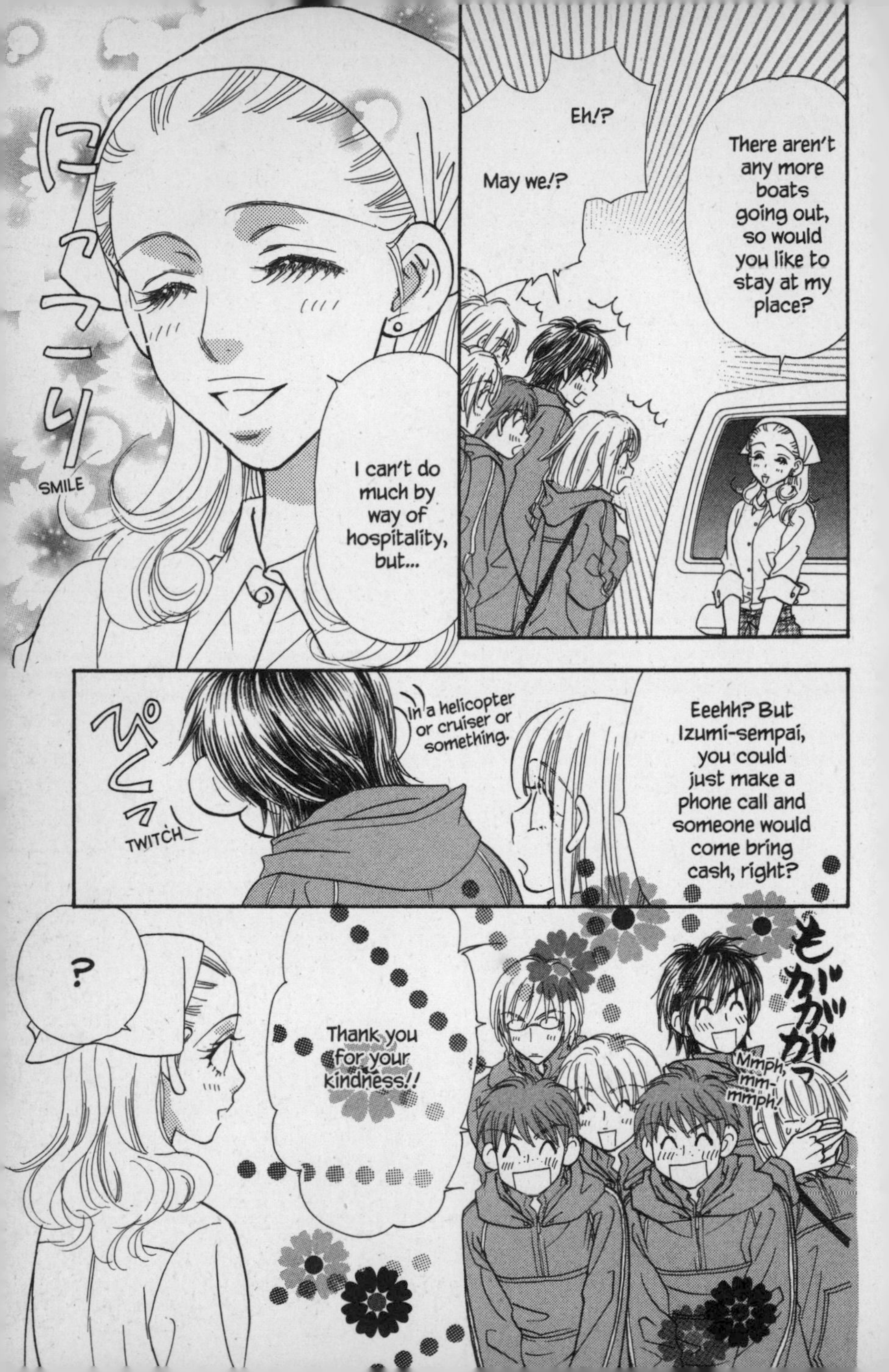
There aren't any more boats going out, so would you like to stay at my place?
Eh!?
May we!?
I can't do much by way of hospitality, but...
SMILE
Eeehh? But Izumi-sempai, you could just make a phone call and someone would come bring cash, right?
In a helicopter or cruiser or something.
TWITCH
Mmph, mm-mmph!
Thank you for your kindness!!
?

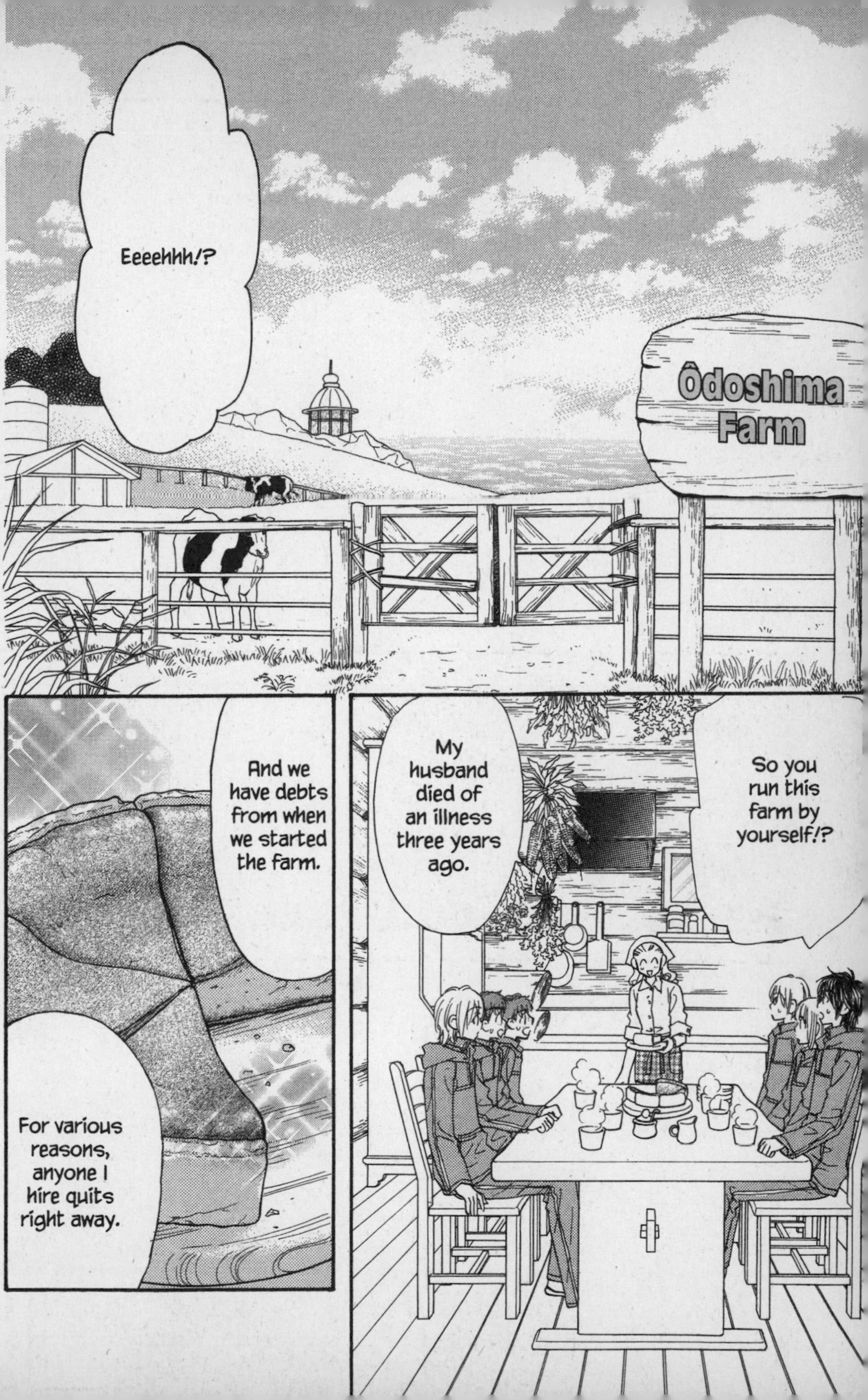
Eeeehhh!?
Ôdoshima Farm
So you run this farm by yourself!?
My husband died of an illness three years ago.
And we have debts from when we started the farm.
For various reasons, anyone I hire quits right away.

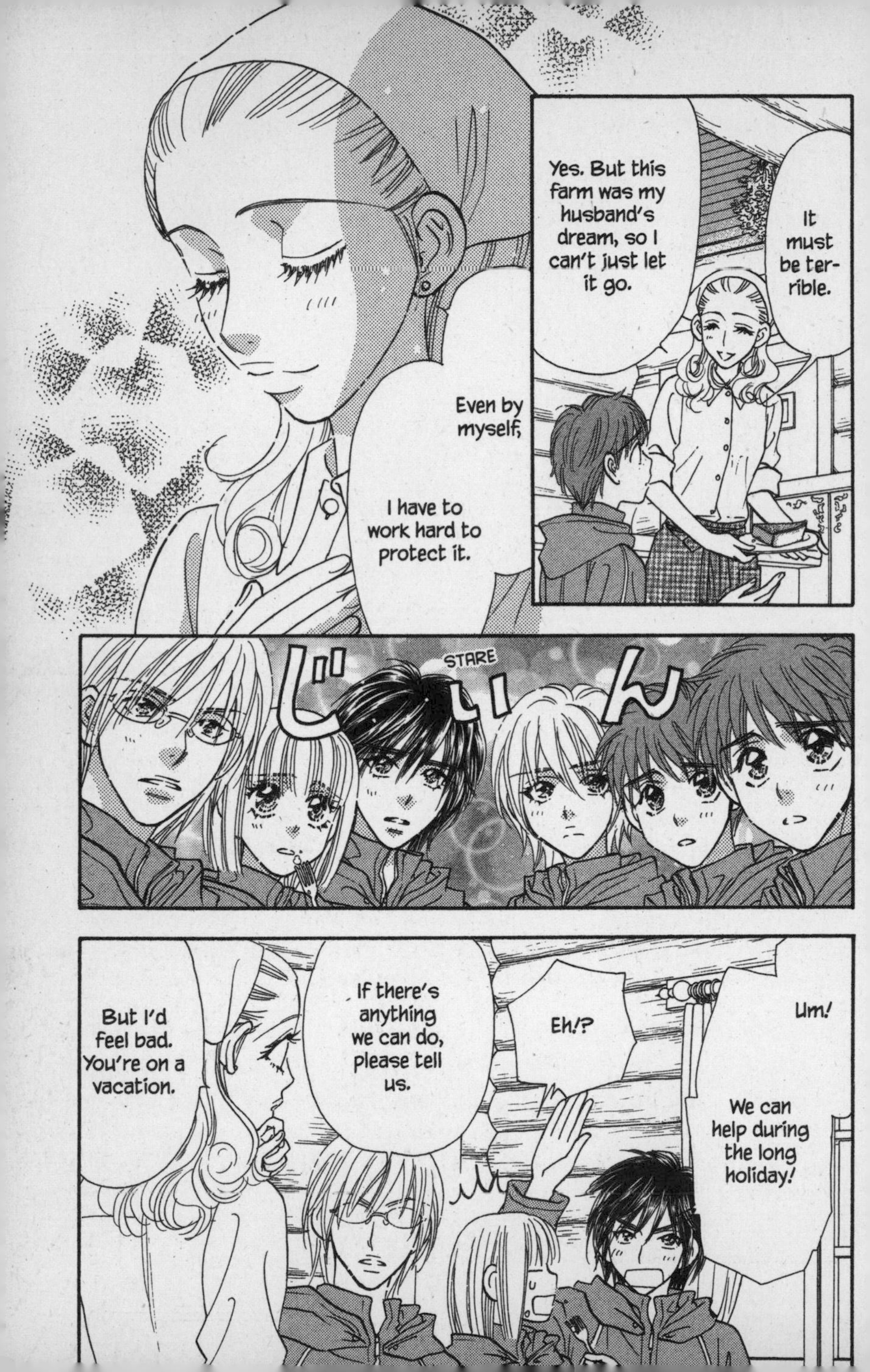
It must be terrible.
Yes. But this farm was my husband's dream, so I can't just let it go.
Even by myself,
I have to work hard to protect it.
じぃん
STARE
Um!
We can help during the long holiday!
Eh!?
If there's anything we can do, please tell us.
But I'd feel bad. You're on a vacation.

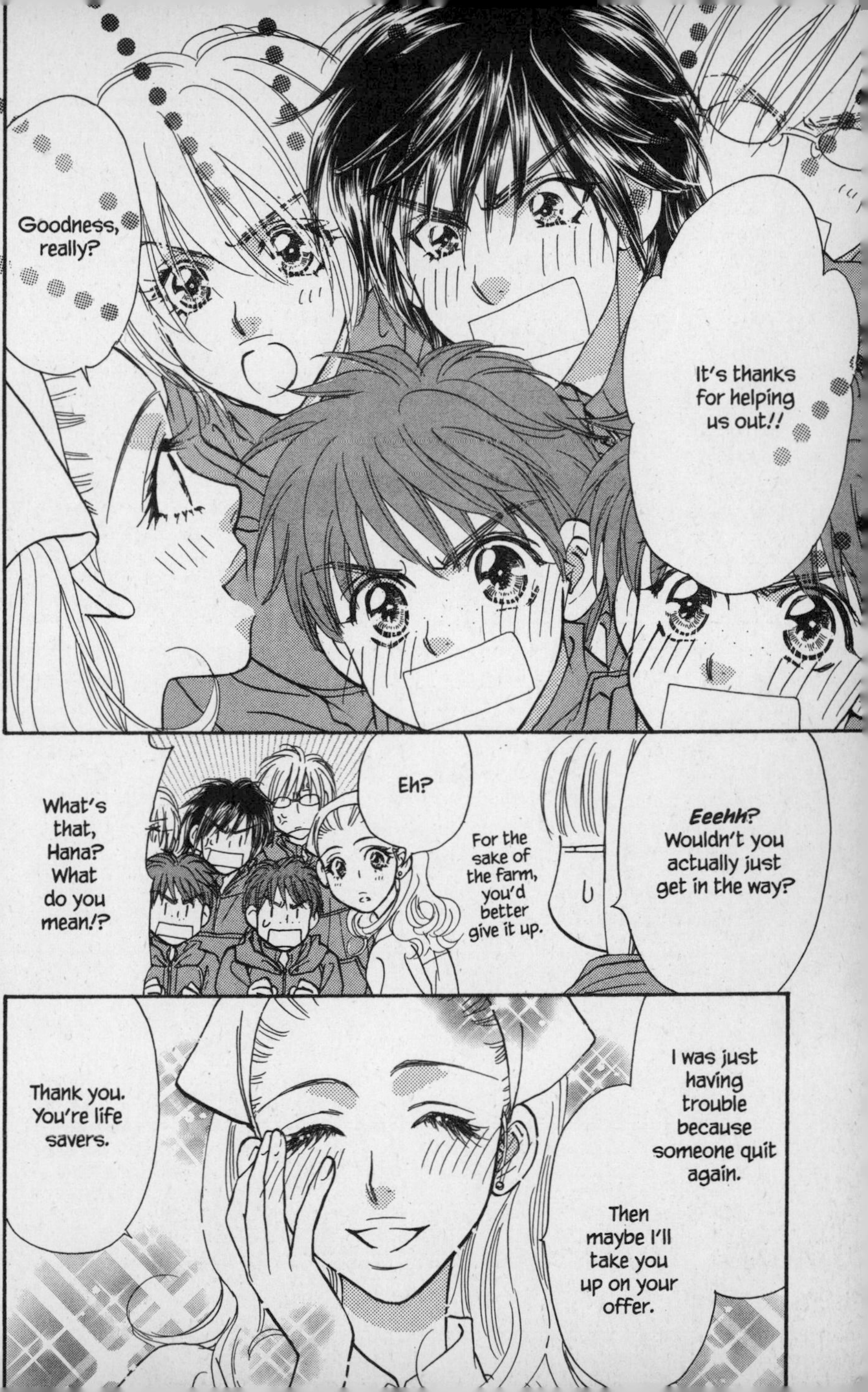
It's thanks for helping us out!!
Goodness, really?
Eeehh? Wouldn't you actually just get in the way?
Eh?
For the sake of the farm, you'd better give it up.
What's that, Hana? What do you mean!?
I was just having trouble because someone quit again.
Then maybe I'll take you up on your offer.
Thank you. You're life savers.

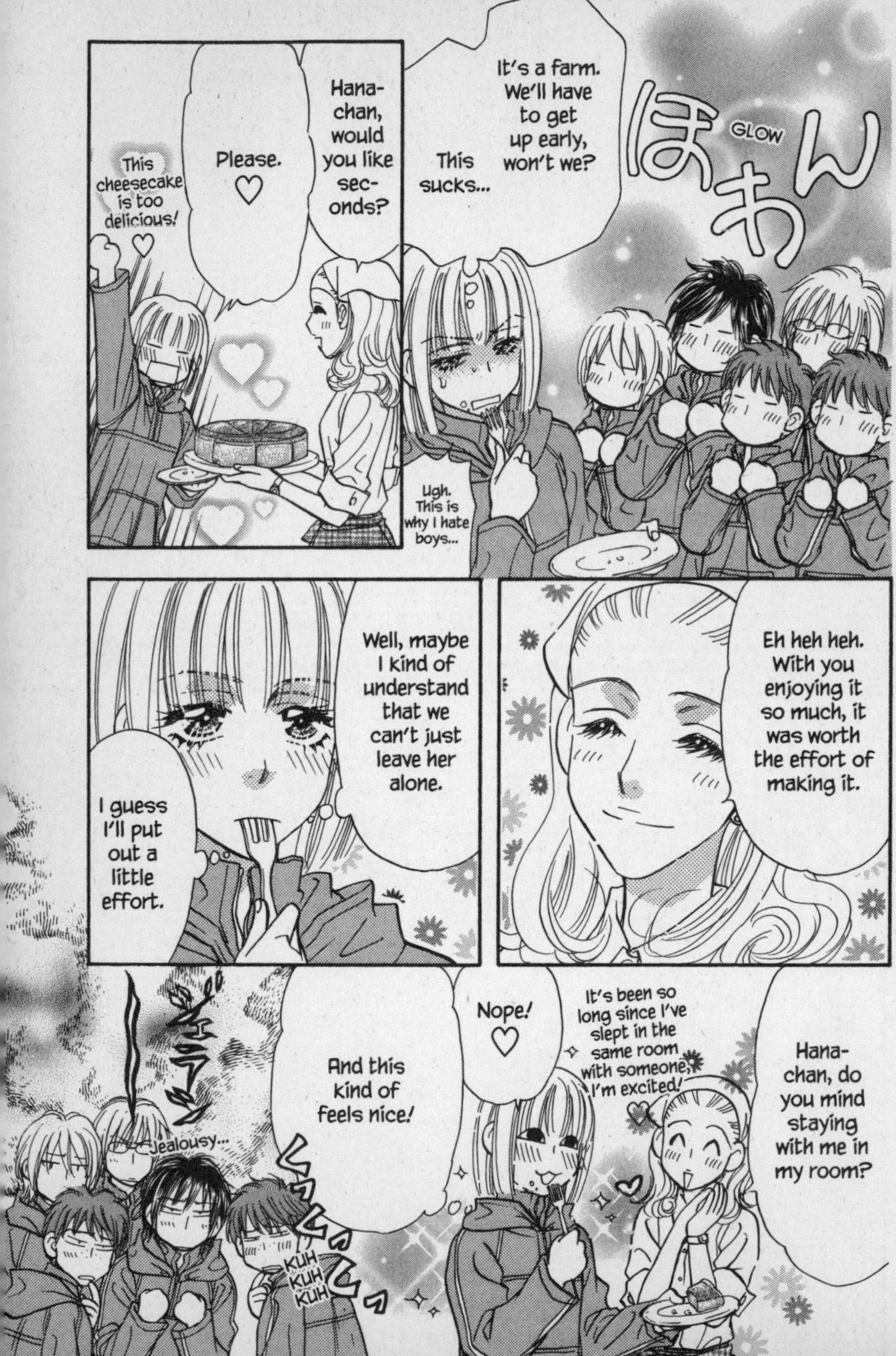
ほわん
GLOW
It's a farm. We'll have to get up early, won't we?
This sucks...
Ugh. This is why I hate boys...
Hana-chan, would you like sec-onds?
Please. ♡
This cheesecake is too delicious! ♡
Eh heh heh. With you enjoying it so much, it was worth the effort of making it.
Well, maybe I kind of understand that we can't just leave her alone.
I guess I'll put out a little effort.
Hana-chan, do you mind staying with me in my room?
It's been so long since I've slept in the same room with someone, I'm excited!
Nope! ♡
And this kind of feels nice!
KUH KUH KUH
Jealousy...

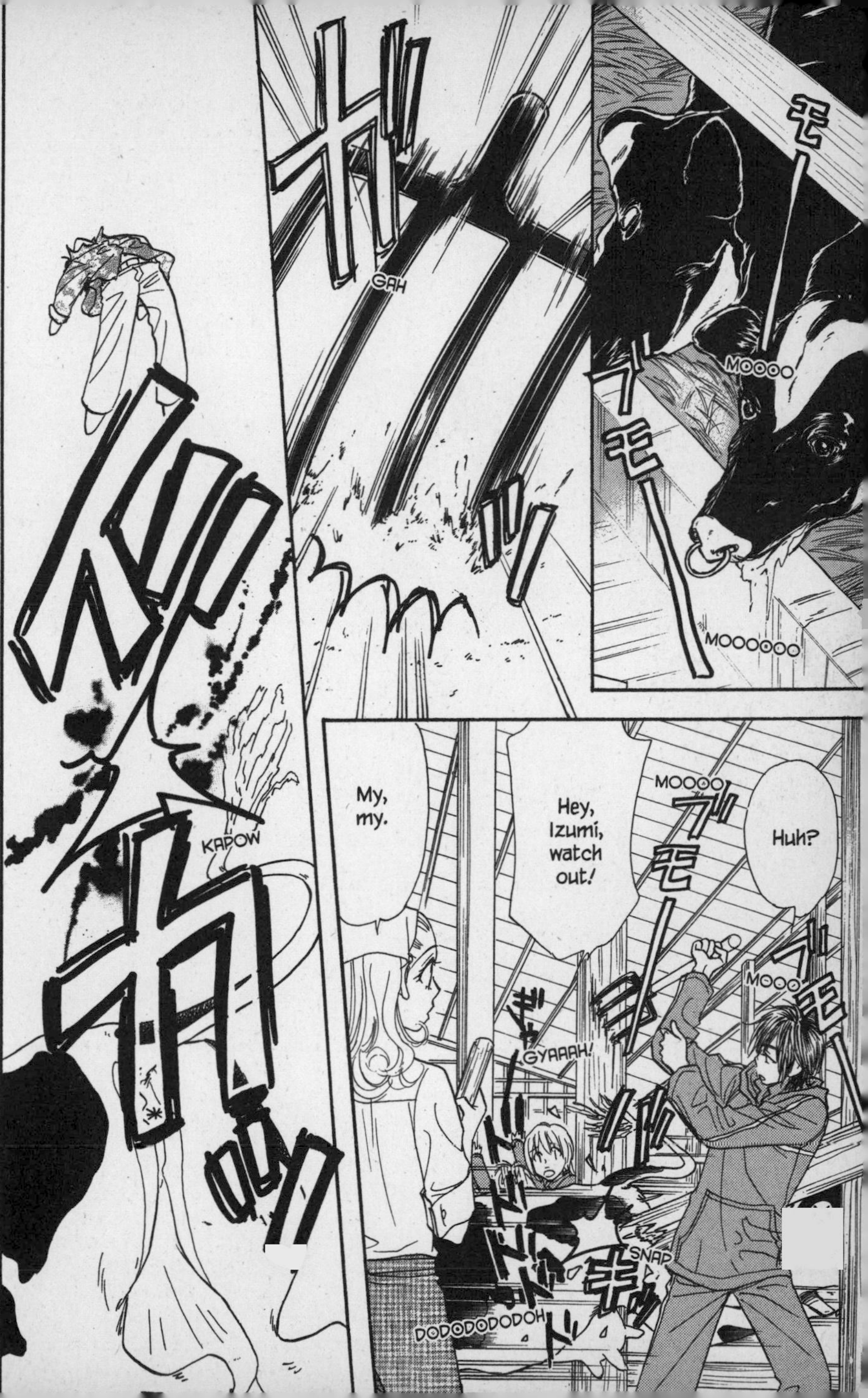

MOOOO
MOOOOOO
GAH
Huh?
MOOOO
Hey, Izumi, watch out!
My, my.
MOOO
GYAAAH!
SNAP
DODODODODOH
KAPOW

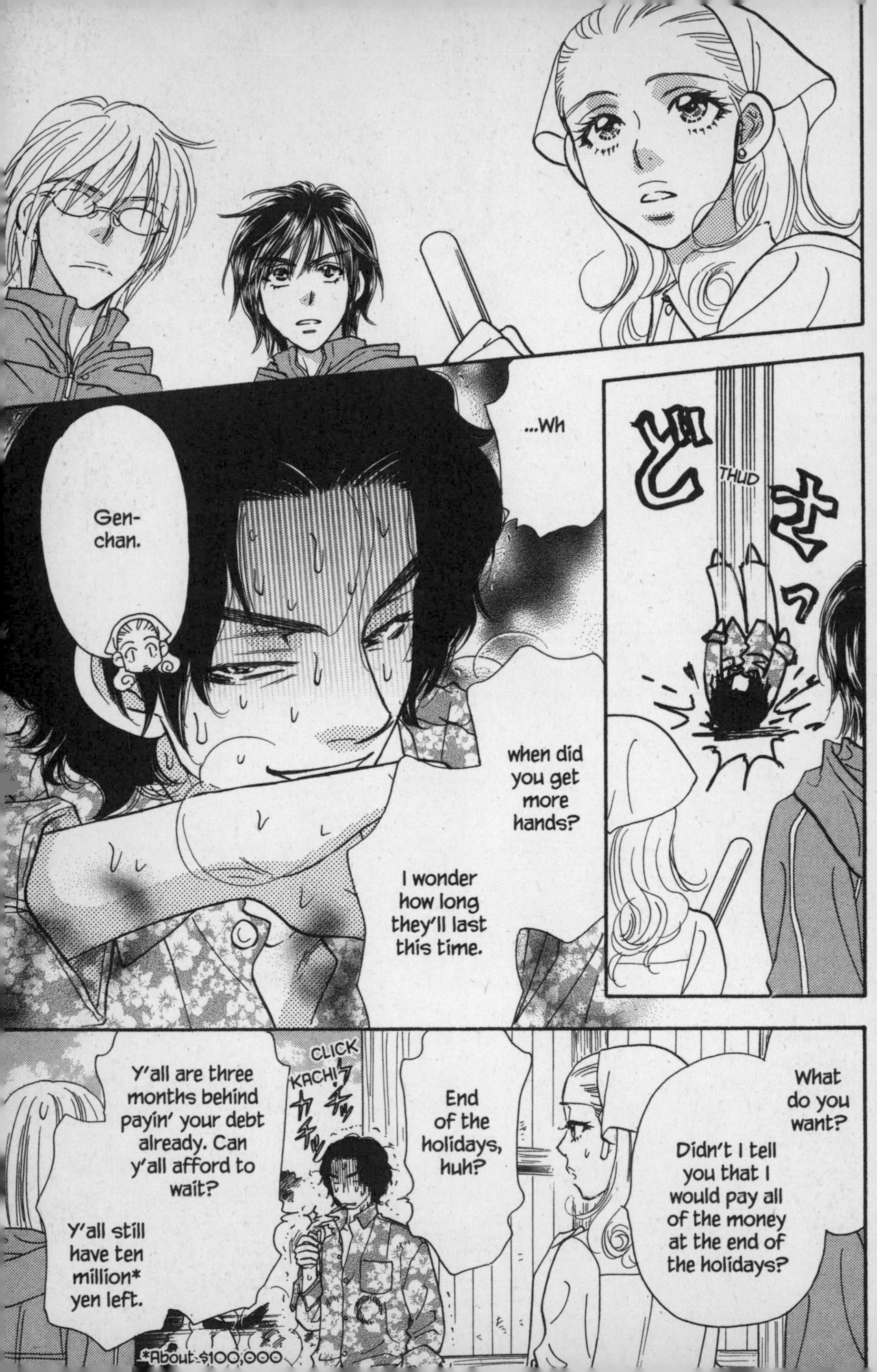
どさっ
THUD
...Wh
when did you get more hands?
I wonder how long they'll last this time.
Gen-chan.
What do you want?
Didn't I tell you that I would pay all of the money at the end of the holidays?
End of the holidays, huh?
CLICK
KACHI!
カチッ カチッ
Y'all are three months behind payin' your debt already. Can y'all afford to wait?
Y'all still have ten million* yen left.
*About $100,000

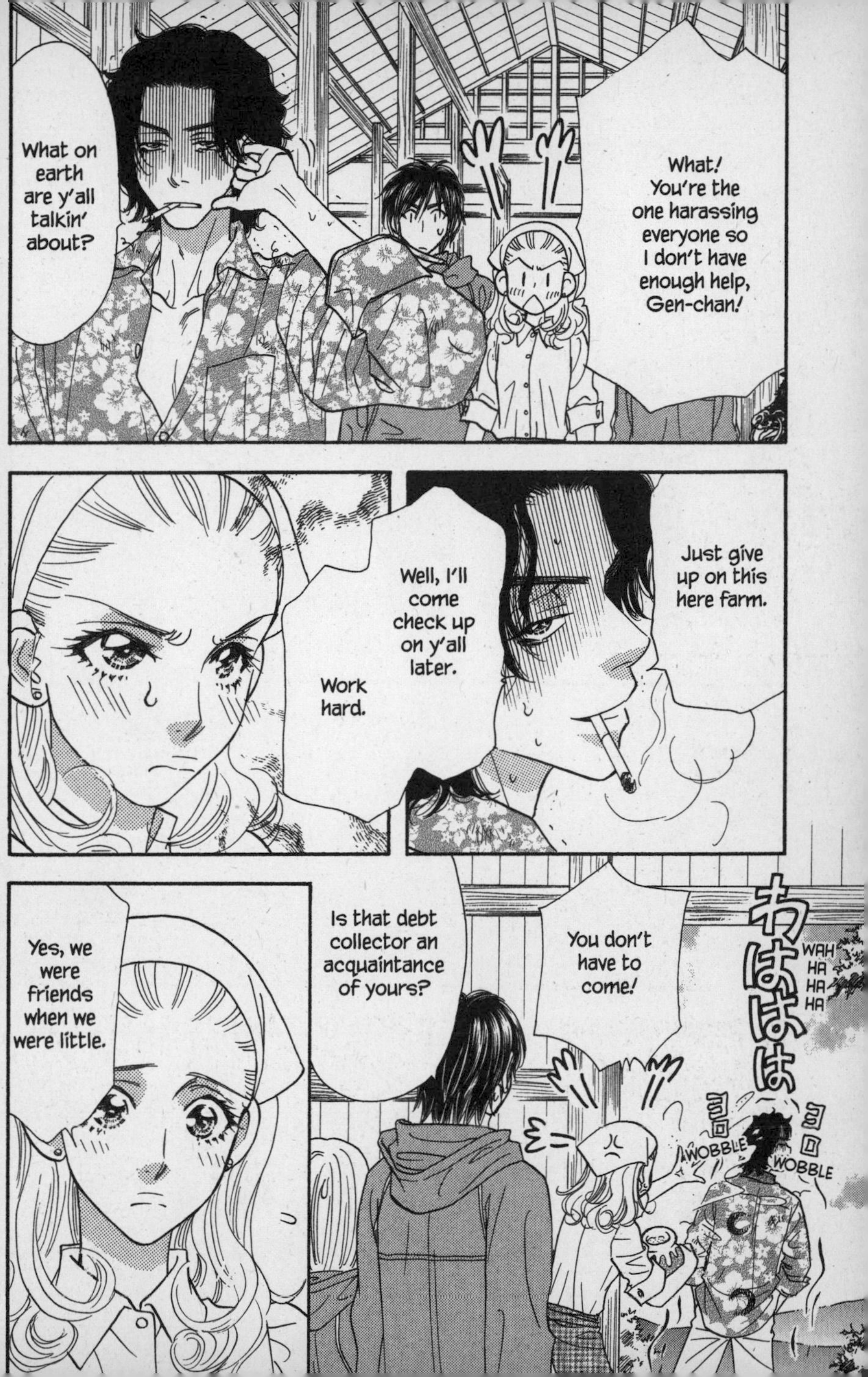
What! You're the one harassing everyone so I don't have enough help, Gen-chan!
What on earth are y'all talkin' about?
Just give up on this here farm.
Well, I'll come check up on y'all later.
Work hard.
わははは
WAH HA HA HA
You don't have to come!
Is that debt collector an acquaintance of yours?
ヨロ WOBBLE
ヨロ WOBBLE
Yes, we were friends when we were little.

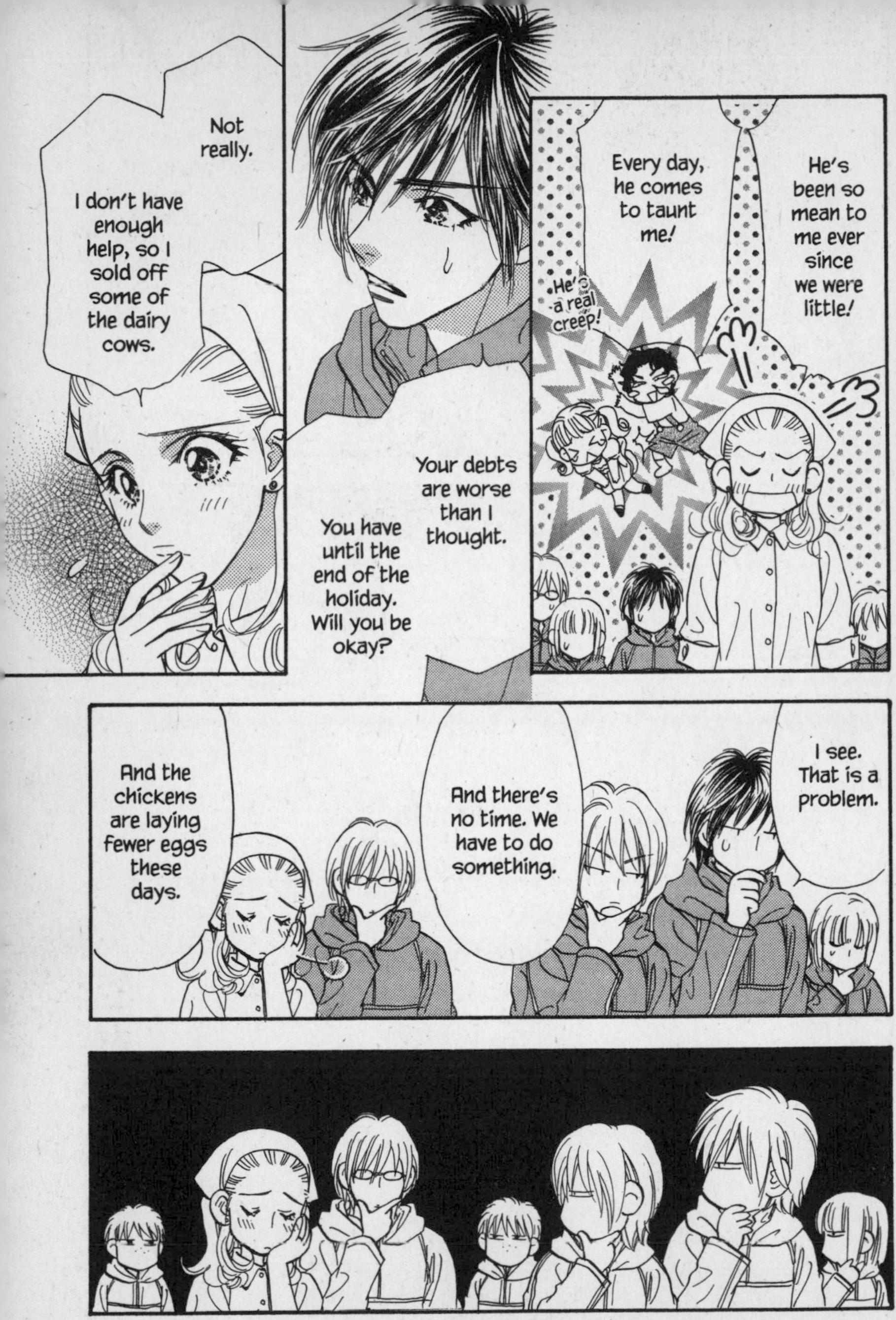
He's been so mean to me ever since we were little!
Every day, he comes to taunt me!
He's a real creep!
Your debts are worse than I thought.
You have until the end of the holiday. Will you be okay?
Not really.
I don't have enough help, so I sold off some of the dairy cows.
I see. That is a problem.
And there's no time. We have to do something.
And the chickens are laying fewer eggs these days.

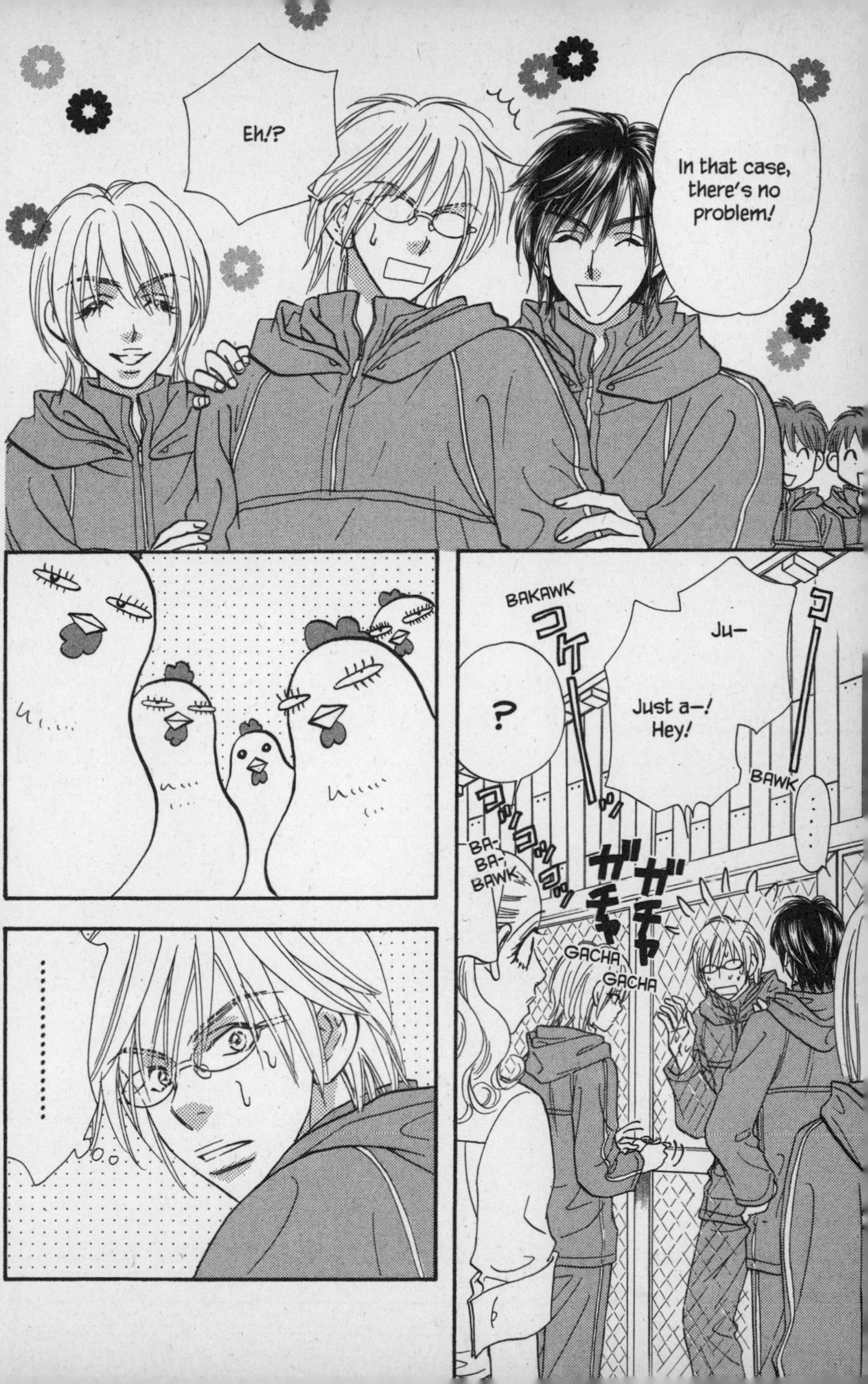
In that case, there's no problem!
Eh!?
BAWK
Ju–
Just a–! Hey!
BAKAWK
?
...
BA-BA-BAWK
GACHA
GACHA
......

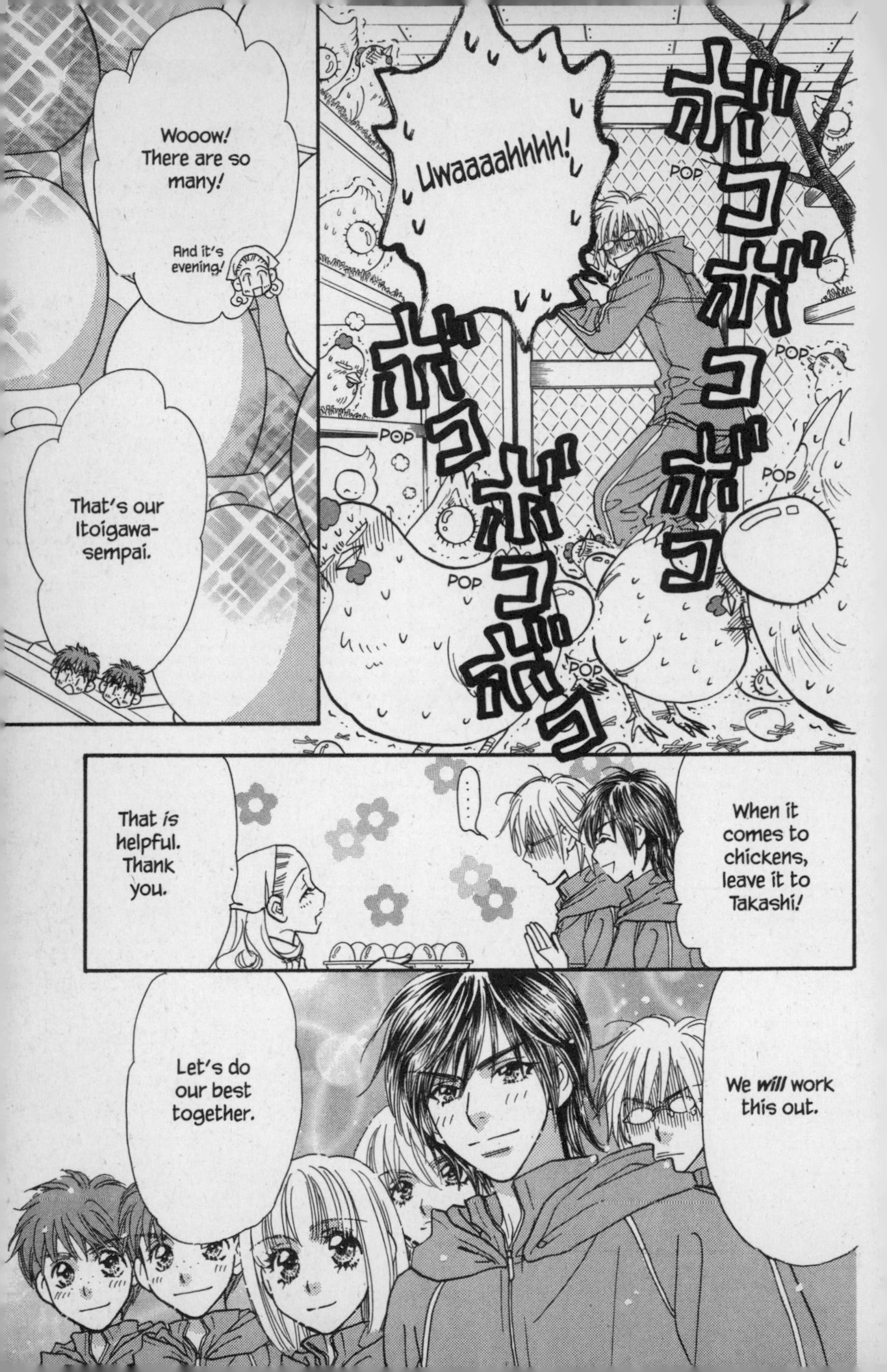
Uwaaaahhhh!
POP
POP
POP
POP
POP
POP
Wooow! There are so many!
And it's evening!
That's our Itoigawa-sempai.
When it comes to chickens, leave it to Takashi!
...
That *is* helpful. Thank you.
We *will* work this out.
Let's do our best together.

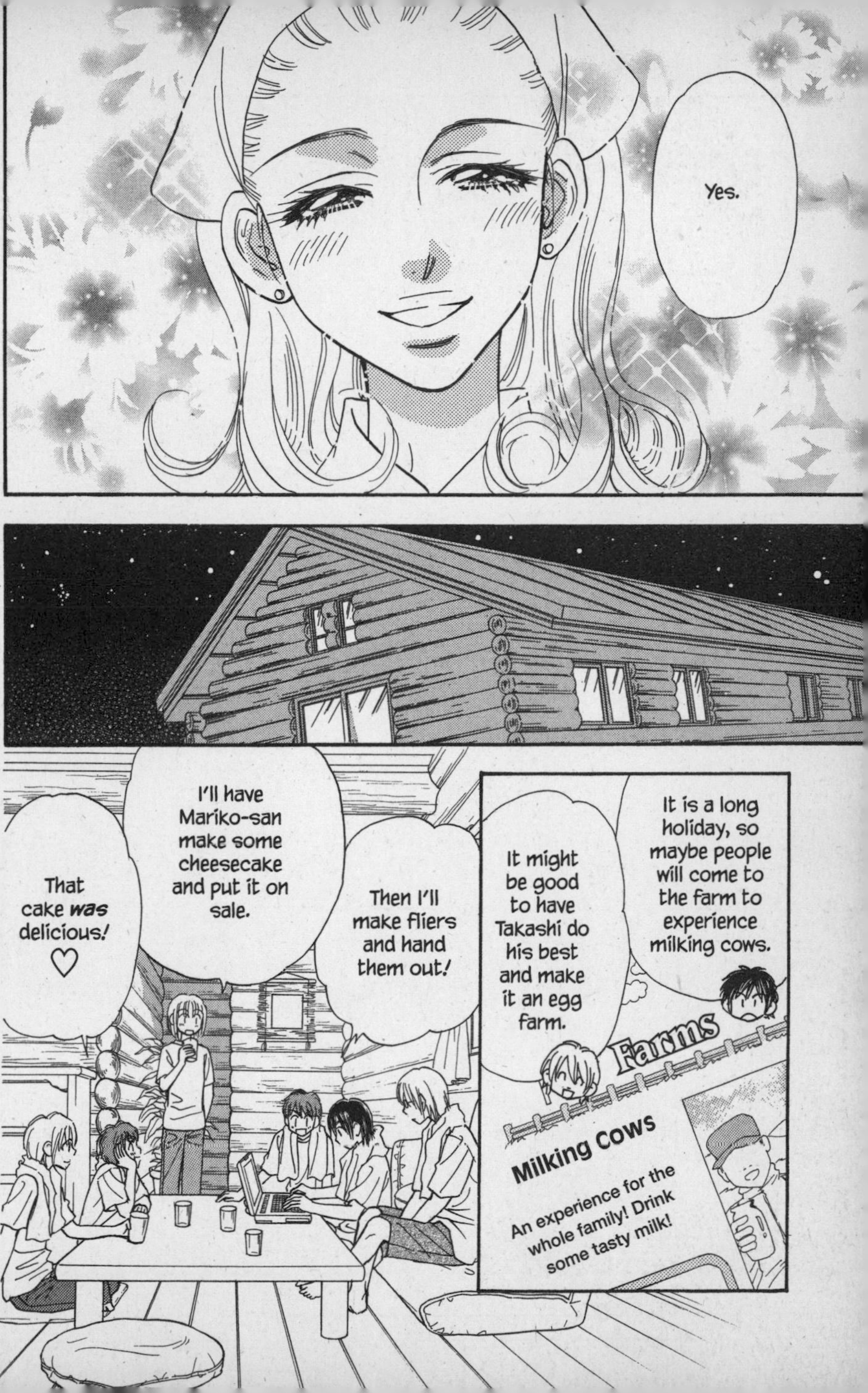
Yes.
It is a long holiday, so maybe people will come to the farm to experience milking cows.
It might be good to have Takashi do his best and make it an egg farm.
Farms
Milking Cows
An experience for the whole family! Drink some tasty milk!
Then I'll make fliers and hand them out!
I'll have Mariko-san make some cheesecake and put it on sale.
That cake *was* delicious! ♡

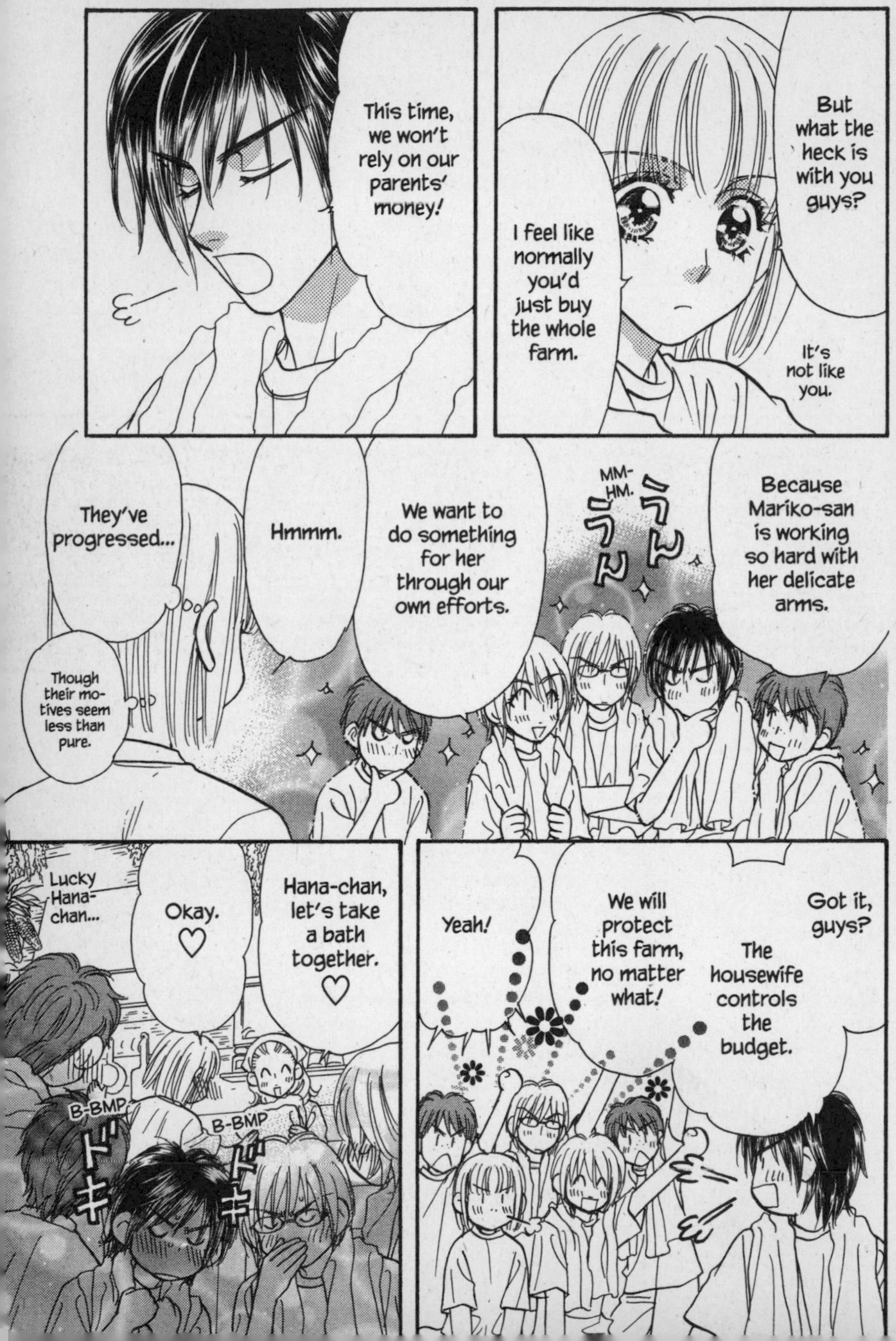
But what the heck is with you guys?
It's not like you.
I feel like normally you'd just buy the whole farm.
This time, we won't rely on our parents' money!
Because Mariko-san is working so hard with her delicate arms.
MM-HM.
うん うん
We want to do something for her through our own efforts.
Hmmm.
They've progressed...
Though their motives seem less than pure.
Got it, guys?
The housewife controls the budget.
We will protect this farm, no matter what!
Yeah!
Hana-chan, let's take a bath together. ♡
Okay. ♡
Lucky Hana-chan...
B-BMP
ドキ
B-BMP
ドキ

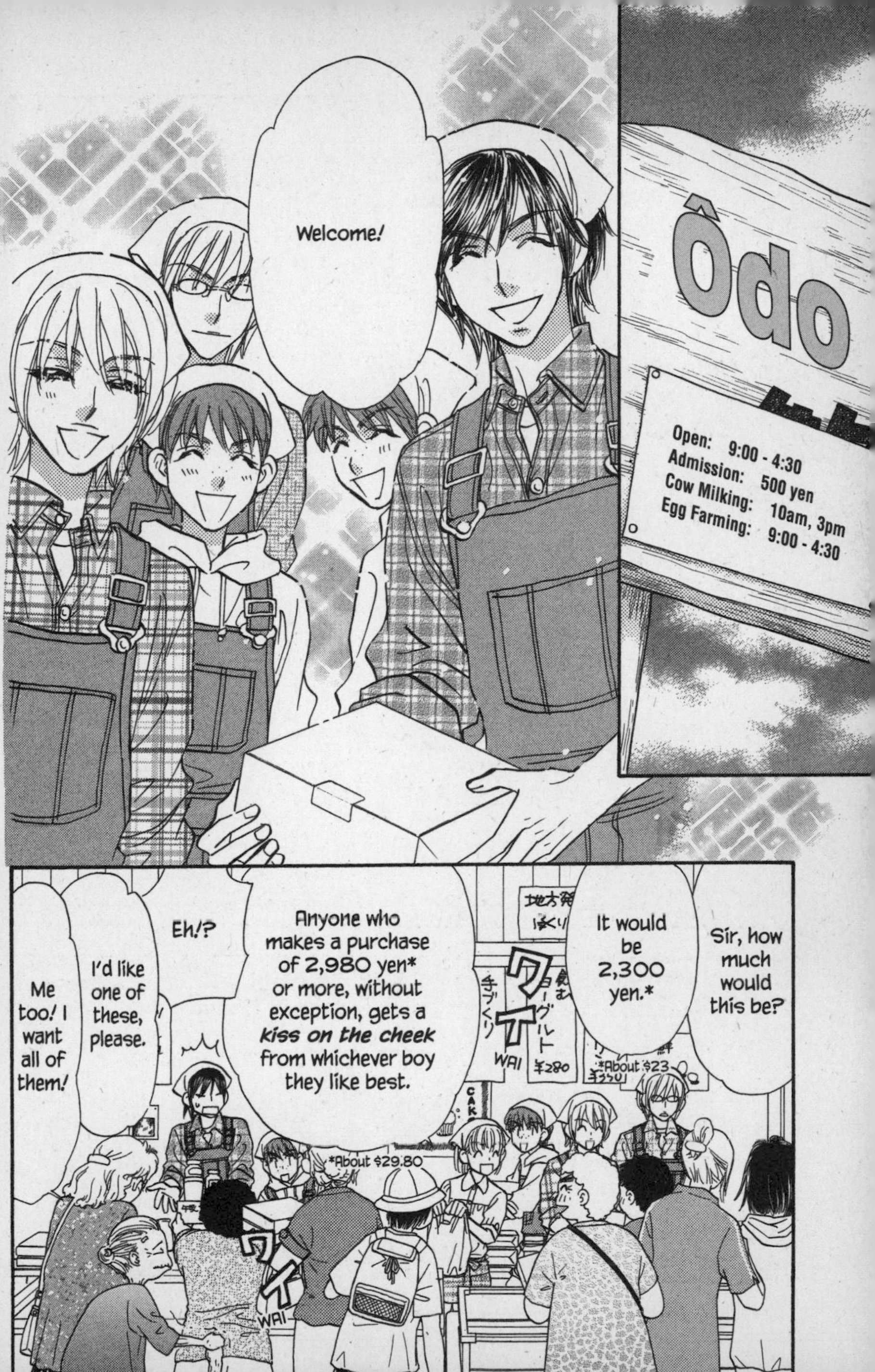
Ôdo
Open: 9:00 - 4:30
Admission: 500 yen
Cow Milking: 10am, 3pm
Egg Farming: 9:00 - 4:30
Welcome!
Sir, how much would this be?
It would be 2,300 yen.*
*About $23
ワイ
WAI
Anyone who makes a purchase of 2,980 yen* or more, without exception, gets a ***kiss on the cheek*** from whichever boy they like best.
*About $29.80
Eh!?
I'd like one of these, please.
Me too! I want all of them!
ワイ
WAI

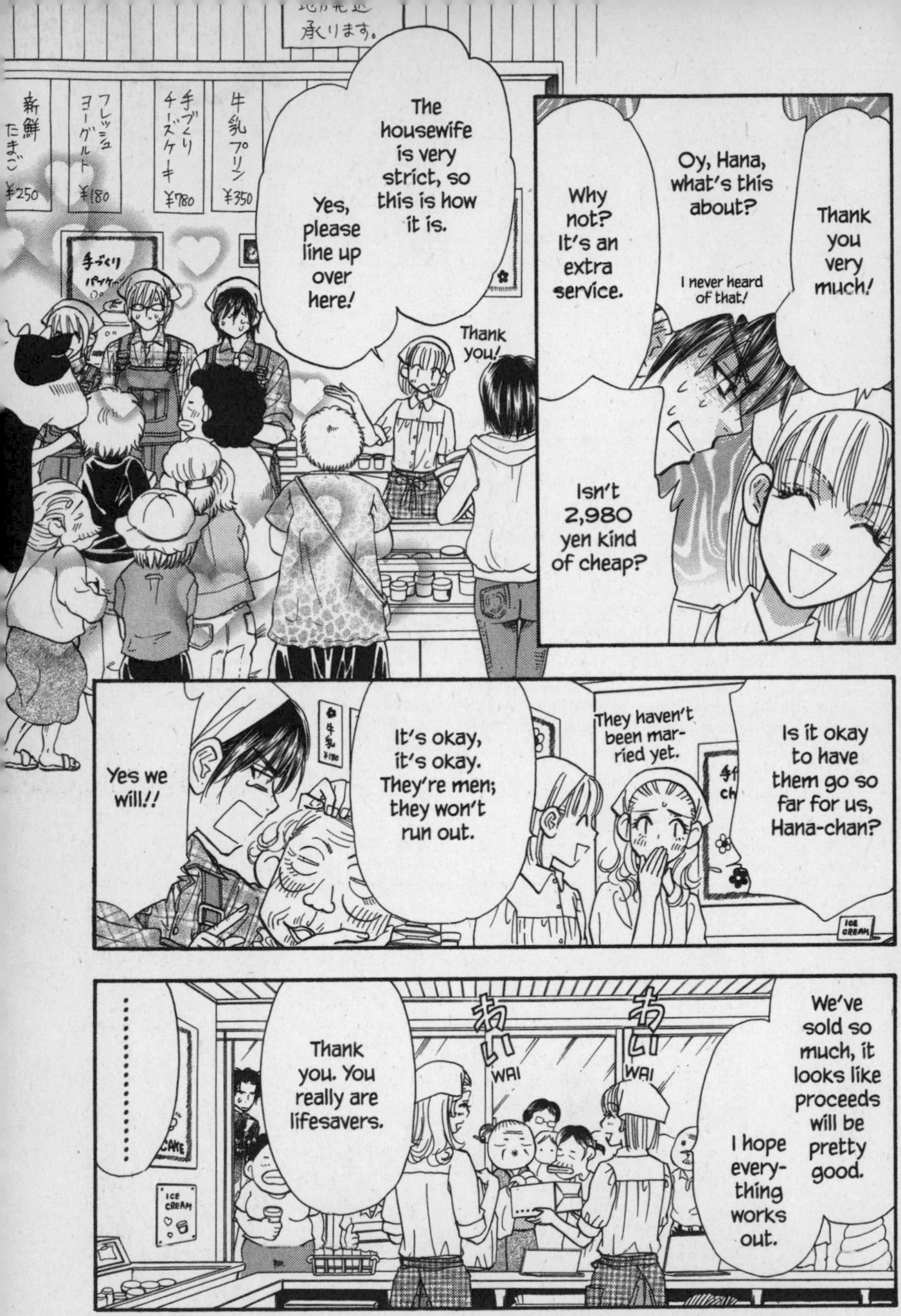
Thank you very much!
Oy, Hana, what's this about?
I never heard of that!
Why not? It's an extra service.
Isn't 2,980 yen kind of cheap?
牛乳プリン ¥350
手づくりチーズケーキ ¥780
フレッシュヨーグルト ¥180
新鮮たまご ¥250
The housewife is very strict, so this is how it is.
Yes, please line up over here!
Thank you!
Is it okay to have them go so far for us, Hana-chan?
They haven't been married yet.
It's okay, it's okay. They're men; they won't run out.
Yes we will!!
We've sold so much, it looks like proceeds will be pretty good.
I hope everything works out.
わい WAI
わい WAI
Thank you. You really are lifesavers.
……

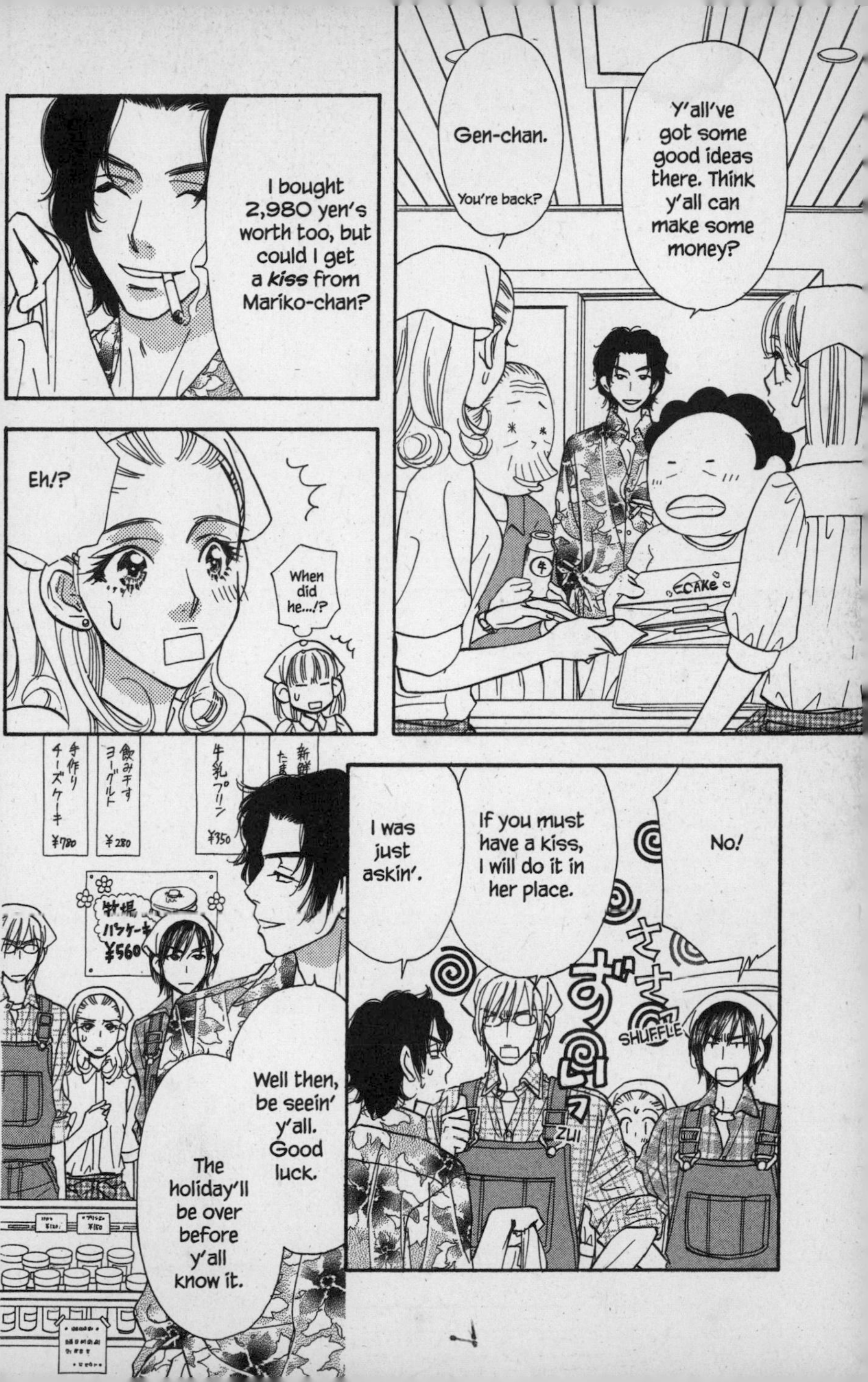
Y'all've got some good ideas there. Think y'all can make some money?
Gen-chan.
You're back?
CAKE
I bought 2,980 yen's worth too, but could I get a *kiss* from Mariko-chan?
Eh!?
When did he...!?
No!
If you must have a kiss, I will do it in her place.
I was just askin'.
SHUFFLE
ZUI
牛乳プリン ¥350
飲みやすヨーグルト ¥280
手作りチーズケーキ ¥780
牧場パンケーキ ¥560
Well then, be seein' y'all. Good luck.
The holiday'll be over before y'all know it.

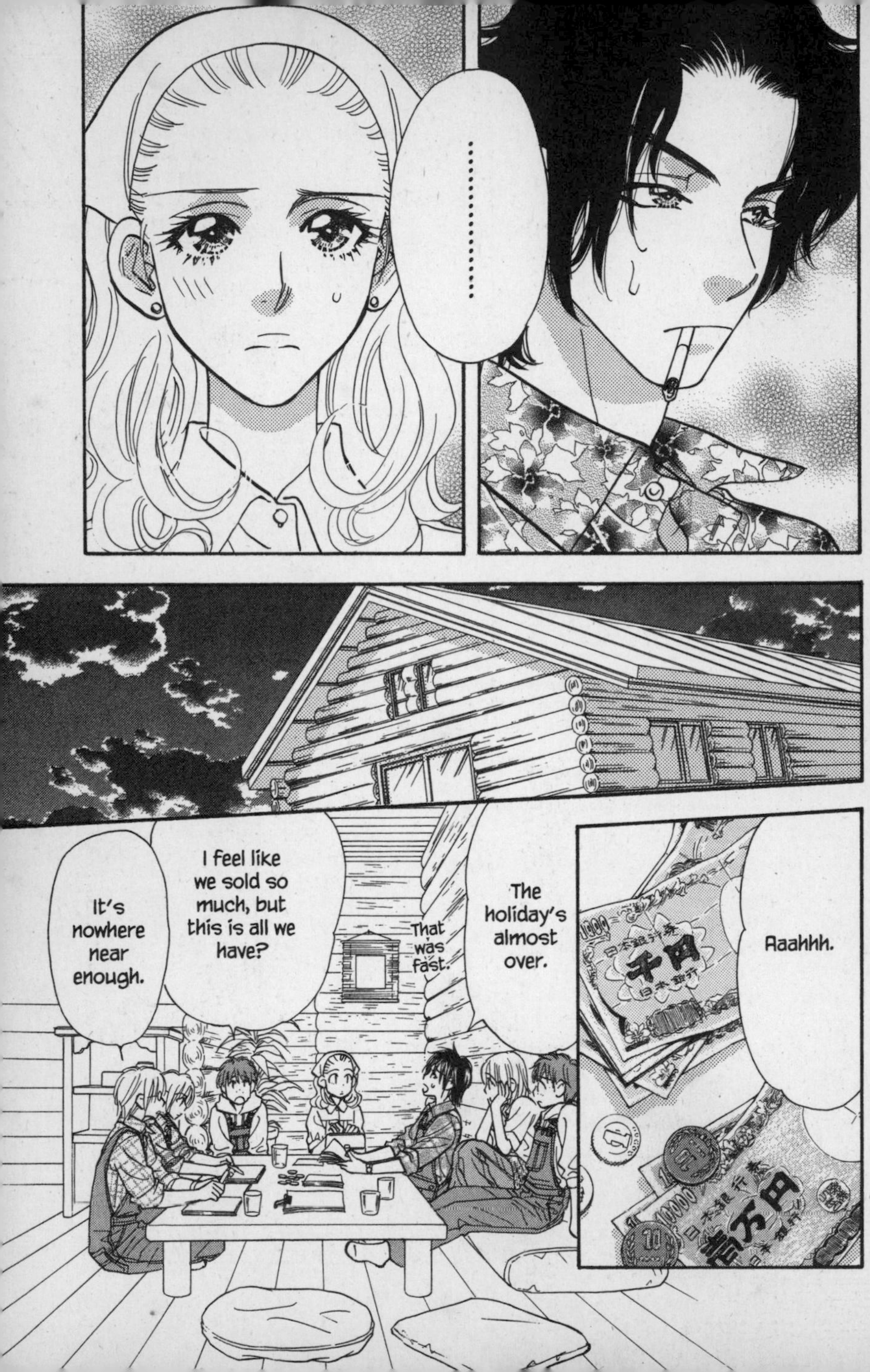
......
Aaahhh.
The holiday's almost over.
That was fast.
I feel like we sold so much, but this is all we have?
It's nowhere near enough.

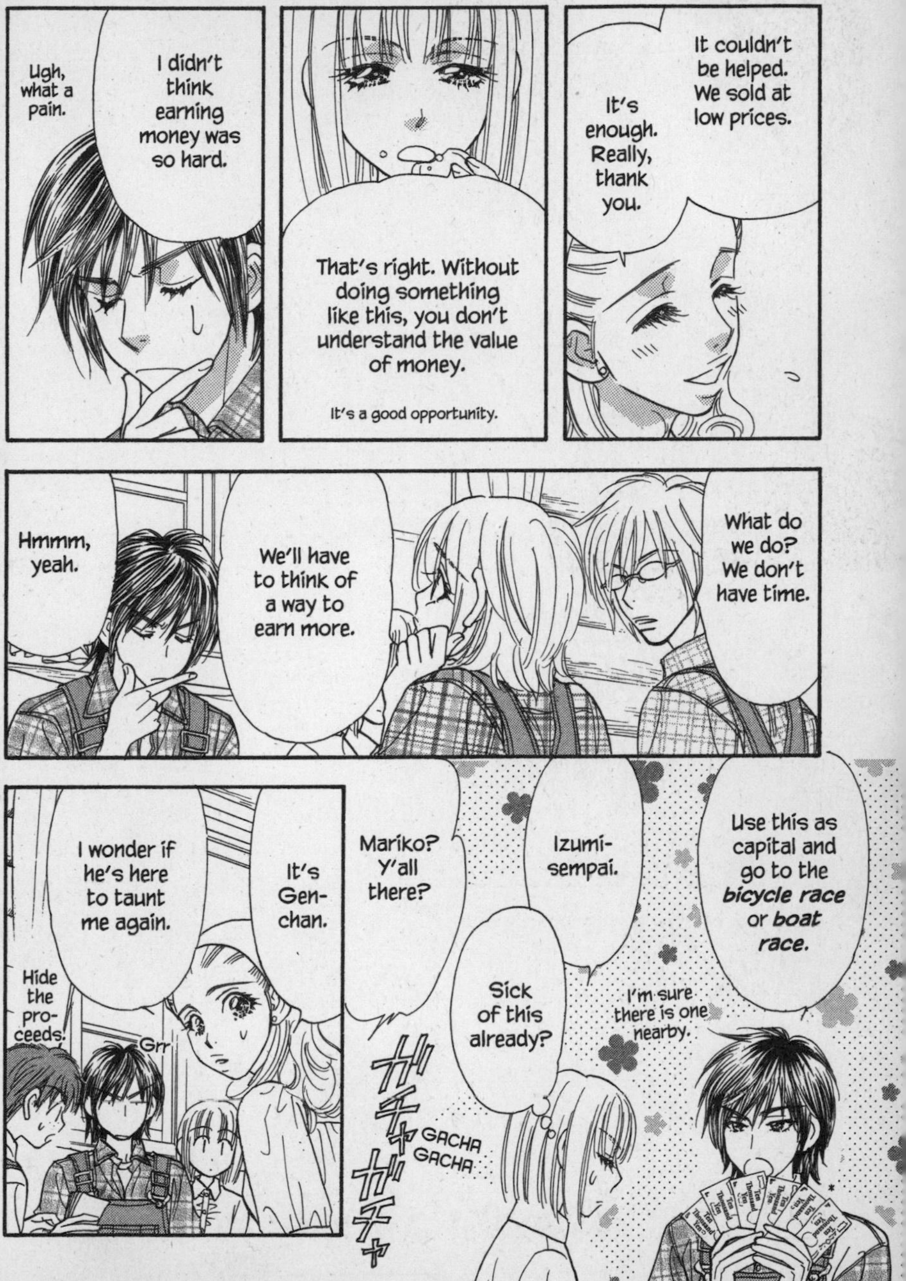
It couldn't be helped. We sold at low prices.
It's enough. Really, thank you.
That's right. Without doing something like this, you don't understand the value of money.
It's a good opportunity.
I didn't think earning money was so hard.
Ugh, what a pain.
What do we do? We don't have time.
We'll have to think of a way to earn more.
Hmmm, yeah.
Use this as capital and go to the *bicycle race* or *boat race*.
I'm sure there is one nearby.
Izumi-sempai.
Sick of this already?
Mariko? Y'all there?
ガチャガチャ
GACHA GACHA
It's Gen-chan.
I wonder if he's here to taunt me again.
Hide the proceeds.
Grr

*About $100 each

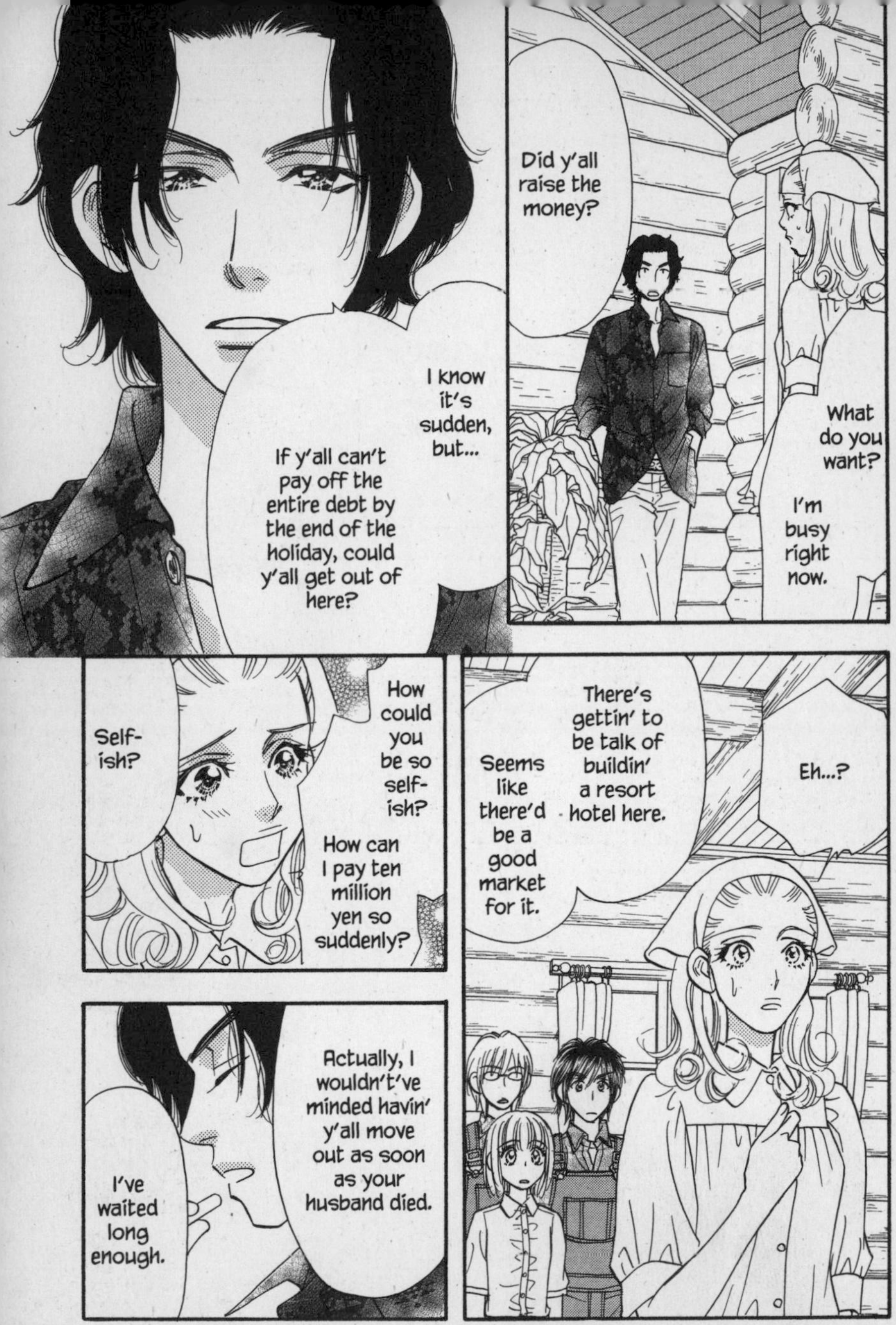
Did y'all raise the money?
What do you want?
I'm busy right now.
I know it's sudden, but...
If y'all can't pay off the entire debt by the end of the holiday, could y'all get out of here?
Eh...?
There's gettin' to be talk of buildin' a resort hotel here.
Seems like there'd be a good market for it.
How could you be so self-ish?
How can I pay ten million yen so suddenly?
Self-ish?
Actually, I wouldn't've minded havin' y'all move out as soon as your husband died.
I've waited long enough.

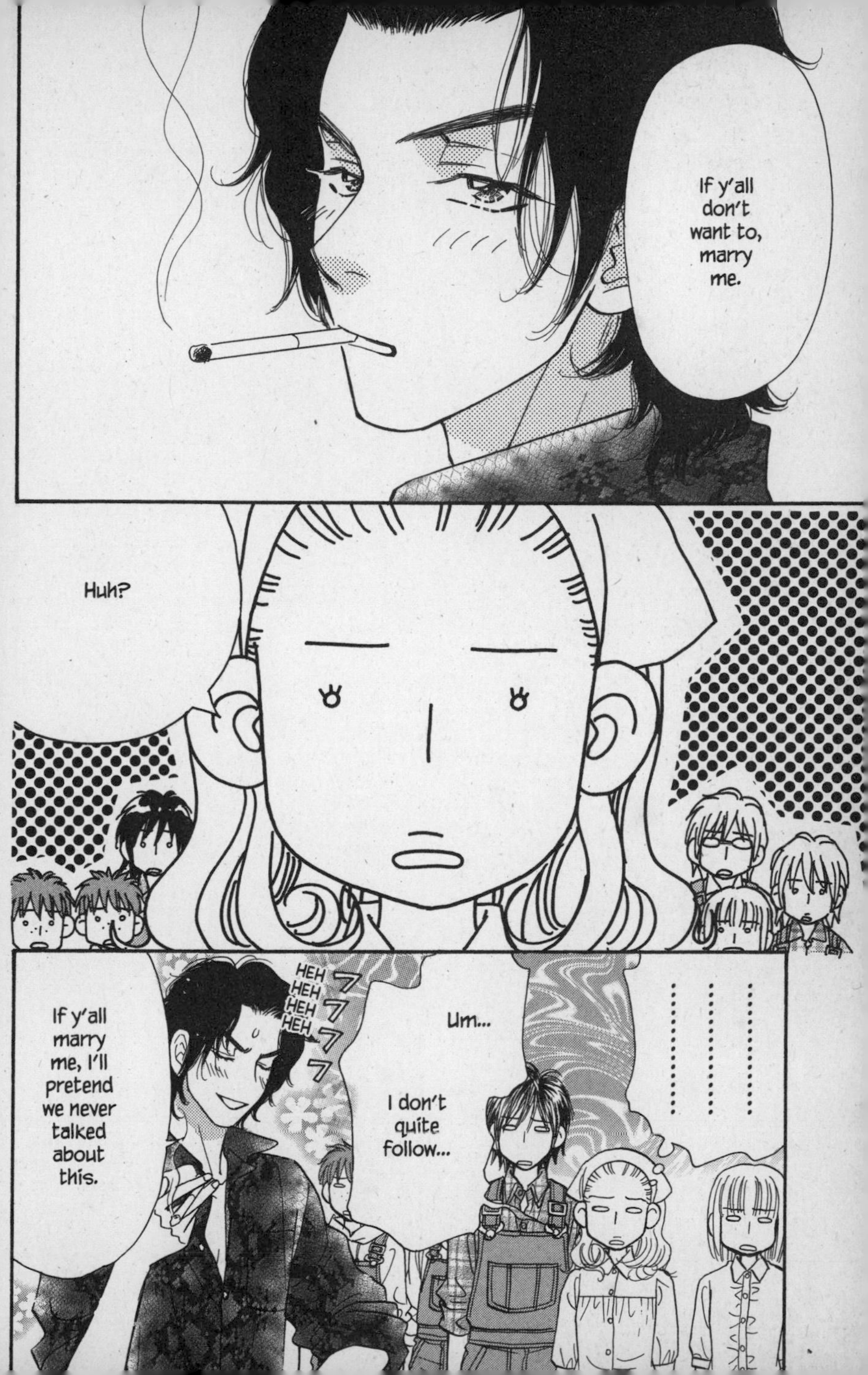
If y'all don't want to, marry me.
Huh?
......
Um...
I don't quite follow...
HEH HEH HEH HEH
If y'all marry me, I'll pretend we never talked about this.

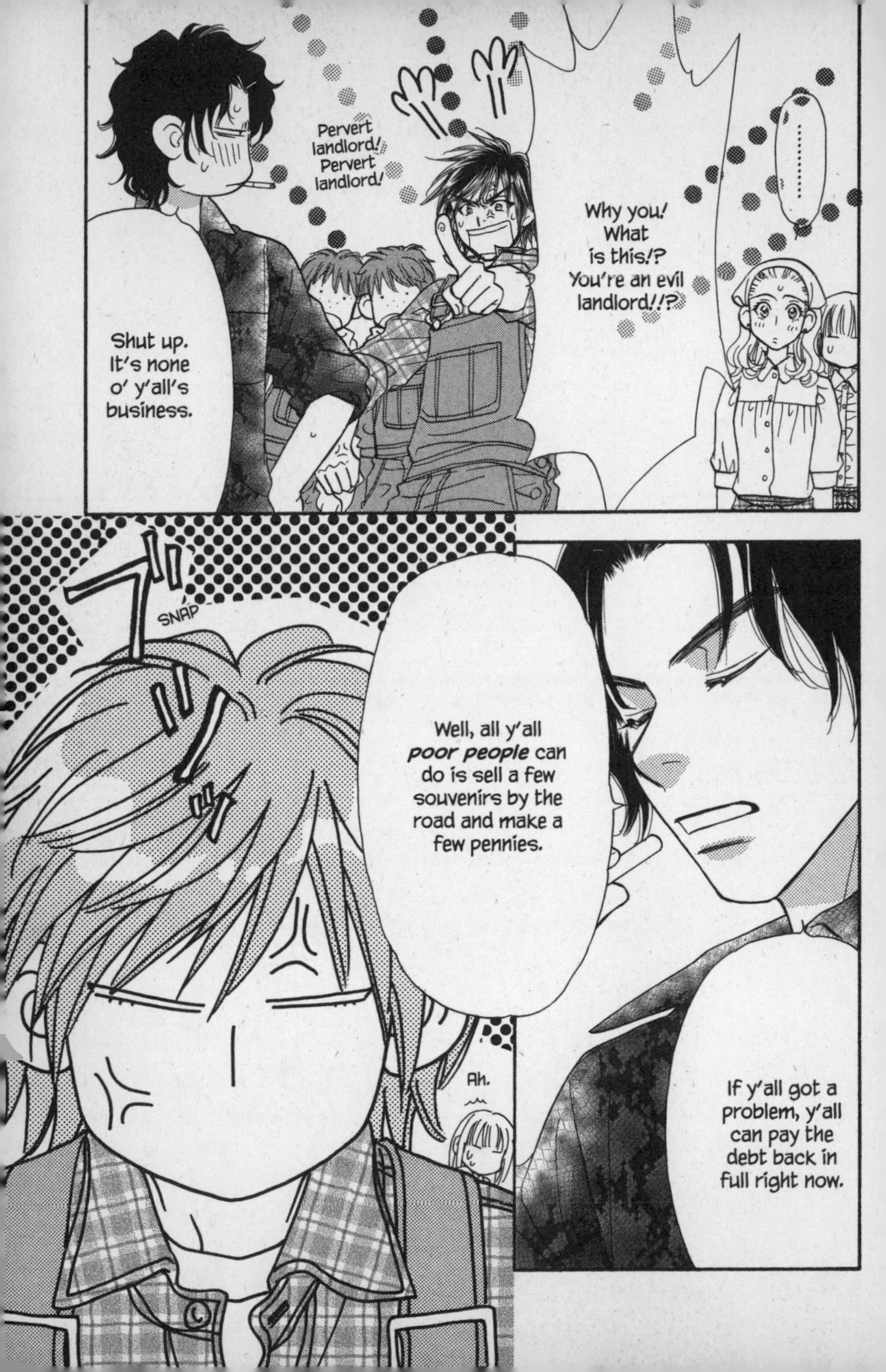
......
Why you! What is this!? You're an evil landlord!!?
Pervert landlord! Pervert landlord!
Shut up. It's none o' y'all's business.
Well, all y'all *poor people* can do is sell a few souvenirs by the road and make a few pennies.
If y'all got a problem, y'all can pay the debt back in full right now.
SNAP
Ah.

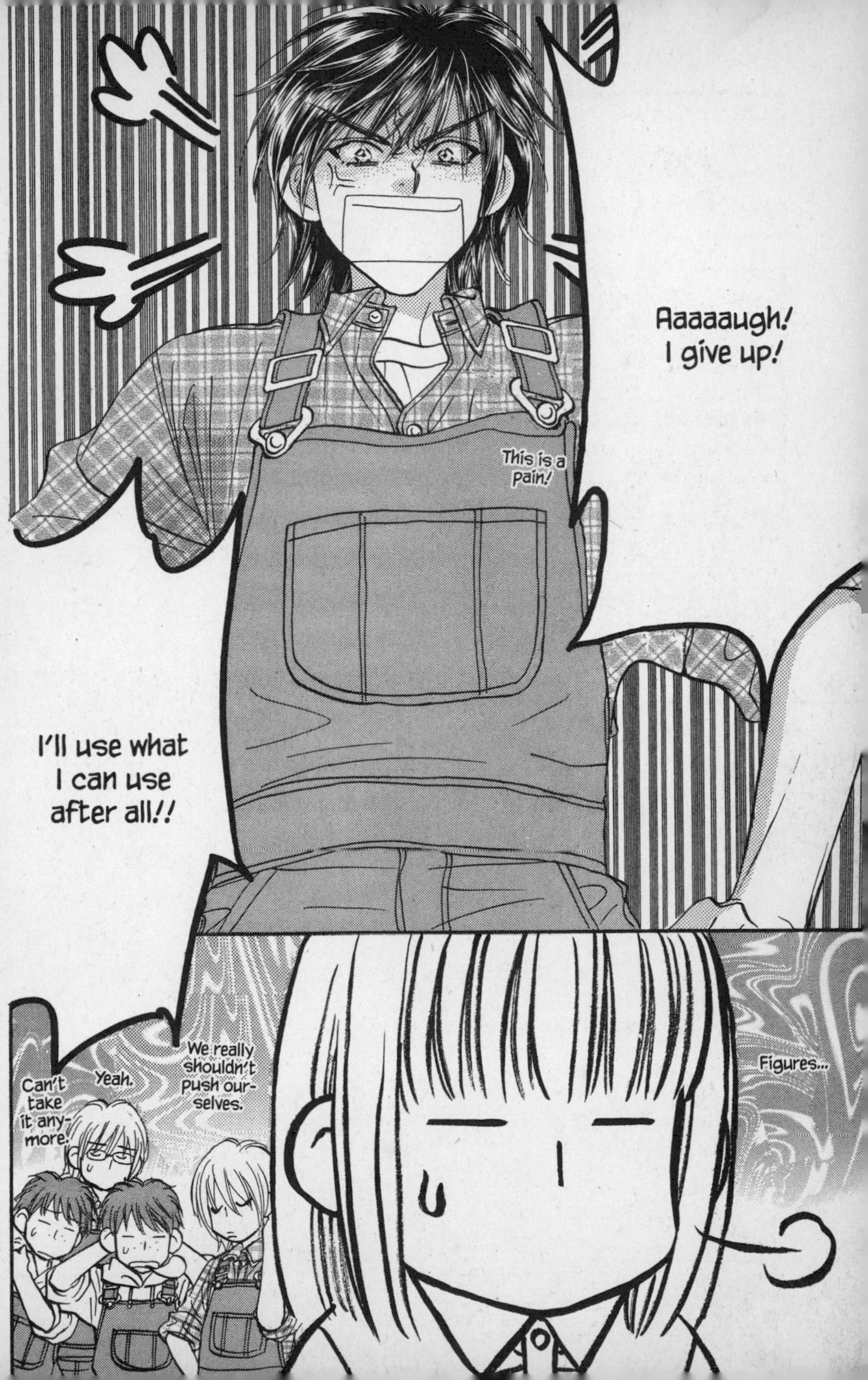
Aaaaaugh! I give up!
This is a pain!
I'll use what I can use after all!!
Figures...
We really shouldn't push our-selves.
Yeah.
Can't take it any-more.

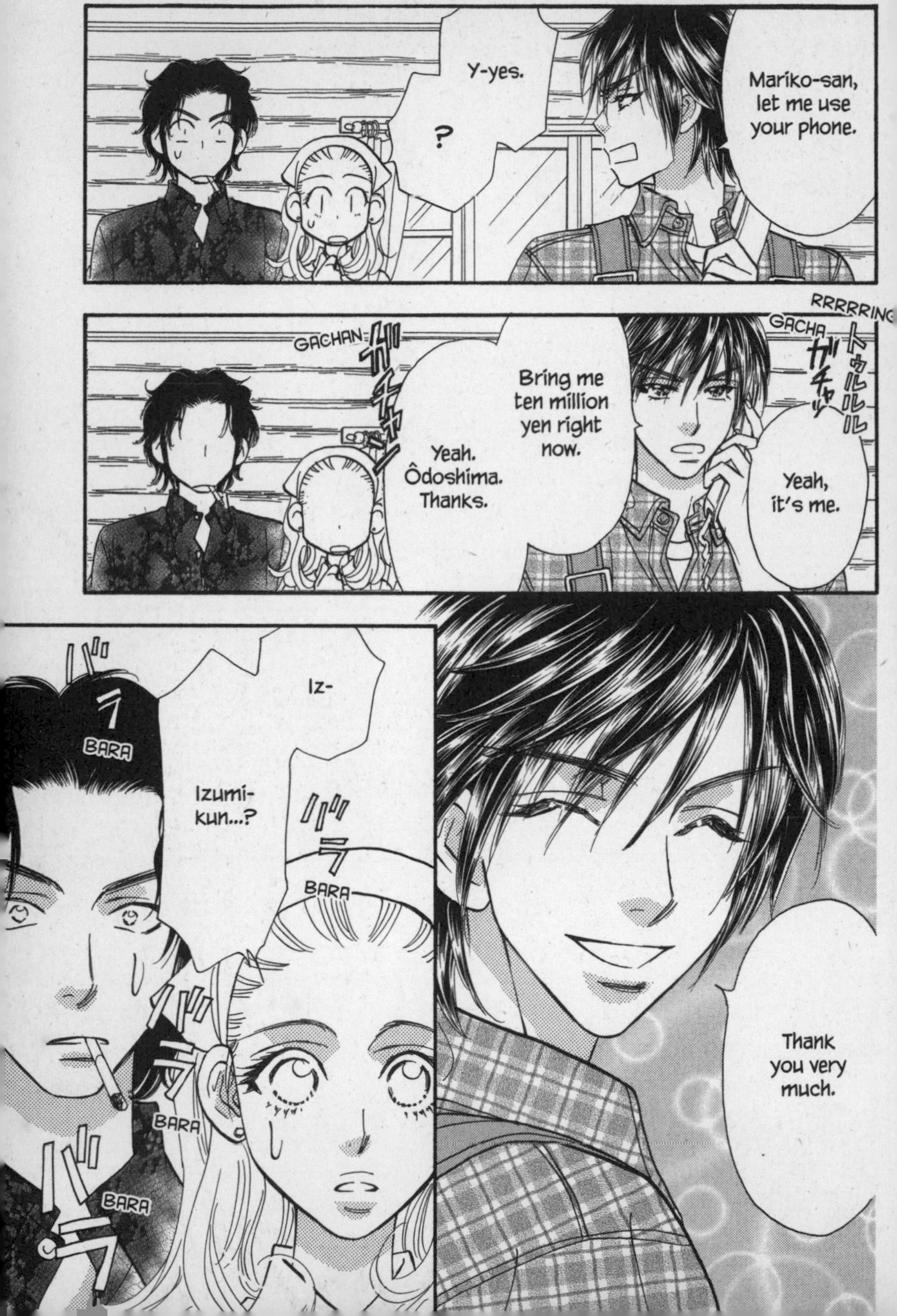
Mariko-san, let me use your phone.
Y-yes.
?
RRRRRING
GACHA
Yeah, it's me.
Bring me ten million yen right now.
Yeah. Ôdoshima. Thanks.
GACHAN
Thank you very much.
Iz-
Izumi-kun...?
BARA
BARA
BARA
BARA

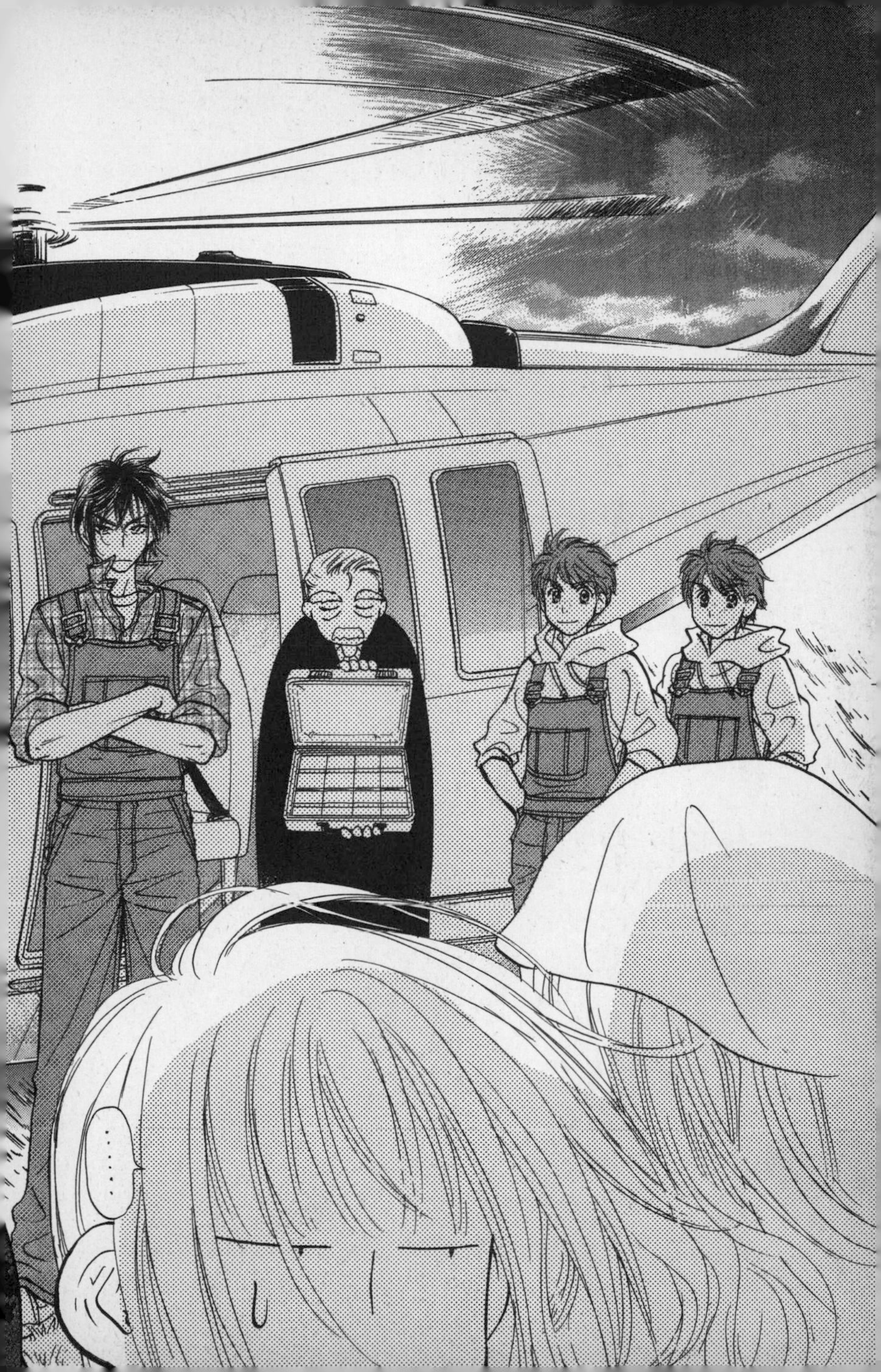
……

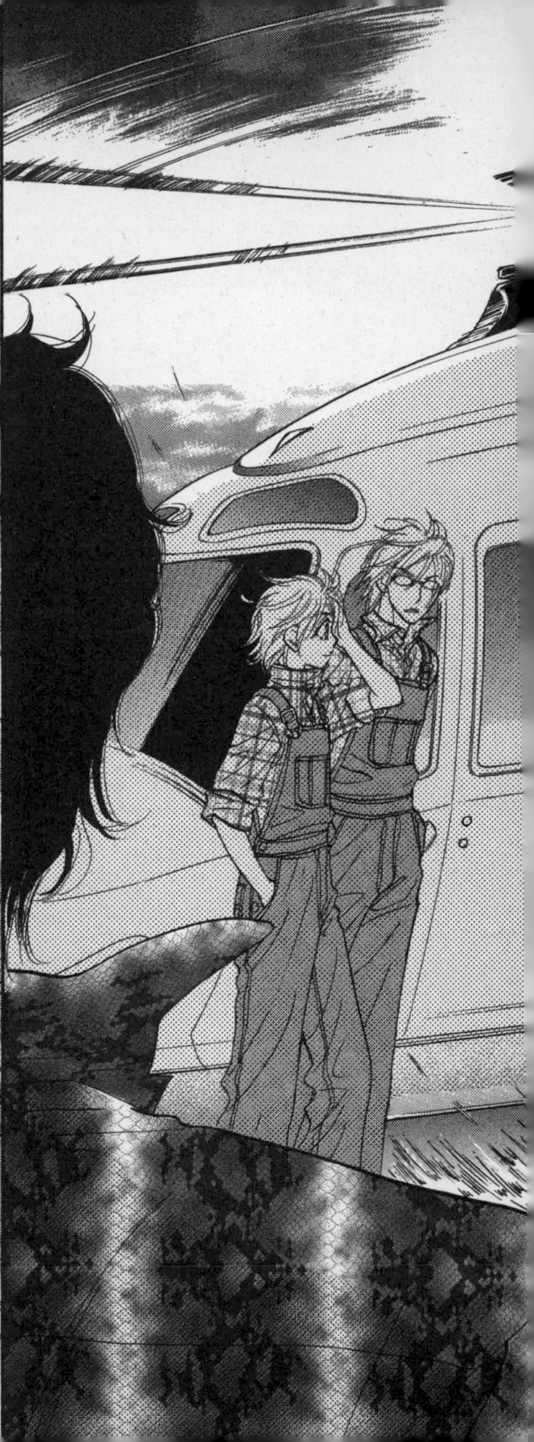
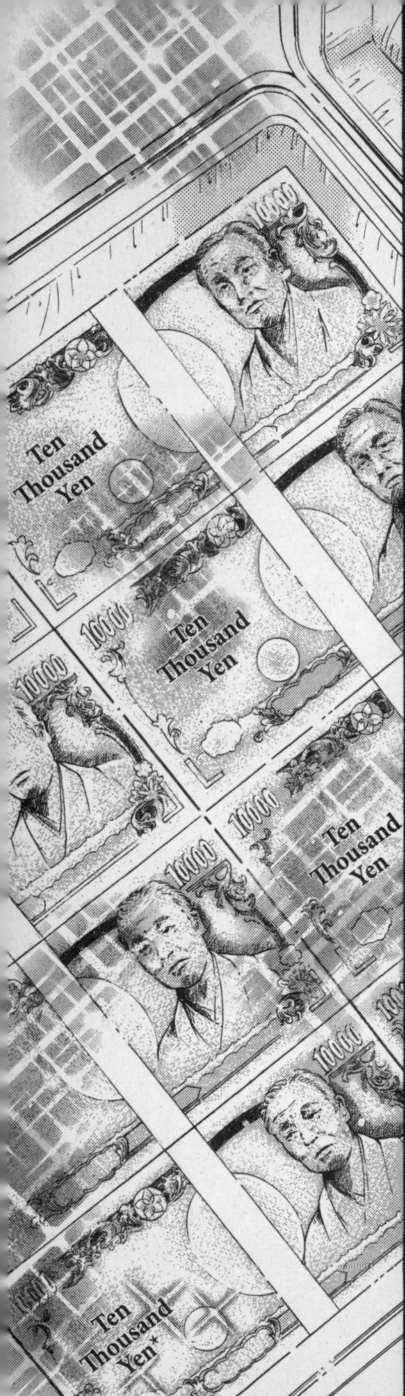
10000
Ten Thousand Yen
Ten Thousand Yen
Ten Thousand Yen
Ten Thousand Yen*
*About $100

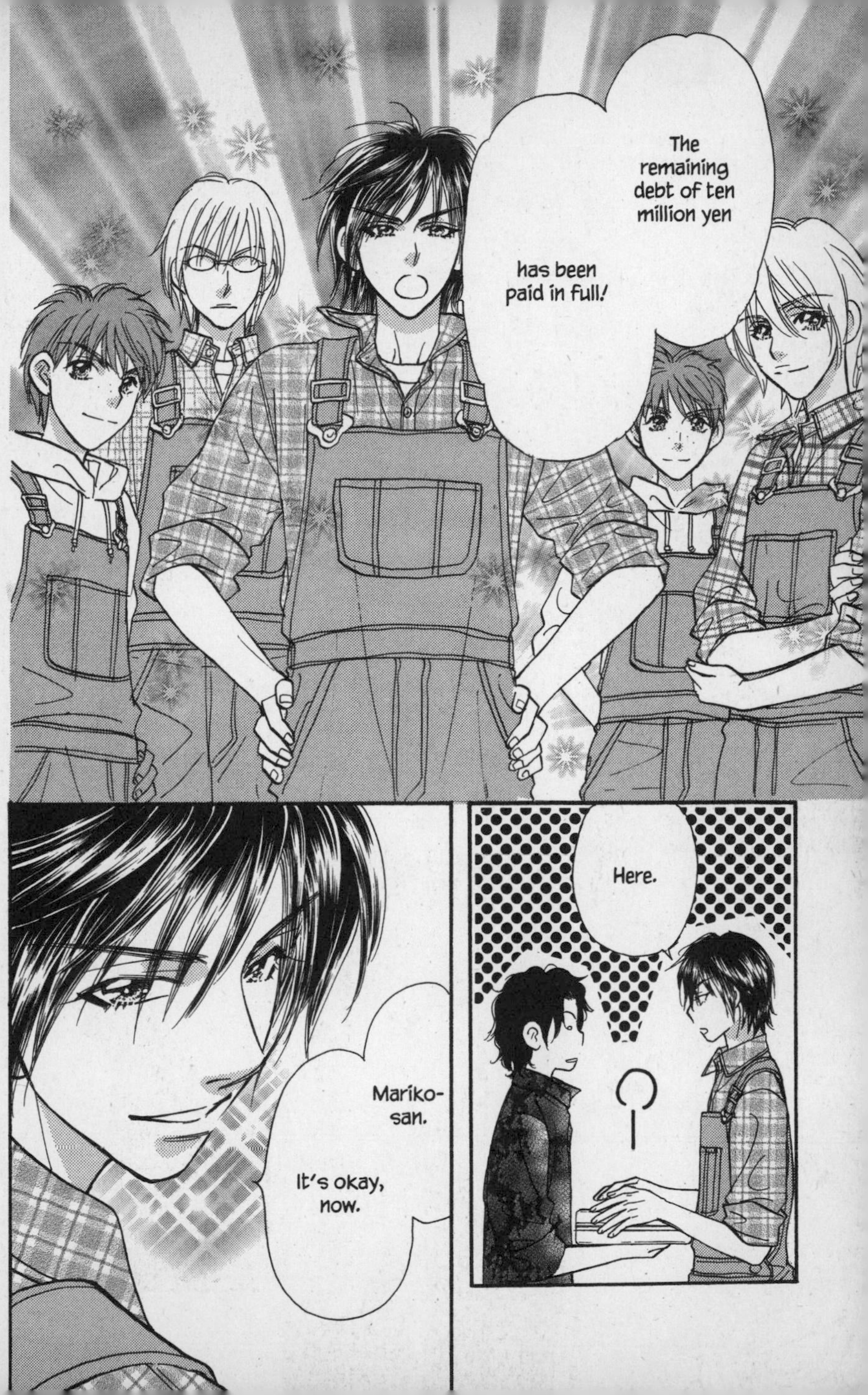
The remaining debt of ten million yen
has been paid in full!
Here.
Mariko-san.
It's okay, now.

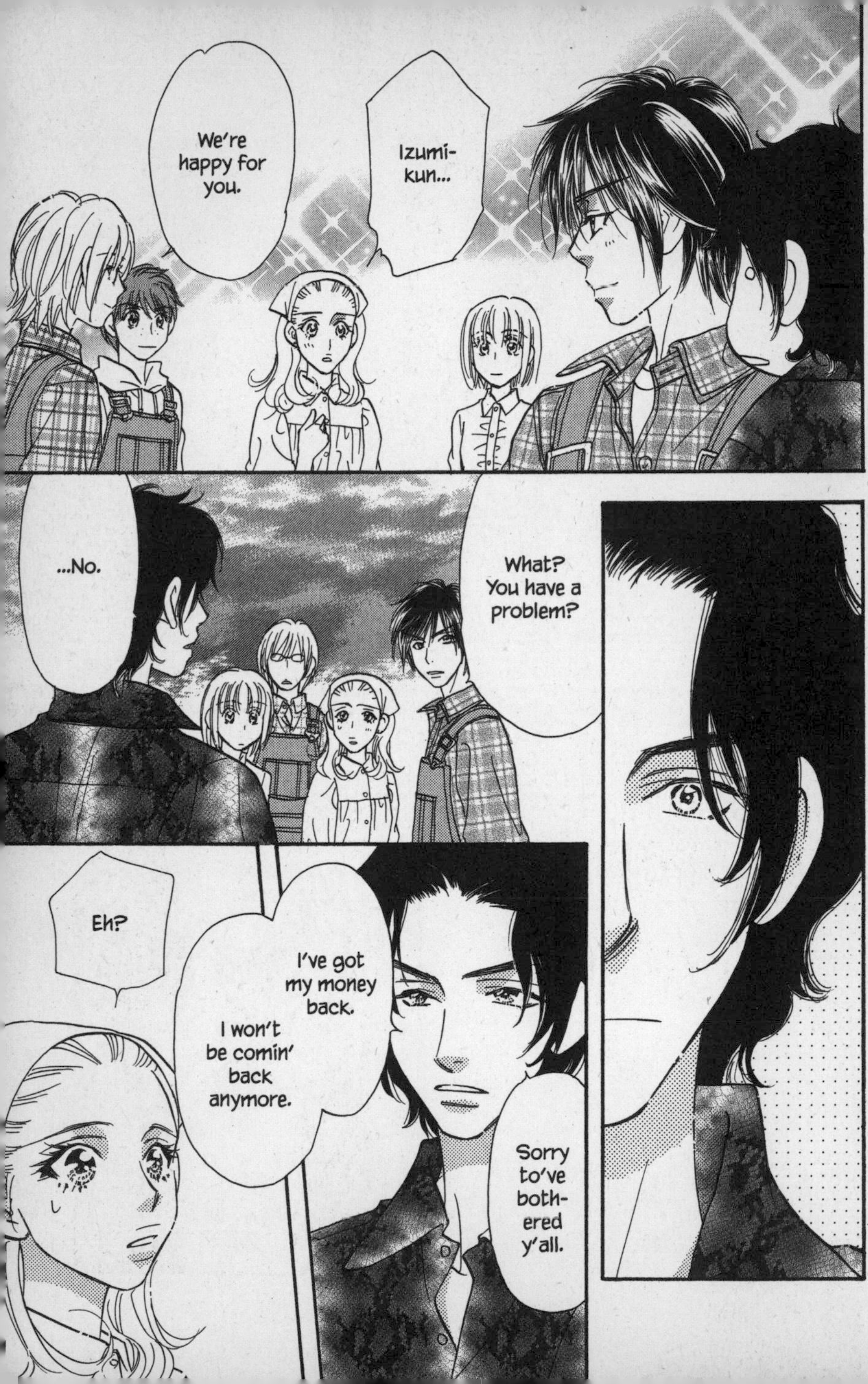
Izumi-kun...
We're happy for you.
What? You have a problem?
...No.
I've got my money back. I won't be comin' back anymore.
Sorry to've bothered y'all.
Eh?

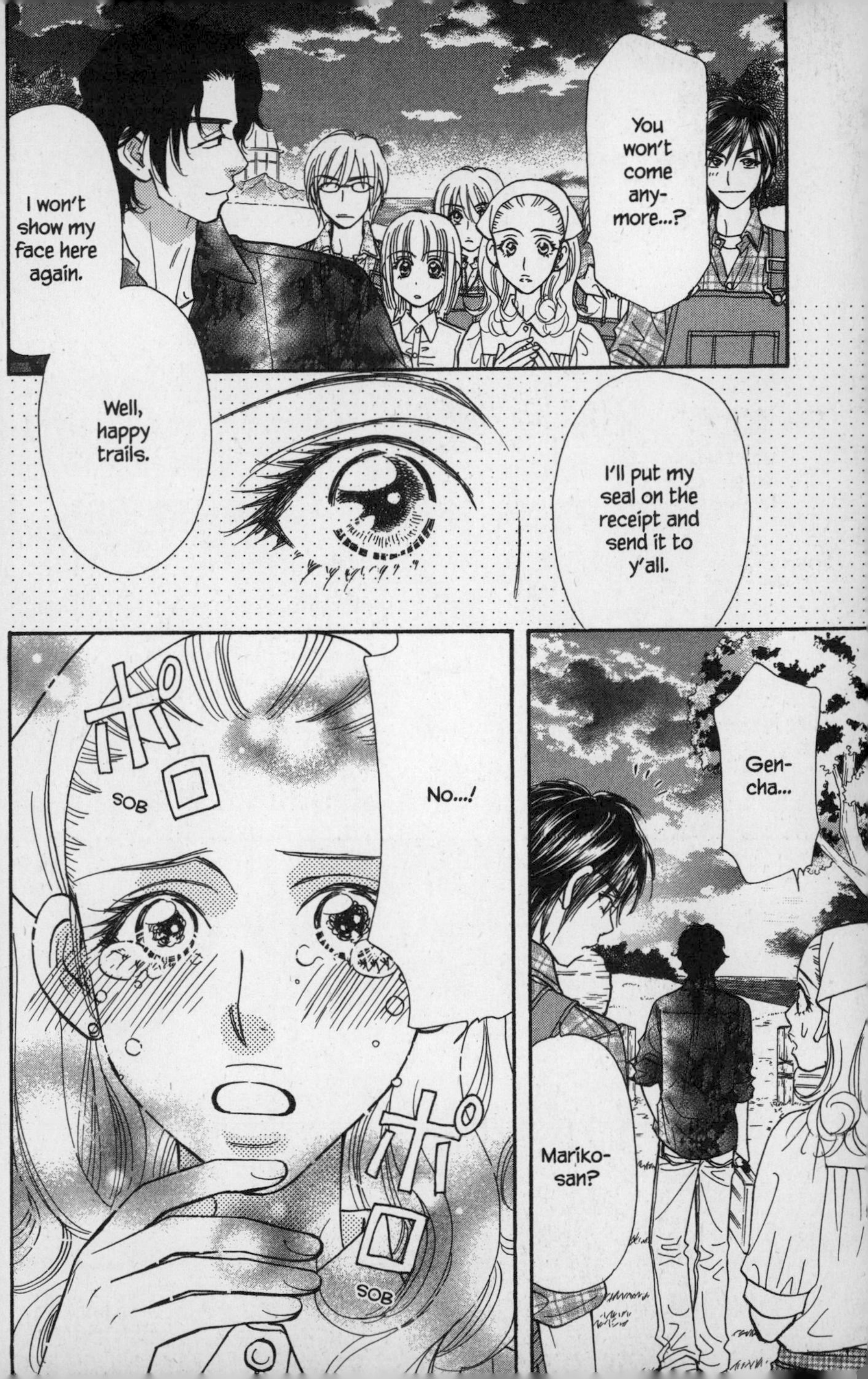
You won't come any-more...?
I won't show my face here again.
I'll put my seal on the receipt and send it to y'all.
Well, happy trails.
Gen-cha...
Mariko-san?
No...!
ポロ
SOB
ポロ
SOB

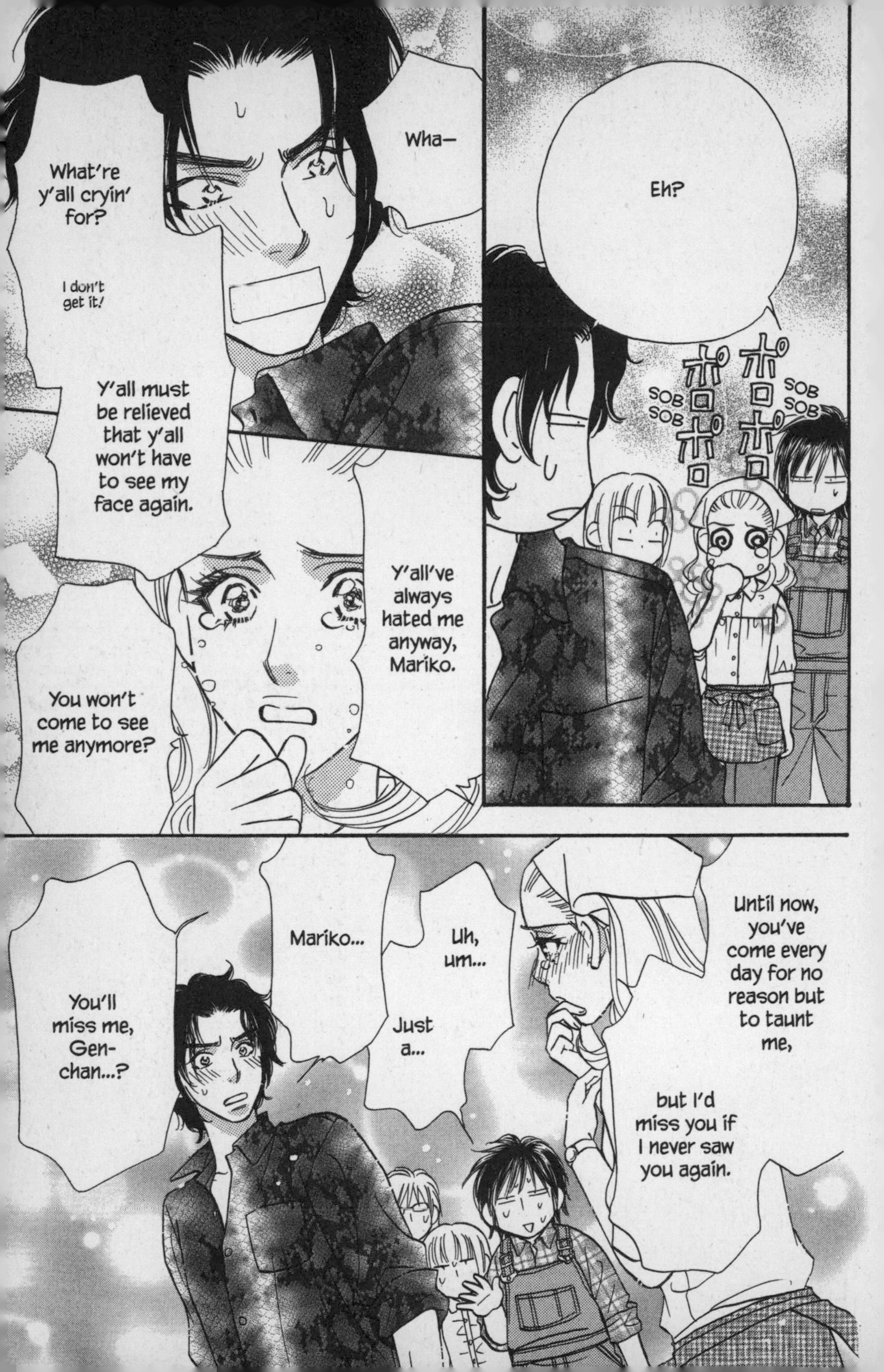
Eh?
SOB SOB
ポロポロ
ポロポロ
SOB SOB
Wha—
What're y'all cryin' for?
I don't get it!
Y'all must be relieved that y'all won't have to see my face again.
Y'all've always hated me anyway, Mariko.
You won't come to see me anymore?
Until now, you've come every day for no reason but to taunt me,
but I'd miss you if I never saw you again.
Uh, um...
Just a...
Mariko...
You'll miss me, Gen-chan...?

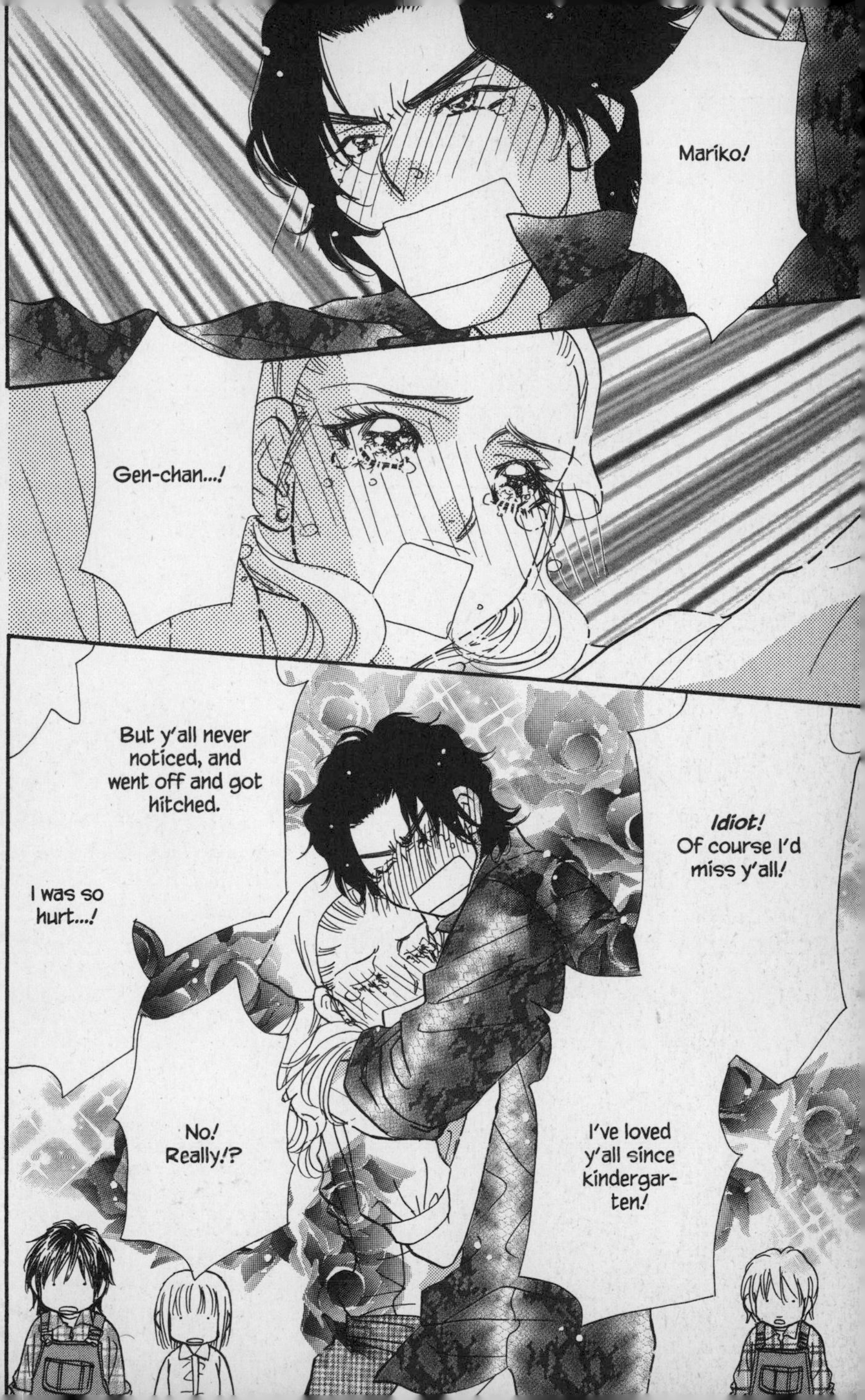
Mariko!
Gen-chan...!
Idiot! Of course I'd miss y'all!
I've loved y'all since kindergar-ten!
But y'all never noticed, and went off and got hitched.
I was so hurt...!
No! Really!?

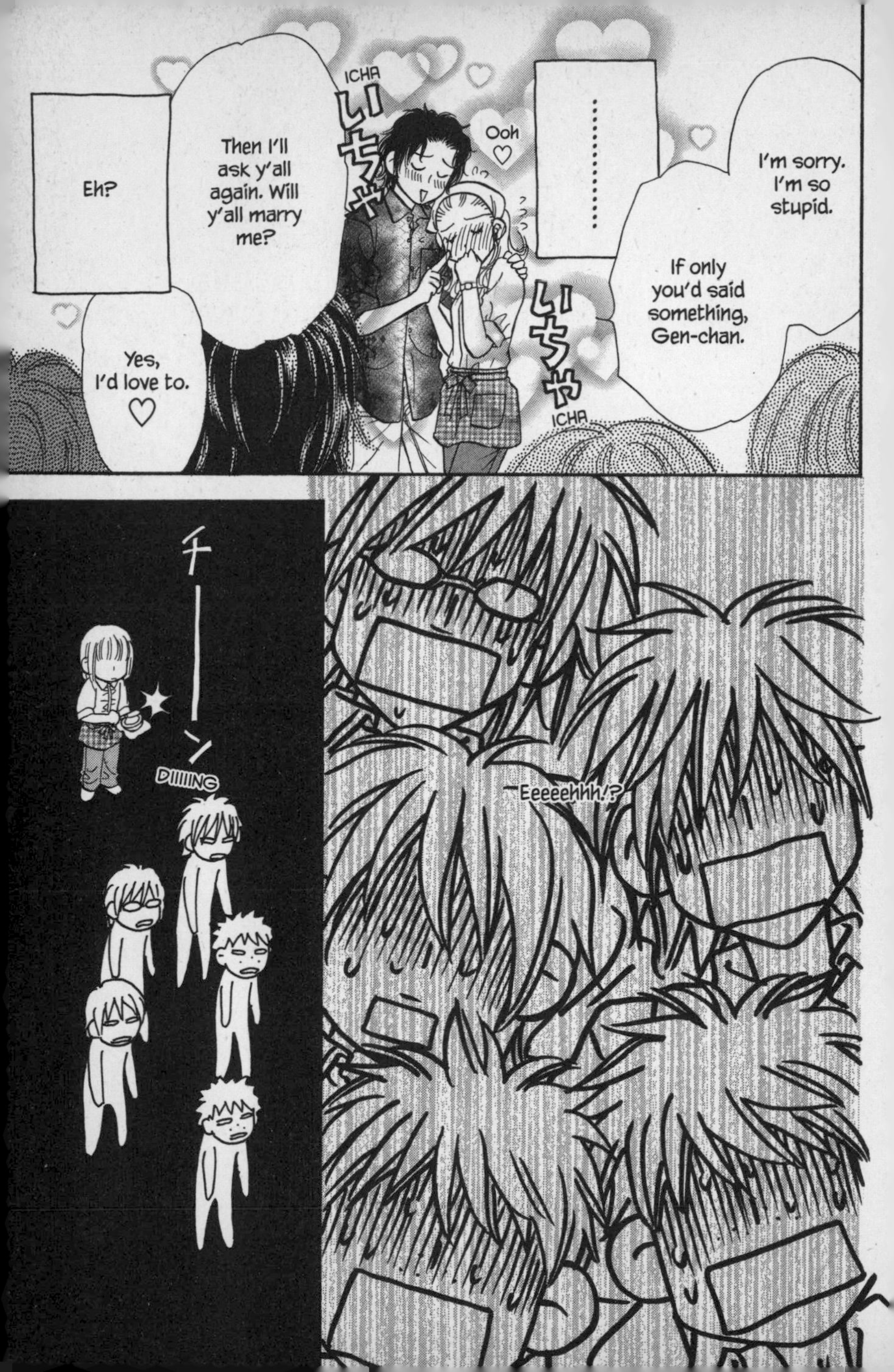
I'm sorry. I'm so stupid.
If only you'd said something, Gen-chan.
……
いちゃ
ICHA
Ooh ♡
いちゃ
ICHA
Then I'll ask y'all again. Will y'all marry me?
Eh?
Yes, I'd love to. ♡
Eeeeehhh!?
チーン
DIIIING

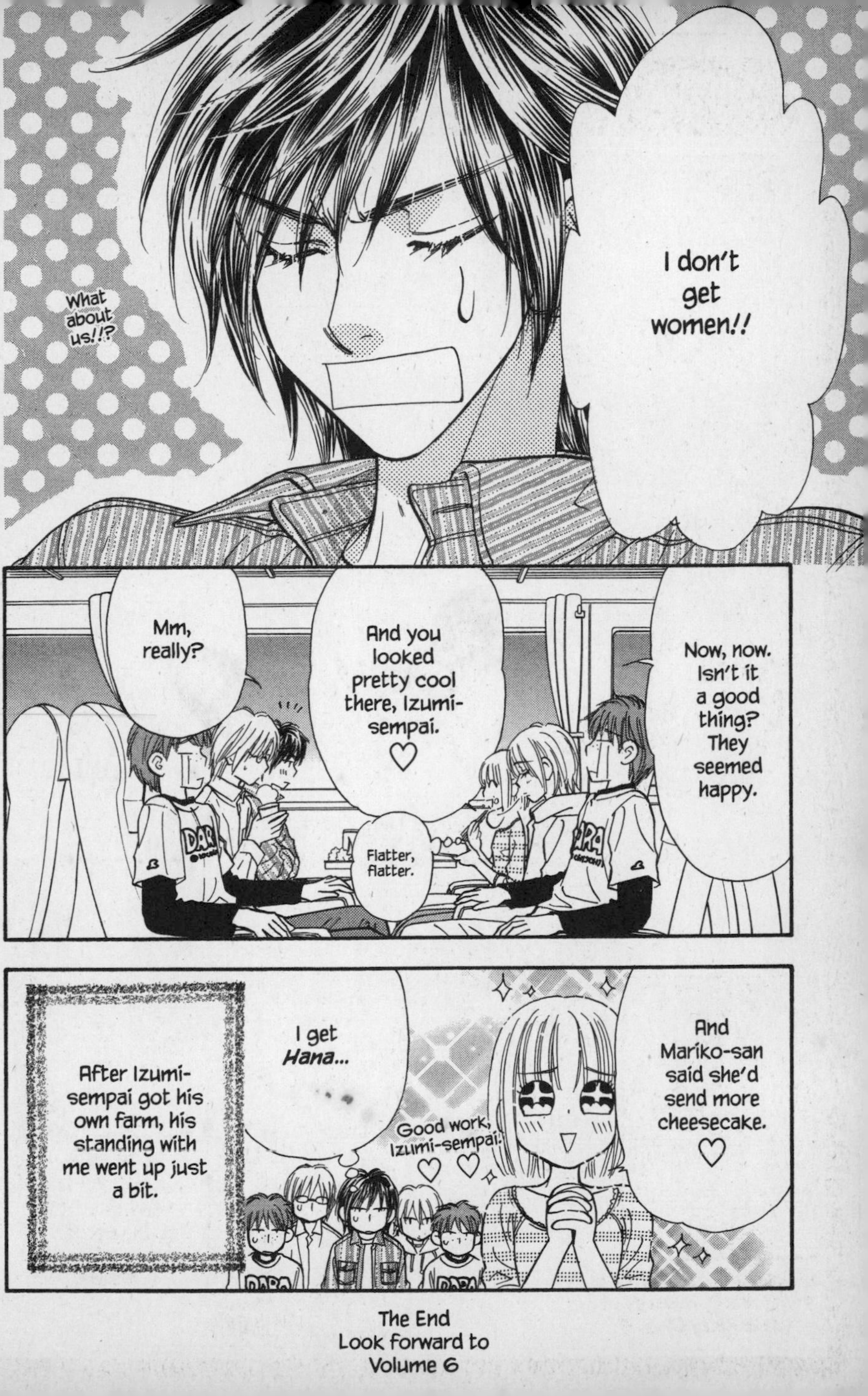
I don't get women!!
What about us!!?
Now, now. Isn't it a good thing? They seemed happy.
And you looked pretty cool there, Izumi-sempai. ♡
Flatter, flatter.
Mm, really?
And Mariko-san said she'd send more cheesecake. ♡
Good work, Izumi-sempai! ♡ ♡
I get *Hana*...
After Izumi-sempai got his own farm, his standing with me went up just a bit.

The End
Look forward to
Volume 6

Hockey Club ♨ Character Profile No.4

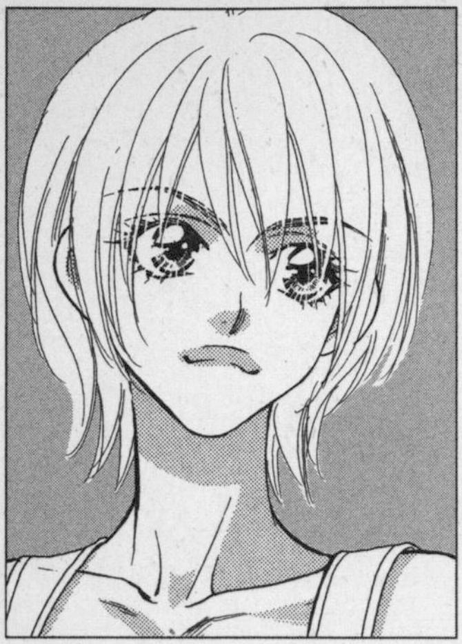

Natsuki Serizawa

Birthday	November 9th
Blood type	AB
Height	175 cm (about 5'9")
Hobbies	Reading, watching movies, bathhouse tours
Special skill	Feeding animals, making tea
Favorite food	Raw food
Least favorite food	He'll eat anything
Favorite subjects	Math, biology
Least favorite subjects	Nothing in particular
Favorite type of girl	Smart girls
Other (notes)	Quick to undress

Motto

Be open in relationships

♨ Famous Scene Selections ♨

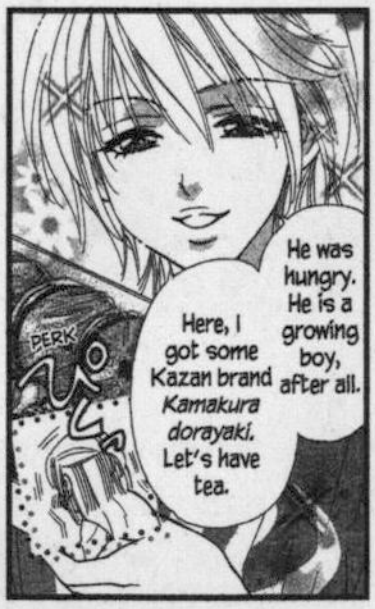
He was hungry. He is a growing boy, after all.
Here, I got some Kazan brand *Kamakura dorayaki.* Let's have tea.
PERK

▲ For some reason, he has been appointed as the person in charge of Hana's snacks.

▼ Despite his feminine appearance, it would seem he possesses something quite admirable....

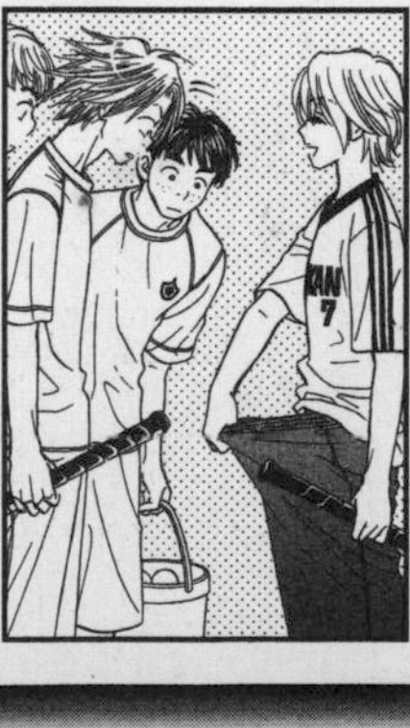

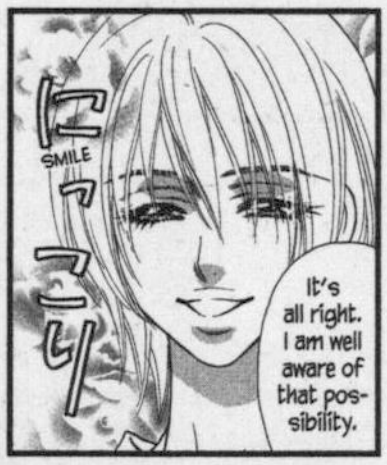
SMILE
It's all right. I am well aware of that possibility.

▲ With the face of an angel, he speaks the words of a devil....

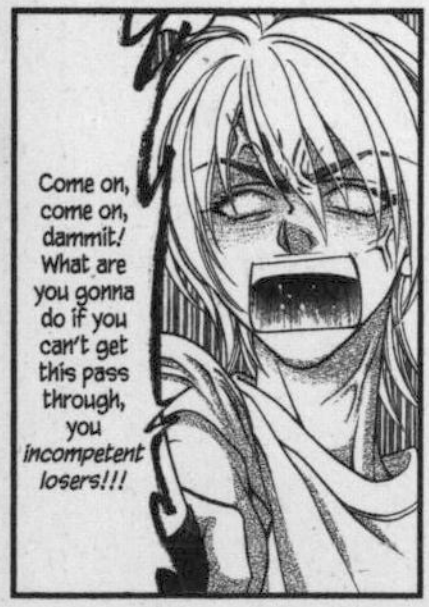
Come on, come on, dammit! What are you gonna do if you can't get this pass through, you *incompetent losers!!!*

▲ Natsuki is actually the most manly member of the Hockey Club. ♥

Find the differences. ♪ Can you tell them apart!?

Hockey Club ♨ Character Profile No.5

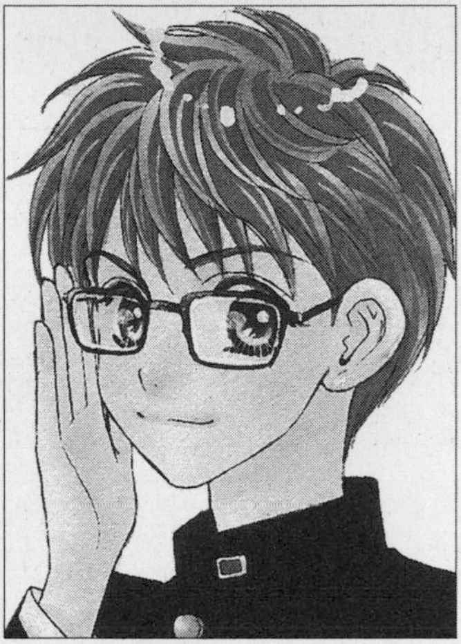

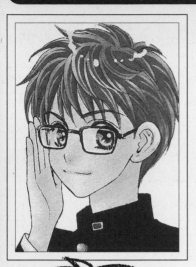

Kinta Ayuhara

Birthday	June 6th
Blood type	O
Height	169.1 cm (about 5'6.6")
Hobbies	Traveling, trying food at various restaurants, hockey
Special skill	Imitating Ginta
Favorite food	Hashed meat with rice
Least favorite food	Insects
Favorite subjects	P.E., English
Least favorite subject	Chinese literature
Favorite type of girl	Cute, laid-back girls
Other (notes)	He hates being mistaken for his younger brother!

Motto

A man's gotta have guts!

♨ Famous Scene Selections ♨

▼ He's the older brother.

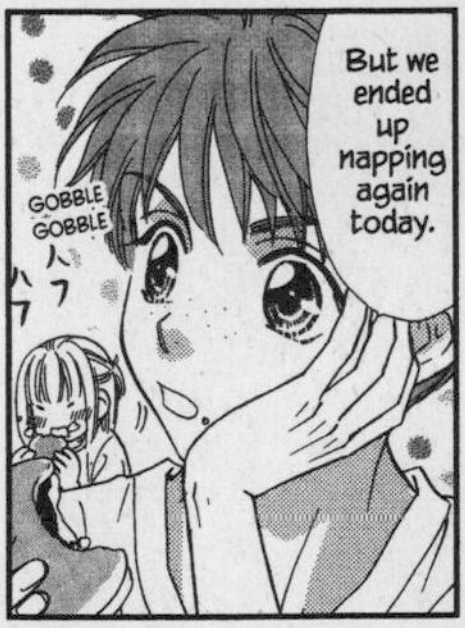
But we ended up napping again today.
GOBBLE GOBBLE

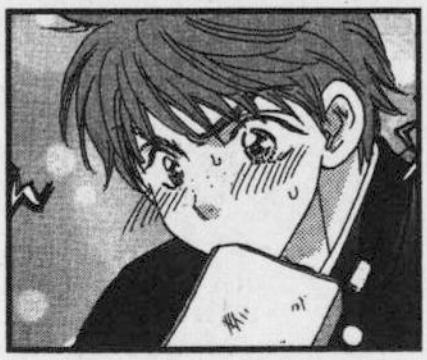

▲ The older brother's first love is...

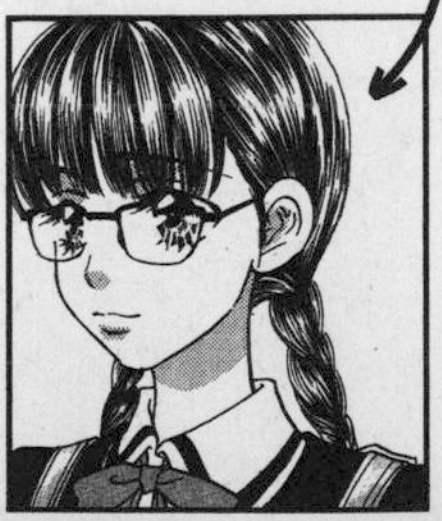

◀ Rin-chan from St. Johannes Girls Academy.

▼ He transformed into an Akiba-type, and suffered an honorable defeat.

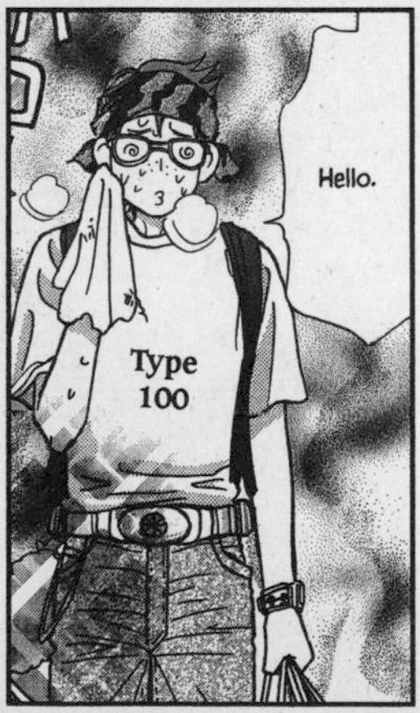
Hello.
Type 100

Note: These two pages are not copies!!

Hockey Club ♨ Character Profile No.6

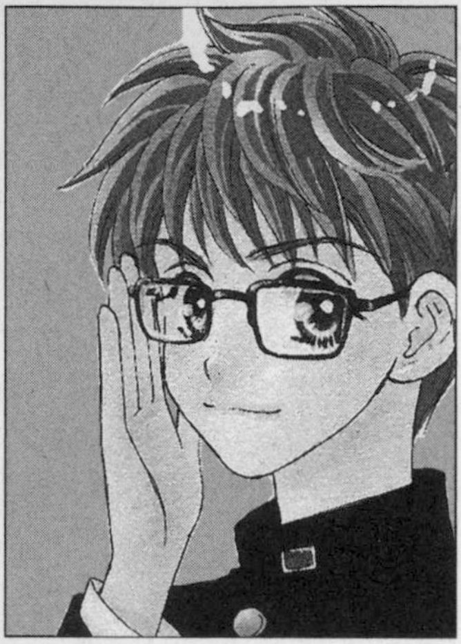

Ginta Ayuhara

Birthday	June 6th
Blood type	O
Height	169 cm (about 5'6.5")
Hobbies	Trying food at various restaurants, traveling, hockey
Special skill	Imitating Kinta
Favorite food	Curry with rice
Least favorite food	Bizarre foods
Favorite subjects	P.E., English
Least favorite subject	Classical literature
Favorite type of girl	Cute, spaced-out girls
Other (notes)	He hates being mistaken for his older brother!

Motto

We're all brothers!

♨ Famous Scene Selections ♨

▼ He's the younger brother.

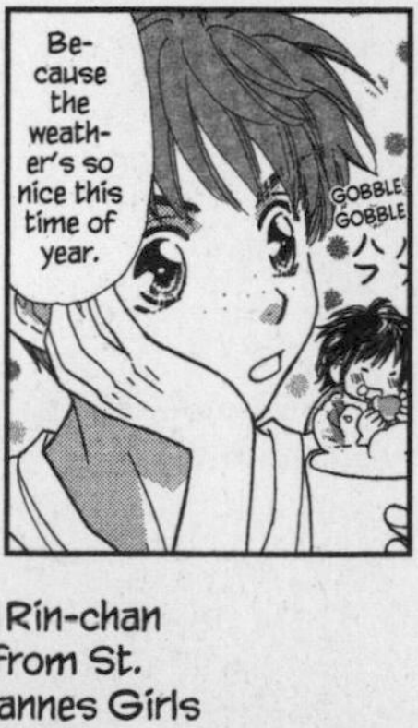
Because the weather's so nice this time of year.
GOBBLE GOBBLE

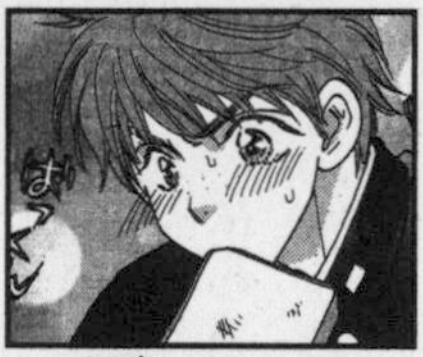

▲ The younger brother's first love is...

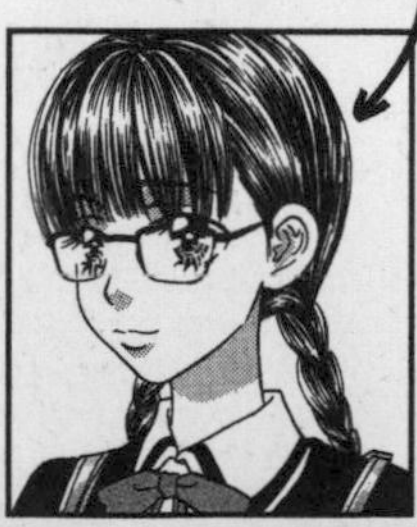

◀ Rin-chan from St. Johannes Girls Academy.

▼ He transformed into a minstrel, and suffered an honorable defeat.

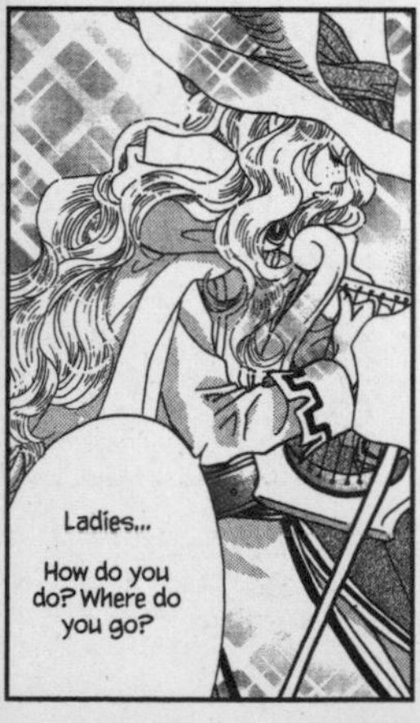
Ladies...
How do you do? Where do you go?

Translation Notes

Japanese is a tricky language for most Westerners, and translation is often more art than science. For your edification and reading pleasure, here are notes on some of the places where we could have gone in a different direction with our translation of the work, or where a Japanese cultural reference is used.

Mogo'o-kun, page iv

Mogo is the sound of munching, and *o* is a common suffix for boys' names. Morinaga-sensei probably named him while watching him munch leaves.

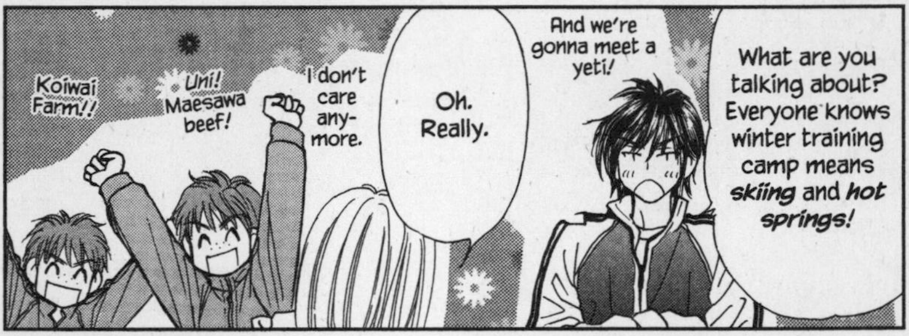
What are you talking about? Everyone knows winter training camp means *skiing* and *hot springs!*
And we're gonna meet a yeti!
Oh. Really.
I don't care anymore.
Uni! Maesawa beef!
Koiwai Farm!!

Uni, Maesawa beef, page 6

Uni means "sea urchin," and is a local delicacy of Iwate Prefecture. Iwate is also a good place to raise cattle, and the beef raised in the town of Maesawa is known for being delicious as well as low in fat.

Koiwai Farm, page 6

Koiwai Farm is a dairy and egg farm at the foot of Mt. Iwate. It's also a great tourist attraction.

Manjû, page 10

Manjû are steamed yeast buns with filling. In this case, they're shaped to look like yeti.

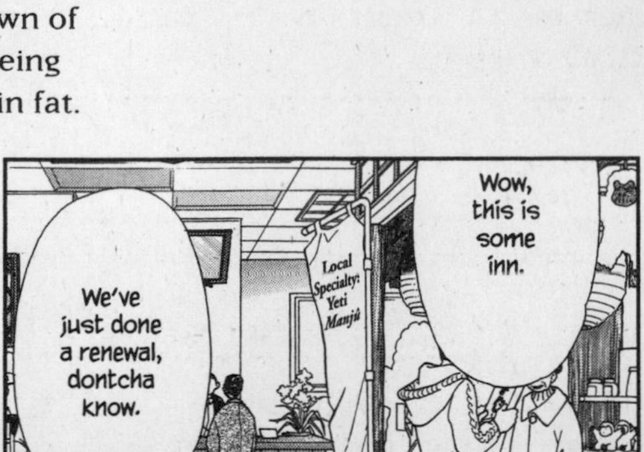
Wow, this is some inn.
Local Specialty: Yeti Manjû
We've just done a renewal, dontcha know.

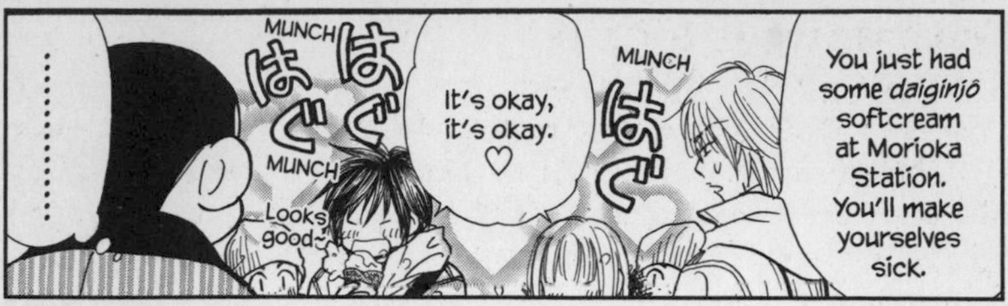
You just had some *daiginjô* softcream at Morioka Station. You'll make yourselves sick.
MUNCH
はぐ
It's okay, it's okay. ♡
MUNCH
はぐ
MUNCH
Looks good~
......

***Daiginjô* softcream, page 11**

Rice-wine-flavored soft ice cream.

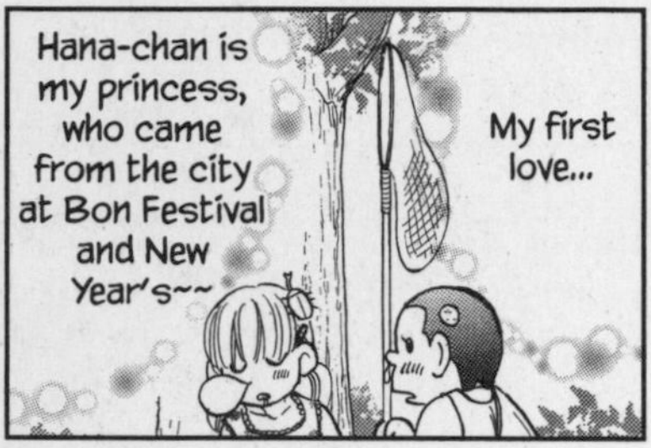
My first love...
Hana-chan is my princess, who came from the city at Bon Festival and New Year's~~

Bon Festival and New Year's, page 11

In Japan, the two big family holidays are the Bon Festival and New Year's. The Bon Festival is a Buddhist festival to honor one's ancestors.

***Kurione*, page 21**

A *kurione* is a type of shellfish that lives in the waters of northern Japan. Because of its appearance, it is called the "angel of the ice floes." It surprises its prey—and then devours it quickly—with the mouth on top of its head.

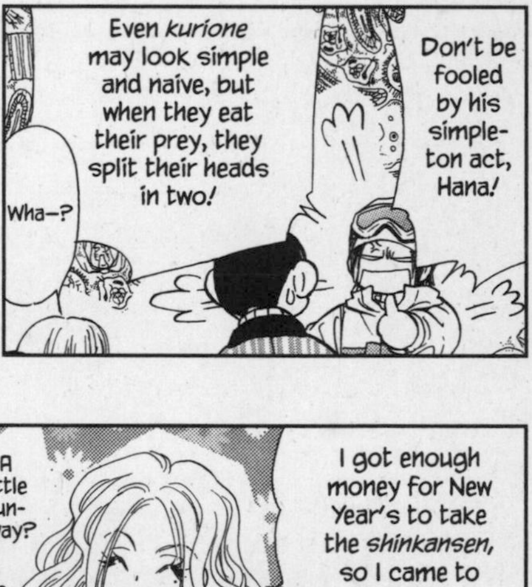
Don't be fooled by his simpleton act, Hana!
Even *kurione* may look simple and naive, but when they eat their prey, they split their heads in two!
Wha—?

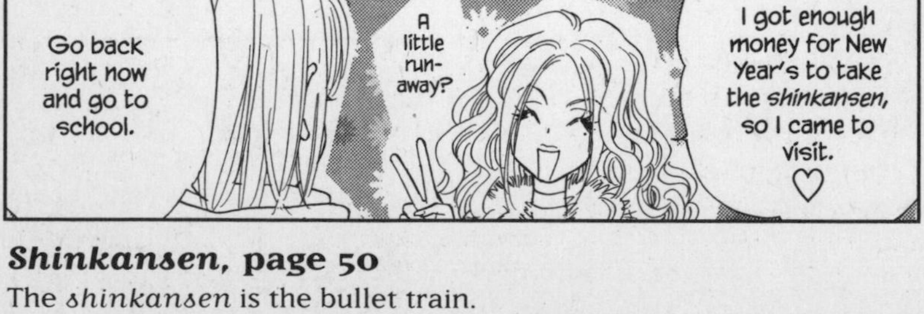
I got enough money for New Year's to take the *shinkansen*, so I came to visit. ♡
A little run-away?
Go back right now and go to school.

***Shinkansen*, page 50**

The *shinkansen* is the bullet train.

Kanô Sisters, page 51

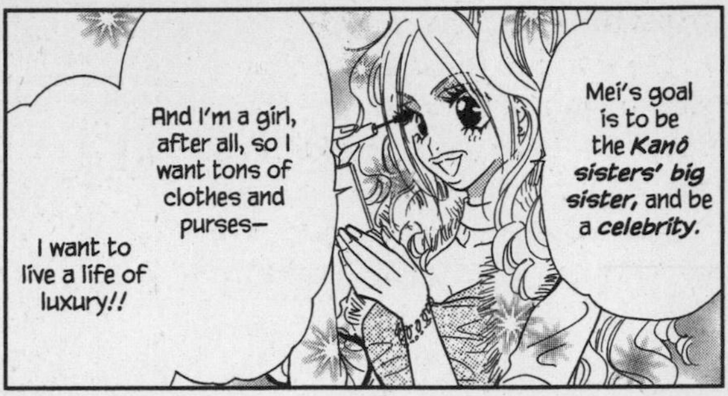

Mei's goal is to be the *Kanô sisters' big sister,* and be a *celebrity.*
And I'm a girl, after all, so I want tons of clothes and purses—
I want to live a life of luxury!!

The Kanô sisters are Japanese celebrities who claim to be half sisters, but no one knows if it's true. They also refuse to answer questions about their real ages, so it is possible for Mei to become their "big sister," despite being only eleven.

Backpack, page 55

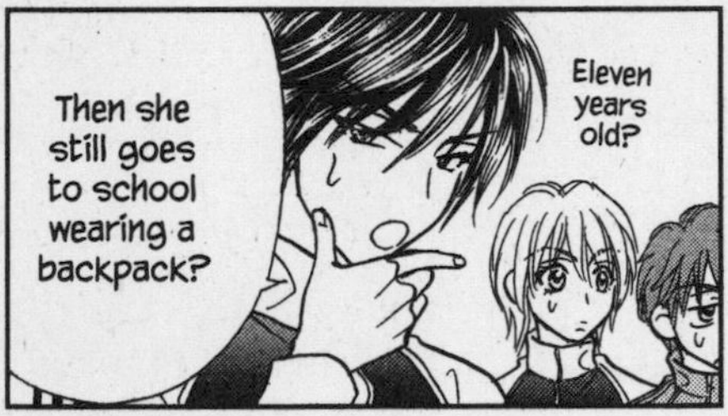

Eleven years old?
Then she still goes to school wearing a backpack?

In Japan, kids wear backpacks to elementary school, but when they get to higher education, they usually carry bookbags instead.

***Ukokkei*, page 56**

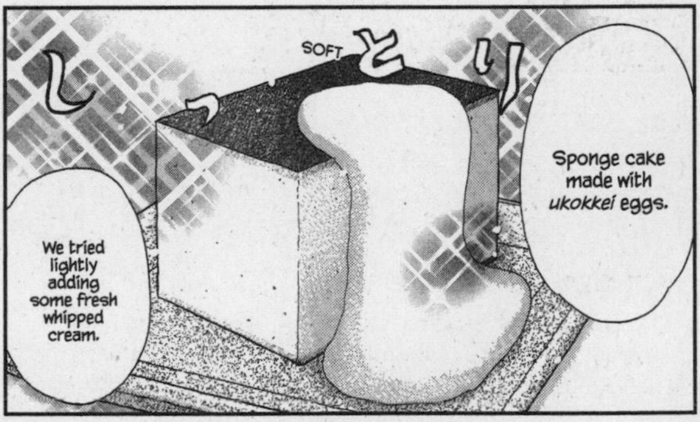

Sponge cake made with *ukokkei* eggs.
しっとり
SOFT
We tried lightly adding some fresh whipped cream.

Ukokkei, or silkie, chickens are a breed of ornamental chicken with fluffy white feathers, found in Asia. In China, their meat and eggs are thought to have medicinal properties.

Mobile suit, page 67

In the world of Gundam, "mobile suit" originally referred to a moving space suit used for the building of space colonies. But since that time, humanoid military spacecraft have come to be called "mobile suits" as well.

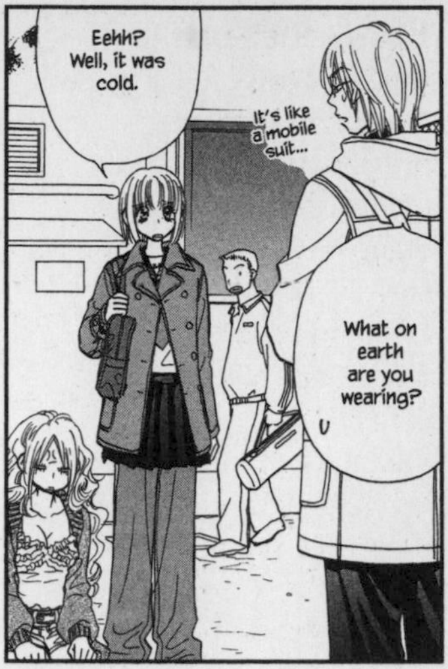
What on earth are you wearing?
It's like a mobile suit...
Eehh? Well, it was cold.

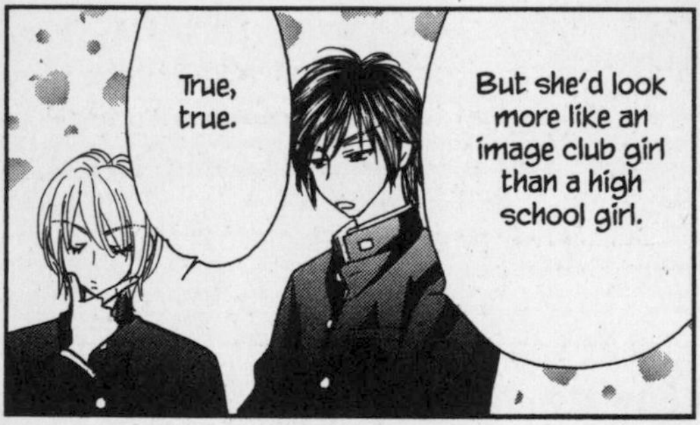
But she'd look more like an image club girl than a high school girl.
True, true.

Image club, page 72

An image club is basically a cosplay brothel, or a brothel where the prostitutes dress up as nurses, maids, high school students, etc.

Haramaki, page 74

Haramaki, or stomach wraps, are used to keep the stomach warm.

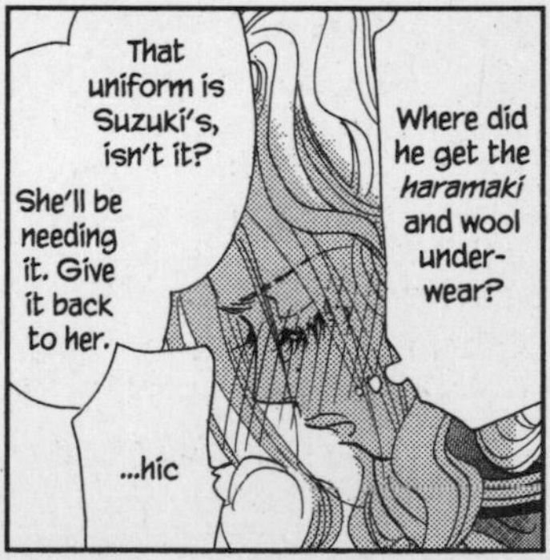
Where did he get the *haramaki* and wool underwear?
That uniform is Suzuki's, isn't it?
She'll be needing it. Give it back to her.
...hic

Mel Fisher, page 94

Mel Fisher is an American treasure hunter. He is famous for salvaging the wreck of the Spanish galleon *Nuestra Señora de Atocha*, which sunk while carrying lots of treasure.

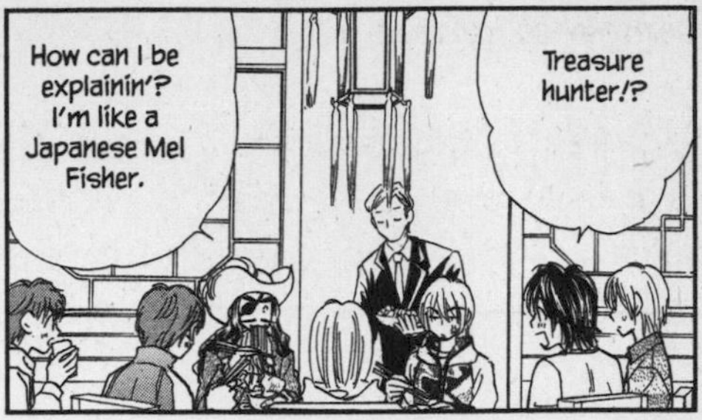
Treasure hunter!?
How can I be explainin'? I'm like a Japanese Mel Fisher.

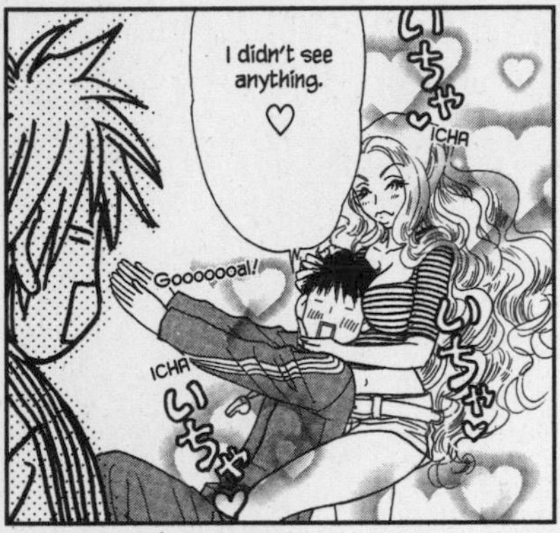
いちゃ♥
ICHA
いちゃ♥
I didn't see anything. ♡
Goooooal!
ICHA
いちゃ♥

Icha, page 114

Icha is the sound of being all over somebody in a flirtatious manner.

Natsuki's "this," page 117

The gesture Natsuki's father is making is Japanese sign language for "woman," so he's asking if Hana is Natsuki's woman, or girlfriend.

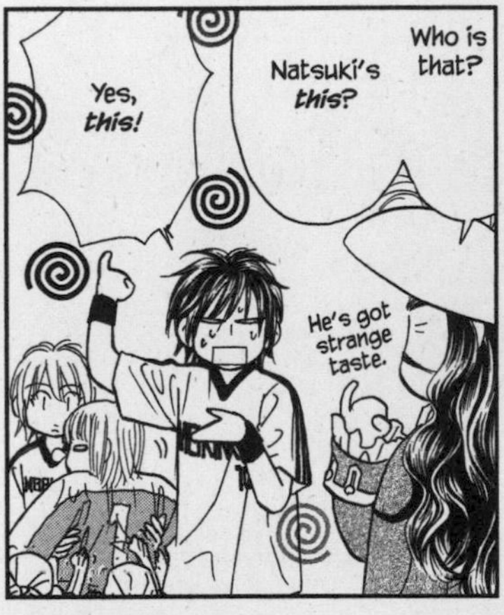
Who is that?
Natsuki's *this*?
Yes, *this*!
He's got strange taste.

Preview of Volume 6

We're pleased to present you a preview from volume 6. Please check our website (www.delreymanga.com) to see when this volume will be available in English. For now you'll have to make do with Japanese!

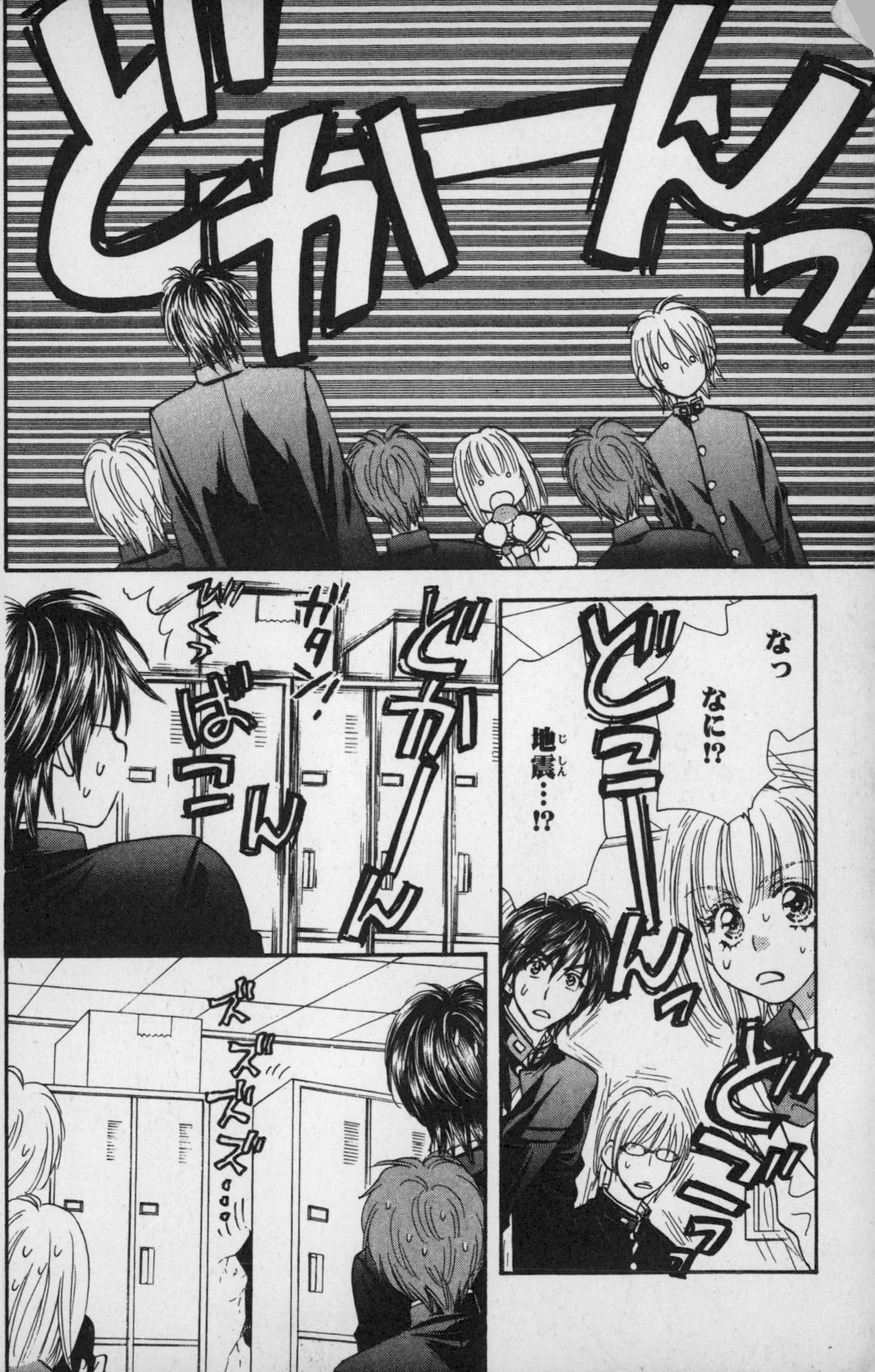
どかーんっ
なっ
なに!?
地震…!?
どっごんっ
どごっ
どかーん
ガタン!!
びくっ
ばっこん
ズズズズズ

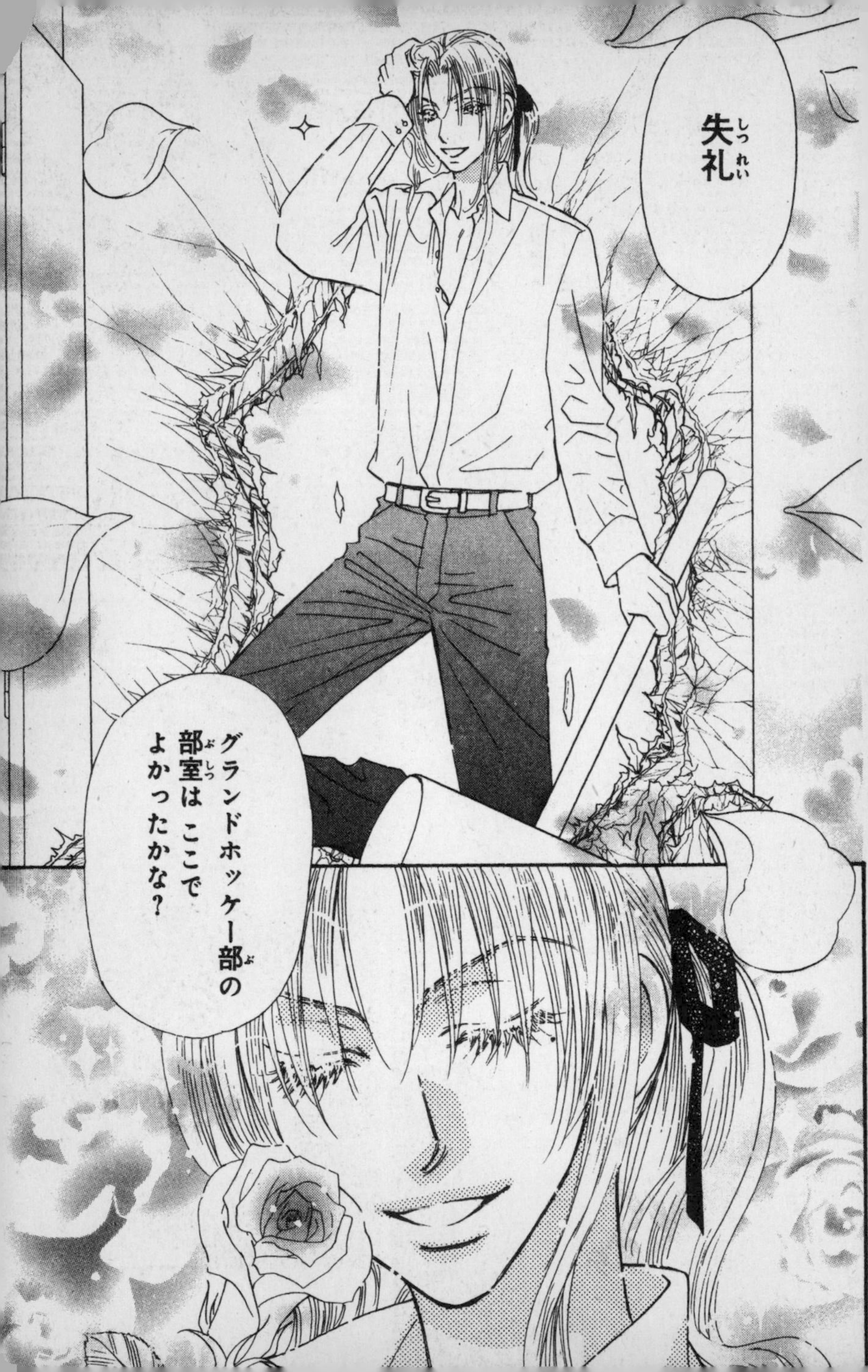
失礼
グランドホッケー部の部室は ここでよかったかな？

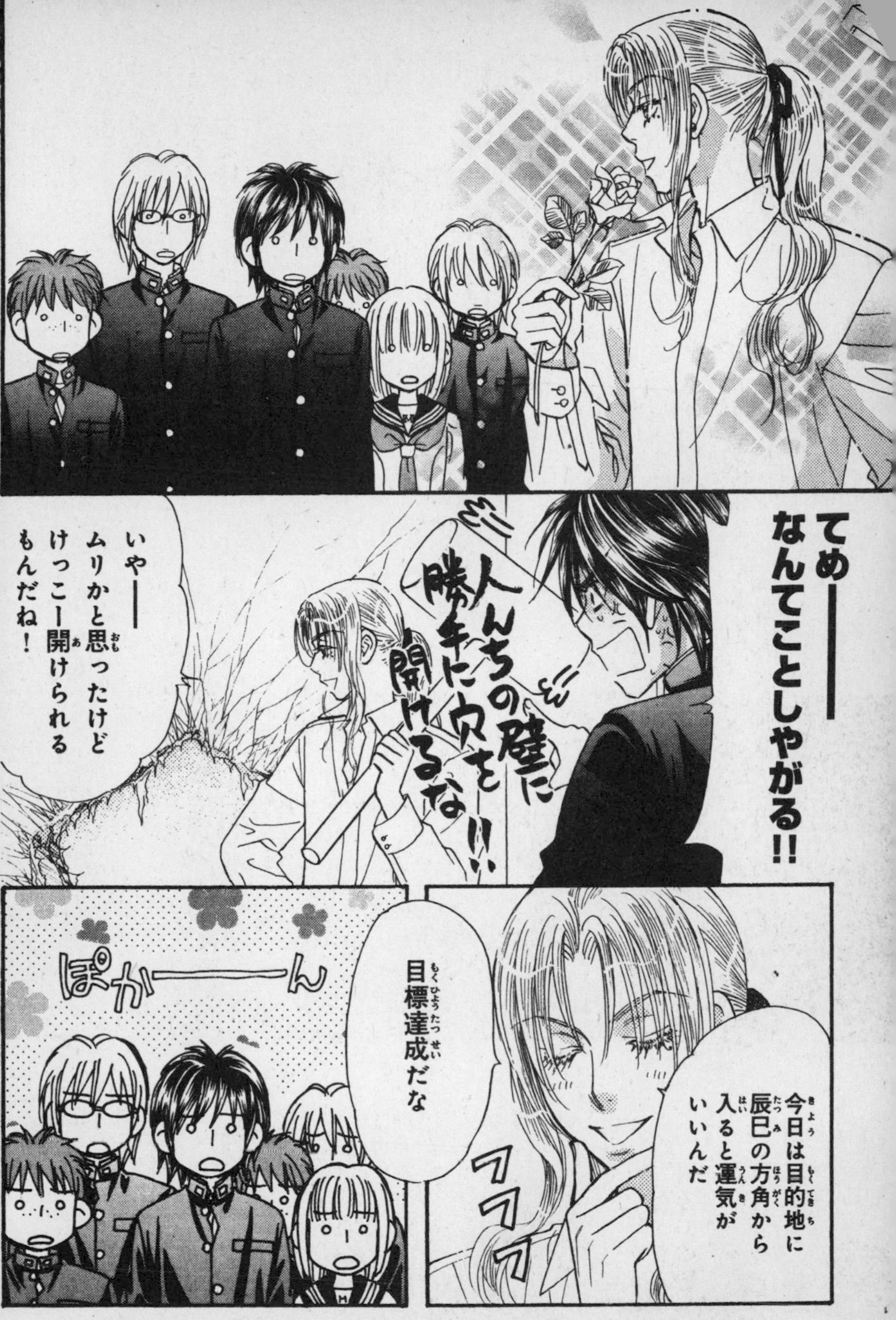
てめ―――
なんてことしやがる!!
人んちの壁に勝手に穴を開けるな!!
いや―――
ムリかと思ったけど
けっこー開けられる
もんだね!
今日は目的地に辰巳の方角から入ると運気がいいんだ
フフフ
目標達成だな
ぽか―――ん

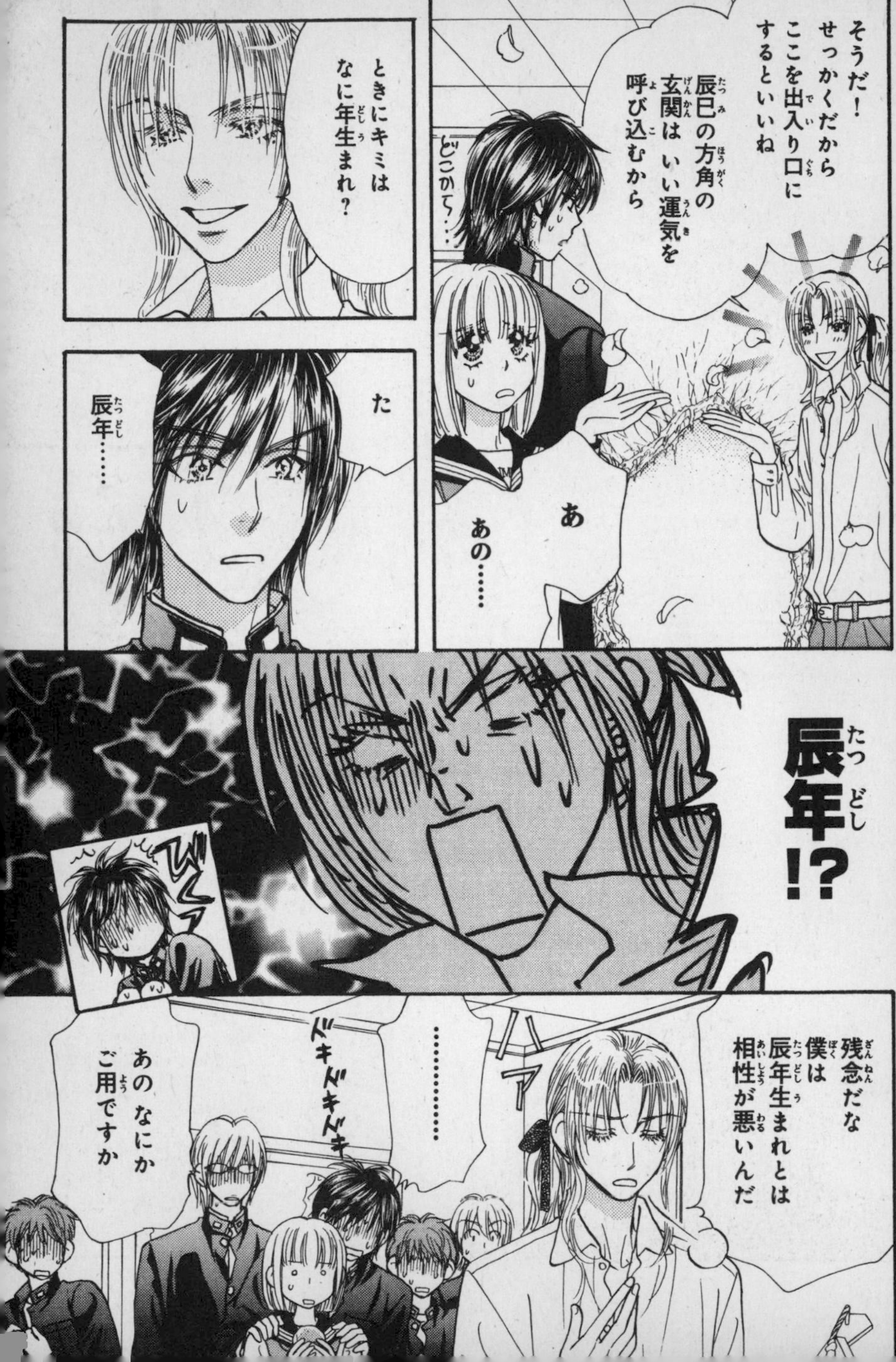
そうだ！ せっかくだから ここを出入り口にするといいね
辰巳の方角の玄関は いい運気を呼び込むから
どこかて～……
あ
あの……
ときにキミは なに年生まれ？
た
辰年……
辰年!?
残念だな 僕は辰年生まれとは相性が悪いんだ
ハァ
………
ドキドキドキドキ
あの なにか ご用ですか

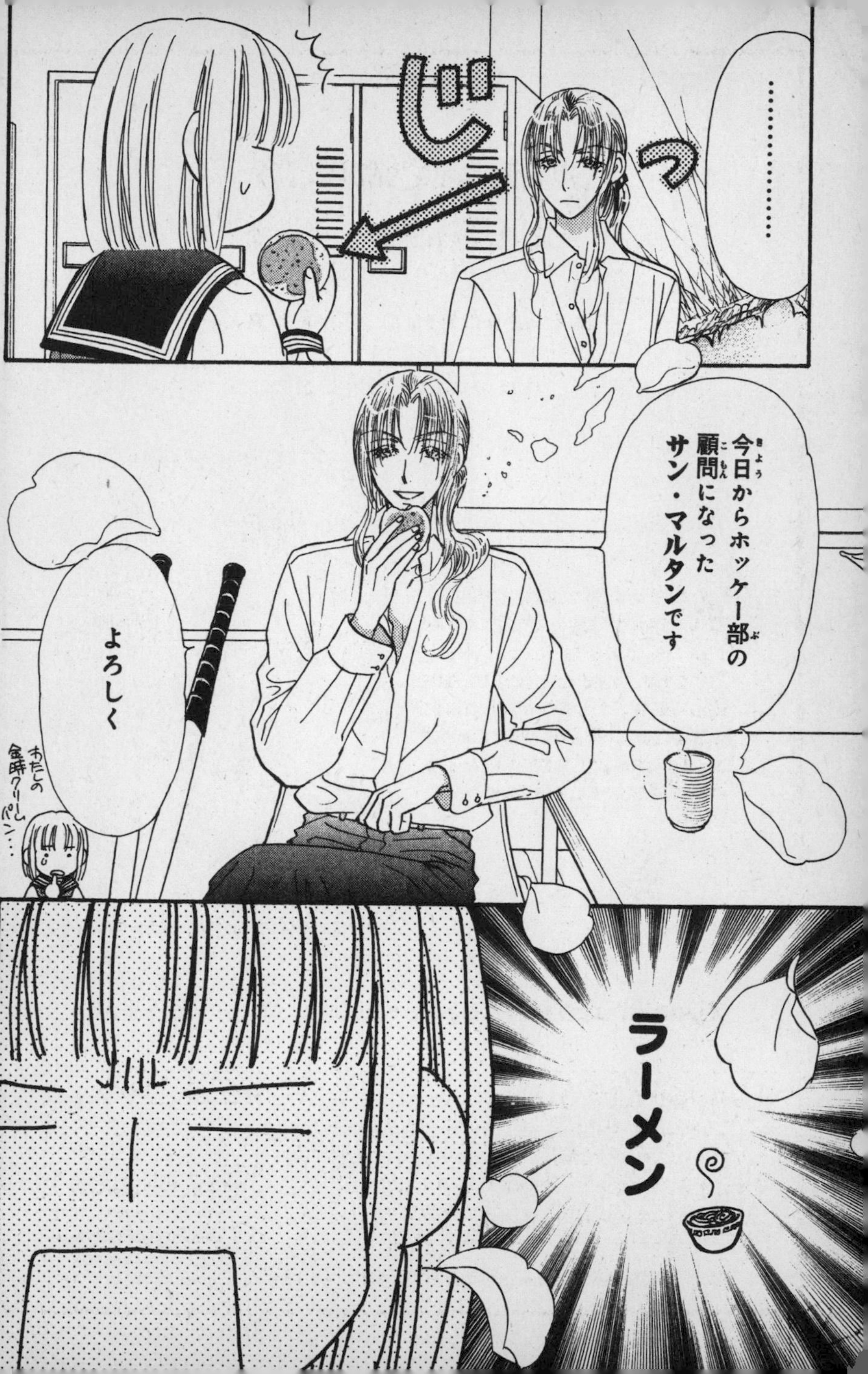
……
じっ
今日からホッケー部の顧問になったサン・マルタンです
よろしく
わたしの金時クリームパン……
ラーメン

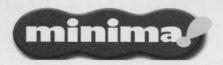

minima!

BY MACHIKO SAKURAI

A LITTLE LIVING DOLL!

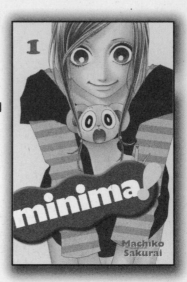

What would you do if your favorite toy came to life and became your best friend? Well, that's just what happens to Ame Oikawa, a shy schoolgirl. Nicori is a super-cute doll with a mind of its own—and a plan to make Ame's dreams come true!

Special extras in each volume! Read them all!

VISIT WWW.DELREYMANGA.COM TO:
- Read sample pages
- View release date calendars for upcoming volumes
- Sign up for Del Rey's free manga e-newsletter
- Find out the latest about new Del Rey Manga series

RATING   T AGES 13+

DEL REY MANGA デルレイ

The Otaku's Choice™

Yozakura Quartet

BY SUZUHITO YASUDA

A DIFFERENT SET OF SUPERTEENS!

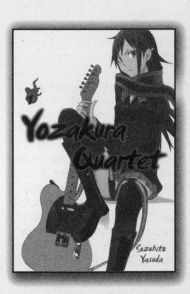

Hime is a superheroine. Ao can read minds. Kotoha can conjure up anything with the right word. And Akina . . . well, he's just a regular guy, surrounded by three girls with superpowers! Together, they are the Hizumi Everyday Life Consultation Office, dedicated to protect the town of Sakurashin. And with demon dogs and supernatural threats around every corner, there's plenty to keep them busy!

Special extras in each volume! Read them all!

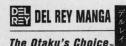

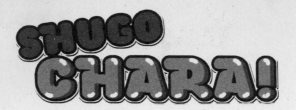

SHUGO CHARA!

PEACH-PIT

Creators of *Dears* and *Rozen Maiden*

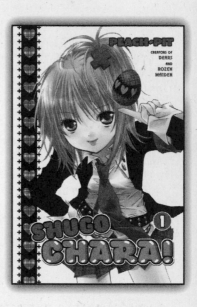

Everybody at Seiyo Elementary thinks that stylish and super-cool Amu has it all. But nobody knows the *real* Amu, a shy girl who wishes she had the courage to truly be herself. Changing Amu's life is going to take more than wishes and dreams—it's going to take a little magic! One morning, Amu finds a surprise in her bed: three strange little eggs. Each egg contains a Guardian Character, an angel-like being who can give her the power to be someone new. With the help of her Guardian Characters, Amu is about to discover that her true self is even more amazing than she ever dreamed.

Special extras in each volume! Read them all!

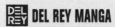
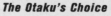

KITCHEN PRINCESS

STORY BY MIYUKI KOBAYASHI
MANGA BY NATSUMI ANDO
CREATOR OF ZODIAC P.I.

HUNGRY HEART

Najika is a great cook and likes to make meals for the people she loves. But something is missing from her life. When she was a child, she met a boy who touched her heart— and now Najika is determined to find him. The only clue she has is a silver spoon that leads her to the prestigious Seika Academy.

Attending Seika will be a challenge. Every kid at the school has a special talent, and the girls in Najika's class think she doesn't deserve to be there. But Sora and Daichi, two popular brothers who barely speak to each other, recognize Najika's cooking for what it is—magical. Could one of the boys be Najika's mysterious prince?

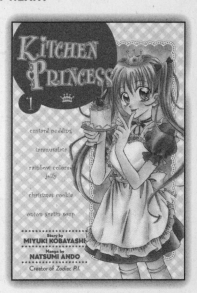

Special extras in each volume! Read them all!

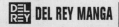

TOM

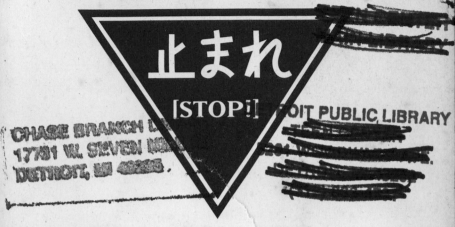

止まれ

[STOP!]

You're going the wrong way!

Manga is a completely different
type of reading experience.

To start at the *beginning,*
go to the *end!*

That's right! Authentic manga is read the traditional Japanese way—
from right to left. Exactly the opposite of how American books are
read. It's easy to follow: Just go to the other end of the book, and read
each page—and each panel—from right side to left side, starting at
the top right. Now you're experiencing manga as it was meant to be!